THE THREE GREAT CLASSIC WRITERS OF
MODERN YIDDISH LITERATURE

THE
Three Great Classic Writers
OF
Modern Yiddish Literature

VOLUME II

SELECTED WORKS OF

Sholem-Aleykhem

EDITED BY

Marvin Zuckerman & Marion Herbst

Joseph Simon   *Pangloss Press*

Illustrations by Manuel Bennett
Design by Joseph Simon

Library of Congress Cataloging-in-Publication Data

Sholem-Aleykhem, 1859-1916,
  [Selections, English, 1994]
  Selected Works of Sholem-Aleykhem / Edited by Marvin Zuckerman &
Marion Herbst.
     p.   cm. — (The three great classic writers of modern Yiddish litera-
ture : v. 2)
  Includes bibliographical references.
  ISBN 934710-24-4 (hard bound) : $37.50
  1. Sholem-Aleykhem, 1859-1916—translations into English.
I. Zuckerman, Marvin S. II. Herbst, Marion, 1932- . III. Title.
IV. Series.
PJ5129.R2A287   1994
839'.098309—dc20   94-582
                                         CIP

Contents

ACKNOWLEDGEMENTS

Thanks and acknowledgements are due the following:

Autobiographical Selection: From *From the Fair* by Sholom Aleichem trans., ed. by Curt Leviant, translated by Curt Leviant, Translation copyright © 1985 by Viking Penguin, Inc. Used by permission of Viking Penguin, a division of Penguin Books USA, Inc.

Autobiographical Selection: From *The Great Fair* by Sholom Aleichem, translated by Tamara Kahana, copyright © 1955, The Noonday Press. Reprinted with the kind permission of the Family of Sholom Aleichem.

"The Election" translated by Louis Fridhandler.

"Legboymer" translated by Louis Fridhandler.

"Stempeniu: A Jewish Romance" from *The Shtetl* translated by Joachim Neugroschel, copyright © 1979 Joachim Neugroschel. Published by the Overlook Press, Lewis Hollow Road, Woodstock, New York 12498, $25 cloth, $13.95 paper.

Selection from *The Nightingale:* Reprinted by permission of The Putnam Publishing Group from *Yosele the Nightingale* by Sholom Aleichem. Translation copyright © 1985 by Aliza Shevrin.

Selection from *Wandering Star:* Translated by Frances Butwin, 1952, Crown Publishers; reprinted by permission of Frances Butwin.

Tevye the Dairyman by Sholem Aleykhem reprinted by permission of Miriam Katz from *Sholom-Aleichem: Tevye the Dairyman and Other Stories,* translated by Miriam Katz, published by Raduga publishers, Moscow, 1988.

Selection from *Menakhem-Mendl* by Sholem-Aleykhem: reprinted by permission of the Putnam Publishing Group from *The Adventures of Menakhem-Mendl,* translated by Tamara Kahana, copyright 1969 by the children of Sholom Aleichem.

Selection from *Adventures of Mottel the Cantor's Son* by Sholom Aleykhem, translated by Tamara Kahana, copyright © 1953. Reprinted by kind permission of the Family of Sholom Aleichem.

Selection from *In The Storm:* Reprinted by permission of the Putnam Publishing Group from *In The Storm* by Sholom Aleichem. Translation copyright © 1984 by Aliza Shevrin.

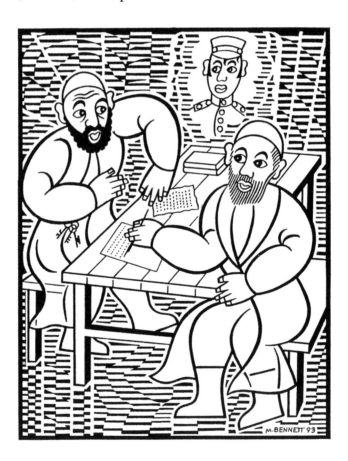

In Praise of Sholem-Aleykhem

"…The most popular and beloved Jewish writer…"
—Zalmen Reyzin.

"Sholem-Aleykhem taught his people to laugh; he enchanted tens of thousands of his readers with his language, which sparkles with humor…" —Ba'al Makhshoves

"The great natural genius of Yiddish literature.

"One of the very few modern writers who could be said to speak for an entire people.

"Sholem Aleichem is the great poet of Jewish humanism and of Jewish transcendence over the pomp of the world.

"Sholem Aleichem's Yiddish is one of the most extraordinary verbal achievements of modern literature."
—Irving Howe and Eliezer Greenberg

"Sholem Aleichem taught a people steeped in tragedy to laugh at its troubles….His laughter still reverberates in Jewish homes wherever Yiddish is read or understood." —Sol Liptzin

"…That great Jew who has in his stories brought us more joy than anyone else." —Irving Howe and Ruth Wisse

"…Sholom Aleichem, perhaps more than any other writer who has ever lived, writes about Jewishness as if it were a gift, a marvel, an unending theme of wonder and delight." —Alfred Kazin

"He writes to entertain, and not to instruct…. With him the last spark of the didactic ideals of the Haskala has entirely vanished. He is above all else a litterateur who is addressing an audience with a decided taste for good literature." —Leo Wiener

"…The most beloved Yiddish author." —Charles Madison

"Rarely in the history of literature has a writer come along who could be said to have captured the total identity of a people. Such a writer becomes a folk-hero in his own time, to his own people.... Sholom Aleichem...is one of those rarities.

"The most beloved of all Yiddish writers."   —Sol Gittleman

"...aspects of Jewish life were masterfully delineated by [Sholem-Aleykhem]...in many stories, always with an eye to brighten that life and evoke a hearty laugh at its foibles, tricks, and pranks."
                                                    —Meyer Waxman

The last photograph of Sholem-Aleykhem,
Bronx, New York, 1916.

Preface

The main lines of Yiddish literary history are firmly drawn: almost everything in the modern era stems from the "classical" trio of prose writers,
Mendele, Sholem-Aleykhem, and Perets. So dominant are their literary
personalities, so powerful the thematic and stylistic precedents they established that even those who try to break away from them generally succeed
in doing little more than confirm the very influence they would reject.
— Howe and Greenberg, *A Treasury of Yiddish Stories*

*   *   *

This is Volume Two of a trilogy presenting selected works in translation of the three great modern Yiddish classicists: Mendele
Moykher-Sforim, Sholem Aleykhem, and Y. L. Perets.

Volume One, an anthology of some of the works of Mendele,
appeared in 1991 and was well received; it was cited as "making an
important contribution ... filling a terrible gap in Jewish literary
history."

This second volume contains two of Sholem-Aleykhem's complete novels—*Stempenyu* and *Tevye the Dairyman* (the basis of the
famous musical *Fiddler on the Roof)*—substantial excerpts from
seven other Sholem-Aleykhem novels and from his artful autobiography, *From the Fair.* Two of his short stories, never before translated, are also included (for one of these, written in 1883, he used the
pen-name "Sholem-Aleykhem" for the very first time), as well as
two of his extremely popular "folksongs"; an amusing letter to the
great national Jewish poet, Khayim Nakhman Byalik; an essay on
Zionism ("Why Do the Jews Need a Land of Their Own?"); a new
translation of his moving last will and testament; and a new translation of the revealing epitaph he wrote for himself and which
appears on his tombstone in the Workmen's Circle cemetery in
Brooklyn.

This volume is also copiously illustrated with artwork and photographs.

There are many anthologies in translation of Sholem-Aleykhem's works, but none of them brings together in one volume such a broad cross-section of his work.

Many collections of his short stories are also available and are continually being reprinted (these stories have, therefore, been omitted from this collection).

As can be seen from the selections in this anthology, the pace of translation of Sholem-Aleykhem into English has been accelerating. A great deal more still remains to be done. What this volume hopes to accomplish is to provide a kind of "Viking Portable" of Sholem-Aleykhem, so that readers can, in one volume, hold in their hands enough of his varied writings to gain a fuller understanding of the scope and range of his achievement.

In no other single volume has the reader available such a representative sampling of Sholem-Aleykhem's work.

After the chronology and a biographical sketch (neither of which are provided in such detail in any Sholem-Aleykhem anthology); a treatment of Sholem-Aleykhem's medical history, revealing little-known facts suggesting that Sholem-Aleykhem could have survived his last illness; a memoir about Sholem-Aleykhem by his son-in-law; some letters from Sholem-Aleykhem from on-board ship on his way to America; an analysis of some famous fictional place names and their meaning in the works of Sholem-Aleykhem; and a general introduction by the editors, the volume begins with an introduction to Sholem-Aleykhem by Sholem-Aleykhem himself, namely a selection from his autobiography, entitled in Yiddish, *Funem Yarid (From the Fair)*. Why "From the Fair"? Because, as he explains it:

"From the Fair" implies a return trip, or the results of a great fair. A man heading for a fair is full of hope. He has no idea what bargains he will find and what he will accomplish. He flies toward the fair swift as an arrow, at full speed... don't bother him, he has no time. But on the way back he knows what deals he has made and what he has accomplished. He's no longer in a hurry. He's got plenty of time. No need to rush. He can assess the results of his venture. He can tell everyone about the trip at his leisure—whom he met and what he has seen and heard at the fair.

—Leviant's translation

From the Fair is his autobiography, but is not in the usual autobiographical form. As Sholem-Aleykhem himself puts it: "...I chose a special form of autobiography: memoirs in the form of a novel. I'll talk about myself in the third person" (Leviant's translation).

The next selection, in Part II (Two Early Stories) "The Election," translated here into English for the first time, is also self-referential. Published in 1883, it is the first time Sholem Rabinowitz signed a work of his as "Sholem-Aleykhem." This piece is followed by another early story, also translated here for the first time into English, *"Legboymer."* Both these stories are introduced by their translator, Louis Fridhandler.

Part III presents two poems Sholem-Aleykhem wrote that became incredibly popular, were set to music and sung (one in a "theatrical version"). Isn't it remarkable that Sholem-Aleykhem, never a great poet, should have written two poems that became so widely known and sung among the people.

In Part IV, we present three novels that, in Sholem-Aleykhem's mind, constituted a kind of trilogy, three works that all dealt with the lives of Yiddish performing artists. One deals with a singer, one with a musician, and the third with an actor. *Stempenyu,* the one about the musician, is presented here in full. Selections are given from the other two. Preceding *Stempenyu* in our volume is a dedicatory "open letter" to Mendele Moyker-Sforim that was included as a sort of preface to his novel by Sholem-Aleykhem and is presented here for the first time in an English translation by the editors of this anthology.

In Part V appear Sholem-Aleykhem's three greatest characters: Menakhem-Mendl, Motl Peysi the Cantor's Son, and Tevye the Dairyman. *Tevye the Dairyman* is given here in its most complete form to date (previous translations, including the latest one before this (1987) have left some things out which are here included). Carefully chosen selections from the other two novels (and a reading of our introductions) will give the reader a foretaste of what a reading of them in their entirety would be like.

Part VI presents sizable selections from three other Sholem-Aleykhem novels, one of which deals with the 1905 revolution and its aftermath; another of which satirizes middle-class shtetl-type Jews disporting themselves in the famous central-European spa, Marienbad; and the third of which deals with antisemitism in Russia and in particular with the Mendl Beilis blood libel.

Part VII allows us to eavesdrop on an amusing bit of correspondence from Sholem-Aleykhem to his good friend and fellow

Zionist, the great national Jewish poet, Khayim Nakhmen Byalik. We present it here in our own translation.

Part VIII shows us a side of Sholem-Aleykhem that is often overlooked: the dedicated, passionate, devoted Zionist side. Written in 1898, it presents his argument on "why the Jews need a land of their own."

Part IX, the final section, contains Sholem-Aleykhem's last will and testament, his "ethical will." A great human document, it was entered into the Congressional Record and reprinted in the *N.Y. Times*. We present it here in our own translation, along with our translation of the epitaph he wrote for himself which appears on his tombstone in the Workmen's Circle Har Karmel cemetery in Brooklyn where he lies buried.

The volume ends with a bibliography and a glossary.

*   *   *

We want to heartily thank Dr. Louis Fridhandler here, not only for his contribution of two never-before-translated Sholem-Aleykhem stories and their introduction, and his two other contributions (Sholem-Aleykhem's medical history and the piece on Sholem-Aleykhem's fictional place-names), but also for reading through our introductions and offering valuable suggestions.

The "Fiddler on the Roof"—an American imagination.

L'khayim!

Chronology*

1859 Born Sholem Rabinovitsh, March 2nd, in Pereyaslav, Ukraine, a Jewish town about 60 miles southeast of Kiev.

1861 Moves to Voronkovo, a small town nearby (the model for *Kasrilevke*). Spends his childhood and receives his *kheyder* · education there. Father considered well-off by the community (a grain and lumber merchant; also had government privilege of mail delivery).

1871 Moves back to Pereyaslav because father's business goes bad; there father runs a poor inn. Sholem employed as "puller-in." Poverty now his lot. Begins study of *gemore*.

1872 Mother dies of cholera. Lives for several months with maternal grandfather in Boguslav, across the Dnieper. Father remarries.

1873 Enters Russian gymnasium in Pereyaslav on a scholarship. Writes first Yiddish composition: a dictionary of his stepmother's curses, arranged alphabetically.

1874 Writes biblical romances in Hebrew à la Abraham Mapu; father delighted.

1876 Graduates gymnasium. Application to the Jewish Teachers' Institute at Zhitomir rejected. Tutors Russian, Hebrew, and other subjects privately in poor Jewish homes in and around Pereyeslav.

1877 Becomes tutor to Olga Loyeff, the not-quite-13-year-old daughter of a rich Jewish landowner, Elimelekh Loyeff, who owns a big farming estate in Sofievka in the province of Kiev.

1879 Begins to publish journalistic pieces in Hebrew.

---

*Based on a variety of sources, including Dan Miron's article in the *Encyclopedia Judaica* and an unpublished chronology by Louis Fridhandler.

1880 Evicted by Loyeff when he discovers romance blooming between Sholem Aleykhem and Olga. Returns to Pereyaslav. Wins competition to become government-appointed *rabiner* (crown rabbi) in Lubny (Louben), a small town about 80 miles east of Kiev. Attempts to correspond with Olga are frustrated.

1882 Publishes Hebrew articles calling for help to the poor and dealing with other social issues.

1883 Against wishes of Loyeff, marries Olga Loyeff (a Rabbi Zuckerman officiating); after reconciliation with Loyeff, quits his job as a government-rabbi. Decides to write almost exclusively in Yiddish rather than Hebrew. Moves to Byela Tserkov (in the province of Kiev). First Yiddish story, "Tsvey Shteyner" ["Two Stones"] published in the weekly *Dos Yidishe Folksblat* (St. Petersburg). Publishes second story in Yiddish, *Legboymer,* using pseudonym, "Sholem-Aleykhem," for the first time.

1884 First Yiddish novel, *Taybele,* appears.

1885 Elimelekh Loyeff, his father-in-law, dies. According to Russian law, as the sole surviving male heir, the entire Loyeff estate, which amounts to a large fortune, devolves to Sholem-Aleykhem. He is now a very rich man.

1887 Moves to Kiev (the model for *Yehupets*) and plays the stock exchange. Summers with his family in nearby Boira (the model for *Boyberik*). The short story, "The Pocket Knife," appears; he is encouraged by Shimen Dubnow's favorable review of it.

1888 Joins *Hibbat Zion* movement. *Sender-Blank un zayn gezindl* (*Sender Blank and His Little Household*) a novel, appears. Promotes, edits, and publishes, using his own money to pay authors and printing costs, a new kind of anthology of Yiddish literature, soliciting manuscripts from many fine new Yiddish talents. (The great Yiddish classicist, Perets, for example, publishes his first Yiddish work there, a long narrative poem called *Monish.*) The anthology was called *Dos Yidishe Folks-bibliotek,* a landmark in Yiddish literature.

1889 *Stempenyu,* another novel appears.

1890 *Yosele Solovey* (*Yosele the Nightingale*), still another novel, is published. His feuilletons, articles, stories also appear during these years in Yiddish, but also in Hebrew and Russian. Produces a second volume of *Dos Yidishe Folks-bibliotek.*

Loses his fortune on the Kiev stock exchange. Forced to flee Kiev to avoid creditors; travels in Europe. Mother-in-law settles debts as best she can in his absence.

1891   Returns to family, which had, in the meantime, moved to Odessa.

1891-1894   Plays the stock exchange in Odessa and again in Kiev (moves back there in 1893); then tries to make it as a broker around the Kiev sugar factories. Writes several propaganda pieces for the Zionist movement.

1892   First *Menakhem-Mendl* letters appear.

1894   Writes first *Tevye* story (published, 1895); also writes first play, *Yakhnehoz.*

1898   Publishes beginning of a novel with a Zionist theme, called *Moshiyakh's Tsaytn* (*Messiah's Times*).

1900-1906   Supports himself almost entirely with his pen.

1905   Witnesses pogrom in Kiev; decides to leave Russia.

1906   Gives successful readings of his work throughout Europe to create additional income. Accompanied by his wife and youngest son, Numa, goes to New York, with brief stop-over in London.

1907   Tries to write for Yiddish stage in New York. Two plays open on same night, one performed by Jacob Adler, the other by Boris Tomashevsky. They close quickly. Returns to Europe with stop-over in Holland to participate in the Zionist Congress meeting there, then rejoins his family in Geneva, Switzerland.

1908   Spends time in Berlin with Max Reinhardt trying, unsuccessfully, to persuade him to perform his comedy, *Der Oytser* (*The Treasure*). Then goes on another successful reading tour throughout Russia. During reading tour, collapses in Baronovitsh (in present-day Poland) with tuberculosis. Is confined there for a couple of months. Enters sanitorium in Nervi on the Italian Riviera.

1909   Begins writing his novel, *Blondzhende Shtern* (*Wandering Stars*). (Finishes it in 1911.) His fiftieth birthday celebrated worldwide. Copyright to most of his works restored to him. Works translated into Russian.

1910   Son-in-law, I.D. Berkowits, begins work of translating his works into Hebrew. S-A suffers apparent heart attack.

1913   Suffers from urinary problems. Recovers. Writes *Der Blutiker Shpas* (*The Bloody Hoax;* published in 1914).

Continues writing *Menakhem-Mendl, Tevye,* and *Motl Peysi dem Khazns.* Begins work on *Funem Yarid,* his unfinished autobiography.

1914 Completes another successful reading tour of Russia. In summer, is vacationing with family at Baltic Sea when World War I breaks out. As "enemy alien," must leave Germany. Makes it to Copenhagen, then to New York in December, where he writes for the Yiddish press. Diagnosed as having diabetes insipidus.

1915 Son Misha dies of tuberculosis in Copenhagen. Writes "ethical will." Sholem Aleykhem's health deteriorates. Continues work on *Motl* and *Funem Yarid.* Finishes comic play, *Dos Groyse Gevins* (*The Big Win* [or, *The Jackpot*]).

1916 Lack of income forces him to go on another reading tour of the U.S., despite failing health. Dies May 13. New York witnesses its largest funeral before or since as hundreds of thousands accompany him to his place of burial.

THE THREE GREAT CLASSIC WRITERS OF
MODERN YIDDISH LITERATURE

M.BENNETT 93

Introduction

If Mendele was the first of the three great classicists, the founding "grandfather," so to speak, of modern Yiddish literature, the "eynikl" ("grandchild"), Sholem-Aleykhem, was by far the most read and best loved.

In some ways, Sholem-Aleykhem almost single-handedly created the era in the history of Yiddish literature we call "modern Yiddish literature." It was Sholem-Aleykhem who, with his essay "Shomer's Mishpet" ("The Trial of Shomer"; 1888), attacked the kind of sentimental clap-trap being written by Shomer (N.M.Shaykevitsh; 1849-1905) and others, and called for a new kind of literature to be written in the Yiddish language.

Holding up Mendele Moykher-Sforim (Sh.Y. Abramovitsh; 1864-1917) as an example of what could be accomplished in the mother-tongue—in Yiddish—he dubbed Mendele the *"zeyde"* ("grandfather") of the new Yiddish literature and himself the "eynikl" (grandson). (I.L. Perets came to be called the "father" of the new Yiddish literature—even though Sholem-Aleykhem preceded Perets chronologically as a Yiddish writer and was the one who paid Perets for his first serious Yiddish literary effort.)

There is no doubt that Sholem-Aleykhem's *"zeyde,"* Mendele Moykher-Sforim, exerted a great influence on him. Yiddish critics have, for example, always taken for granted the similarities between Sholem-Aleykhem's character, Tevye, and Mendele Moykher-Sforim's character Mendele-the-Book-Peddler.* The Yiddish critic, Ba'al Makhshoves (1873-1924), says the following (Reyzin, 641; our translation) of Mendele's influence on Sholem Aleykhem:

---

*Dan Miron, in *A Traveler Disguised,* stresses the great difference between Mendele-the-author (Abramovitsh) and his creation, the literary character, Mendele-the-Book-Peddler.

Sholem-Aleykhem portrait

Engraved by M.A. Gershmann

A realist through and through, with great powers of observation and with a very lively spirit, Sholem-Aleykhem is, after Mendele Moykher-Sforim, the most significant portrayer of the Jewish mass....in this, one senses to a certain extent Abramovitch's [Mendele's] influence, just as it can also be sensed in various places in Sholem-Aleykhem's style.

But then he adds:

Nevertheless, Sholem-Aleykhem remained quite independent and original in his work...and even his descriptions of Jewish small-town life [the Kasrilevke stories]...in which Abramovitch's [Mendele's] influence is most strongly discernible, belong not only to the best things of Sholem-Aleykhem's, but also to those most characteristic of him.

In 1888, Sholem-Aleykhem announced he was editing an anthology of new Yiddish literature and would pay for contributions—which he did, handsomely, using his own funds. The anthology was published and contained not only his own novel, *Stempenyu*, but also a long narrative poem, *Monish*, by I.L. Perets, his first published piece in the Yiddish language, as well as other fine pieces by other new, young Yiddish talents. After that (if not entirely because of it) the "modern" period in Yiddish literature began in earnest; there was a virtual outpouring of fresh, new, talent on the Yiddish literary scene.

Irving Howe and Eliezer Greenberg in their *A Treasury of Yiddish Stories* refer to Sholem-Aleykhem as "the great natural genius of Yiddish literature." He is often thought of as a primitive folk artist. This is far from the truth. He was, as Irving Howe says later in *The Best of Sholom Aleichem*, "a self-conscious, disciplined artist rather than merely a folk-voice..." He was well-read, and influenced by some of the other great masters of European literature, such as Dickens, DeFoe, Swift, Balzac, Heine, Chekhov, Gorki, Turgenev, and Tolstoy. Sholem-Aleykhem's great genius consisted in his ability to use the Yiddish language in such a way, to portray Yiddish types in such a way, to employ the monologue in such a way—in such an artistic, skillful way—as to create the illusion that his stories, characters, and dialogue somehow issued forth from the folk itself.

Another prevalent misconception sees Sholem-Aleykhem as a sentimentalist, someone who tickles the feet of the folk. He is seen through a haze of nostalgia, or he is perceived as someone who sees or protrays the shtetl and its folk in a sugary, sentimental way. This is also far from the truth. As Irving Howe and Ruth Wisse have

5

pointed out in one of their introductions, there is a "dark side" to Sholem-Aleykhem. One can easily see this in the *Tevye* stories, which are really tales of one disaster after another: in one, his daughter marries a revolutionary who is being sent to Siberia where she goes to join him and who Tevye will never see again; in another, his daughter commits suicide because she was dallied with and then abandoned by a false lover; in a third, another daughter throws herself away on an unattractive rich man so she can provide for her aged father, who watches her wither as a result; still another daughter marries a poor tailor, only to have him die of tuberculosis, leaving her (and Tevye) with several children to support; another is lost to Tevye because she marries out of the faith and Tevye feels compelled to consider her "dead"; and in a final episode, Tevye himself is driven out of the home he and his fathers, and theirs before them, lived in for generations. This is hardly the stuff of sweet sentiment and nostalgia.

Sholem-Aleykhem's biography (see our Biographical Sketch, p. 9) is interesting to us not just because it satisfies our natural curiosity about the life of a great writer, but also because it, as might be expected, sheds some light on the sources for his fictional characters, stories, and situations. In the most obvious instance, it is clear that Sholem-Aleykhem's dealings on the Kiev stock exchange gave him much material for *Menakhem-Mendl*. It is safe to say that he could not, nor would he have, written the *Menakhem-Mendl* pieces the way he did without his own experiences on the *bourse*. As for *Motl, Peysi the Cantor's Son*, it is also clear from his own descriptions of himself as a boy that much of Motl's mischievousness and his quirky outlook on people and life derive from the way Sholem-Aleykhem himself was as a boy. And as for *Tevye The Dairyman*, it again is clear, we think, that Sholem-Aleykhem in his own lifetime experienced the same kind of social, linguistic, religious, and cultural distancing from his own roots that Tevye had to confront with each of his daughters—and that that was the source from which he drew the travails of Tevye.

At one point, Sholem-Aleykhem was working on an edition of his collected works. It was to contain 40 volumes. He never lived to complete it. In 1917, just one year after his death, an edition of his collected works began to appear in New York. When it was finished in 1923, it contained only 28 of the 40 volumes.

According to the *Encyclopedia Judaica*, over 6000 books, articles, and reviews have been written on Sholem-Aleykhem's works.

Perhaps it is Sholem-Aleykhem's sense of the tragic in Jewish life in the East European Pale—along with his marvelous ear for the way his people talked, his intimate knowledge of their lifestyles, their characters, their outlook—perhaps even more than his justly acclaimed sense of humor—that makes Sholem-Aleykhem the proclaimed "folk-hero" of the Jewish people

Sholem-Aleykhem has been called "the great genius of Yiddish literature...a great humorist...a supreme story teller...a master of world literature...a folk hero...a word-genius *par excellence*...one of the great writers of world literature...a writer who captures the spirit of a whole people in his works, who gives voice to their deepest feelings, aspirations, and spirit...and a humorist with a 'dark side.'"

All of these things are, of course, true. His humor, his humanity, his skill with the language, his fine ear for Yiddish speech, his knowledge of his people—their outlook, their suffering and their ways—all of this are what made him great, caused him to become a "household word," caused his people to love him so, even caused him to become known to the other peoples of the world (*via Fiddler on the Roof*—but he was read and was popular in translation long before that, in Chinese, for example, as well as in Russian and in many other languages).

The editors of this anthology—although they love Sholem-Aleykhem and his works, and although they have steeped themselves in his life, writing, and writings about him, and have presented the fruits of their work in this anthology—must confess that the reasons for Sholem-Aleykhem's success as a writer are on the one hand so obvious as to need no explanation, or on the other hand so mysterious as to elude all explanation.

What is left then is to read him here, albeit, "through the veil" (Byalik once said that reading a poem in translation is like "kissing the bride through her veil"—but too many of us have no *breyre* [choice]).

We invite you, then, to read, laugh, cry, and enjoy, to savor the work of this "second" of the Yiddish classicists, the self-styled "eynikl," master of the Yiddish word, whose work will live as long as the Jewish people lives.

Sholem-Aleykhem!

Sholem-Aleykhem talks things over with Tevye the Dairyman.
Illustration by David Labovski

Biographical Sketch

Sholem-Aleykhem was born Sholem Rabinovitsh in the town of Pereyaslav (now called Pereyaslav-Khmielnitski [Chmielnicky]* in the Ukraine (Poltava province) in 1859, on the 18th of February (old-style calendar) or the 3rd of March (present-day calendar).

At the age of two, he and his family moved to the little town of Voronko, nearby. There he was raised until the age of 12, when the family, due to the collapse of Sholem-Aleykhem's father's business dealings, was forced to move back to Pereyaslav.

But it was Voronko that was his beloved home, the locus of his fondest childhood memories, the model for his archetypal shtetl of the Jewish Pale as he portrayed it under its fictional name, Kasrilevke (Poortown).

In Voronko, Sholem-Aleykhem attended *kheyder;* enjoyed his status as the son of one of the most prominent citizens of little Jewish Voronko—his father traded in lumber and grain, and also received income as the government postal agent for the town; experienced the various types who came to visit in his father's house and absorbed their talk and mannerisms; soaked up legends and stories from his best friend, the orphan Shmulik; and generally lived the life of a Jewish boy in a Jewish small town surrounded by friends and family, subjected to the love and slaps meted out to boys to make them learn and listen. Sholem-Aleykhem got his share of the love and slaps.

He was a boy who learned well and also got into a lot of mischief. One of his chief bits of mischief was to mimic the mannerisms, both verbal and nonverbal, of his teachers and other adults; this evoked lots of hilarity...and slaps.

His father was a traditional Jew with a happy and unusual combina-

---

*It is a typical kind of Sholem-Aleykhem (and Jewish)irony, that his birthplace should be renamed in this particular way: Bogdan Chmielnicky, the son of a Polish nobleman, became a Cossak and Ukrainian leader who led an uprising against the Poles in 1648. A national hero to the Ukrainians, he is remembered by Jews as the murderer of hundreds of thousands of Jews and the brutal annihilator of over 700 Jewish communities. His name lives in the common Yiddish expression, "Khmielnitski'z tsaytn" [Chmielnitsky's times].

tion of traits: he was a khassidic Jew who at the same time loved and admired the *haskole,* the East-European Jewish enlightenment of the time, including the developing modern Hebrew literature that it fostered. As a boy, Sholem-Aleykhem read novels by one of the early pioneers of this literature, Abraham Mapu, and translations of world literature into Hebrew (e.g., *Robinson Crusoe*).

Sholem-Aleykhem's father early recognized his son's exceptional intelligence and talent, praising, encouraging, and protecting him, if necessary.

At one point in the young boy's life, it did become rather necessary. When he was thirteen, Sholem-Aleykhem's mother died during a cholera epidemic, leaving her twelve offspring behind (Sholem-Aleykhem was child number three). After the requisite period of mourning, his father sent about half his brood—Sholem-Aleykhem among them—off to his wife's parents in Boguslav to be looked after. In the meantime, Sholem-Aleykhem's father, Nokhem, without revealing the total number of his offspring, took another wife to run his household and raise his young ones. This stepmother, of an already irascible temperament, was, as can be imagined, made even more choleric when she realized the full extent of her new responsibilities. Life was hard; the inn they were running outside Pereyaslav brought in only a subsistence amount. When she protested loudly (as only she could do) that Sholem was wasting money by burning kerosene late at night (he was writing a romantic novel in Hebrew in the manner of Mapu), his father came to his rescue, telling her not to bother this one, to leave this one alone, that she could scold and supervise his other children as she thought necessary, but that this one was special. She respected this wish of her husband's and thereafter did not bother Sholem.

This poor and irascible stepmother also became the unwitting inspiration for Sholem-Aleykhem's first literary effort in Yiddish. His stepmother was a master of the Yiddish oath, as were so many mother's of the Jewish Pale. She laid about her not only with the traditional slaps, when necessary, but also with those most artful and colorful Yiddish curses. Characteristically, Sholem was inspired to write these curses down, verbatim, and arrange them in alphabetical order, calling the list, "The Abusive Tongue of a Stepmother." His father and stepmother discovered him laboring over this early literary *oeuvre* one night, and instead of the slaps, curses, and scolding he expected, much to his surprise, his list of oaths provoked laughter and amusement.

Another moment from Sholem-Aleykhem's childhood is of some significance. When he was still a small boy, as he was sitting in his home with his father and some of his cronies as they drank tea from the samovar and shmoozed, one of the company read to the group from a Yiddish booklet he had brought along. It was a humorous piece, and Sholem watched as these grown men were absorbed in it, would burst out in laughter from time-to-time, and would slap their knees in their exuberance, shouting out such things as "that rascal!" "what a rogue!," meaning the author. Sholem tells us he envied the author of that Yiddish booklet who could so entertain and provoke to such amusement grown men. At that moment, he tells us, he wished he would someday be able to do the same.

It is important, we think, in this sketch to take note of the remarkable nature of Sholem-Aleykhem's education up to the age of about fourteen. It is only remarkable to us, here and now, but it was fairly typical then and there, typical, that is, for a boy of Sholem-Aleykhem's gifts and social standing.

Until the age of fourteen Sholem received only the traditional Jewish religious education. This consisted of, first, instruction in the reading and writing of Biblical Hebrew; then the reading and translating (into Yiddish, of course)—and even memorizing—of large parts of the first five books of the Bible (i.e., the Pentateuch or *Toyre* [*Torah*]); then "advanced" studies of the rest of the Bible; and ending with the study of various parts of the Talmud, with its exegesis and interpretation of the Bible, and with its eye to the application of the intent or meaning of the Bible to life. Included also in this education was an emphasis on penmanship. Sholem mastered all of this beautifully. Note, however, that this education included almost nothing of what we now think of as elementary and secondary education: no history, no world literature, no foreign languages (and that included the language of the land, i.e., Russian or Ukrainian), no science, in short, no "secular" subjects at all. And yet it seemed to have prepared Sholem exceedingly well—well enough to permit him to bone up on all these secular subjects quickly, sufficiently well to gain him admittance to the provincial Russian School, where admission of Jewish Students was severely limited, and to permit him to do so well there as to win him a scholarship (of which he was allowed to receive only half by the school administration because he was a Jew).

The next step for Sholem would have been the university, but he was persuaded to apply instead to the Jewish Teacher's Institute in Zhitomir. Much to his chagrin (and to his family's, of course), the Institute rejected him. It was a matter of his age. The Institute course of study ran for four years; Sholem would be eighteen on admission; that meant that in three years he would be drafted and would be unable to finish the course. On these grounds his application was rejected. What now?

Because Sholem was now so well-versed, not only in traditional Jewish learning but in secular subjects as well, i.e., Russian language and literature, history, world literature, mathematics, etc., he began to hire himself out as a tutor. This was a hard life: meager pay and miserable conditions in the poor Jewish households of the region. But one day he got lucky. Through a chance meeting, he ended up as a member of a wealthy Jewish household and as tutor to a pretty 13-year-old girl.

Elimelekh Loyef, his new employer, was an unusual kind of Jew for that time and place. He was a proprietor of a huge landed estate. It was a large working farm, with peasants, fields, orchards, and an elegant farmhouse with household servants. He wanted a highly qualified tutor for his daughter, who at the same time could perform secretarial and bookkeeping services for him in the daily management of his estate. In Sholem-Aleykhem he found just the right young man.

For Sholem-Aleykhem his new employment meant a vast step away from the darkness and gloom of his previous existence into the brightness, joy, and prosperity of a new life. He was living in what it's possible to think of as the setting for a Chekhov play: the light and air and flowers and fields of the estate with its comfortable house and its comfortable rooms, lots of good food, served by obsequious servants, money and clothes too—and to top it all off, a charming, intelligent young girl to tutor. It was heaven.

But if it was Paradise Found, it was soon to become Paradise Lost. A cousin of Loyef's came to stay for a couple of weeks and brought Loyef's attention to the fact that his young tutor and his daughter were spending entirely too much time together in an unseemly fashion. Was this proper? What kind of a father was he? Loyef felt betrayed by his trusted employee. One morning shortly thereafter, Sholem-Aleykhem came down for breakfast to find the house deserted, an envelope of money left for him, no note, but a coachman with instructions to take Sholem-Aleykhem away, with his baggage, to the train station. After three years, he was being cast out of Paradise.

He and Loyef's daughter, Olga, had indeed grown fond of each other during their three years together. They missed each other terribly. Sholem had tried to arrange for his letters to be delivered to Olga by the Postmaster, but this false friend betrayed him and delivered them to Loyef instead, who kept them from his daughter. The two sweethearts had no way of communicating with each other.

Sholem-Aleykhem passed a requisite examination and succeeded in a competition to become "government rabbi" in the town of Louben. He now had a way to support himself. At the same time, as a true son of the Haskole, with literary ambitions, he wrote essays in Hebrew and submitted them to the Hebrew publications of the time. One of these was published in the Hebrew Journal, Ha-Melits, and was signed, "Sholem Rabinovitsh." Olga's cousin, a reader of these journals, spotted his name and brought it to his cousin's attention. In this way, the two young lovers were reunited. Olga joined Sholem in Kiev and was married to him there (by a Rabbi Zuckerman) without her father's consent.

Not long after that, Loyef was reconciled with his daughter and new son-in-law. Sholem was persuaded to leave his job as "government rabbi" and return with his bride to Sofievka. After a few months there, they moved to Belaya Tserkov, where they lived for three years, supported by Loyef. There, in 1884, the first of their six children was born.

Then Elimelekh Loyef died. In 1885, under czarist law, legal ownership and managemant of the wealthy estate fell to Sholem, not to Olga. Managing such an estate was not something he was prepared for. It was decided instead to sell the estate. This was done, and Sholem-Aleykhem became a whealthy man. The family, including his mother-in-law and some servants, then moved to Kiev (1888). There Sholem-Aleykhem invested his family's inheritance in the stock exchange. When he wasn't preoccupied with speculating on the exchange, he was writing. And when he wasn't writing he was editing and publishing his new literary project, the *Yidishe Folksbibliotek*.

Then the crash of 1890 hit the Kiev stock exchange, and Sholem-Aleykhem lost everything. Not only was he now a relatively poor man again (Paradise Lost again), but he had to run away from Kiev to Paris, Vienna, and Czernowitz while his mother-in-law, with what little was left to her of the inheritance, held his creditor's at bay.

Sholem-Aleykhem was now thirty-one years old. he rejoined his family in Odessa, where they had moved in the meantime. He tried his hand at the stock exchange again, but to no avail. He now turned entirely to writing in an attempt to make his living. Now there was a large reading public for Yiddish with a more elevated taste than before, so the possibility of so doing did not seem as remote as it had once seemed. From this time on (around 1900), Sholem-Aleykhem devoted himself solely to writing Yiddish, relying only on his pen to earn a livelihood. This he was able to do, sometimes not very well (more often than not the printers and publishers exploited him, not paying him the loyalties to which he was entitled, until the copyrights were regained, after great efforts, in 1909) until his death in the Bronx, New York, on May 13, 1916.

Sholem-Aleykhem was a prolific writer. he wrote almost nonstop. He could write almost anywhere, oblivious to his surroundings. He could write on the train, trolley, marketplace, exchange, waiting rooms, city, countryside, with the noise of the city or of family and friends around him—anywhere and everywhere. He wrote on a little clipboard of his own devising (perhaps we can claim him as the inventor of the clipboard), a narrow piece of wood to which he attached narrow strips of paper with a rubber band. This he carried inside his coat pocket and removed to write on whenever something came to him. When Sholem-Aleykhem began to prepare his collected works for the press in 1913, it was projected to fill 40 volumes; when the collected works were finally published between 1917 and 1925, they were incomplete at 28 volumes.

In 1905, Sholem-Aleykhem witnessed from a hotel window overlooking a Kiev street some of the horrors of the pogrom that the Russians, with governmental incitement and support, carried out in that city and in many other cities and towns all across Russia. It was the czarist government's reply to the cries of the people for bread and freedom and its cynical way of dealing with the constitution and the shortlived Duma it granted to quell the disturbances: blame the Jews; unleash the anger of the Russian people on the Jews, rather than on the government.

Partly as a result of this experience, and partly because he was being told that the Yiddish theater was flourishing in New York and that he could make a big success there, in 1906—after giving a successful reading tour of his work throughout Europe (like Dickens, he was a marvelous interpreter of his own work—people flocked to his readings)—he went with part of his family to America (he was very much a family-man who loved to have his children around him, calling his family his "republic"; if they were not with him for any reason, he carried on an intense correspondence with them). There he gave two plays to the two greatest actors/impresarios of the Yiddish stage at the time: Jacob Adler and Boris Tomashefsky. To Adler he gave *Pasternak;* to Tomashefsky, *Stempenyu.* Although it is an interesting story how these plays fared in their hands, it cannot be told here: the jealousies, the rivalries, not only between these two theatrical giants, but also among the various Yiddish newspapers, with their differing political/ideological positions, and how this affected the reviews and the success of Sholem-Aleykhem's plays. At any rate, both plays failed at the box office; they both closed within a week of their openings. Sholem-Aleykhem left New York a disappointed man. He had arrived to great fanfare, to a tremendous and warm welcome: there were banquets and meetings and speeches; he was hailed in the American newspapers as "the Jewish Mark Twain." But in the end, with the failure of his two plays, it came to nothing. He decided to return to Europe.

Before rejoining the rest of his family in Geneva, he stopped off in Holland to participate as a delegate from New York to the eighth Zionist Congress meeting at the Hague. Ever since he had joined the Khovevei Zion movement in 1888, he had remained a committed and fervent Zionist, writing many pieces, from novels to short stories to essays to journalistic articles, in the service of this cause. In 1907 at the Hague, as a delegate to the Zionist Congress, he met for the first time the great national Jewish poet, Khayim Nakhmen Byalik, who was also serving as a delegate; they remained fast friends.

*　　　*　　　*

In 1908 Sholem-Aleykhem goes on another highly successful reading tour. He is met by crowds at the railroad stations, students carry him back to his hotel on their shoulders, the readings are given to packed houses, young people and workers unhitch the horse to his droshky and pull him along the streets to the lecture hall. In the middle of this tour, at a town called Baronovich, in present day Poland, he coughs, spits up blood, is diagnosed with tuberculosis, and is confined to bed in that town for the next two months.

After that rest, and for the next five years, Sholem-Aleykhem winters in Nervi, on the Italian Riviera, and summers in Switzerland and in the Schwartzwald in Germany, trying to cure his tuberculosis. He does so. A year later he gives another successful reading tour in Russia.

In 1914 he is vacationing with his "republic" at the shore on the Baltic in Germany when World War I breaks out. As a Russian citizen, he is considered an enemy alien and is forced to leave Germany at once. Like many others, he decides to escape Europe's war and emigrate with his family to America. He makes it there with all his family except Mischa and Emma: Mischa is ill and Emma remains with him in Copenhagen. Another daughter, Lyala, and her husband, return to Russia.

In America, he is again warmly received. He writes for the Yiddish newspapers, is even published in translation in the Hearst papers, and continues working. He lives first in an apartment in Manhattan and then on Kelly Street in the Bronx. In 1915 he receives the sad news of his beloved son Mischa's death from tuberculosis. He is devastated. He rewrites his will. Five months later he is dead.

New York witnesses the largest funeral the city has every seen before or since. Hundreds of thousands accompany their folk writer to his grave in a funeral procession that winds its way from Kelly street in the Bronx all the way down through Manhattan and across the Brooklyn Bridge to the Har Nebo cemetery in Cypress Hills, Brooklyn.

He is later interred in the Workmen's Circle Har Karmel cemetery in Brooklyn, where he is, according to his wishes, buried, not among aristocrats and upper class people, but among the common folk, "workers, the real Jewish people, so that the gravestone which will be placed on my grave will beautify the simple graves around me, and the simple graves will beautify my grave, just as the simple, honest folk during my life beautified their folk-writer."

The Orphan. The ordinary Jew is orphaned by Sholem-Aleykhem's death. He is buried in the Workmen's Circle cemetery in New York.

Was His Death Too Soon?

by Louis Fridhandler

There is no answer, yet the question gnaws. Sholem-Aleykhem was only 57 when he died on May 13, 1916. It was one day after his 33rd wedding anniversary. What went wrong?

He was plagued by illnesses, but the evidence outlined below suggests there could have been time for more creativity for a spirit that thrived, grew vigorous, while at work. In writing, he washed away pain.

*   *   *

His broken heart, after learning in New York of his son's death in far-off Copenhagen from tuberculosis of the brain, hastened his death. The most critical factor in his last couple of weeks, however, was his failure to drink enough water, despite urgent appeals by his physicians. To a degree he stopped listening to them, as he felt they did not or could not listen to him.

First, a brief review of some relevant medical history:

1. July 28, 1908, at age 49, he fell acutely ill with hemorrhagic pulmonary tuberculosis in Baranovitch, Poland. This interrupted a tour of cities and towns where he read his works before enthusiastic audiences. He was forced to remain in a hotel for two months before moving to a sanitorium in Nervi, Italy.

2. Nervi, Spring, 1910: Sholem-Aleykhem was lying on a couch enjoying the sun when he fainted. He recovered enough to travel to Switzerland, where a Professor Sahli diagnosed a heart attack and advised a long rest in Badenweiler. Reference to this episode has been found in only one place.[1] There is oblique confirmation in a letter from Sholem-Aleykhem to Gershon Levin[2] where he writes that he is feeling better and that Professor Sahli discovered that he "had a heart."

3. Perhaps his urinary tract symptoms of 1913 began around *khanike,* 1912. Gershon Levin, in his memoir, mentions a "bladder problem" which interfered with Sholem-Aleykhem's plans to travel to Russia during *khanike,* and cites a letter of late January, 1913, in which Sholem writes, "...ill for the last nine days.... my shouts [of pain] must at times be heard all the way to Warsaw. Haven't you heard? After all, you have an ear for music."[3]

Other letters from a clinic in Bern, Switzerland, during January and February, 1913, describe his terrible pains and premonitions of dying. The best medical summary is given in his letter of late March, 1913, to Gershon Levin, a physician, in which Sholem-Aleykhem writes, "...I suffered from urinary blockage.... Kocher,...a butcher, said I must have a [prostate] operation without fail. As it turned out, it was simply a spasm of the sphincter due to nervousness and strain. The great urologist, Professor Zuckerkandel, prescribed compresses and much walking.... thank God, I've forgotten that I have a bladder. It is much more normal than it used to be."[4]

This susceptibility to physical symptoms of "nervous" origin is especially relevant to his final weeks.

4. At the outbreak of World War I, Sholem-Aleykhem and family were in Germany, where they were considered enemy aliens. They managed to flee to Copenhagen through Berlin and Malmo, Sweden. On the northward train from Berlin they were under the watchful eyes of German soldiers. Berkowitz describes how he wanted to get water to slake Sholem-Aleykhem's dreadful, nagging thirst, but his way was blocked by hostile soldiers waving threatening bayonets. In Copenhagen, Sholem-Aleykhem was given a diagnosis of diabetes insipidus (no relation to sugar diabetes[5], it is due to insufficient anti-diuretic hormone secretion from the posterior pituitary). It may have been caused by a tubercular infection of the pituitary gland. With diabetes insipidus, one must drink much water to avoid dehydration and its complication. This, too, was an important factor in his final weeks.

5. The news from Copenhagen of his son's death, September 15, 1915, was a dreadful shock to the family. Berkowitz writes of a sudden change in appearance and spirit, from an impression of eager youthfulness, to one of disheartened old age. The family moved from Harlem to the Bronx in the hope that a change of location might ease the pain.[6] The severest sting came from the thought that he had to say *kadish* for his son instead of the other way around.

6. In March, 1916, he fell ill with an acute inflammation of the pericardium, the outer casing of the heart.[7] it was a serious illness, but he followed doctor's orders and recovered. He soon gave up listening to his doctors, and lived only six or seven weeks more.

*   *   *

The circumstances of his father's death in January 1888, and a piece of fiction of 1913, become relevant here. His father died of esophageal cancer at age 57. A letter from Sheyne-Sheyndl to Menakhem-Mendl contains a description of her father's death that seems a fictional revisitation by Sholem-Aleykhem of his own real and awful experience, that of watching his own father die. An excerpt:

> Pa had not been feeling well for some time. He complained that something was growing inside him and that he could not eat. The doctors fed him pills, told him it would soon pass. As time went on, Pa ate less and less. The doctors fed him pills, took money (may they sicken), until he

18

stopped eating and slowly faded away from starvation. He went out like a flickering candle, quiet as a dove, no groan, no peep, just closed his eyes and—finished.

A description of Sholem-Aleykhem's last two weeks bears a haunting similarity to Sheyne-Sheyndl's report about *her* father's final days. After Passover, Sholem-Aleykhem complained of frequent nausea. *He* thought something was growing inside *him*. His physicians told him it was "nerves," and it would soon pass. He ate less and less, drank little, and his condition steadily deteriorated.

His identification with his father was strong and clear. In secret, he told his nurse (who had attended him in 1908 in Baranovitch) that he knew that he had a cancer of the esophagus growing inside him, just like his father. Another sign of his approaching end was that he was 57, the age at which his father and grandfather had died. Though the doctors told him he was only suffering from "nerves," Sholem-Aleykhem didn't believe them and resented the diagnosis. Berkowitz reports:

> …His doctor was still optimistic. He argued with Sholem-Aleykhem that he must take himself in hand, because he is not sick just nervous. Sholem-Aleykhem listened with a sad, tired, remote look in his eyes, and said, "All right, you've ended your speech. Now go home to sleep in peace." As the doctor left the room, Sholem-Aleykhem said to me, "What a dolt! I feel my life ebbing, and he talks to me of nerves." In the last days of his illness, he told his nurse, "I'm being called 'there,' and this time, arguing won't help. I'll have to go."[9]

This conversation was in Russian. Had Sholem-Aleykhem felt free to converse in his beloved, homey Yiddish, his mother tongue, he might have felt more deeply understood through a kinship with the doctors. That might have encouraged his cooperation with them. Would he have drunk enough water in time?

Worth noting is that, as was his habit, Sholem-Aleykhem used the formal "you" when speaking with his son-in-law, I.D. Berkowitz, who never understood why. The obvious distance Sholem-Aleykhem felt in that room with Berkowitz and the doctors must have been painfully chilling and depressing.

During a troubled night, well before the dawn of May 9, Sholem-Aleykhem shakily penned his last writing: a short, unfinished chapter for *Motl Peysi dem khazns*. He wrote:

> In America, everyone must move. If he doesn't want to move, he is made to move.

Was he fictionalizing his confession to his nurse that this time, he knew arguing wouldn't help, he would have to go?

The chapter also features a nameless, poorly-dressed customer of a news-stand who mutely picks up a newspaper and reads without a word to anyone. When told in anglicized New York Yiddish *"Es kost a peni"* [it costs a penny], a sound still foreign to Sholem-Aleykhem's European ears, the customer replaces the paper, remaining mute. Is it possible the customer represents Sholem-Aleykhem, who apparently gave up hope of being understood by those not ready to use his *mame-loshn* [mother tongue], the sounds of his childhood?

On May 9, there was an attempt to nourish and rehydrate the patient with a nutrient enema, termed by Berkowitz, *nourishment by artificial means.* It worked. The treatment made him feel a great deal better, but the improvement was short-lived. On May 10, he grew much worse. Specialists ruled out gastrointestinal disease and diagnosed terminal kidney failure due to the history of diabetes insipidus.[10] On May 12, another doctor offered the slim hope that eight glasses of water might get the kidneys working again.[11] Sholem-Aleykhem drank only a little, and he died early the next morning.

*   *   *

What, then, did Sholem-Aleykhem die of? The physiological answer is, "kidney failure due to dehydration resulting from diabetes insipidus"; add to this Sholem-Aleykhem's close identification with his father and his heartbreak at the death of his elder son, Mischa. Could he have lived more productive years if he had been able to understand the true nature of his illness and had drunk lots of water? Based on what we now know, very likely.

REFERENCES

[1] Berkowitz, I.D., Volume 4, p. 82, *Undzere Rishoynim,* Tel Aviv: Hamenorah Publishing House, 1966.

[2] *Dos Sholem-Aleykhem Bukh,* ed. I.D. Berkowitz, New York: IKUF, pp. 272-273, 1926, 1958.

[3] *Dos Sholem-Aleykhem Bukh,* p. 278.

[4] Ibid.

[5] *Undzere Rishoynim* 4: 155.

[6] *Undzere Rishoynim* 5: 207.

[7] *Undzere Rishoynim* 5: 214.

[8] *Menakhem-Mendl,* by Sholem Aleykhem, Tel Aviv: Beth Shalom-Aleykhem, I.L. Peretz Publishing House, 1976, p. 56.

[9] *Undzere Rishoynim* 5: 221.

[10] Epilogue to *Motl Peysi Dem Khazns* by I.D. Berkowitz, in Book 2 of *Motl Peysi Dem Khazns, Ale Verk Fun Sholem-Aleykhem, Folksfond Oysgabe,* xix: 205-207.

[11] *Dos Sholem-Aleykhem Bukh,* p. 371.

Sholem-Aleykhem with his clip-board, 1913, *at age* 54.

Sholem-Aleykhem at his desk in 1905.

Sholem Aleichem As I Knew Him*

by B.Z. Goldberg

(Translated and abridged from the Yiddish by Max Rosenfeld)

Ben-Zion Goldberg (1895-1972), Yiddish publicist, was married to Sholem Aleichem's daughter, Marie [1892-1985], author of My Father, Sholem Aleichem *(1968). The Yiddish essay appeared in* Yiddishe Kultur, *May 1951. —M.R.*

Let me describe him as I knew him the last year and a half of his life.

He was a bit shorter than average, broadboned, slender, round-shouldered. But his stature depended upon his mood. In good spirits, he looked taller, stronger, more energetic, full of *joie de vivre.* In poor spirits, he seemed smaller, thinner, bent-over, wrapped in a dark cloud.

His face, typical Jewish-Ukrainian: wide across the forehead, narrowing toward the chin. His skin—yellow as parchment, with deep furrows. An old face, but with a youthful glow in his blue eyes. His teeth, white, strong. His hair, not as blond as it had once been, grew long and thick and fell in waves across his large head. His voice, also youthful, firm, vibrant. His diction, remarkably clear. He spoke with the cadences and pauses of a skilled orator.

His attire, not foppish, but definitely different. He dressed according to his mood. When his health was bad, he put on a dark-gray suit and an old sweater. When he was working, he wore a velvet jacket, a colored cravat, and in his breast-pocket, two or three fountain pens, which he called his "tools." When he completed a piece of writing and—as was his custom—was about to read it to his family, he dolled up, as if he were going to a formal banquet.

Sometimes, on a Saturday morning, if he felt like it, he put on his cutaway, his ulster with the velvet collar, and a top-hat, and walked to the Hungarian Synagogue at 116th Street in Harlem to hear Cantor Yossele Rosenblatt. (It was only a few blocks from his home on Lenox Avenue.) Trolley cars clanged. Automobiles raced by—there were no traffic lights in

*Reprinted by permission of *Jewish Currents* (May 1991), p.25.

23

those days. Throngs of people pushed and shoved on a mundane street in the most mundane city in the world. And in the midst of all this he strolled along—a bit of the Jewish Sabbath in a top-hat.

People would stop and stare, but he was used to that. Sunk in his *shabbos* mood, he wasn't bothered.

Why did he go to shul? He was not an observant Jew. He did not keep the Sabbath. His home was not "kosher." He did not fast on the designated days. And yet one could hardly call him an *apikoyres,* a non-believer. Other great Jewish artists of his time, like Mendele Moykher-Sforim or Bialik, acted much the same way. What he observed were the esthetic-emotional parts of Jewish ritual, and in intimate moments—when he wrote his will, for instance—he even called upon the name of God. It had nothing to do with theology. It was not the God who lives up in heaven but down below in the hearts of human beings.

Sholem Aleichem was always writing. He loved his work. It came easy to him. It bubbled like the water in a spring, fresh, clear, delicious. And he was the first to savor what he had written. I could tell by his facial expression whether the sentence he was working on was happy or sad. If it was comical, he laughed out loud.

But the first draft was only a step in the process. He was a great believer in Mendele's dictum: "A real writer must polish every word." Sholem Aleichem, however, did not find this laborious. He did it in a relaxed way, like an artist putting the finishing touches on a painting. When he was writing the first draft, he worked standing up at a high desk. For the send draft he would lounge in a big easy chair, his little notebook in one hand, and touch his pen lightly to the paper.

He could write anywhere—in the train that he often took from New York City to Belmar, NJ; on the ferry to New Jersey; on the subway. Had you been watching him you might have thought he was dozing. But suddenly he would take his notebook out of his inside pocket, then his pen, and start writing. In good health and in bad, he wrote. I once saw him writing while a family member held an ice-bag to his head. So long as he had the physical strength to move his hand, he wrote. And in his final days, when he was no longer able to do that, his hand moved of its own accord.

He is lying mortally ill. He falls asleep. His right hand, resting atop the blanket, moves. Three of his fingers come together, as though grasping a pen, and start moving slowly across the blanket...

Two passions Sholem Aleichem had—his writing, and his family. He needed his family around him as he needed air to breathe. His fantasy: to have all of them nearby—his sons, his daughters, his sons-in-law, his daughters' boy friends—everyone within walking distance. Better still, under one roof, and they would all come to lunch in his apartment at precisely one o'clock every day (and feel free to bring a friend or two).

That's why, here in America, he felt trapped, could hardly breathe— the family had been torn apart. One daughter and a son in Denmark. Another daughter and her husband and child in Russia. The rest in the U.S. How could he gather them all together when the war was a chasm between them?

Still, at one o'clock every day, the table was set, and whoever was in the city was expected to be there. If you had been downtown on business, you had to be back home for lunch, whether you were hungry or not. Papa sat at the head of the table. The maid brought the food in from the kitchen. Mama served everyone their portion. You watched Papa's eyes. If he was feeling good, it was a joyous occasion. If not, the food stuck in your throat, no matter how hard he tried not to spoil the mood. But no one ever talked about it.

Evenings the family would gather too, but not by pre-arrangement. They simply enjoyed being together, so if at all possible, they would drop in. What did we talk about? The latest news, maybe. All the Yiddish news-papers came into the house, and even some from abroad. And Sholem Aleichem read them all, front page to last, including the ads. We talked about new books that had come out. Mainly about Yiddish writers and their work. We praised and we criticized—but only the work, never the writer himself. To speak sneeringly of a writer—that was off limits.

And we never talked about the past, about the days when Papa was rich. We never mentioned the sacrifices he had made for Yiddish litera-ture, the generous fees he had given to young writers. Or that his wife had sold her diamond ring for half its value in order to ransom the second vol-ume of his *Folks-Bibliotek* from the binder. (I had to learn about this later from an article in a Soviet newspaper!)

Sholem Aleichem never spoke about the standing-room-only recep-tions for him all over Europe. Or here either, for that matter. What he did like to talk about were the comical incidents that happened to him at these events. And when he told us these stories in his own inimitable manner, who could help but laugh?

I often wondered: Where did this relationship between Sholem Aleichem and his family stem from, so rare in our days. I believe there was a series of psychological reasons, as well as the particular circumstances of his life. Primarily it was because he led a life in which he had never done anything he wanted to hide from them. Add to that his natural love for children, his talent for getting along with them as an equal. He never struck any of his six children, never even raised his voice to them. One word from him that he was displeased with something they had done— and that was enough. When they grew up, he never tried to dominate them, tell them what to do. From a very early age they considered him a friend whom they loved and respected.

And then, he fell ill at such a young age, and he became an object of solicitude. In this "foreign" land only his family could provide a safe milieu for him to live in...

Alarming news from his children on the other side of the ocean about the impending death of his son. His own illness here, and unremitting financial worries. His relationship with editors of Jewish publications was not good. They resented him because he earned more than they did—which still did not prevent him from falling immediately into debt, so that he was financially unable to do some of the things that might have cured his illness.

Despite all that, he was intensely interested in everything going on around him, especially in Jewish life. He could stand on a street corner for a long time and talk with a Jewish newspaper dealer. He could walk into a dry-cleaning store and "interview" the owner—how do they clean the clothes, how much do they pay their workers? He went to learn first-hand how the more prosperous Jews lived. All his live he had gotten his "sustenance" from the people; he did not want to lose it here.

But he needn't have worried. All sorts of Jews came to visit him, to share their troubles with him, to ask for advice. He did not hide from them. Instead of the root seeking the soil, the soil came to the root.

*   *   *

A cool autumn evening. He and I were taking a walk along a street in Lakewood. He was feeling better. The cool air seemed to invigorate him. We walked briskly. He talked about his writing plans—plans that would have taken years and years to fulfill. He was especially excited about giving his young hero Motl a musical career in America. But Motl the orphan was twice orphaned. His story was never completed, just as Sholem-Aleykhem's own autobiography remained unfinished. On May 13, 1916 the Master Yiddish Writer died at age 57, his favorite pen still in his hand...

Sholem-Aleykhem Comes to America

Letters on Board Ship from London to New York in 1906

These letters are in the form of a diary kept by Sholem-Aleykhem on board S.S. St. Louis, going from London to New York. It was Sholem-Aleykhem's first journey to the United States (he was there again in 1914), traveling with his wife and their small son, Numa.

Addressed to his children. Translated from the Yiddish translation of the Russian.*

Between Sky and Earth, Atlantic Ocean   Tuesday, Oct. 16, 1906

Dear Ones:

I am writing these pages to you while lying in bed in a second-class cabin. This is the first day that it's possible to use a pencil. All day Saturday it was calm...Sunday morning...the ocean began to cut capers, tossing the boat up and down like a chip of wood...Woke up at seven o'clock Monday morning. Bad. The ocean was furious. We couldn't get up. We rang. A steward and nurse entered. Brought coffee. We couldn't drink it. We lived on water, oranges and Madeira. Numtchik woke up and asked: "Where are we?" He doesn't want to go to America; he wants to go to Geneva....

Wednesday October 17, fifth day out.

...We took mother out on deck. Seated her on a chair. The ocean—just like a mirror. We wrapped her all up. The view is wonderful. The weather—magnificent. Sun. Numtchik and I watch a card game which is in full swing. Americans play cards. Germans swill beer. Englishmen gorge themselves....

On deck. Sun. The ocean—a sheet of mercury. The boat—do you know what it is like?—It's a small moving colony, with streets and alleys and little houses and families and children and shouting and bustling.... The population of our colony is said to number 3,500. In short, a miniature Bohuslaw....

---

*From *Jewish Currents,* December 1958, p. 14-15; reprinted from Melech Grafstein's *Sholem Aleichem Panorama,* published by *The Jewish Observer,* London, Ontario, Canada, 1948, p. 341.

...Few Jews on board boat and therefore lonesome. There is this peculiarity about Jews: when there are a lot them they are hard to stand; when there aren't any, you long for them....

Thursday, Oct. 18, Morning

...The joy of the passengers in the knowledge that land is near is boundless. Tomorrow, we're told, we shall see land.

Just sent a telegram to New York by wireless.

About 12 noon we went down "to the people" in third class. Good God! How horrible! Humans are treated not better than animals. Soon I was surrounded by the entire Jewish colony. This was immediately noticed by the attendants who asked me to be good enough to return to second class. After this our cabin (second class) seemed like paradise.

Moral: Son of man, look beneath thyself....

Saturday, Oct. 20, 3 o'clock

At last we are in New York! The pier is jammed full of people. The boat pulls up slowly. There are loud shouts of *haydad!* Hats are tossed up into the air, a mass of hats. What is the occasion? Shouts of "Sholem Aleichem!" made everything clear. The crowd consisted of delegates of Zionist and other organizations. We were surrounded by representatives of the Yiddish and English press. I was raised up in the air. Numtchik began to cry. Cameras were trained on the three of us. Among the people who rushed up to kiss me, there was a young gentleman with a short yellow beard. It was my brother Bernard. This gentleman exclaimed: There is a telegram! Tisay (Ernestina) gave birth to a girl!" It was more than a solemn moment!

Addressed to literary friends in Odessa; the critic I.H. Ravnitzki (1859-1944), the poet Hayim Nachman Bialik (1873-1934), the writer E. L. Levinsky (1858-1910) and Moishe Polinkovsky. Translated from the Yiddish.

New York, Nov. 4, 1906

Dear Friends Ravnitzki, Bialik, Levinski, Polinkovski, and others:

This is the first opportunity I have to write you a few words, but no more than a few. The enclosed clippings will tell you everything. The honor I was given upon landing, from the first day I came here until the so-called reception, was really a bit too much. But the recognition that has been accorded our Yiddish literature and our beloved folk speech has truly given me much pleasure and it has sweetened my life in the long wander-

ings that I have undertaken. I hope that this will be the end of my wanderings. There are prospects of a very brilliant future here for me, and brother
Levinski was right in telling me so as far back as a year ago.

Write!

Your, Sholem-Aleykhem

I am here with Olga and Numtshik, just the three of us. The rest of the
family is still in Switzerland.

PLACE NAMES AND THEIR MEANING
IN SHOLEM-ALEYKHEM'S WORK

by Louis Fridhandler

Sholem-Aleykhem's fictional town names are worth examining. Insights may be gained. Let's look "behind the scenes" at his better-known towns: 1. *Kasrilevke,* 2. *Mazepevke,* 3. *Yehupets,* and 4. *Boyberik.* (An analysis of *Finsternish* and *Hrebinka,* the place names Sholem-Aleykhem used for his two early stories, "The Election" and "Legboymer," respectively, can be found at the end of the introduction to those two stories (p. 74 in this volume).

1. *Kasrilevke*

The Slavic suffix *-evke* denotes a small town. *Kasril* is of Hebrew origin. Sholem-Aleykhem's original spelling of *Kasril* indicates it to be *Katriel* in the Sephardic pronunciation. *Katriel* signifies "Crown of God"; but it came to mean "pauper" in Yiddish. And so *Kasrilevke* may be deciphered to mean: "The townlet of miserable paupers who are nevertheless a treasured adornment of God himself!"* As the townspeople of *Kasrilevke* might say, "Thanks, but we'd just as soon forego the honor and have money." The contrast between noble appellation and mean reality is rather striking. How did he synthesize it?

Kasrilevke resonates with *Krasilovka,* a non-fictional small town close enough to Kiev to be a suburb.** The transposition of two consonants and two minor vowel changes transform *Krasilovka* into *Kasrilevke.* He apparently juggled the sounds, took them apart, played with them, until they fell into place to create a townlet whose name expressed that bitterly ironic compliment: God should indeed regard as noble adornments the denizens of *Kasrilevke* for holding true to Jewish values despite degrading poverty, persecution from hostile gentile neighbors, and an oppressive government. Sholem-Aleykhem "connected" with Yiddish readers everywhere, whose

---

*These suggestions are based on an insight by Dovid Berglson who pointed out that the first three Hebrew letters of *Kasrilevke* spell *Keser:* a crown, a Torah ornament, a *shayndling,* a glistening gem. In folk-speech, it means, "a merry pauper." [*Sovietishe Literatur* (Kiev) 1: 65-78, 1939]. Further, *Akatriel Yah* is one of the names of God used in the *Talmud* (*Gemore, Berakhot* 7a). *Akatriel* begins with the letter aleph, whose function is not clear. The rest, *katriel,* is spelled exactly as *kasril* by Sholem-Aleykhem in *Di shtot fun di kleyne mentshelekh.*

**Many years before he created *Kasrilevke,* Sholem-Aleykhem mentioned the town of *Kriselevke* in "Shomers Mishpet" (1888, p. 69). The similarity in sound strongly suggests he meant *Krasilovka,* near Kiev, where he lived in 1888.

daily lives were troubled by such factors. Jews were proud to claim kinship with the beloved and worthy inhabitants of *Kasrilveke,* who endured and lived honorable lives.

2. *Mazepevke*

Rather than reaching for irony, Sholem-Aleykhem at times used fictional names to simply and directly stress a townlet's social and cultural ambience, a well-worn device among authors.

Mazepevke was an awful place. In a Hebrew piece of 1889, *Don Quixote of Mazepevke and his Side-Kick, Pincus,* Sholem-Aleykhem portrays *Mazepevke* as a heap of garbage. The place owes its name to Ivan Stepanovich Mazepa, a Cossack hetman of the seventeenth century (successor to Khmelnitski, perpetrator of the massacre of at least 100,000 Ukrainian Jews in 1648-49). Furthermore, in Yiddish, *mazepe* means "a slovenly person" (Harkavy's dictionary). As if to underscore ambience, Sholem-Aleykhem dubbed a *Mazepevke* stream, *Der Taykh Shtunkeylo.* A close English equivalent might be, "The Stinkola River." There is no mistaking the general "air" of the town.

Mazepevke was invented at east thirteen years before *Kasrilevke.* The great popularity of beloved *Kasrilevke* led to replacement of *Mazepevke* (with its unpleasant connotations) by *Kasrilevke* in later editions of some pieces. It was a bad idea. An example: the original setting for the 1901 version of "Legboymer" is *Mazepevke* (Sholem-Aleykhem's *Ale Verk,* Vol. 2, pp. 69-88, Warsaw, 1903). Later (perhaps posthumously by I.D. Berkowitz), the setting was changed to *Kasrilevke. Der Taykh Stunkeylo* was retained, however, producing a jarring, discordant note. The stream did not belong in beloved *Kasrilevke* (*Folksfond Oysgabe,* Vol IX, pp. 99-120, 1918).

Menakhem-Mendl comes from *Kasrilevke* in the most accessible editions. It was originally *Mazepevke,* and that made it easier to understand why he avoided returning home to wife and family.

Tevye's wife, Golde, originally came from *Mazepevke.* However, the change to *Kasrilevke* was not overly discordant.

The earliest mention of *Mazepevke* seems to be in 1888 in *Di Yidishe Folks-Bibliotek,* Vol. I. It was a set of book reviews dated *Mazepevke,* 1888, signed with the pseudonym *S. Bikherfreser* ("Gobbler of Books"). The next mention of *Mazepevke* seems to occur in the Hebrew tales written in 1889 for *Hamelits,* "Images and Shadows of Jewish Life in *Mazepevke.*"

3. *Yehupets*

Sholem-Aleykhem's "ear" helped him create a name for the city of Kiev which echoed the whooping and hollering so characteristic of the big city's noise and bustle, the shouts of droshky drivers and Jewish street traders who were excluded from the stock exchange building. *Yehupets* is certainly Kiev. The street names remain authentic, leaving no doubt.

4. *Boyberik*

Sholem-Aleykhem and his family spent many a summer in the town of Boyarka, near Kiev, where they, and many other Kiev Jews, rented a *dacha*. He changed the name, making it sound more homey and Yiddish.

Around the samovar in the shtetl.

32

A NOTE ON TRANSLITERATION AND TRANSLATION

Yiddish is, of course, written with the letters of the Hebrew alphabet. This poses a problem to the translator/transliterator. How to present Yiddish words which are left untranslated—or Yiddish names—in the alphabet system of another language?

In 1937, the YIVO Institute for Jewish Research in New York instituted a standard system for the transliteration of standard Yiddish. It approximates the sounds of standard Yiddish. It is much to be preferred to the haphazard, inaccurate attempts at transliteration previously practiced, some of which persist even today.

A case very much in point is the transliteration of the pen-name of the author of the works presented in this anthology. His name has been variously transliterated as *Sholom Aleichem; Shalom Aleichem; Sholem Aleichem; Scholom Aleichem;* etc.

According to the system devised by the YIVO, his pen-name is most accurately rendered as "Sholem-Aleykhem." (The hyphen is inserted because that is how this very common expression of greeting—meaning, roughly, "Hello!"—is spelled in Yiddish: with a hyphen.)

We have chosen to follow YIVO's system in the transliteration of our author's name. This of course causes all kinds of problems, but we believe it is worth it: to draw attention to the existence of a standard system of transliteration which we wish were as widely employed as possible—and to more accurately reflect the original Yiddish pronunciation.

The problems are various.

The Library of Congress, many years ago, adopted "Sholom Aleichem" as the standard transliteration; also, the differing works we drew on for this anthology used differing transliterations of Sholem-Aleykhem's name.

What we have done is to use our transliteration (based on the standardized YIVO system) in the title, in our biographical sketch, and in our introductions. But in the selections and quotes from other sources we have allowed the differing transliterations of Sholem-Aleykhem's name to stand.

*   *   *

A similar problem arises in the transliterating of Yiddish words that the translators of various selections chose, for one reason or another, to transliterate rather than to translate.

Some of these transliterations are so old now and so commonly employed that any other transliteration looks odd, even incomprehensible. A good example is the transliteration "matzoh." This has become the standard way to write this word in English, but to a speaker of Yiddish it seems an abomination. It gives a totally false idea of how this word is pronounced in any dialect of Yiddish. In the YIVO system, it would be written as "matse."

The problem with this is that Jews (or others) will not recognize this transliteration as referring to the familiar, unleavened, Passover flatbread.

Undaunted, however, we have decided, come what may, to stick with the YIVO system. But...where the original translator put "matzoh," for example, we have let it stand. In our Glossary, we have listed it as "matzoh," and referred the reader to "matse."

We hope in this way to make a small contribution to the wider adoption of the YIVO system of transliteration.

*   *   *

Much has been written about the difficulties of translating Yiddish into English, or any other language for that matter.

The problem seems to inhere, not just in the ordinary problems of translating from one language to another—e.g., idioms, words, expressions, that somehow lose their savor when translated—but in the difficulty of translating words and expressions that are steeped in alien or remote cultural or religious traditions.

Another difficulty usually cited is the problem posed by the richness of a Yiddish vocabulary which draws, etymologically from so many different linguistic sources (Hebrew, Slavic, Germanic, etc.), each with its own flavor, overtones, and nuances.

With Sholem-Aleykhem, these problems seem to treble. The richness of his language, his word-play, his ear for the speech of the folk—all of these make the task of the translator particularly difficult.

As for the "cultural/religious remoteness," often cited as a difficulty for the translator, with Sholem-Aleykhem's *Tevye* stories this problem becomes especially apparent. The chief problem is that Tevye, the ostensible narrator of the stories, often quotes from Hebrew scripture or from other sacred Jewish writings—to make a point, to get a laugh, or to comment on a situation. Sometimes he quotes quite accurately; other times he garbles the quote or applies the quote inappropriately (often on purpose).

How is the translator to deal with these Hebrew interpolations, these quotes? How to convey the humor of their "garbledness"?

Various translators have taken various approaches. Some have deleted them; some have translated them; some have transliterated them and then followed their transliteration with a translation. We believe that Miriam Katz, the translator of *Tevye the Dairyman* in this anthology, chose an original and readable approach: she translated them directly, but indicated that they are scriptural, learned, or sacred quotations by putting them in italics.

No solution is completely satisfactory. But we think Miriam Katz has handled the difficulties of translation extremely well, as have the other translators in this anthology (we must exclude ourselves), each in her/his own way. Better to kiss the bride through her veil, than never to kiss her at all.

I
Autobiography

INTRODUCTION TO
FROM THE FAIR

In 1908, Sholem-Aleykhem decided the time had come to write his autobiography. As he himself put it, "You may die suddenly. People who think they knew and understood you will turn up with cock-and-bull stories about you. What will you gain by it? Better to do the job yourself, for nobody knows you as well as yourself" (Tamara Kahana's translation).

But it wasn't until 1914, in America now, on Kelly street in the Bronx that Sholem-Aleykhem began to tell his own story. He told it in the third person, as if writing about someone else. And he told it in episodes, rather than as one continuous tale.

Originally he intended for it to have ten parts (or volumes). He only lived to write the first three parts, taking the autobiography up to his twenty-first year. He was working on it up to a few days before his death.

From the Fair is not only a book from which we learn much about the great Yiddish classicist, it also remains one of his most charming and entertaining works.

For this volume we have chosen two selections by two different translators. The first selection consists of Chapters 1 through 6, translated by Tamara Kahana, Sholem Aleykehm's grand-daughter; the second selection, Chapters 68 through 73, are from near the end of *From the Fair*, translated by Curt Leviant.

In the first selection, we learn about Sholem-Aleykhem's boyhood in Voronko (the prototype for his fictional Kasrilevke); his parents; and his dear childhood friend, a spinner of fascinating tales, the orphan, Shmulik.

In the second selection, we watch as Sholem-Aleykhem meets his *basherte* (destined wife), is admitted to "paradise," and is expelled therefrom.

The complete *From the Fair* consists of seventy-eight chapters and 278 pages in translation. The original Yiddish version appeared serially in *Der Tog* from mid-June 1915 until his death.

He wrote the following dedication as a preface to this, his autobiography. It is reproduced below (our translation):

FOR MY CHILDREN—A GIFT

Dear, beloved children of mine:

I dedicate to you the work of my works, the book of my books, the song of songs of my soul.

I know that my book is, as is every human being's work, not free of faults, but who knows better than you what it cost me? I have given and invested into it the best that I possess: my heart.

Read it from time to time.

Perhaps you or your children will learn something from it—how to love our people and how to value its spiritual treasures which lie strewn about in all the dark corners of our great exile all over the great world.

That would be the best recompense for more than thirty years of faithful work in the field of our mother-tongue and literature.

Your father,

The author,
Sholem-Aleykhem,
February 1916, New York

1. Why "The Great Fair"?

In lieu of an introduction • Why has the author undertaken to write an autobiography? • Sholom Aleichem, the writer, tells the story of Sholom Aleichem, the man.

When a man starts out for a fair, his heart is full of hope; he does not know yet what bargains he may make nor what his achievements may be. He flies toward it like an arrow. Don't stop him—he has no time to dally!... But after he returns from the fair, he has already made his bargains, accomplished his achievements; he is no longer in a hurry, for now he has plenty of time. He is now able to sum up the result of his journey, and he can tell about it unhurriedly, dwelling on every detail: whom he had met at the fair, what he has seen, what he has heard.

My friends have often insisted that I should recount the story of my life. "The time has come," they said, "and it may even be interesting...." I tried to listen to their advice. Several times I set myself to work, but each time put the pen aside until... finally the right time came. Before I had reached the age of fifty, I had the honor of meeting His Majesty, the Angel of Death, face to face. I was almost dispatched to that place whence one cannot write letters nor even send a greeting by messenger. In short, having been practically gathered unto my forefathers, I said to myself, "Now the time has come. Snatch the opportunity and write, for no one knows what the morrow will bring! You may die suddenly. People who think they knew and understood you will turn up with cock-and-bull stories about you. What will you gain by it? Better do the job yourself, for nobody knows you as well as yourself. Tell the world what you are like, what you have done, what you have seen—write your autobiography!..."

It is easy enough to say *write your autobiography*, a truthful, unembellished story of your life. But it would be like giving an account of my entire life, or holding a confessional before the world! In fact, writing an autobiography and making a spiritual will are practically the same. Besides, it is difficult for a human being to rise to such a height that he can resist the temptation to show himself in the most flattering light, to paint himself as a "good fellow" who deserves a pat on the back. I have therefore chosen a special form of autobiography—that of a biographical novel. And so I shall speak of myself in the third person; that is, *I, Sholom Aleichem, the Writer,* shall relate to you the true life-history of *Sholom Aleichem, the Man,* as unceremoniously as I can, without embellishment or affectation, as an impartial observer might tell it, an absolute stranger—but still as one who had been with the hero continuously and had passed with him through all the seven circles of hell. And I shall tell it to you, little by little, dividing it into separate stories or episodes. And may He, who grants man the gift of Memory, grant me this gift, that I may not omit a single occurrence of interest that I have experienced, nor one person whom I have met at the Great Fair where I have passed almost fifty years of my life.

2. The Village

The little village of Voronko. • A kind of Kasrilovka. • A legend from the days of Mazepa. • The old synagogue, the old cemetery, the two affairs.

The hero of this biographical novel was raised and bred in Kasrilovka, which is already somewhat familiar to my readers. It is to be found, if you are curious to know, in Little Russia, in the county of Poltava, not far from the old historic city of Pereyaslov. But its real name is Voronko, and not Kasrilovka.

Strictly speaking, I ought to mention the city where he was born and the date of his birth, as is customary with biographers. I confess, however, that such details have no interest for me. What does interst me is the little village of Kasrilovka—or Voronko— because no other town has so impressed itself upon my hero's mind as that blessed Kasrilovka-Voronko, and no other city in the

38

world has endeared itself to him to such an extent that he cannot, nor ever will, forget it.

And come to think of it, what other city is there in the wide world—be it Odessa, Paris, London, or even New York—that can boast of such a great market place, and of so many Jewish shops, large and small; stands, of all sizes, stacked with mountains of freshly picked aromatic apples and pears, cantaloupes and watermelons, which goats and pigs are always trying to nip, so that market wives must constantly war against them?... And we, the schoolboys, certainly longed to taste these unattainable delicacies but could not come near them.

What other city contains an old humpbacked synagogue which has such a beautiful ark of the covenant carved with two lions that could be mistaken for birds, were it not for their long tongues and the rams' horns in their mouths? It was in this synagogue (so the old inhabitants tell us) that our grandfathers once locked themselves from the cursed Mazepa, the chieftain of the Ukrainian Cossacks; for three days and three nights they sat there wrapped in prayer shawls and phylacteries and read the Psalms, and that is how they escaped certain destruction. Those old inhabitants also tell us that the rabbi blessed the synagogue against fire; indeed, no matter how great a fire rages in the village, it never touches the synagogue! What other city can boast of a bathhouse which stands at the foot of a hill, on a river bank, and draws its water from an inexhaustible well? And the river! Where else is there such a river where generation after generation of Jewish schoolboys, as well as Gentile urchins, bathed, splashed, learned to swim, fish, and perform extraordinary tricks? Old Jews have plenty to tell about this wonderful old bathhouse. Once a peasant was found there who had hanged himself while drunk. This even led to a terrible calumny; the Gentiles claimed the Jews had hanged him. Oh, the village had trouble enough on its hands! They were prepared to whip the most prominent citizens—perhaps they actually whipped them, but I do not want to delve too deeply into this matter because I dislike sad stories, no matter how ancient.

What other city is graced by such a high hill, on the other side of the synagogue, the top of which almost reaches the clouds and where, as everybody knows, a treasure has lain hidden since the days of Chmielnicki—Chmielnicki, who led the Ukrainian rebels against Polish rule in the seventeenth century? Many times, we are told, people have begun to dig for the treasure, and each time have had to stop because human bones—legs, arms, skulls, and skeletons in shrouds—were turned up. These were obviously the remains of Jews, and perhaps even of martyrs…who knows?

In what other city will you find such excellent citizens? It may appear, at first sight, that they are no more than petty merchants and innkeepers living off the Gentiles and off each other. And yet they all behave with dignity; each has a home of his own, family prestige, and a pew in the synagogue—what difference whether it is at the east wall or the one opposite? And those who are less well born or less well off, no doubt have some distinguished relative of whom they can tell endless, exaggerated yarns.…

And what an old cemetery there is, what a large magnificent ancient cemetery where most of the graves are so overgrown with grass that no one is certain they contain human bones! You may be sure there are plenty of stories concerning this cemetery, and not very cheerful ones—in fact, rather terrifying stories of the past. But let us not talk of cemeteries before bedtime.…

The village of Voronko is small, but how lovely and appealing it is! If your legs are strong enough, you can walk its length and breadth in half an hour. You'll find no railway, no seashore, and no noise.… But it has two fairs a year, created specially so the Jews can carry on their trade and earn a living. A tiny, humble village— yet full of lovely stories and legends, enough to fill a whole volume! You are no doubt very fond of stories and legends. But we must keep within the limits of this biography, and so first we must introduce you, as is customary, to the father and mother of our hero. Be thankful that it is with his parents and not with his grandparents or great-grandparents, as most biographers do, that we begin.

3. In Father's Home

The rich man of Voronko, the man of many occupations. • A horde of children. • The tyranny of Fruma, the servant girl. • The hero is a mimic and a scamp.

A tall man with a broad, white, wrinkled forehead, a thin beard which seemed to smile, and a constantly worried expression! A man of means and an amateur cantor, a scholar and a man well versed in the Bible, a pious man and a lover of Hebrew, a disciple of the Hasidic Rabbi of Talna, and a secret admirer of the more "worldly" writers like Mapu, Slonimsky, and Zederbaum; philosopher, arbiter, counsellor, chessplayer, and connoisseur of diamonds and pearls— this describes the hero's father, Reb Nahum Vevik's [that is, Nahum, son of Vevik], who was considered the richest man in town.

It is hard now to determine how great a fortune a "rich" man could amass in Voronko, but occupations he had in abundance. He was a lessee of properties, supplied beets to the sugar mill, ran the rural post office, dealt in wheat, freighted barges on the River Dnieper, cut lumber, and fattened oxen for sale. But his main source of livelihood was the dry goods store. That is, it was called a "dry goods" store, but besides dry goods, one could also find groceries, hay and oats, homemade medicines for the peasants, and even hardware. Father did not interfere in the dry goods store. It was managed entirely by Mother, Haya Esther, a woman of character, an efficient, quick worker and a very strict mother. And of children there was no dearth—there were more than a dozen, of different sizes and complexions: black-haired, flaxen-haired, red-haired children.

Generally speaking, no one paid much attention to this host. They had not been greatly wanted, and had they failed to enter this world, it would not have been considered a misfortune. But once they were there, then, "Who are they disturbing? May they have long and happy lives!" The ones who were lucky enough to get safely through smallpox, measles, and the other childhood diseases, were sent off to *cheder*, the Jewish school—first to Noteh Leib, who taught the youngsters, and afterwards to Reb Zorach'l, teacher of the Talmud. The child who did not escape the thousand-eyed monster which devours fledglings returned whence it had come. Then mirrors were draped; parents sat on the floor as a sign of mourning, their shoes off, weeping bitterly. They wept until…until they stopped weeping. They quoted the usual passages, "The Lord giveth, and the Lord taketh away," dried their eyes, rose from the ground, and—forgot…. In the constant noise and bustle made by more than a dozen children, one already married and sprouting a beard, another still an infant at the breast, it could not have been otherwise.

For the mother to rear such a host, to nurse each through illness, was quite a feat. A child received as many spankings, pokes, and slaps as he could absorb. But let him fall ill, and Mother did not leave his bedside. A mother's lot! And no sooner was the child well enough to leave his bed than, "Off to *cheder*, you rascal, off to *cheder!*"

41

Every boy attended *cheder* from the age of four until…almost until he was led to the marriage canopy. And it was the one who stood midway as to age in this horde who distinguished himself most in mischief—the hero of this biography, Sholom by name, or Sholom Nahum Vevik's.

Really he was not a bad boy, this Sholom Nahum Vevik's. Yet, although he surpassed the others in studies, he received the largest share of slaps and pokes and spankings. Very likely he deserved them.

"Wait and see, no good can come of this child! Look at him, obstinate, self-willed, greedy, growing up to be a good-for-nothing!"

So spoke Fruma, the pockmarked maid. Fruma was blind in one eye, but, nevertheless, she was a thrifty, honest, devoted servant. So devoted was she to her mistress that she took great pains to bring up the children to be good, pious, and devout in the eyes of God and man by whipping them black and blue and underrationing their food. As Mother was a very busy woman, constantly occupied in the shop, it was Fruma the Maid who ruled the house with an iron hand and "educated" the children. She woke them, gave them breakfast, sent them to *cheder*, brought them back from *cheder*, slapped them, fed them, repeated the evening prayer with them, slapped them again, and put them to sleep in bed with her—that is, the children lay in the bed, and she lay at their feet.

Fruma the Maid was an enormous trial to the children, and, when her wedding day came, they celebrated a great holiday. Long live curly-haired Yideleh the Thief (he was a horse thief), who oiled his hair with goose-fat and who could never properly blow his nose because his nostrils had grown together! Blessings on him, fool that he was, for deciding to marry blind Fruma! And the truth is he didn't marry her just because he didn't have "anything better to do," but "out of love." He had been violently smitten by her, body and soul. It wasn't because she had only one eye and a pockmarked face, God forbid, but because, by marrying her, he became, in a sort of way, related to Reb Nahum Vevik's. Such a match! That was no joke. Mother Haya Esther herself arranged the wedding; she was the bride's entire family: She baked the pastry, brought musicians from the neighboring city, danced till daybreak, and finally became as hoarse as a crow.

How the youngsters laughed that day! What mischief they made! Their joy was not due so much to the fact that a noseless thief was marrying a blind spinster, but because they were rid of Fruma's tyranny forever. They also laughed because that rascal Sholom made them laugh with his pranks: he imitated the bridegroom whistling through his nose, and the bride squinting at the bridegroom with her one eye and licking her lips like a cat that has just eaten cream.

Sholom was a master at mimicking others, at copying their mannerisms and ridiculing their foibles. At his first meeting with a person, he immediately discovered some weakness—something "funny"—and he would mimic it there and then. The horde would roar with laughter, but his parents would complain to his teacher, "He's a regular monkey. We've got to break him of the habit."

And so his teacher undertook the task of "breaking him of the habit"—but with no appreciable result. A "devil" must have entered into the child, an imp intent on mocking everyone— absolutely everyone. Even the rabbi was included—his manner of taking snuff and of shuffling his small feet. And the rabbi's wife— the way she pursed her lips, blushed, and fluttered one eye when she asked the rabbi for money for the Sabbath, her way of mispronouncing the word "Sabbath," which came out always "Sabbas"…. Hands struck, slaps resounded, rods whistled. Oh, those whippings! What whippings!

In short—some life!

4. Shmulik the Orphan

Stories, fantasies and dreams. • Magic and the Kabbala.

Some faces are created to bewitch you at first sight. Such faces cry out, "Love me!" And before you know it, you do love them.

Shmulik the Orphan had such an endearing face. He was a fatherless, motherless boy who was being raised by the rabbi.

Sholom Nahum Vevik's became attached to this boy from the moment they met. He shared breakfasts and lunches with him and they became friends—such friends! They were one being, one body, one soul. And all because of Shmulik's stories.

No one knew as many stories as Shmulik. It is not enough, however, to know stories; one must be able to tell them. And Shmulik told them best of anyone.

Where did this strange boy, with the red cheeks and dreamy

eyes, get his fund of stories—lovely, fanciful tales, adorned with fantastic images? Did he hear them somewhere? Or were they all fruits of his fancy? Even now, I do not know. There is only one thing: they flowed out of him like water from an everlasting spring. They flowed as smoothly as oil. He drew them out like a long silken thread. His voice was sweet; his manner of talking was honey-sweet; his cheeks were red, eyes liquid and dreamy, as if veiled by a light mist.

On a Friday afternoon or Sabbath after lunch—sometimes on a holiday at twilight—having climbed the high Voronko hill "the top of which almost reaches the clouds," the two comrades would lie face down on the grass or look up at the sky, and Shmulik would begin his stories. One was about a king's son and a king's daughter; another concerned a rabbi and a rabbi's wife; still another was about a prince and a hunting dog; there were stories about a princess in a crystal palace, about twelve thieves in the woods, about a ship that sailed the "frozen ocean," about a pope who held religious disputes with great rabbis. There were stories about animals, devils, imps, evil spirits, magicians and sorcerers, wood-demons and werewolves, half-animals, half-men, and a story about the "hanging candlestick of Prague".... Every story had a smell and taste of its own; all of them were permeated with magic.

And Sholom Nahum Vevik's would listen open-mouthed, never once taking his eyes off this wonderful boy with the red cheeks and the dreamy eyes.

"How do you know all this, Shmulik?"

"Dumbbell, you haven't heard anything. I know how to draw wine from a wall, and oil from a ceiling!"

"How do you do that?"

"Dumbbell, it's simple! I can make gold out of sand, and jewels and diamonds from broken glass!"

"How do you do it?"

"Why, with the Kabbala, of course, Didn't you know that our rabbi is a Kabbalist? Everyone knows that! He never goes to sleep."

"Well, what does he do?"

"All night long, when everyone else is in bed, he's up. He's all by himself, and he studies the Kabbala."

"You see everything he is doing?"

"How can I, dumbbell? I'm asleep."

"Then how do you know he studies the Kabbala?"

"How do I know? Why, even a baby knows that. Just ask! The rabbi can do the impossible. If he wanted, the twelve springs of quicksilver would open for him, and the thirteen gardens of saffron; and gold, silver, diamonds, and jewels, as many as there are

44

grains of sand in the sea, could all be his. So many, you'd never want any more."

"Well, how come that you're always hungry, then? And why doesn't the rabbi ever have enough money for the Sabbath?"

"Because! Because that's how he wants it! He wants to suffer in this world, do penance here. But if he wished, he could be as rich as Korah in the Bible. He could be richer than a thousand Rothschilds, because he knows how. He knows every secret. He even knows where the treasure is hidden."

"Where is it hidden?"

"Don't ask me! If I knew, I'd have told you long ago. I'd have wakened you in the middle of the night and said, 'Come, Sholom, let's get the treasure!' and we would have gathered the gold in our hands and stuffed it into our pockets...."

And when Shmulik spoke of the treasure, his dreamy eyes glowed, his cheeks flamed, and he became so excited that his friend burned with the same fire. Shmulik spoke, and his friend Sholom stared at his mouth, drinking in every word.

5. Treasures

What is a treasure? • A legend from Chmielnicki's times. • Magic stones.

The fact that there was a treasure right here in our little village was indisputable.

How did we come by a treasure? Chmielnicki brought it, that Ukrainian who rebelled against Polish rule. Chmielnicki buried it here a long time ago. For thousands of years, people had been collecting treasure after treasure, and then Chmielnicki came and took them away and buried them.

"Who was Chmielnicki?"

"You don't know about Chmielnicki? Why, he was a monster, the Haman of his time.... Any baby knows that.... Well, this monster, this Chmielnicki robbed the nobles and wealthy Jews. He stole millions, and he brought it here, to Voronko, and buried it one dark night in the ground under the light of the moon, on the other side of the synagogue. The spot is now overgrown with grass, and a spell has been cast upon it so that no one can find it."

45

"So then it's lost for good?"

"Who says for good? Why do you think God created the Kabbala? The Kabbalists know a trick or two for this sort of thing."

"What kind of trick?"

"You can be sure it's the right kind. They have a magic spell where a certain verse from the Psalms must be repeated forty times forty...."

"Which verse?"

"If I only knew! But even if I knew, it wouldn't help much. The way it goes, you have to fast for forty days, and you have to recite forty chapters from the Psalms on each of these days, and on the forty-first day, right after the sun has set, you've got to sneak out so that no one sees you, because if anybody does, God forbid, you have to start fasting all over again.... Well, if you make it and no one sees you—and it must be on a dark night, just before the new moon—you must go downhill to the other side of the synagogue, and there you stand for forty minutes on one leg, counting forty times forty, and, if you don't make a mistake in counting, the treasure will appear before you, just like that...."

So, very gravely, Shmulik the Orphan would explain to his friend Sholom the secret of the treasure, and he would gradually lower his voice, speaking as if he read, not pausing for breath.

"...and the treasure will appear through a small flame. When you see the flame, you have to walk up close to it at once. You don't have to fear getting burned because the flame only gives off light—it doesn't burn. Then all you have to do is lean over and gather in the treasure with both hands." (Shmulik would demonstrate how with both hands.) "You gather in the gold and the silver, and the diamonds and the jewels, and those precious stones called *Kadkod* and *Yashpoh*...."

"What's the difference between those two?"

"Such a difference! *Kadkod* is a stone which throws light like a candle. And *Yashpoh* makes white out of black, yellow out of red, green out of blue, dry out of wet, a well-fed man out of hungry one, young out of old, the living out of the dead.... All you have to do is rub it on the right hem of your jacket and say, 'Let a good breakfast appear before me!' And a silver tray will appear, and on the tray two fried pigeons and fresh white rolls, everything first class! Or else you say, 'Let a good dinner appear before me!' and a golden tray with all kinds of food and dishes fit for a king appears before you—right in front of your eyes are fried tongues and stuffed *kishke*, smelling deliciously, and fresh crisp *chalah*, and lots of wine of the best quality, and nuts and carobs and mountains of candy—such an enormous lot that you've had too much already!"

Shmulik would turn his head to one side and spit an excess of saliva. His friend would see by his dry lips and his pale dreamy-eyed face that Shmulik would not have refused a piece of fried tongue, nor a stuffed *kishke*, nor even a slice of white bread.... And he would make a vow that the very next day he would bring to Shmulik a few nuts and carobs and a candy stolen from Mother's shop. But, in the meantime, he would beg Shmulik to relate more and still more. Shmulik did not have to be coaxed. He would moisten his lips and speak on.

"...and after you are stuffed with all these fine things, after you've drunk down the excellent wine, you take the stone, rub it, and say, 'Let a soft bed appear!' Immediately you have a bed of ivory, decorated with gold, with a feather quilt as soft as butter, and with silken pillows at the head, the whole covered with a satin blanket. You undress and fall asleep, and you dream of angels and cherubs, of seraphs of the Upper and Lower Paradise.... Or, if you prefer, you rub the stone, and suddenly you rise into the clouds and then above the clouds, and you fly like an eagle, way up, far far away...."

Did the writings of his friend Sholom Nahum Vevik's, many years later when he had become Sholom Aleichem, reflect the spirit of this poor orphan with his wonderful stories? Who knows? One thing is certain—Shmulik had enriched Sholom's imagination, broadened his understanding, and to this day, deep in his heart, he treasures Shmulik's dreams and Shmulik's fantasies of riches and magic stones... although perhaps in a different guise

—Translated by Tamara Kahana

68. An Unexpected Examination

It was near twilight when the young maskil, Joshua Loyev, and his
young protégé entered the town of Bohuslav. At their inn they met
old man Loyev, who was waiting for his son. Old Loyev impressed
Sholom. He had never expected a Jew to look like a general, a field
marshal with a leonine voice. Joshua briefly described the young
teacher, and where and how they had met. After listening to his
son, the old man saddled his nose with a pair of white silver spectacles. Without undue ceremony, he earnestly contemplated
Sholom and inspected him as if he were a fish in the market. Then
Loyev stretched out a warm hand and greeted the teacher with a
friendly look, as amicable a look as such a stern field marshal could
muster.

"What's your name?" he asked Sholom.

Learning the young man's name, Loyev now spoke as softly as
his leonine manner allowed him to:

"Now listen here, my dear Sholom, please be good enough to
step into the other room. I have to discuss some matters with my
son. Then I'll call you in and we'll continue our chat."

The other room was a guest parlor in the European fashion.
Here sat Bereleh Etels, the innkeeper. A former dry goods merchant, in his old age he had become the owner of an inn. Bereleh,
a man with a blue nose ribbed with tiny red veins, stood with
hands folded, doing nothing. After speaking of his guests and their
business, he said of himself: "God has punished me. In my old age,
I have to sell noodle soup!"

His short, thin wife wore a bowtie-shaped headdress and a
chain of little yellow pearls around her neck. She wandered around
the house vituperating the innkeeper's children (she was a second
wife), cursing the servants, abusing the cat, apparently dissatisfied
with the entire world—a pessimist of the first order! At the window, reading a novel by Spielhagen, sat their youngest daughter,
Shivke, a beautiful and extremely coquettish girl with a round,

pale face. A few young men with trimmed beards—the cream of Bohuslav's intelligentsia—came to visit her and discuss literature. The blue-nosed innkeeper introduced the young teacher to this group. How the old man knew who the teacher was is a riddle. To prevent his being bored, the beautiful young girl turned to Sholom with a sweet smile.

"Did you read Spielhagen's *On the Sand Dune?*"

"Yes, I know all of Spielhagen."

"How about Auerbach?"

"Yes, Auerbach too?"

"And Bogrov's novel, *Memoirs of a Jew?*"

"That I know by heart!"

"How about the novel *What Is to Be Done?*"

"Who hasn't read Chernyshevsky?"

"What did you think of the heroine?"

"Vera Pavlovna? What sort of question is that?"

The beautiful young girl and her cavaliers were enchanted. One of them a private attorney with the imposing name of Mendelssohn, tugged at his just recently sprouted mustache. It turned out that he was head over heels in love with the girl, and was fuming with envy at the young guest who had all of literature in his back pocket. The lawyer stared daggers at Sholom and deep in his heart probably wished that the newcomer break all his bones the next time he took a step.

But all this emboldened our young hero, and he began to speak trippingly on the tongue, citing entire passages by heart and throwing around names like Buckle's *History of Civilization in England* and John Stuart Mill's *On Liberty*. (An out-of-town young maskil has to reveal what he knows when he visits people he doesn't know.) And then right in the middle of Sholom's impassioned discourse, old man Loyev and his son Joshua entered and overheard the young Pereyaslav teacher's lecture to the assembled company. Loyev and Joshua exchanged glances, apparently pleased.

"Listen here, young fellow, let me ask you something," old Loyev sang out. "My son tells me that you're just as knowledgeable in our holy Jewish books as in their secular ones. Do you remember what Rashi says about the daughters of Zelophehad?"

Then commenced a long-winded discussion on Rashi. And Rashi led to the Talmud. At which followed a learned disquisition about scholarship and Haskala, as is usual among Jews who are at home in all the commentaries. This caused a sensation, a furor so great that old man Loyev placed his hand on Sholom's shoulders and said:

49

"Experience has taught us that despite all this learning and knowledge, when it comes to writing a letter, for example, one's tongue is tied. So, if you'll forgive me, please take this pen and write me a letter in Russian, addressed to the director of a sugar factory. Tell him that until he forwards a certain sum of money we will no longer provide him with sugar beets."

Obviously, this little letter was just a pretext to test Sholom. The letter was passed from hand to hand; the exquisite calligraphy amazed everyone. Here the merit of his teacher, Monish of Pereyaslav, stood Sholom in good stead. Reb Monish Volov had a natural gift for calligraphy. A golden hand. People displayed his handwriting all over town. He didn't write—he painted. Despite his total ignorance of the Russian language, this devout, God-fearing Jew competed with the writing teacher at the state school. It was incredible that such beautiful penmanship was done by a hand and not a machine. His students, including the Rabinowitz children, had suffered enough under Reb Monish's tutelage. But they drew sustenance from his handwriting and his beautiful Russian script, which in time became so useful to them.

But the examination did not end here either.

"If you don't mind," old Loyev added, "please translate this letter into Hebrew; you see, the director of the sugar factory is a Jew!"

That's how the old man explained his request, which of course was also connected with the exam. Without giving it too much thought, Sholom translated the letter into flowery Hebrew. He tried to make the script beautiful and artistic, and the lines thick, measured, gemlike and exquisite. And here too the merits of a former teacher, Reb Zorechl, came into play. What Reb Monish was for Russian calligraphy, Reb Zorechl was for Hebrew.

In short, Sholom passed the improvised exam with flying colors. His head spun from the effort. One of his ears burned. Fantasy took him on her wings and bore him to the world of sweet dreams and enchanted thoughts. He was beaming and happy. The old dream of a treasure had begun to be realized, and quite naturally: Sholom imagines that he arrives at his new home and becomes acquainted with Loyev's daughter. They fall in love, disclosing their secret to the old man. He places his hands on their heads and blesses them: "Be happy, dear children!" Sholom writes his father in Pereyaslav: "This is the story, dear father, please come." They send a carriage for him drawn by fiery steeds... Then smack in the middle of the dream his reverie was broken. Old man Loyev approached, called Sholom aside, and began to talk of mundane matters—that is, wages.

"Or would you rather we postpone it for later?"

"Yes, later."

Sholom felt like a man who had just fallen asleep and begun to dream—when suddenly someone came and woke him. The sweet dreams went up in smoke. His overheated imagination vanished like a shadow and the charm of the treasure and all the good, sweet thoughts disappeared.

Meanwhile, night had fallen and it was time to leave. Several miles still separated the town of Bohuslav from the village. A two-hour journey. The horses were already harnessed, and Andrei the coachman carried Sholom's valise into the carriage. The outside air was cool.

"Is that how you're going?" old Loyev asked Sholom. "Why you're as naked as Adam! You'll freeze, for goodness sakes! Andrei! Give me a cloak!"

From under his seat Andrei drew out a warm woolen cloak. The old man himself helped Sholom put on the garment, which made him warm and comfortable. But he didn't care about that. Something else concerned him. Shivke, Bereleh's daughter, and her cavaliers were standing by the window, looking on, watching old Loyev help Sholom on with the cloak. It seemed to Sholom that they were laughing. Andrei too made him feel discomfited and ill at ease. He wondered what the peasant thought of him.

69. A Jewish Leaseholder

A Wealthy Jewish House • Learning Etiquette • Old Man Loyev's Library • An Extraordinary Jewish Landowner

It was night when all three entered the village: the elder Loyev, his maskil son Joshua, and Sholom, the young teacher from Pereyaslav. After passing many squat, dark, peasant huts, a large field, and a threshing area stacked with piles of straw, hay and grain, the carriage slowed down in front of an imposing courtyard. Before the coachman could stop the horses, the wooden gate opened of its own accord. A hatless peasant bowed low to the master and admitted the carriage. It glided briefly as if on a soft carpet and came to a halt in front of an imposing white mansion. The

51

roof of this large, wide house was thatched with straw. Two big porches (one on each side) graced the front, and a garden the back. The house had many windows and was whitewashed inside and out. The furniture was simple. There seemed to be dozens of rooms. Servants scurried about like silent shadows. They wore soft shoes to lessen the noise. No one dared say a word while the old man was at home. The discipline was tight. The landlord alone was heard. His leonine voice rang out like a bell. At a long finely decked table in the first spacious room sat a beautiful, tall young woman. She was the old man's second wife. Next to her sat a girl of thirteen or fourteen, their one and only daughter, a copy of the mother. Old Loyev introduced them to Sholom and they sat down to supper.

This was the first time that the young teacher found himself at a patrician table where the meal was conducted with great formality and served by a white-gloved lackey. This servant was only a simple peasant named Vanka, but Loyev dressed and primped him like a nobleman's retainer. For one unaccustomed to an assortment of plates, and to spoons and glasses of varying sizes, it was rather difficult to maintain aristocratic decorum and not violate the tenets of etiquette. One had to be constantly on guard.

It must be admitted that Sholom had never known that while at table one had to obey an entire corpus of etiquette. In an average Jewish home this was not strictly observed. There everyone ate from one plate, dunked his fresh challa in the gravy, or even ate with his hands. In a middle-class Jewish home, one was oblivious to special rules pertaining to dining and negotiating knives, forks and spoons. In a middle-class Jewish home it sufficed to know that you have to leave a piece of fish or meat for the sake of good manners. Otherwise, one could sit the way one pleased, eat as much as one wanted, and, without fear of reprimand, pick one's teeth with the fork.

Who was it that introduced etiquette to the world? Who indited such a code of law, and where was it written? No, the young tutor had never read these rules of etiquette. His sole thought was to watch carefully what other people were doing. Naturally, he could not enjoy his food if he had to be constantly on guard, always careful not to take an extra mouthful, hold fork and knife improperly, sip the soup too loudly, or have someone hear him chewing.

The teacher also passed the etiquette exam with flying colors, but the first few times he left the table hungry. After all these fancy formalities, plentiful courses and excellent food, Sholom longed for a piece of fresh bread and herring and onion, hot baked potatoes in their jackets, still gritty with sand, and a dish of cabbage whose odor wafted in the air for a full day and night....

It took some time for Sholom to get used to the discipline of finicky formality. In the meantime, the youth had to keep up appearances and not display his democratic manners and proletarian habits, God forbid. In a word, he had to be like everyone else. Indeed, from the very first day he was not considered a stranger but an equal—one of the family. After all, he came from a good family. That was Loyev's decision. In fact, the old man expressed his opinion concerning the teacher directly to his face, telling him that he came from a good family, and that such a person must be treated with special consideration.

First, Sholom was given a private room simply furnished but with all the comforts and the finest service. Tutoring his pupil took up two or three hours a day. The rest of the time was Sholom's own and he could do what he pleased—read books or write. He read everything that came his way. Old Loyev himself liked to read and constantly spent money buying new books. And since the old man read no other language but Hebrew, most of his library consisted of Hebrew titles. (Yiddish was not fashionable at that time.) Among the writers who adorned the library of this village magnate and landowner were Kalman Schulman, Mapu, Smolenskin, Mandelkern, Gottlober, Yehalel (the pen name of Yehuda Leib Levin), Isaac Ber Levinsohn, Mordecai Aaron Guenzburg, Isaac Erter, Dr. Kaminer and Chaim Zelig Slonimsky.

Old Loyev knew all these books almost by heart. He loved to cite passages from them, and to speak about them again and again. Only rarely does one meet a man with such a memory, such a commanding manner of speaking. An orator! He also had an extraordinary sense of humor. He had a true talent for retelling a tale in his own fashion. A man of experience, he told stories that were interesting and full of suspense. Not only did he narrate, but he also poeticized, creating multicolored pictures. Wherever he was, no matter how many people were present, he alone was heard.

In brief, he was a rare sort, an original, a Jew like no other. It was amazing that a man who was raised in a pious Jewish home, in the Jewish town of Bohuslav, turned out the way he did. How did a Bohuslav Jew learn to conduct such an aristocratic household, to love the soil, and to devote himself to farming? It was fascinating to watch him in the morning as he stood next to the threshing machine by the river, in his high shiny boots and velvet knee-length coat, giving orders to his workers, throwing the sheaves into the feeder, or operating the winnow and the sieve. He took part in every phase of the work himself: plowing, sowing, weeding, digging, reaping and processing the grain; he was with the horses, the oxen and all the domestic animals. He worked everywhere.

If we ever had to show other people an exemplar of a Jewish landowner, an authentic farmer, old Loyev could have been chosen. Christians said openly that people ought to learn from this Jew how to manage a farm, work the soil in the best possible fashion, and make poor workers content. All the village peasants, without exception, would have done anything in the world for him. Not only did they fear him and stand in awe of him—they loved him. They simply loved him because he treated them like human beings, like friends, like his children. These gentiles had never experienced such good treatment from previous landlords—the Polish noblemen. One should remember that the older generation of peasants had not yet forgotten the feel of serfdom on their bodies; they still bore the marks of beatings and blows. And now they were being treated like human beings, not like animals. That explained their trust in their landlord. Hardly a soul among them could multiply two by two. When it came to reckoning, they relied on the old man completely. They were confident that he wouldn't cheat them even out of a penny.

It's hard to imagine the different course Jewish history might have taken and the role we could have played in the economic and political life of the land, had it not been for the Russian minister Ignatiev's edicts against the Jews, edicts forbidding them to settle in villages, or to buy or rent land for farming. I say this because leaseholders like old Loyev were no rarity either in this region or in others of the blessed Pale of Settlement. Jews from Bohuslav, Kaniev, Shpole, Rzhishtchev, Tarashtche, Zlatapolye, Uman and many, many other places left their little towns and headed for the villages. They leased large and small tracts of land from the noblemen and did wonders with them. They took poor soil and neglected ruins, and converted them into veritable Gardens of Eden. This is no exaggeration. The author of this autobiography heard these very words from the famous Russian landowner Vasily Fyodorovitch Simorenko, a Christian and a close business associate of old Loyev, whom we shall soon meet again. In a word, Loyev was a kind of nobleman, a Jewish landowner. Because of an evil decree, his kind has been uprooted and wiped from Jewish history, perhaps for many, many years.

70. Life in the Village

The Village Sofievke • Sholom Gets to Know the Outside World • Three Good Years
Tutor and Pupil • Like Brother and Sister • With Books, Fields and Neighbors

The village, Sofievke, belonged to Count Branitski. Sholom came as an employee, a temporary tutor, but stayed on permanently and found his second home. Here, as we shall see later, the course of his life and future happiness were determined forever.

Meanwhile, the teacher spent almost three years at the village. He considered them the best, the most blissful years of his life. In every respect this was truly the springtime of his life. Here he was closer to nature, to God's world, and to God's earth—the earth from which we all came, and to which we shall all return.

In Sofievke Sholom realized that our place was here, in nature—and not there, in town. Here he became convinced that we are a part of the great outside world; that we always longed for and will always long for mother earth; that we always loved and will always love nature; and that we were always drawn and will always be drawn to the village. I hope that the kindhearted reader will forgive my short introduction. I can't think of Sofievke without expressing the feelings bound up with it. Having said this, we can now go to the village itself and depict in detail the happy village life.

Sholom slept in a large, bright room with closed shutters; when he woke in the morning, one thrust of his hands opened the window and the shutters. A shaft of light streamed in, bringing with it the warmth of the sun. The aroma of mignonette mingled with the scents of mint and wormwood, and with the fragrances of other unknown grasses once sown (so people claimed) by Count Branitski. But now nettles and thornbushes grew along with the tall grass of the steppes. It grew so high during the summer that both tutor and pupil often played hide-and-seek in six-foot-high grass and had to look for a long time until they found each other. The noise of the opening window prompted a cackling hen and her family to dash off to a side. But soon she returned, scratching and pecking at the dirt, teaching her little chicks to do the same.

It didn't take long to wake, dress and wash. Although it was still early when Sholom left his room, he found no one in the house. Old Loyev had long since departed for the threshing area and the noisy machine. Mrs. Loyev was with the turkeys, geese, ducks and other fowl—they had an entire kingdom of winged creatures. From the large fields came a slow procession of ox cars laden with grain. From afar, one could see the wheat field at a glance. Much of the wheat was already harvested and bundled into sheaves. The rest stood in ripe, yellow stalks, bending and waving in the breeze.

On the other side of the meadow, where the grain ended, were straight rows of beets with large green leaves. Spaced well apart between the rows stood the tall sunflowers, their fuzzy yellow heads like soldiers on guard. Birds loved to gather around the sunflowers and one by one pick out the already sweet white seeds. Beyond that lay the dense oak forest. When the noblemen still resided in Sofievke, they would hunt game there. Now that the land was leased by a Jew, the innocent rabbits and birds had no worries. Jews did not hunt. Jews found other uses for the forest. Old Loyev felled timber, and built barns, chicken coops, storehouses for the grain, sheds and stables for oxen and horses, wagons, sleighs, and numerous other farm implements.

After breakfast, when his first lesson was done, Sholom strolled in the garden, sometimes alone, sometimes accompanied by his pupil. It was hard to say when the garden was more beautiful—at Shevuos time, with the trees in full bloom, or in the summer, when the currants and gooseberries turned red. Or perhaps late in summer, when ripe apples fell from the trees and only the late-blooming, round black plums remained.

Each season had its own special charm and enchantment. The strolling tutor and his pupil always found something new in the garden, even if the gooseberries were still green as grass and sour as vinegar—it didn't matter. They pricked their hands and plucked the largest gooseberries, the ones that hung down and were translucent in the sunlight. Later, when the currants became red as wine and sparkled in the sun, they seemed to plead with you: Take some more, taste another bunch! And so it went, until one's teeth were set on edge. The same held true for the sour cherries and the sweet cherries and the other fruits, which ripened at different times. True, all these could be bought in town too. But they didn't have the same taste and smell as when you plucked them fresh from the tree. And especially if you were not alone but accompanied by a girl who was dear and precious to you, a girl who also considered you dear and precious, like a member of the family, a brother…

56

How could the pupil not have related to her teacher like a brother, when her parents treated him like a son? Sholom was not treated any differently than the Loyevs' own children. Like the Loyev children, the tutor too was surrounded with plenty, lacked nothing, had no worries and no concern with money. In that house, money did not exist at all. That is to say, there was money—and plenty of it. But with the exception of the old man, no one knew its worth nor felt any shortage of it. Everything was prepared lavishly and generously. Food, drink, clothing, shoes, even the rides in the gleaming horse-drawn carriage. There was a servant at every step, an unending supply of people and horses whenever you wanted them. When you appeared in the village, all the gentiles bowed and removed their caps. Born noblemen could not have felt better, freer and more honored.

The old man returned from work covered from head to toe with dust, straw and bits of stalks. He pulled off his long boots, washed, changed his clothes, and took on a new look. He sat down at his desk and looked through the mail. A young peasant lad had brought it on horseback from the nearest post station (in Baranyepolye), carrying the mail in a sack on his shoulders. After reading through his letters, Loyev summoned Sholom to write replies to them. The tutor did his work quickly because he understood old Loyev at a glance and knew all the correspondence by heart. The old man hated to repeat anything, and liked to be understood even before he had finished. Himself a quick worker, he liked to see work swiftly done.

When the correspondence was finished, the family sat down to eat. Invariably, there were several guests at the table. Most of the time they were neighbors, leaseholders or merchants who had come to buy wheat, oats, barley or other grains. As I said, a stern discipline reigned at the table. No one dared say a loud word; only the old man sounded forth like a bell. He never ran out of things to say. For everything he had a story, a parable, a proverb which made you think and laugh. He had no equal at telling an interesting story, imitating and mimicking everyone down to the last detail. He had true talent, even though other Jews considered him strange, an oddball, a crank, a madman.

Nevertheless, the merchants loved to deal with him because his word was a sacred bond; even if the price increased after a deal was made, you could be sure he would not renege on the sale. He acted this way not out of principle or pretension—it was plain and simple natural honesty, which knew of no chicanery and hated false, underhanded behavior. In the business world, a man like that was called a "crazy loon" (behind his back, of course), but merchants preferred to deal with such a madman than with any other who was sane.

After the meal, when the old man and his guests talked and arranged business deals, the teacher and his pupil left to study, learn and read. Most of all to read. They read everything that came their way, indiscriminately, without system. Mostly, they read novels and plays of the great classic writers, Shakespeare, Dickens, Tolstoy, Goethe, Schiller, Gogol, along with potboilers by French writers, such as Eugéne Sue, Xavier de Montépin, Von Born, Achard and other hack scribblers of the French boulevard.

After satiating themselves with books, they went to see the thresher in action, or to the meadow where the men harvested grain and bundled the stalks. It made Sholom want to roll up his sleeves and take part in the work. But standing on the side and watching was much easier than bending your back cutting grain and binding stalks. Looking didn't make you perspire or raise blisters on your hands.

But what an appetite it prompted later! They came home, had buttermilk and black bread, then went out for a stroll in the garden. Or they asked for a horse and carriage and rode with Andrei to the neighboring estates: to Guzipke, Kritohorbe, Zakutenitz. Everywhere they went they were warmly welcomed as beloved guests. The hosts didn't know what to give them first, so they were served tea from the samovar and fruit preserves. Sometimes they rode to Baranyepolye to see Postmaster Malinofsky. There they were treated to a bottle of liquor which the postmaster himself drank up, one little tumbler after another, for Malinofsky was a goy who loved to drink.

At other times, they would visit Dodi the Steward, who lived nearby—in fact, on the estate itself. Dodi's little house was much more fun than their big mansion. The treats one got there one couldn't manage to get at home. For example, only Dodi's wife would serve green garlics with sorrel schav. And where else could they indulge in fresh young pickles right out of the barrel, eaten with hot potatoes in their jackets? Or stuff themselves with sweet cabbage stems which Dodi's wife cut up, ready for sauerkraut? Or drink their fill of apple cider which had the taste of Paradise? A visit delighted Dodi's wife, and Dodi himself was in seventh heaven! But Dodi the Steward was a character in his own right and deserves a separate chapter.

58

71. Dodi the Estate Steward

Dodi the Steward was a strong, well-built man—neither tall nor husky, but rather solid and muscular. He had yellow hair and somewhat squinty blue eyes. His shoulders—steel. His chest—iron. A hand like a hammer. Not every horse could take him. When he straddled a horse's back he seemed part of it; you couldn't tell where Dodi ended and horse began.

All the gentiles were in awe of Dodi. They were scared to death of his hand, although he rarely raised it to strike anyone. Except if necessary. Only when words no longer availed. The minute someone said, "Here comes Dodi," the peasants, their wives and their daughters (all of whom had been standing around gossiping) quickly set to work. When he was with the workers, he didn't just talk. He took the plow or sickle, the shovel or pitchfork, and with his own hands showed how the work should be done. It was hard to fool Dodi; stealing was impossible. For theft there was no punishment great enough. Drunkenness also incensed him. A glass of whiskey was all right, but becoming drunk, brawling and rioting—that was out. You took your life in your hands!

But you'd hardly recognize this manly Dodi, before whom an entire village of peasants trembled, when he stood in the presence of old Loyev. He was smaller than a child, meeker than a lamb. His hands at his sides. Holding his breath. No soldier stood in awe and respect before a field marshal as Dodi did before the old landlord.

Dodi had come to the village as a youngster and stayed on permanently. He grew in size and responsibility until old Loyev crowned him with the title "steward"—that is, he made him the foreman of the entire estate. Here Dodi married; here he earned his bread. He was given his own little house and garden, and provided with flour, straw, wood and two milk cows. He became a householder and a father of children. Still, he never dared to sit in the old man's presence. Not even for a minute. Only once in his entire life had he sat down in Loyev's presence, and an incident occurred that Dodi never forgot.

I think I mentioned that old Loyev loved to explain, to teach everyone, to share what he knew with others. One long winter night, Dodi presented a report of the estate finances, standing before the old man as usual. When he finished, Dodi waited to be dismissed. But old Loyev was in a good mood. He wanted to chat a while, not about estate affairs, but about peripheral matters and about his Polish neighbors.

Finally, the conversation turned to Poland and the Polish Rebellion. Then Loyev discussed the Russians and Russian history before Peter the Great. And since a book on Russian history in a Hebrew translation by Mandelkern lay on Loyev's desk, he began to read, translating the entire story of Peter the Great into Yiddish for Dodi. As he read, Loyev told Dodi to sit down. Dodi didn't dare. The old man repeated his command. This time Dodi had no choice. He sat on a chair next to the door, under the old grandfather clock. Dodi's head was not used to such lectures, and to top it off, he was seated. So gradually he began to nod. His eyes closed, stuck fast, and with the drone of the old man's voice, he slowly fell into a sweet sleep. Now we'll let Dodi sleep and say a few words about the grandfather clock.

The clock was an old invalid that had provided many years of service, and should long have been retired for a well-deserved rest in the attic among old, decrepit junk. But Loyev always had a strange affection for superannuated things—for an old, faded and cracked mirror that reflected a double image, for an old collapsed chest of drawers, from which pulling out a drawer was as hard as splitting the Red Sea! Among other such antiques was an old-fashioned inkwell that had been on his writing desk for years. Made of glass, it was shaped like a little boot and set into a black wooden container filled with sand. No money in the world could persuade the old man to chuck this old inkwell and buy a more civilized-looking one. But it had nothing to do with stinginess. Old Loyev was not stingy at all. On the contrary, he purchased only the best and most expensive. He just couldn't bear to part with an old object. The same held true for the clock, which on account of its advanced years needed a heavy weight. New weights were constantly being added. Before this clock tolled the hours, it wheezed and rattled like an asthmatic old man before he begins to cough. But when it rang out the hours, the clock really sounded off like a church bell. The "bong, bong, bong" was even heard outdoors.

Now let's return to Dodi. Dodi snoozed and Loyev read the history of Peter the Great and his wife, Anastasia. Suddenly the old clock decided to chime the hour of ten. Dodi no doubt thought it was fire—the granary was ablaze. So he quickly jumped to his feet and shouted: "Water!"

Frightened, the old man put down the history of Peter the Great and looked at Dodi through his spectacles.

"I'm going to remember that look," said Dodi, "till my dying day…"

Sholom liked Dodi for his simplicity and calm. He was convinced that this man of nature had never uttered a lie in his life. Dodi's loyalty and devotion to his boss and his family was limitless. And because the teacher was treated by the Loyevs as a member of the household, Dodi too considered him family, and was prepared to go through fire and water for him.

In Dodi's view, everything connected with the Loyev family was on a higher plane. In any case, they weren't like other, average folk. Dodi simply deified the Loyevs—and this helped Sholom too. During the hot summer days or the long winter nights, Sholom and his pupil loved to drop in on Dodi and his wife for a quick visit. In that small house with its low ceiling that one could touch with a fingertip, they always felt better than at home. The schav with young garlics that they ate at Dodi's house during the summer, and the baked potatoes and fresh sour pickles or frozen sauerkraut that were served during the winter, were mouth-watering delicacies a thousand times better than the most exquisite dishes at home. Not to mention when Dodi's wife, Pessi, baked honey cake or rendered chicken fat—that was a holiday for the youngsters. Hot honey cake just out of the oven, or fresh fatty cracklings that melted in your mouth like the manna the Israelites ate in the desert—these were no small matters.

Most of their visits were in the winter, when the trees were wrapped in white, like frozen corpses in shrouds. At such time Sofievke lost its summer charm and splendor. There was nothing better to do than slip into Dodi's well-heated little house and refresh oneself with Pessi's delicious treats. Outside, awesome silence reigned. The snow was deep. No one came to visit the Loyevs. Sholom's heart was filled with gloom, his soul with melancholy. One solution was to ask Andrei to harness the horses to a wide sleigh. The youngsters buried themselves in fur coats and, covered with sheepskin blankets, rode to one of the neighboring estates, where they had a glass of tea from a hot samovar and then returned home.

But winter had its advantages too. There was plenty of time to

61

read and write. During the nearly three years that Sholom spent in the village, he wrote much more than during a later ten-year period when he was already a writer named Sholom Aleichem. Writing never came so easily to him as then. Throughout the night he would write long, heart-rending novels, impassioned dramas, and complicated tragedies and comedies. Ideas poured from him as from a barrel. His fantasy spurted like a fountain. He never asked himself why he wrote all this. When he finished a work, he read it to his pupil and both were enchanted. Both were convinced that it was a masterpiece—but not for long. As soon as Sholom completed a new work, it became a masterpiece, and the earlier one was considered pale and wan by comparison. The best place for it was the stove. And so, up in flames went more than a dozen novels and scores of plays.

Neither of them doubted that the young man was born to be a writer. Both tutor and pupil spoke of this, fantasized, and they built the most beautiful dream castles. Discussing different plans and various works, they forgot their own plans. About this they never exchanged a word. It never dawned on them to articulate their feelings or to ponder the fate of their own romance.

The word "romance" was too clichéd, the word "love" too banal for what the young couple felt. Their relationship was so natural they could not have felt any other way. Would a brother ever dream of declaring his love for his sister? It wouldn't be an exaggeration to say that objective observers knew and constantly talked about the young couple's romance more than the two protagonists themselves. Both were too young, too naive, and too happy. Not a cloud specked their blue sky. They saw no opposition from anywhere. And most important—they never thought of it. During the nearly three years of their acquaintance, they never dreamed for a moment that they would ever separate. Nevertheless, the day came when they had to part. Not forever, but for a short time.

This happened when our hero had to report to the draft board.

72. The Draft Board

Talk of the Draft • Saying Good-bye • A Letter of Recommendation • Fantasies
Results of the Letter • Story of a Crippled Son • The Return

One can confidently say that during these three years hardly a day passed in Sofievke without hearing the word "draft." For old Loyev the draft was a sickness, a mania that didn't let him rest by day or sleep at night. It cost him a fortune. How? When his son Joshua had to report to the draft board, the father first went to the provincial seat, in Chernigov, stayed a long while, and after much anguish managed to get an exemption certificate for him. This was one of several documents that exempted its possessor from military service. With such a certificate one never had to serve in the active military, only in the reserves. The cost of that piece of paper could have made a pauper wealthy. But for the sake of his son nothing was too expensive for old Loyev.

As soon as the certificate affair ended, another tumult began. The Russo-Turkish War broke out, and rumors spread that the reserves might be called up. In that case, Loyev had to get his son a white card stating that the bearer was unfit for military service. This meant that the candidate had to undergo a physical examination to determine if he was fit for duty. And, as might be expected, the examination revealed Joshua was not suitable, and he was given the white card. In other words, disqualified, thank God.

Not only was he not qualified for military service, but the physicians also suggested that he be sent to a warm climate, to Menton and Nice, for a cure, because he had a serious heart ailment. Indeed, within several years (as we will see a bit later), Joshua died from this illness. In the meantime, however, all hell had broken loose in the house. Father and son traveled to Kaniev and became acquainted with the district police chief, and other local officials, and with doctors. The officials and the draft board doctors kept taking loans from Loyev. Friendly Jews and advice givers had also latched on to the gravy train. Everyone under the sun was pumping money into his pockets from Loyev's. In short, the only word you heard in the house was draft, draft, draft.

63

When Sholom had to report to the draft board, old man Loyev became nervous. He made every effort to transfer quickly the teacher's residence from Pereyaslav to Kaniev, and to register him with the Kaniev draft board, where Loyev had great influence. One's own father couldn't have been more solicitous to his son than old Loyev was to Sholom. But curiously, Sholom himself feared the draft less than the Loyevs. For him, traveling to Kaniev and reporting to the board was actually a festive occasion. He ordered a new pair of high boots and a soldier's hood; indeed, he was quite prepared to be drafted. He was certain he would excel in the army, would please the officers, and would soon become a noncommissioned officer or a sergeant-major. No Jew could attain any higher rank. But at the last minute, when Sholom had to leave, all his courage suddenly melted. He felt embarrassed and ashamed. Yet he must admit that when he had to bid farewell to the family, perhaps forever, a strange longing pressed his heart and he shut himself in his room, buried his head in his pillow, and wept bitter tears…

But he wasn't the only one in that house to cry bitterly. In her room his pupil wept even more. Her eyes were swollen from crying and she couldn't even appear at the table. On the pretext of a bad headache, she remained in her room all day long and refused to see anyone.

Saying good-bye was a very sad ordeal. A Tisha B'Av mood encompassed the house. Sholom's heart was dark and desolate. In the carriage, as Andrei was about to whip the horses, our young hero looked up to the window for the last time and saw a pair of bleary eyes that silently said to him: "Go in good health, my darling, but come back quickly because I can't live without you!"

Sholom heard these words with all his senses and his eyes replied: "Be well, my beloved. I'm coming back to you because I can't live without you!" And only now did he realize how attached he had become to this house. No force in the world but death could tear him away from here.

He sank into a reverie; his heated imagination took wing, and he began to dream. When he returned he would reveal himself first to her and then to her parents. He imagined turning to old Loyev and saying: "I love her. I love your daughter. Do what you want with me!" Then the old man would embrace him and say: "It's good you told me. I've been expecting it for a long time." And then began the wedding preparations. Tailors were brought from Bohuslav and Tarashtche to sew garments for the bride and groom. They baked honey cakes and prepared fruit preserves. A huge carriage normally kept in the barn and used only for special occasions was sent for members of the groom's family. His father, Uncle Pinny and other relatives came. Though no one knew how he got there, Shmulik too appeared at the wedding. Shmulik, the rabbi's son. Shmulik the Orphan who had so many wonderful stories to tell. "Well, Sholom," he said as he kissed the groom, "didn't I tell you that the treasure was yours?"

Sweet childish dreams and golden fantasies of this kind fused in Sholom's mind until he came to Kaniev. There he stayed with a hunchbacked relative of old Loyev, a rich wine merchant who sold wines to the surrounding nobility. His name was Berach Bertchik. Sholom at once attended to his draft board affairs and presented his letter of recommendation to the local police chief. In this letter old Loyev stated: "I'm sending our tutor to the draft board with the hope that I'll have him back within a week, freed of all obligations."

The chief read the letter and gave a one-word reply: "Fine!" And that sufficed to calm Sholom. He went to the board and drew a number, which happened to be 285. True, this number was not a very high one, but the examination list at the draft board closed at 284. Sholom was free. Because of him, several other Jewish lads with higher numbers were also freed. That year there was great joy in Kaniev.

For this celebration, Sholom's father traveled to Kaniev from Pereyaslav. If I remember correctly, Uncle Pinny came too—he had an in-law in Kaniev—and the festivities grew tenfold. Berach Bertchik fetched some wine from his cellar, and the celebrant sent a telegram to Sofievke through the Baranyepolye Station:

"Mazel tov. They didn't get to me. I'm free. Coming home tomorrow morning."

However, more than one day passed before our hero could leave Kaniev. For was it possible that a Jewish celebration not be marred? A certain man appeared whose name was Vishinsky or Vishnefsky. A Jew, a shouter, a loudmouth. He had a crippled son who he was sure would be disqualified. But it turned out he was declared fit for military duty. This vexed the father, and he began to raise a fuss:

"What? My crippled son will go and serve instead of those privileged snobs who bought their freedom?"

When people asked him not to yell, he shouted, "What? Am I yelling? Seems to me I'm talking rather softly."

He began to shout even louder. "I know why the chief took

only cripples into the army." And he secretly told everyone the reason—but so loudly that the entire town knew it down to the last detail. Even the exact language of Loyev's letter to the chief. (There are no secrets where Jews are concerned.)

This Vishinsky or Vishnefsky proclaimed that he would not remain silent. "I'm going to bring everyone to court," he said, "the chief, the doctors, the entire draft board!"

People then called this Vishinsky aside and told him that a collection would be made and that his crippled son would be freed from military duty. But he didn't want to hear promises.

"In the Yom Kippur service, Jews bow down seven times between the words 'thus he said' and 'thus he counted.' I don't want promises. I want to see cash on hand." He then repeated these demands in Russian. Nothing helped. Then some good folk intervened. They called one meeting, another meeting, and two more meetings, and all the exempt candidates contributed. One gave fifty rubles, another a hundred, and they gathered up a sufficient sum, which would be divided among the drafted Jewish men. The largest share was taken, of course, by the shouting Jew. He argued that he deserved more than anyone else because his son was more of a cripple. Logic of course would have dictated otherwise: on the contrary, *because* he was a cripple, it would be easier to exempt him. But what could you do with such a loudmouth, shouting at the top of his lungs?

Seeing that everyone gave in to his whims, like a spoiled brat Vishinsky continually increased his demands. He began to bargain like a fishwife. Luckily, the above-mentioned relative, Berach Bertchik, had carte blanche from old Loyev to give the prospective draftee as much money as he needed. Who thought of money at such a time? Freedom was the only thing that mattered; freedom was the only blazing star. Sholom felt free only when he sat in the carriage that had been sent to the railroad station in Mironovke. Andrei the coachman brought him regards from home: everyone was well, thank God, and everything was in order.

"Giddyap," said Andrei and began a conversation with the horses in their language. The horses understood him and the carriage almost flew through the air. It was a warm, mild autumn day. The sun was hot but did not burn. It patted and caressed. Sholom's eyes closed. The web of dreams began again. Silken dreams. Castles in the air, golden castles. Soon he would be home. As soon as he arrived, he would reveal his cards to old Loyev: "I'd like to inform you that I love your daughter and your daughter loves me." Soon. Within half an hour. Fifteen minutes. Here was the familiar Baranyepolye, the forest, the pastureland, the cemetery, the windmills that looked like giants from afar, waving their hands and calling, "Come here, come here!"

A few minutes more and he saw the courtyard. The great white mansion with its two porches. There could be no greater joy than when a child comes home to his parents freed from the draft. Sholom had many, many stories to tell about the miracles and wonders of the draft—a virtual Exodus from Egypt! But he did not tell the most important matter, the one he had rehearsed. He did not reveal his cards before old Loyev. He postponed this for the next day, for later…

Meanwhile, one day passed and then another, one week and then another. Then an unexpected catastrophe struck, brought on by an outsider who opened up the old man's eyes to the ongoing romance. This person happened to be a wise, far-seeing woman, a relative of old Loyev from Berditchev named Toive. We call her "Auntie Toive from Berditchev." When you get to know her, you'll see how appropriate her name is. To her we'll devote a separate chapter.

73. Auntie Toive From Berditchev

Actually, Toive wasn't an aunt to anyone. She was no more than a cousin to old Loyev. But, as I mentioned, the name Auntie suited her. She was a rather homely woman with a pockmarked face and a long nose. Her clever-eyed glance, however, seemed to penetrate you. People said that she wore the pants in the family. She managed the business affairs and was quite wealthy. Now, after an absence of many years, Auntie Toive came to visit the Loyevs.

Naturally, for an aunt from Berditchev the aristocratic life in the village seemed new and strange: she saw everything through her Berditchev eyes and marveled at everything. She talked familiarly to old Loyev and told him explicitly what she thought, what pleased her, and what did not.

For example, she liked the life in the village, the air, the cows, the horses, the fresh milk that smelled of the pasture, and the bread made of homegrown wheat. Everything smelled of the earth, of one's own labor. Everything was good, top-notch. She even liked Dodi, a man of nature. But she disagreed with her cousin's discipline; it smacked too much of a nobleman's antics. The way she saw it, being a Jew and a lessee of land was a contradiction. On the other hand, she liked the fact that Loyev was a good farmer and loved the earth. Why not? As long as God helps, one can make money and become a rich man. Why not? Perhaps she too wouldn't have refused this opportunity. But she didn't understand why one had to live so far from Jews. Why didn't Loyev go to Bohuslav when a Jewish holiday came? And she reproached him for his mocking a beggar with a green scarf who had wandered into the area, the sort that claimed to be a grandson of a noted Jewish scholar, when he asked for a donation. Sure, Loyev had given one, and with a generous hand too. But still, he had poked fun at the man. "Rather don't give and don't mock," Auntie Toive from Berditchev contended.

And another thing. Auntie Toive liked the teacher. Sholom was a fine lad—she had nothing against him, and he knew his stuff too. And what's more, he came from a good family—that made it even better. But where was it written that a tutor had to be so close to his pupil? In her opinion, this teacher was too chummy with his charge. How did she know this? Auntie Toive had an all-seeing eye. Auntie Toive appointed herself to watch the young couple's every step. In fact, with her own eyes she had witnessed them eating from one plate. Auntie Toive from Berditchev noticed from the very first day that the girl was dying for the lad and that he was head over heels in love with the girl.

"It's plain as day to anyone," she declared, "except for someone who's either blind in both eyes, or simply doesn't want to see what's happening under his nose. All I had to do," Auntie Toive continued, "was take one look at the the two of them sitting at the table, exchanging glances, talking with their eyes. From that moment on," said she, "I didn't stop watching them for a second." Indeed, Auntie Toive zealously watched when they sat and studied, when they went for walks, or when they went riding in the carriage.

Once—so Auntie Toive told the old man—she noticed them walking into Dodi the Steward's house. That she didn't like from the start. "What business do children like that have in his poor house?" But lazy she was not, Auntie Toive from Berditchev, and she peeked in through Dodi's window and saw the young couple eating from one plate. What they ate, she didn't know. But she did see them—may she see good things the rest of her life!—eating and talking and laughing…

"So it's either one thing or the other. If it's a match—why well and good, but the mother and father have to know. And if it's a love affair? A romance? Then the parents should certainly know—for it's much healthier and better and nicer to give your daughter to a poor teacher who has no more than a couple of shirts to his name than to wait until this selfsame teacher runs off with the daughter on some dark night to set up a quick wedding canopy in Bohuslav, Tarashtche or Korsun."

These were Auntie Toive's complaints, as they later became known. She revealed them to her cousin in absolute secrecy half an hour before her departure. Her words reverberated in old Loyev's heart, for when he left to escort his cousin, he was furious and didn't say a word to anyone for the rest of the day. He secluded himself in his room and didn't show his face.

That night, his son Joshua arrived in Sofievke and spent the night there. Something was going on. Something was brewing. They locked themselves into the old man's room, discussing something in whispers. They were evidently holding a family council. The pupil, ready to go for a walk with her tutor, was stopped at the last minute. The family didn't come to eat all at once, as usual; they came separately, at various times. Each one finished eating, rose, and went on his way. Something extraordinary was happening in the house. A strange silence that precedes a storm…

Who would have thought that a couple of ambiguous words from Auntie Toive from Berditchev would cook up such a storm and prompt such a revolution in the house? Had Auntie Toive known sooner what repercussion her words would cause, perhaps she wouldn't have butted in where she wasn't needed. Much later they learned that Auntie Toive from Berditchev immediately regretted the whole thing and wanted to take back what she had said, but by then it was too late. She made an about-face and began to argue with the old man that it really wasn't such a great misfortune, and that there was really nothing to get upset about. Was it the boy's fault that he was poor? "Being poor is no shame" and "Happiness is in the hands of God" were among the proverbs she fed him.

Words, however, no longer availed. The old man maintained that actually he had nothing against Sholom. But how dare they conduct a romance in his house without his knowledge? His daughter's possible engagement to a poor lad didn't bother him. Then what did? It was he, her father, who was supposed to introduce such a young man to her. And she must not choose him herself, without having consulted her father! This is what vexed him more than anything else.

The young couple became aware of all these complaints and remarks only much later. But at this time, like a pair of innocent lambs, they did not know who had betrayed them. They only felt that something was brewing. What could come of it—they would see tomorrow. The next day would tell.

The next morning when our hero awoke, he found no one at home. Not the old man or his wife, not the son or the daughter. Where were they all? They had gone. He didn't know where and none of the people in the courtyard would say. On the table he saw a package prepared for him. He opened it, hoping for a letter, an explanation, but he found no message. Not a word. The only thing the packet contained was money—wages that had accumulated throughout his entire stay. Nothing more. In the courtyard, the sleigh stood waiting (this incident happened during the winter) with a warm sheepskin blanket to cover his legs. Sholom couldn't get a word out of the household retainers.

Even Dodi the Steward, who would have willingly chopped off his hands for Sholom and his pupil, answered all questions with only a shrug and a deep sigh. His fear of the old man overrode everything else. This made the humiliated teacher even angrier. He felt lost and didn't know where to turn. He made several attempts at writing a letter, first to old Loyev, then to his son Joshua, and then to his pupil. But the words didn't come. It was a great catastrophe. He had never expected such a slap in the face. He felt disgraced for himself and embarrassed before the others. But he didn't hesitate too long. He sat in the sleigh and let himself be brought to the station in order to leave—but where to? He himself still didn't know. Wherever his legs would take him. In the meantime, before he arrived at the railway station, he asked the coachman to stop in Baranyepolye—the post station from which Sofievke got all its mail. In Baranyepolye Sholom had a friend. You know him—the manager of the station, Postmaster Malinofsky.

By nature, Malinofsky loved to have his palm greased. And as we already know he also loved to drink. He frequently got presents from old Loyev's lands: a bag of wheat, a wagonload of straw and, in honor of the holiday, a coin or two. Malinofsky made common cause with the teacher and his pupil and, generally speaking, was a good goy.

Sholom stopped by for a short visit and unburdened his heart. Sholom wanted Malinofsky to be a smuggler of contraband—he'd send a letter to Loyev's daughter and have her reply, if there was one, forwarded to him. After hearing Sholom's request, Postmaster

Malinfsky stretched out a hand and swore to God. And in case Sholom didn't believe him, he crossed himself too. He would do his absolute best. And since a business deal was being concluded between good friends, said agreement had to be wetted down with a bit of whiskey and a piece of herring. Nothing else would do. Both sat down and did not rise again until the bottle was empty and Malinofsky was full, at which he began to embrace and kiss the teacher. Once again he swore and crossed himself, and said that Sholom's letters would be given over to Loyev's daughter—rest assured. For when Malinofsky gives his word, it's his sacred oath…

And so it was: The first few flaming and impassioned love letters that Sholom sent him, one after another, Postmaster Malinofsky (as Sholom later learned) placed squarely in the hands of old Loyev. Hence it is easy to understand why no reply was ever received to these flaming and impassioned letters. And it is also easy to understand why he continued writing these letters—until he stopped writing.

. . . .

What do these dots mean? They stand for a long, dark night. Everything was wrapped in a thick mist. The lonely wanderer was groping for his way. He kept stumbling over stones or falling into a pit. He fell, scrambled up, continued on his path, tripped over another stone and fell into another pit, taking no notice of the bright world around him. He did foolish things, made mistakes, one greater than the other. A blindfolded man cannot possibly find the right road. A blindfolded man must go astray—and Sholom went astray. He strayed for a long, long time, until he found the right road. Until he found himself.

— Translated by Curt Leviant

71

A caricature of Sholem-Aleykhem in the English language journal, Jewish Quarterly (1959) *for the* 100*th birthday of the writer.*

II
Two Early Stories

INTRODUCTION BY LOUIS FRIDHANDLER TO
THE ELECTION AND *LEGBOYMER*

Sholem Rabinowits wrote his second Yiddish story, "The Election," in 1883, the first ever signed with his pseudonym, "Sholem-Aleykhem." "Legboymer" was written in 1887. In the foreground of both pieces are social commentary, criticism, protest, and confrontation of harsh realities. His celebrated talent for rib-tickling was then barely discernible—although "The Election" opens with a slapstick scene.

The Election   *   *   *

This piece concerns a lively and acrimonious debate about candidates for election to the post of *rabiner.* Sholem-Aleykhem had been *rabiner* in the town of Loubny since mid-1880. Jews were required by czarist law to elect a *rabiner* to record local births, deaths, marriages, sales and exchanges of property, and other Jewish community statistics. He was paid by the Jews, but worked for the Czar. On national holidays, the *rabiner* (or *crown rabbi*) was expected to deliver orations praising the czar and his regime. It could not have been a comfortable position. Sholem-Aleykhem was married on May 12, 1883. Bending to the wishes of his wealthy father-in-law (who surely felt the position was not suited to someone with good family connections), Sholem-Aleykhem left that job in August 1883. "The Election" appeared in early fall of 1883, written while he was probably still smarting from serving for three years in an official capacity that garnered no respect from fellow Jews.

In "The Election," the incumbent *rabiner* is a learned free-thinker, beloved by the common folk for helping the poor and ill. The challenger, a writer, is supported by the town's well-to-do movers and shakers because he is expected to collaborate and serve *their* interests rather than the towns-people's.

In his autobiographical novel, *From the Fair* (see excerpts in this volume, p. 35), Sholem-Aleykhem describes his own successful candidacy for *rabiner* and his dismay in realizing he had caused the incumbent to lose his job. At the end of part three of *From the Fair,* Sholem-Aleykhem tells of his resolve to be unlike all other *rabiners:* "Why must a *rabiner* be a hypocrite, a flattering toady to the rich, and a servile functionary for the regime?"

"The Election" is obviously autobiographically grounded. It is especially interesting to note, however, that Sholem-Aleykhem appears to split himself into two separate fictional characters: he was, indeed, a writer, as is the challenger. He was also a true devotee of the *haskole,* that is, a learned free-thinker, as is the incumbent. The piece seems to reflect his pain in being pulled in opposing directions.

Legboymer

Young boys of the *kheyder* suffer pain of body and soul inflicted by a teacher demoralized by his own humiliating poverty and shallow learning, traits of the ordinary *melamed.* *"Dos Meserl"* ("The Penknife"), written earlier, deals in part with a similar theme. Dubnow, the historian, then a commentator on Jewish literature in the Russian-Jewish press, praised "Dos Meserl" as a rare gem among the tawdry pieces then appearing. That must have encouraged Sholem-Aleykhem to produce something in a similar vein.

The piece was extensively revised for a 1901 publication. The theme remained a similar one, but a hellfire sermon was eliminated. Further, the names of people and places were changed, and the boys' alcoholic consumption was not emphasized. The revision was so extensive, that the 1901 version should be considered a separate peace with the same title.

*   *   *

Finsternish and Hrebinka

"The Election" is set in *Finsternish.* The message is not hidden. The name, "Darkness," directly suggests a benighted place with benighted inhabitants.

The townlet in *"Legboymer"* is *Hrebinka.* On the surface it has no explicit connotations. A more careful probe, however, suggests meanings. *Hrebinka* is a transliteration of the Yiddish. The expected Russian form would be *Grebinka.* That resonates with the town of *Grebenka,* a railway junction between Loubny—where, as noted earlier, Sholem-Aleykhem worked as *rabiner* for three years—and Kiev. Side-roads led to Pereyaslav, where his father and stepmother lived. He must have passed by or stopped in *Grebenka* numerous times. *Grebenka,* means comb in Russian. A related word, *grebenku,* means to have one's hair cropped. One is thus reminded that groups of hostile gentiles would pin a Jew down, cropping his hair, knowing full well how serious a violation of Jewish religious custom that was and how painful a humiliation. The boys in *"Legboymer,"* so proud of their Jewish heritage, suffer severe humiliation in *Hrebinka.*

The town of the little people.

A caricature of Sholem-Aleykhem with friends and ordinary Jews.

The Election *

TRANSLATED BY LOUIS FRIDHANDLER

A bustling crowd, elbow to elbow, jostled for space at the house of Reb Fayvl Knok. Old Fayvl's beard was flecked with bare patches, and he sported two thick earlocks, tufts of hair running down each cheek. His skullcap tapered to a point. As he rose to face the milling crowd, he blocked a man's mouth with one hand while his other hand held another one's beard. Fayvl shouted hoarsely, "We've had this educated-shmeducated rabiner long enough! What good to us is his education? That'll just make him better at denouncing us to the police! We've had him six years. Isn't that long enough? Better elect Isaac instead! He's one of us. We can deal with him and plug all the loopholes. Maybe he's not too smart when it comes to books, but...."

"What's the use of talking and talking?" cried Ref Yosef Indik, who liked to throw cold water on everything. "The main question is: Can he fill out the official forms?"

Reb Faytl Glok, whose mouth had been shut by the hand of Fayvl Knok, managed to pull free and hollered, "Do what you like, but wouldn't it look better all around if we kept a *rabiner* who reads books? The Christians, too, would respect that. Yes, I know, I admit it—he's lazy when it's time to come to the synagogue. Not exactly pious. But listen: if a Jew is down and out and needs help, he helps. And remember how, somehow, he managed to have a school built for poor children. He arranged a home for the sick, and lots of other things.

---

*The Yiddish title is *"Di vibores"*; it was reprinted in *Fargesene Bletlekh*, pp. 37-41, and in *Ale Verk,* Moscow, 1948, pp. 50-53, from which this translation was made. It was his second piece in Yiddish, and the first use of his pseudonym, "Sholem-Aleykhem."

"Can't you let anybody else talk?" asked Fayvl Knok as he blocked Faytl's mouth again. "We already know the favors he does. Some favors! What did we get from that freethinker? Secular schools! Old Reb Tsodek (the rich one) has been saying again and again that our educated *rabiner* is just too cheeky. What gall! At his school Jewish children walk home two-by-two, just like gentiles in a mygnasium, er, gymnasium.

Then he called to his wife, "Dvosi-Leye, come set up the drinks, and let's have a bite to eat. It's a holiday, you know. *Election day!* Well, take a look at who just breezed in. Fridl Blits! What's new in town, Fridl?"

Fridl Blits is a roly-poly little man with tiny hands whose eyes never seemed to focus on any one spot. He's always cheerful, always busy, but has no definite occupation. How he supports a wife and children, only God knows.

Fridl reported at once: "The rich people want a new *rabiner* and endorse his rival, Isaac-the-writer. The regular folks—the tailors, shoemakers, draymen, wedding musicians, teachers of the little boys, and all the poor people—are ready to risk their necks for the old *rabiner.* They say they won't trade him in even for the 'real' rabbi himself. Meanwhile, all wine merchants and taverns are crowded with customers. Velvl Zyika has ordered fifty roasted geese from Pesi-Shprintse, along with eighty ducks and ten turkeys. Raphael-Yoyne-the-baker made a few thousand cookies, and the town is really living it up, and I don't have any more time so I have to get going."

*   *   *

At three tables covered with worn, green table clothes sat the recording secretaries bent over, scratching pens on paper. At a corner table sat the executive secretary with a sour face. Near him stood a tall man with a long, serious face, a thin nose and scrawny shoulders. He kept jabbing the executive secretary with his sharp fingers. That was Isaac-the-writer, Isaac-the-talebearer, who hoped to become the new *rabiner* that day in the town of *"Finsternish."**
The hall was filled with people standing around, jammed together like a flock of sheep. They were of the lower class, the masses who must earn their piece of bread with their last bit of strength. At the sides, in arm-chairs and on benches, sat the well-bred, well-fed

---

*Darkness

78

men with smooth, round bellies and finely groomed beards. These were the town's rich men, the elite intelligentsia. Everybody was waiting for the mayor, speaking at the same time like a congregation between afternoon and evening prayers. What confusion! Through the buzz you could hear only: "Right? No, left. Isaac, the new one? O.K., let it be Isaac. And do you vote for the old one, the one we have? Yes, that's the one!" An elderly man, one of the rich ones, heatedly said to the crowd:

"Friends, apparently you want to keep the old *rabiner,* that heretic, even though he writes secular stuff for the newspapers, and doesn't even wear a hat; and his children go to the gentile *gymnasium;* and he even writes on the Sabbath. That upstart has sold you a bill of goods. But! I warn you, if you elect him you'll live to regret it! You need to know your place! You're only unimportant people who should recognize those who are better than you. What do you see in that freethinker that makes you support him so long? *Six years is enough!*

"Forgive me, Reb Tsodek, for what I'm about to tell you," shouted an old, grey-haired tradesman from among the crowd, "but the old *rabiner* really needs our support now. He has earned it. Let him be a freethinker or whatever he wants. We won't suffer for *his* sins. He hasn't hurt anyone. If not for him, our children would have nowhere to go and nothing to do; and the old, the sick would still lie about in the streets as they used to. We gave him our word. We can't back out now!"

"I see that he has bedazzled you," declared Reb Tsodek, taking up where he left off. "I tell you again: don't do something you'll be sorry for. Seems to me I've earned more from you than that penniless heathen who arrived with nothing but a worn hat. But look what I've done for you! I set up a bank to loan you money. My cash box is always open to everybody, and I don't charge high interest. I've been the tax-collector here for 28 years! Who helped you repair the synagogue and built you a bathhouse (pardon me for mentioning both in the same breath)? Who brought you a cantor from Brody along with eight choirboys? Who gave your little town seven ritual slaughterers and three rabbis? Who gave you...?

Just then the mayor arrived, and the voting began. The crowd murmured, "Shhh," as they elbowed each other to cast their ballots. First, Isaac stood up to hear his vote-count: 22 white and 76 black ballots. Rejected! Then the old rabiner stood to hear his winning total: 22 black and 76 white. Reb Tsodek burned with rage.

The crowd began to leave for their celebration. They got drunk and stayed drunk the rest of the day and night.

Next morning Fridl Blits spread the word all over town that:

1. Reb Tsodek added three kopeks to the tax on three pounds of meat;
2. The bathhouse door is now locked; and
3. Reb Tsodek denounced his very poorest debtors to the police who confiscated the goods of some, and packed others off to jail.

—Fintsternish, 1883

Legboymer*

A Cheerful Story With a Sad Ending
In memory of May 12,1883, *Legboymer***

Translated by Louis Fridhandler

1

"Do you have the impression that when we were children in *kheyder* we had only rotten times with never a single day of happiness to brighten our lives? Well, if that's what you think, you're making a big mistake! Sure, nowadays it's different. It's better. Your gymnasium children, or those who go to secular school, have two months at liberty, a vacation on top of other holidays. Your young ones can recharge their energies, fling off the burden of study from their weary heads, and devote themselves to *living:* jumping, clambering over rocks and hills, drifting along in a boat, shooting play guns, munching candy, swimming the length and breadth of the creek, and plenty more such devilment. In the old days we boys in the *kheyder* were not used to that. We were really at the mercy of our teacher, Moti-the-Bandit or Mayer-the-Whip, who scourged our flesh, whose weighty fists afflicted us. We were made to understand that:

> Our teacher hath led us to paths of righteousness, and along the byways of Torah study. He shed a wise light by whose glow we drew from the fountain of knowledge for the delight of all human hearts. And in that light, we obeyed the will of God, Ruler over all realms.

Such gaudy words were penned by my friend, Fishl-the-

---

*Translated from the Yiddish from *Yudishes Folksblat*, St. Petersburg, 1887.
**It was Sholem-Aleykhem's wedding day.

Bridegroom, soon after his engagement party, when he wrote his first fancy letter to his future father-in-law, the leaseholder of a farming estate. The family displayed it proudly for three whole years, until Fishl was married and opened a tavern in a village somewhere. Today he's burdened with a family and desperately poor. God protect us and all Jews from that! But that's not really what I want to tell you. I just wanted to explain that we *kheyder* boys *did* have our bright moments, a joyous hour, even one full day of happiness during a troubled, melancholy childhood. That day was *Legboymer.*

*   *   *

"Rally 'round, little children," said my *rebbe* to us, putting aside the iron rods with which he used to flog our tender young hides. A cheery smile appeared on his creased, shriveled face. "Listen, little children. Get yourselves together and have a feast tomorrow, all of you, big ones and little ones, poor and rich, each according to the fortune with which God has blessed him. Go out to the open countryside. Go. Be happy and spirited on the day which God, blessed be He, has granted you with His generous Hand. *Legboymer,* children, *Legboymer* is *your* holiday, and you must lift up your hands to heaven. With all your heart, clear of mind, strong of voice, thank and praise the Almighty for the great mercy and generosity with which He blesses us out of great love for Israel, His chosen people, whom he delivered from the land of Egypt and Who fed us manna in the desert for forty years and Who gave us the Torah through His servants, Moses and Aaron, at Mount Sinai, in the midst of thunder and lightning. Moreover, children, do not forget that you are Jewish children who are descended from Abraham, Isaac, and Jacob, and are not like any other children in the whole world.

"You well know, children, that if you forget about God for a minute, a moment, then you slide into error and sin against Him. That only prolongs the Jewish exile, and hell gains a multitude of the wicked and depraved for their well-deserved punishment. And in hell, burning lashes are always ready for you, and the fire blazes forever under you, and you are hurled back and forth by the *Slingshots of Hell.* Your screams resound from one end of creation to the other, and a howling roar rumbles from above in a mournful wail, 'Woe is Me, for I see not a single saint on earth who might redeem his unfortunate, sinful people.' Are you crying, little children?

(We are crying.)

"Cry, cry! Let your tears become a river as deep as an ocean to submerge your evil sins. Perhaps that will draw mercy for us from above to bring our suffering to an end. Perhaps then, from this day forward, we shall hear good news of deliverance and consolation for Jews, so that, with clear minds, we may offer God, in fear and with love, the wholehearted service He has earned from us, as it is written."

We shook with sobs. We were drenched in our own tears. The *rebbe* spoke without a pause, citing verse after biblical verse. He incessantly admonished and reprimanded us with terrifying notions. He painted frightful pictures that made our hair stand on end. We shivered like lambs who have spotted a beast of prey nearby. The *rebbe* continued for a long time, until he arose from the table and took up his "whip" again with these words:

"Well, little chums. Lie down one by one. You need a few lashes to make sure you are not distracted from thinking of your obligation, to make sure you don't forget the burden of *kheyder*. If any one of you hasn't yet earned the lash, I'm sure he'll earn it in due time, with the help of God. I know very well, don't you worry, that while I stand before your very eyes, you show some respect; but as soon as you step out of the *kheyder*, you forget me as surely as you forget last year's snowfalls. What? Maybe not? Hah? Yosele, what have you got to say, Yosele? Am I on your mind a lot out there, when you're home, or in the fields, or playing on the hill with all those scamps? Well, Yosele, am I not a prophet? Right? Come now, get down, my child, and we'll whip you a little. Maybe God will be merciful, and you'll remember, if only for a moment, that there is a *rebbe* in your life and a *kheyder*. Yes, that's the way! Now, Gershon, come on over, come! And you, Leybele. And you, Yisrolik. Khaim! Dovidl! Avreyml! Hershl! Menashe! Motele! Down with your britches, Motele! Bentsi! Lie straight, Bentsi; I'm too tired to tangle with you. Well, that's the way! All done? Already? Good! Now say your prayers and go home. Tomorrow, you have the whole day to yourselves! The next day, early, *into the kheyder*. But, just let me see one of you with a scratch, a sleeve ripped off; or if one of you is absent-minded, or doesn't know the *Gemore* lesson,..WHACK! You won't fool around with me! Good night, little children!"

2

The warming sun moved across the bright, blue sky as we forty-four boys (from the *kheyders* of Mayer-the-Whip and of Moti-the-Bandit) began to assemble soon after prayers in the yard of Bentsi the son of Sholem-Isaac who lived on the other side of the mill. How come at Bentsi's house? In the first place, Bentsi was the eldest, and in the second place, his father is Sholem-Isaac, the rich man, whose yard is big enough for our Friday afternoon chats, with room for all kinds of mischief. Besides, there are blocks of wood and burnt bricks scattered about on the other side of the mill. That's a great place to stage all kinds of theater: "Building Pithom and Raamses," "The Gift of Torah," "The Sale of Joseph," "The Exodus from Egypt," and other plays like that.

"Now," said Bentsi who had scampered up on a big log. "Now, let's see what each of you pals has brought for the feast. We'll put it all together and see what we still need. Mendl! Come on, show us! You first, you're older than the others. What did your mama give you? Two bagels, a baked egg, three, four, five, six nuts, and two groschen. Good! Big Hershl, let's see what you have. Not much: part of a bun, a bit of garlic, and six groschen. That's all right! Little Hershl, hand over your hanky. Oho! Your mama wasn't stingy with dried sausage, two cookies, a few pieces of sugar and a jar with plenty of goose fat. Red Yosl, step forward with your package! Three eggs, a roasted chicken, a whole bun, ten groschen, and a bottle of mead. What a haul! Good for you, Yosl, you rascal! Avrom Moyshe! Yes, you, the tailor's son! Show what you brought. Don't be embarrassed. It makes no difference how much it is. You brought a slice of bread smeared with a little honey. Anything else? A groschen. Fine. Ziame the son of Nakhem-Volf! You must have quite a hoard of riches there! Didn't I guess right? See, kids? Five cookies, about ten eggs, a roast duck, two buns, a bottle of whiskey. Hmm! A flask of beer, a pound of sugar, an ounce of tea, a box of first-rate tobacco. Bravo, Ziame! I like you! Good old Ziame!

"All right boys, sit down on the logs and let's start the feast. Eat what you can and don't be too particular. I have the glasses ready so let's drink *lekhayim* the way our daddies drink *lekhayim*. *Lekhayim,* Yosl, *lekhayim*. Fill the glass and drink *lekhayim* to Red Yosl. Avrom Moyshe, why are you making a face? Drink, you devil, drain it! *Lekhayim,* Hershl! *Lekhayim,* Mendl. Again! A full glass. That's the way! *Lekhayim,* children, *lekhayim!* See, I turn the glass bottom up. I drain it just like Gedalye-Ber, the drunkard, on *simkhes-toyre* after dark, after everybody else has already sobered up. Hey, fellas, look, I'm on my fifth glassful. *Lekhayim! Lekhayim!*"

Bentsi the son of Sholem-Isaac goaded us to take drink after drink.

"What'll we buy with the money?" shouted Bentsi.

From all sides came the roar, "Whiskey! Whiskey!"

*　　*　　*

After the meal, Bentsi again hollered, asking, "Where'll we go?" Somebody answered, "To the other side of the graveyard!"

"No! To the brickyard!" cried another.

"No! That's no good. We better go to the fields behind the fence where the general lives!"

"Don't you know about the vicious dogs there?"

"Yeah, we can't go there" cried several voices at once.

"Now, let me tell you where!" hollered Ziame.

"Shh. Quiet! Ziame is going to tell us where!"

"Yes! Let Ziame talk!"

"Okay," said Ziame, "let's split up into two groups. We'll call one group Yehuda and the other Ephraim. Bentsi will lead Moti-the-Bandit's *kheyder*—I mean the army of Yehuda; and I'll be the leader of Mayer-the-Whip's *kheyder*—the army of Ephraim. We'll get weapons: sticks and stones; then we'll march on the Philistines of Hrebinka.

Some yelled, "Yes, that's it! We'll get those Philistines! On to Hrebinka!"

Others warned, "Hrebinka is a big village with a lot of peasants who'll sic their dogs on us!"

"Never mind! Who cares about peasants and their dogs? Dog, Shmog! We are two armies marching on the Philistines!"

"On to Hrebinka! Comrades-in-arms! Get your weapons ready. We march on the Philistines! Hurrah!"

"A song for the march! Sing: *Fear not, My servant Jacob!*"

Etc., etc.

*　　*　　*

You can't expect me to remember exactly what happened to our armies that day. But a few memories have stuck. I'll never for-

85

get our joyous, patriotic pride, as we sang and "advanced" on the "Philistines." I was one of Moti-the-Bandit's smallest students, with old, worn pants full of rips, but on that day I felt as mighty as Og, the king of Bashan.* I imagined the big stick I carried across my shoulders was a sharp sword; and the stones I kept in my pocket were menacing cannonballs that could easily kill many soldiers. Slowly but surely our blood grew hotter, dangerously close to boiling. We all were filled with a zeal for war, to stab, slaughter, butcher, to vanquish the foe and take his land. The dust from our feet became a thick haze which I took for nothing less than the pillar of cloud which accompanied Moses and the Jews of Egypt. We were very proud and became jollier and more eager for the fight we faced when, at long last, we would reach the Land of the Philistines.

"Here comes a Philistine!" cried Red Yosl pointing to a peasant driving an oxcart. "Leave him alone," shouted Ziame. Big Hershl hollered, "We must take him prisoner!" Ziame held us back, shouting, "No! Leave him alone! That's no Philistine. He's probably a woodcutter, or a water-carrier: just one of the rabble. Let him go, or God will punish us! Come on, kids, sing out loud, *Fear not, My servant, Jacob.*"

The peasant stopped his oxcart, removed his hat, crossed himself three times, snorted, and went on his way. This accidental encounter with a Philistine who seemed properly terrified of our two armies gave us so much courage that as soon as we espied the first few houses of Hrebinka, and heard the dogs barking, we lifted our weapons, and dashed forward, roaring our song in menacing tones.

As expected, a host of peasants and village children surrounded us and gazed in awe at our frightful armies. They said (in Russian):

"What's this?"

"A filthy crew!"

"Jews?"

"Carrying sticks?"

"Let's clobber 'em!"

"Sic the dogs on 'em! Let's get 'em! Comrades!"

*   *   *

---

*Numbers 21:33.

The foe came at us from east, west, north, and south, and beat us without mercy. We had to turn tail and run from their land. Worse than the blows of the enemy were the sharp teeth of their mad dogs, who tore at our sides and calves like lions and leopards. Sobbing in pain, we shouted fervent prayers wrenched from the depths of our tormented souls. We begged almighty God to stay with us, just as He did not abandon Daniel. But He hid his face from us because of our sins and the sins of our parents and ancestors. He poured all His fury upon our heads.

My friend, Fishl-the-Bridegroom, set down this story in a very nice, flowery letter to his future father-in-law, the leaseholder. He wrote it soon after his *rebbe,* Moti-the-Bandit, gave him a sound whipping along with the rest of us. We suffered for weeks from the clubbing by the Philistines and the teeth of their vicious dogs and from the awful fright. Only Ziame, the son of Nakhem-Volf, eluded a flogging from our *rebbe.* He lay very sick for about three weeks, then died. That's how sad was the aftermath of our celebration of the only happy day of the year, our very own holiday, *Legboymer.*

—Kiev, 1887

III

Two Popular Songs

INTRODUCTION TO

SLEEP, MY CHILD

The following is a literal (unrhymed, unmetrical) translation of Sholem Aleykhem's famous poem *"Shlof, Mayn Kind"* (*Sleep My Child*).

Published in 1892, the lullaby became so popular and so widely sung throughout the Pale of Jewish Settlement in Eastern Europe that by 1901, only nine years later, it was listed as an "anonymous folksong" in Ginzburg and Marek's major collection of Yiddish folksongs (Kh. Shmeruk, *YIVO Annual*, 216; Mlotek, 152).

As Khone Shmeruk puts it in "Sholem Aleichem and America" (*YIVO Annual*, Volume 20, 1991):

> It was common in those years for families to become separated in the process of emigrating. Clearly Sholem Aleichem had touched an open wound, for his lullaby spread very rapidly...The lullaby expresses bold expectations of America....Basically, however, the lullaby is an expression of the most painful aspects of emigration. Not always was the separation of families a temporary one. (216)

The music for the lullaby was composed by David Kovanovsky (Mlotek, 152).

SLEEP, MY CHILD
(1892)

Sleep, my child, my comfort, my pretty,
Sleep, then, lullaby.
Sleep, my life, my *kadish eyner**,
Sleep, then, little son.

At your cradle sits your mother,
Sings a song and weeps.
You will likely understand someday,
What she meant.

In America
Is your daddy,
You are but a child, for now,
Sleep, then, sleep, lullaby.

That America is for all,
They say, quite a joy,
And for Jews an Eden,
Something extra-special.

During the week they eat there,
Sabbath loaves, little son.
Soups I will cook for you,
Sleep then, sleep, lullaby.

He will send twenty dollars,
And his portrait too,
And will take us, long may he live,
Over there.

Till the good passage-ticket comes,
Sleep, then, little son.
Sleeping is a precious remedy,
Sleep, then, sleep, lullaby.

---

*The *kadish* is the traditional prayer for the dead recited by a son on the anniversary of a parent's death; it is often used as an affectionate, half-ironic way of referring to a son; here, the word *eyner* is being used in its ironic sense, meaning, roughly, "such a"; i.e., *kadish eyner:* "such a" or "some" *kadish*.

INTRODUCTION TO
SONG OF THE KHEYDER

The kheyder played an enormous role in the life of Eastern European Jewry, up until the attempts in the twentieth century to reform and modernize Jewish education for children.

The old *kheyder* was usually a single, dingy room, most often in the poor home of the *melamed* (the teacher). There the life of the teacher and his wife and babes went on—cooking, squalling, disciplining, emptying of slop-pails—while young boys, from the age of three, were taught to read and write Hebrew. They studied the Bible, and later, the gifted ones and/or those who could pay, studied Talmud.

In Yiddish literature and memoiristic the traditional *kheyder* often comes under bitter, satiric attack; but it is also often remembered with nostalgia and sentiment. Despite its many shortcomings, there is no doubt it kept the Jewish people literate (at least the male half of it)—when many of the surrounding peoples were not. The *kheyder* sharpened wits while transmitting a cultural tradition thousands of years old.

In the unrhymed, unmetrical literal translation below of a poem he wrote in 1888, Sholem-Aleykhem describes such a *kheyder* from the boy's point-of-view: how the *rebbe* beats the boys, and how the beautiful wintry outdoors beckons to them with all its diversions. It's true, says the poet, that autumn pushes aside the summer and brings the winter and *kheyder;* but don't forget, he reminds us at the last, in the end winter is in its turn pushed aside by the summer and—*oys kheder!* (no more *kheyder*).

This poem was adapted for the stage and set to music by J. Cherniawsky. It became a very popular song on the stage of the American Second Avenue Yiddish theater in a rendition by Ludwig Satz (Mlotek, 12). (One of the editors of this book vividly remembers hearing a record of it as a three-year-old child—many years ago.) Following the translation of Sholem-Aleykhem's poem "Song of the Kheyder" below, is a literal translation of the theatrical song Cherniawsky made of it, "Ikh vil nit geyn in kheyder."

"I don't want to go to kheyder, because the Rebbe whips us…"

SONG OF THE *KHEYDER**

Bad times come and always
Push out the dear good times.
After the summer,
The autumn stands right behind
With its winds.

In the house it's dark and dank,
It's cold and muddy on the street,
And the nights—they get longer,
And in your heart—things are no better.

And he stands not far from here,
The helper
With a stick and a lantern.
—May he sink into the ground.

And the rebbe constantly whips us,
Big and little, the whole class,
"Study hard, break your bones,"
But no-one wants to study.

The ice-pond calls.
It's smooth, the snow is white!
"You want to skate?—have fun?"
And he bugs us with the "four patriarchs,"**

With "four patriarchs" and with "unkosher."
The cat-o-nine-tails dances on our backs
From before dawn till late at night,
Till we are thoroughly exhausted.

---

*The *kheyder,* traditionally a single dingy room, usually in the poor home of the teacher, where boys were instructed from the age of three in the Hebrew alphabet and the Bible, and later, the Talmud.

**The original says "fir oves": i.e., the children are mixing up the "dray oves"—the three patriarchs (Abraham, Isaac, and Jacob), with "Pirke oves" (the "Sayings of the Fathers").

You want to eat, still more, to sleep,
But here we go with weapons armed:
Stones, sticks of all sorts,
Like soldiers with our shouts.*

And we're told to sing happily,
To shout out loud: "My Lord, King!"
Whoever doesn't sing out loud,
Catches a pinch, a fist too.

Back at home—you fall down,
You want to sleep,
But he comes again, oh, that rebbe,
He comes in your dream and sends his greetings:

"Listen, rascal, it's a point,
It's time for the Talmud!
Let's hear it now: What's Rabbi Pupa's point?
Let's hear it: If not, I'll let you have it!"

In the morning, back to *kheyder*.
Today's like yesterday—and so on, forever.
And the whip thrashes our bones,
But nobody wants to study.

The good rays of the sun
Fall through the dark windows.
Short nights, days getting longer
Our hearts grow easier.

So wait, children, hope for tomorrow,
You must hope, dare not worry!
Our belief, our faith—
Our Jewish triumph...

Good times come and always
Push out the bad, gloomy times:
After the autumn, after the winter,
Comes the spring, dear children!

---

*It was the custom on the holiday *Legboymer* for *kheyder* boys accompanied by their teachers to march in procession, singing, into the woods and there to shoot with bows and arrows.

94

I DON'T WANT TO GO TO *KHEYDER**

Bad times always come
And replace dear, good ones;
Behind the summer stands ready
The autumn, with its winds.

> Chorus:
>
> I don't want to go to *kheyder*,
> Because the teacher whips us all the time—
> I don't want to go to *kheyder*,
> And the cat-o-nine-tails thrashes my bones,
> But no-one wants to study—
> I don't want to go to *kheyder*.

And he stands ready not far away,
His assistant at his side,
With a stick, a lantern—
May he sink into the ground.

> Chorus

The ice is calling,
The ice is smooth, the snow is white,
I want to skate, have some fun!
And he bothers us with the "four patriarchs."

> Chorus

---

*Cherniansky's popular music-hall version of the preceding "Song of the Kheyder."

The flowering of the Yiddish theater in New York: Lazar Freed, Celia Adler, and Maurice Schwartz in Sholem Aleichem's **Stempenyu,** *the Yiddish Art Theater, 1927.* (Courtesy of the Museum of the City of New York.)

96

IV
The Three "Artistic" Novels

INTRODUCTION TO
STEMPENYU

Stempenyu is the first of three novels Sholem-Aleykhem wrote about Jewish performing artists. Its protagonist is a Jewish *klezmer,* a violinist; it is reproduced in its entirety below. The second one, *Yosele Solovey* (*Yosele Nightingale* (p.181), deals with the world of the Jewish singer; the third, *Wandering Star* (p. 202), with Yiddish actors, with the world of the Yiddish theater.

Sholem-Aleykhem subtitled *Stempenyu* "my first Yiddish [or Jewish] novel," but since he had written earlier novels (*Sender Blank,* 1887, for example), "He could not have meant that this was literally his first novel in Yiddish....[but rather that] this [was] his first self-consciously Jewish novel...." (Anita Norich, *Prooftexts* 4 1984: 237).

Sholem-Aleykhem had to solve a self-imposed dilemma: because he felt that a novel must contain a love story, and since romance, in the modern European sense, was not a part of traditional Jewish life, how was he to write a novel with a realistic, East-European, Jewish setting? In contrast to the unrealistic and sentimental romances and cheap novels that he deplored, Sholem-Aleykhem wanted to base *Stempenyu* on the realities of Jewish life of the time, when, with the help of a marriage broker, marriages were arranged by parents. Family, status, dowry, and financial arrangements—not romantic love—were the primary considerations. The young people involved often were not consulted; they might not even have met before the wedding. As Dan Miron's article in the *Encyclopaedia Judaica* ("Sholem-Aleykhem") puts it:

> Though Jewish life was not devoid of romantic love, young lovers who could decide upon the course of their lives were foreign to its milieu and could, therefore, not be expressed aesthetically.... In *Stempenyu* and *Yosele Solovey* Sholem-Aleykhem circumvented the dilemma

through a restrained love story (which he defined as the model of a "Jewish romance"). In both novels he chose the character of a young man from the Jewish "bohemian" circles.... Taking his heroes from the fringes of traditional society allowed Sholem-Aleykhem to create romantic and appealing characters without affecting the social fidelity of the descriptions.

Stempenyu was published in 1888 as a supplement to the first issue of *Di Yidishe Folksbiblyotek* (*The Popular Jewish Library*), the Yiddish literary journal that Sholem-Aleykhem founded and funded with the goal of elevating Yiddish literature.

In depicting the world of the Jewish musician, Sholem-Aleykhem faithfully rendered the particular slang they used. Since this Yiddish musician's argot was unknown to the rest of the Jewish community, Sholem-Aleykhem included a glossary for his readers. The translation of these particular passages presents a difficulty. Our translator (Joachim Neugroschel) attacked the problem by rendering the Yiddish musicians argot into the jive slang of the black American jazz musicians—an original and intriguing approach.

Preceding the novel is an introduction Sholem-Aleykhem wrote for it in the form of a letter to Mendele Moykher-Sforim, here translated for the first time by the editors of this anthology.

IN HONOR OF MY KIND GRANDFATHER
REB MENDELE MOYKHER-SFORIM

Dear, True Grandfather of Mine:

Stempenyu, my first Yiddish novel, written in honor of your name—is yours. It's yours not just because I wrote it in your honor, but also because it is *you* who implanted in me the desire to write such a novel.

In one of your letters you say to me:

> "I would counsel you not to write any novels at all, because your bent, your genre, is something quite different. And especially since, if there does exist in the *life* of our people *novels,* they are something quite different than they are with all other peoples. One must understand this well and write it quite differently...."

Your words penetrated deep into my mind and I began to understand to what extent a Yiddish novel must be different from all other novels, since Jewish life in general and the conditions under which a Jew can love are not the same as they are with all other peoples. And not only

98

that, but the jewish people has its own character, its own Jewish spirit, with its special customs and rules, which are quite different from those of other peoples. These very national traits of ours, which remain forever genuinely Jewish, must display themselves in a Yiddish novel if it is to be truly drawn from life. This is what I understood from your words and this is what I wanted to express through the Jewish daughter, the beautiful Rachel—she who plays the largest role in this particular novel—and through all the other personages that revolve around her. To what extent did I succeed?—that is another question; but my wish was to write a *Jewish* novel (romance) as you, rightfully, demand of every Yiddish novelist.

In addition, *Stempenyu* is yours, dear grandfather, because its name is yours and the idea is yours: it was with you, grandfather dearest, in one of your recent works, that I encountered, in passing, the name "Stempenyu," with a little flask of love potion which all maids and servant girls buy from him in order to... This was sufficient to awaken in my memory all those wonderful stories I absorbed as a boy in *kheyder* about *Stempenyu*—and my fantasy was then ready to assist me in creating this novel.

It is possible that in many regions, as for example in Lithuania, Jews never hear of a "Stempenyu," and therefore the name itself will seem to them strangely wild. By the same token though, this name is very well known among us, in the whole environment of Mazepevke to Yehupets, not to speak of your little towns, in Gnilopyatsk, Tsviyatshits, and Tuneyadevka*—there even a child knows who Stempenyu was, his ancestry, and his status.

But it isn't just Stempenyu that is an aristocrat. My purpose with this novel was to create three people, or, as they are called, "main characters". *the Jewish artist Stempenyu, with his little violin; the Jewish daughter Rachel, the beautiful, with her Jewish honesty; and the young Jewish wife, Freydl* with her shopkeeper's soul and her trembling over every coin—each of these with his/her own little world. Stempenyu, Rachel, and Freydl—these are my personages, the important folks, who sit up front, at the head of the table, in first class, and all the rest are just simply additional characters, who crop up, as it were, from time to time, and sit always off to the side. That's why I settled the additional bunch with just a few words and all of my labor I dedicated to these three important folks.

I think that Jewish musicians, that is to say, our gangs of *klezmorim,* are unto themselves quite a separate world, and it is worth looking into their lives even deeper than I have done in this novel. One needs for this to have your eye, dear grandpa, your pen and your diligence.

Oh, where does one obtain diligence, deliberation? Where is one to get patience?

---

*These are all fictional towns from Sholem-Aleykhem's and Mendele's works.

"A work," you tell me in another letter, "a work, my dear grandchild, one must sweat over; one must work, polish every word; remember what I tell you: polish, polish!"

Polish! That's the very trouble with us, we young guys: we never have time and rattle-off the whole work, standing up, or, as we say, in brief, really, in one breath, not stopping at every thought, at every word, separately, to *work* and to *polish,* as you do. I know, dear grandfather, I feel it, how necessary it was to purify *Stempenyu* in several solutions. Of course, with you *Stempenyu* would have acquired a different appearance; from out of your hands he would have emerged differently, quite differently. With you, dearest little grandfather, there would have been here "a story over a story," a "story within a story," and "the story itself."

"I like," you say, again in a letter, "that besides a pretty little face, a scene should also possess life, sense, and thought, as with a living human being; a scene, besides displaying beautiful, flowery language, *must also say something worth hearing...*"

But the secret for this has been revealed only to you and to no-one else: creating pictures which have within them two figures, a front and a back side, a top and a bottom, so that within the obvious lies hidden something concealed, a quintessence—for this, grandfather dear, you are the only artist in our literature, and who can compare himself to you? We, youngsters, thank God if the story itself comes out in one piece, without a deformity, with all the organs of a literary creation.

Accept, then, gracious grandfather dear, this gift—my first Yiddish novel, which came to pass with God's will, and may it be the good will of God's sweet name that my *Stempenyu* should find favor in your eyes, and that you should derive pleasure, such as you should wish for yourself, from your devoted grandchild,

The Author,
Kiev, 1886

Stempeniu:

A JEWISH ROMANCE
BY SHOLOM ALEICHEM

STEMPENIU'S ESCUTCHEON

Stempeniu. That was a sort of nickname he inherited from his father. His dad, may he rest in peace, was a musician, he was known as Beryl the Bassist or Beryl of Stempeni, a village in the area of Mazepevke. He played the bass and he was also a good wedding Jester, a fine rhymester, a crafty prankster, he disguised himself as a beggar at all weddings, twisted his eyes, danced like a bear, mimicked a woman in labor yelling "Oh God, oh God, I swear on a stack of Bibles it'll never happen again!...." Or else he let out a stream of water in the middle of a room so that all the men rolled up their coattails and the women lifted their skirts. Or else he hung some sort of rubbish on the mother-in-law's apron, and he played further tricks and hoaxes galore.

They had been musicians for generations. Beryl the Bassist or Beryl of Stempeni, as we know, played the bass. Beryl's father, Shmulik the Trumpeter, had played the trumpet. His grandfather, Faivish the Cymbalist, had played the cymbals, and his great-grandfather, Ephraim the Violist.... In short, Stempeniu came from a long line of musicians, and he wasn't the least bit ashamed (unlike many Jewish craftsmen, who, just between you and me, are ashamed of what they are). And no wonder: The name he made for himself in Mazepevke, the renown he acquired throughout the world—those were no mean accomplishments. Now *there* was a musician for you!

It was an honor for Jews everywhere to hear Nissi Belzer sing, Godik the Wedding Jester recite, and Stempeniu play. Which goes to show that Stempeniu was no run-of-the-mill fiddler, no garden-variety performer, and there must have been solid reasons for the fame he enjoyed among the great. Jews love music and have an ear for song—which even our enemies cannot deny.... Though you may counter that Jews don't get that many chances to listen to music—what reasons do we have for celebrating? How often can we just start playing or dancing at the drop of a hat? But, say what you like, we are still mayvens, experts on singing, playing, and everything else. Why, if a cantor should come to town, we all go running for tickets, and having musicians at a wedding is a downright obligation for us, we would give a bag of borscht just to hear the band playing as the happy couple begin to sip the golden broth—not a merry ditty, of course, a merry one comes later. The company sits about in great respect, the musicians play a doleful tune, a mournful, plaintive dirge. The fiddle weeps, and the rest of the band accompanies it very sorrowfully. The audience is seized with melancholy, and everyone feels grief, a pleasant grief, but still a grief. Each guest becomes wistful, lowers his head, and, rubbing his finger on his plate or kneading balls from the fresh challah, he drifts off in his own thoughts, his own sad thoughts, for each guest must have his own worries, and trouble is one thing a Jew doesn't go borrowing. And so, the gloomy playing and the dismal thinking fuse into one, and every moan of the violin touches the hearts of the wedding guests and finds an echo there. Any heart, especially a Jewish heart, is a fiddle: You squeeze the strings and you draw forth all kinds of songs, mostly sad and gloomy songs.... All you need is the right musician, a master violinist, the kind of master that Stempeniu was.

Oh, what a master he was! He would grab the violin and apply the bow, just one stroke, nothing more, and the violin had already begun to speak. And how do you think it spoke? Why, with words, with a tongue, like a living human being—if you'll forgive my mentioning them in the same breath. It spoke, pleaded, crooned tearfully, in a Jewish mode, with a force, a scream from the depths of the heart, the soul. Stempeniu would lean his head to one side, the long, black shock of hair flowing across his wide shoulders, his eyes, his black, burning eyes, peering upward, and his lovely radiant face would suddenly turn as pale as death. Another minute—and no more Stempeniu! All you could see was a hand flying up and down, up and down, and you could hear all kinds of sounds, and all sorts of singing came pouring out, dark, melancholy, cutting to the quick, piercing the soul, shattering the mind. The audience was fainting, languishing, perishing in every limb. Hearts filled up, they overflowed, and tears came to all eyes. Jews sighed, Jews moaned, Jews wept. And Stempeniu? Who cared about Stempeniu? Not even Stempeniu knew where he was. He did what he had to do, he fiddled, and that was that! And when he stopped playing, he threw down the violin and put his hand to his heart. And his eyes burnt like Sabbath candles, and his beautiful face shone in ecstasy. The listeners awoke as though from sleep, a sad but sweet sleep, and they gave voice to their enthusiasm, all of them at once. They oohed, they aahed, they mmmmed, they lauded, they were beside themselves, they couldn't stop praising him.

"Ooh, Stempeniu! Ah, Stempeniu!"

And the women? What can I tell you about the women? I doubt very much whether they shed as many tears on the Day of Atonement as they did for Stempeniu's music. You mustn't even weep as much for the Destruction of the Temple as the women wept during Stempeniu's playing.

"If only God will let me have Stempeniu for my youngest daughter's wedding! Oh, Lord, oh Lord!"

And thus the women made their wishes, wiped their red, swollen eyes, blew what was left in their noses, and, while they made their wishes, their strings of pearls and gold earrings, and rings, and brooches, and necklaces, and all the other Jewish baubles twinkled and glittered and sparkled.

And then there were the girls, the young ladies. They were shackled to the earth, like mannequins, gaping at Stempeniu and his violin, not stirring a limb, not batting an eyelash, but somewhere, inside their corsets, hearts were fluttering, and concealed sighs kept escaping....

STEMPENIU AND HIS BAND

The sensation made by Stempeniu and his band when they came to a little town, the turmoil they aroused, simply cannot be described.

"Hey look! There's a four-horse wagon coming round from behind the mills. It must be the in-laws!"

"Nope! It's the musicians. That's Stempeniu and his gang!"

"What? Stempeniu? Stempeniu's here already? Now that'll be a merry wedding for Haym ben-Tsion—damn his eyes!"

Jewish wives blushed. Jewish girls set about combing their hair and weaving their long braids. Boys rolled their pants up to their thighs and ran to welcome Stempeniu. And even grown men, bearded husbands, let out smiles, which meant they were thrilled that Stempeniu had come to play at Haym ben-Tsion's wedding. Fine! Why not? Why should they care? It wasn't costing *them* any money, was it?

By the time the wagon fetched up at the inn, the street was chock-full of people. Everyone was curious to catch a look at Stempeniu and his gang, and so they stood there for a moment.

"Just look at them shoving!" everyone yelled, and shoved to the front, as Jews are wont to do. "Just look at him elbowing his way, he wants to be the first! What's there to look at? Haven't you ever seen musicians before?"

That's what each Jew said, pushing his way up to the wagon, while the musicians emerged one by one.

The first to step down was Yokel the Bassist (who played the contrabass), a nasty man with a squashed nose and with wads of cotton in his ears. Next came Leybush with his clarinet, a drowsy mannikin with thick lips. He was followed by Haykel Hump, *the* Haykel Hump, the hunchbacked wedding jester. Then out jumped a man with a tangle of black hair and with hair all over like a wild man from the desert, and terrifying bushy eyebrows. That was Shneyer-Meyer the back-up fiddler. A couple of boys came leaping after him, ferocious-looking creatures with swollen cheeks, blackened eyes, dreadful buckteeth the size of shovels. These were the apprentices, who were still working for nothing, but later, in time, they might turn into respectable musicians. Last but not least, who should come rolling out on crooked bowlegs, but red-haired Mekhtshi the Drummer, with a drum that was twice his size. His face was beginning to sprout a beard, a reddish growth, but only on one side, the right side, while the other half of his face, the left side, was naked, as barren as a steppe. Mekhtshi the Drummer, you must know, had first married at thirty, and rumor had it that his wife was a hermaphrodite....

The town scamps had probably spread the news that Stempeniu was coming with his band. Every so often, a schoolboy sneaked in and gave the drum a bop or twanged the *G*-string of

104

the contrabass. The boy got a whack in the nape of his neck from Yokel the nasty bassist. And little by little, the street began boiling and bubbling, for the bridegroom had also arrived in town with dozens of young men who had driven out to meet him on the other side of the mills. *And the town of Yampeli did shout and was glad.*

And: like Yampeli, like Stristsh, and all the other little Jewish towns that had the privilege of having Stempeniu at a wedding, and that's how it was in Mazepevke, where Stempeniu made his home. In short, the whole world was in a turmoil over Stempeniu!

STEMPENIU'S PREPARATIONS

What was all the excitement about in Mazepevke? Haym ben-Tsion Glock was marrying off his youngest daughter, his fledgling, Rivke. So why not celebrate and rejoice with him? His wedding was the place to be. After all, he was, so they say, one of the richest men in town. Everybody and his uncle would be there. Some for friendship, some for envy, some for duty, some to show off their wives' pearls, earrings, or the new necklace brought back from the county fair; but more than anything—for Stempeniu. In short, *everyone* attended the festivities! All of Mazepevke rejoiced at Rivke's wedding. Not to mention Isaak-Naphtali and his wife and children, for Isaak-Naphtali was Haym ben-Tsion's partner in the store and in the mill, as well as a distant relation, that is to say, Isaak-Naphtali's wife Dvosse-Malke was sort of distantly related to Rivke's mother, a cousin once removed on her mother's side.

No wonder Dvosse-Malke was veiled and bedizened like a genuine member of the family. She bustled around and didn't do anything, but she waved her arms and shouted and made a racket as though she *were* doing something. And her beautiful daughter-in-law, Rachel, stood next to the bride, bedecked and bejeweled like a princess, her big blue eyes shone like two big diamonds and her red cheeks glowed like two blossoming roses. Her one hand held the bride's loosened hair, which the women, copiously weeping, had unbraided for the veiling ceremony. And her other hand stroked her white throat. And she never noticed two black burning eyes staring at her all the while....

The servants scurried about like chickens without heads. The in-laws were clamoring: "Oh God! Oh God! It's time for the veiling! How long can we torment the children, they've been fasting for a whole summer's day already!" Everyone shouted: "It's time! It's time!" But no one did anything. Isaak-Naphtali wandered about in a velvet cap, his hands behind his back like a preacher, and Dvosse-Malke was raising the roof. The other relatives on both sides were dashing past one another, sticking out their hands as though they wanted to do something but couldn't get anything to do.

"Well, why aren't they doing anything?" asked the groom's family.

"Why aren't they starting to do something?" answered the bride's family.

"Have you ever seen the like before? Making children starve that long!" shouted the groom's family.

"Have you ever heard the like before? Making children starve this long?" shouted the bride's family.

"Why's everyone chasing back and forth?"

"What's all this running around anyway?"

"Everyone's running, everyone's making a racket, and they're not even budging! A fine state of affairs!"

"Just running and raising a racket—and no one's willing to do anything!"

"Hasn't there been enough talk already? It's time for action! There's a limit to everything!"

"C'mon already! Stop all the talking! Let's get going! Isn't there a limit?!"

"Where are the musicians?" asked the groom's family.

"The musicians! Where are they?" answered the bride's family.

And the musicians were busy getting ready. They polished the bows, they tuned the instruments. Yokel the Bassist yanked a boy along by the ear, warning him softly: "You little bastard, I'll teach you to pluck strings!" Mekhtshi the Drummer scratched the bristly half of his face, not deigning to glance at anyone. Haykel the Jester was talking to an acquaintance, a teacher, he took a pinch of snuff from him with two fingers and poured out a cascade of jokes. And the other musicians, the boys with swollen cheeks and buckteeth like shovels, stood around Stempeniu, discussing an important matter with him in their jargon:

"Who's the chick next to the frau-to-be?" asked Stempeniu in musician's lingo, staring at lovely Rachel. "Hey, Rakhmiel!" he said to one of the swollen-cheeked apprentices. "Go and check her out, but snappy, man, snappy!"

Rakhmiel quickly came back with a clear answer: "That's no chick, man, she's already hitched. Dig, she's Isaak-Naphtali's daughter-in-law, and she comes from Skvirre. That's her ol' man over there. The one with the velvet cap!"

"You're too much, baby!" said Stempeniu cheerily. "You checked it out that fast? Man, she is really dynamite! A righteous chick! Dig those eyes!"

"If you like," the swollen-cheeked boy asked Stempeniu, "I'll go and rap with her...."

"Go to hell!" replied Stempeniu. "No one asked you to be my go-between, dig! I'll do my own rappin' with her!"

"Hey man!" cried Shneyer-Meyer in their jargon. "Just throw those big black eyes of yours out from the fiddle. Pull some Jewish guts out of those strings!..."

Stempeniu picked up his fiddle, nodded to the others, and they got their instruments ready.

STEMPENIU'S VIOLIN

Now, the bride, with loosened hair, was seated in the center of the room, and the girls and women formed a circle around her, and with God's help, Stempeniu began to play.

Ah, how hard it is for my pen to describe what Stempeniu did! This was no scraping, no mere playing. It was like a religious service, a divine labor, with a lofty feeling, a noble spirit! Stempeniu stood opposite the bride and played a sermon on his violin, a long, lovely sermon, a poignant sermon about the bride's free and happy life until now, about her maidenhood, and about the dark, bitter life in store for her, later, later. Gone was her girlhood! Her head was covered, her long, beautiful hair was out of sight, forever and ever.... No more joy! Farewell, youth. Now you're a married woman!... How bleak and cheerless— may God forgive me!...

That was what came from Stempeniu's fiddle. All the wives understood the wordless sermon, all the wives felt it. They felt it and wept for it with bitter tears.

"How long did *I* sit like that? a young wife thought, Swallowing her tears. "How long did *I* sit like that, with loose, undone braids, and I thought that angels were playing with me, that I was the happiest girl in the world. And now, ah, now!..."

"Oh, God," prayed an old woman, the mother of grown daughters. "Oh God, bring my poor daughter her intended, very, very soon, and with better luck than I had, and with a better life than I have with my husband—may God forgive me!..."

Such were the thoughts of the wives, and Stempeniu did his job. He played for all he was worth, and the violin spoke. Stempeniu drew forth a doleful melody, and the band backed him up. The people grew still, the noise vanished, the turmoil was gone. Everyone, everyone wanted to hear Stempeniu. The men fell to brooding, the women held their tongues, boys and girls climbed up on benches and tables—everyone wanted to hear Stempeniu. "Quiet, everyone. Hush! Shush!"

And Stempeniu melted and flowed like wax on the fiddle: That was all that could be heard. A hand flew up and down: That was all that could be seen. And they could hear all kinds of sounds, and it struck every heart, it pierced every soul, it cut to the quick. The audience was dying, its strength was waning, its flesh was perishing. The hearts filled and overflowed, and tears came to their eyes. Jews sighed, Jews moaned, Jews wept....

And Stempeniu? Who cared about Stempeniu? No one even saw him, no one could see Stempeniu, no one could see a fiddle. They only heard sweet sounds, divine singing, which filled the entire room.... And beautiful Rachel, who had never heard Stempeniu play before, Rachel, who had known that there was such a person as Stempeniu, but had never heard such playing before, Rachel stood and listened to the magical singing, to the rare sounds—and she couldn't understand what was happening to her. Something pulled at her heart, something caressed her soul, but what it was—she couldn't understand. She raised her eyes towards where the sweet sounds were pouring from, and she saw two wonderful black eyes, burning eyes, looking straight at her and piercing her like spears, like sharp spears. The wonderful black burning eyes stared at her and beckoned to her and spoke with her. Rachel wanted to drop her eyes again—and couldn't.

"So that's Stempeniu?"

Such were Rachel's thoughts when the veiling ceremony was over and the relatives began to think about leading the bride to the canopy.

"Where are the candles?" asked the groom's family.

"The candles? Where are they?" answered the bride's family.

And the same old hubbub resumed. Everyone ran and no one knew where. They jostled, they shoved, they trod on corns, they tore dresses, they sweated, they cursed the waiters and the beadles, who in turn cursed the families, and the in-laws argued with one another—it was, God be praised, a lively affair!

In the stampede away from the canopy, Stempeniu left the band, re-emerged among the women, right there, next to Isaak-Naphtali's daughter-in-law, beautiful Rachel. He murmured a few words, smiling, and tossing his lovely black curls. Rachel blushed, lowered her eyes to the ground, and replied to only every tenth word. It wasn't proper talking to a musician, and in front of all those people to boot!...

STEMPENIU'S FIRST MEETING WITH RACHEL

People tell so many different stories about Stempeniu. They say he hobnobbed with wizards and with all the demons, and if he wanted to take a bride away from a groom, he knew a special sort of incantation, all he had to do was give her a look, the right kind of look—and the girl was done for, Lord preserve us! A lot of mothers knew about it, and they kept a sharp eye on their unmarried daughters. When the girls talked to Stempeniu, there was always an older sister at their side, an aunt, a sister-in-law, or some married woman.... True, that was no compliment for our hero, but so what? What did that have to do with the price of eggs? It was no skin off Stempeniu's—nose, heaven forbid. Everyone knew that Stempeniu was a fine scoundrel. So what of it? No one was about to marry their daughter off to him, by God, and Stempeniu remained Stempeniu.

Blessed are you, Jewish wives, who have husbands, and blessed are the men who've given you such a precious gift—freedom. And pity the poor girls who are chained and shackled, guarded and protected until they're led to the wedding canopy—and only then do the girls become women, unshackled, free, happy wives....

Rachel, being a married woman, had no reason to run away

109

from Stempeniu when he walked towards her with his fiddle under his arm and a smile upon his lips. Why was she afraid? Who should she hide from? Her father-in-law Isaak-Naphtali was absorbed in the wedding: He was strolling about with his hands behind his back, watching over the waiters, to make sure they stepped lively. And her mother-in-law Dvosse-Malke was so preoccupied, that if someone had taken the veil from her head, she wouldn't have noticed. Running by, Dvosse-Malke did stop to see what Stempeniu was doing with her daughter-in-law. But she quickly thought to herself: "Who cares? It's nothing. Their business. Forget it!" And she hurried on to order the waitresses to step lively. Isaak-Naphtali and Dvosse-Malke were excellent commanders. The servants dashed about like lunatics, the in-laws on both sides made a tumult as is customary, the guests had washed their hands and were beginning to stake out places on the long benches flanking the long tables, where fresh rolls had already been put out, a whole string of them. All at once, an uproar: There was no water left in the kneading trough.

"Where are we gonna get water?" asked the groom's family.

"Water? Where are we gonna get it?" answered the bride's family.

"Water!" screamed Dvosse-Malke, slightly hoarse.

"Water! Water!" Isaak-Naphtali seconded her screams, pulled up his coattails, and imagined he was doing something.

This new panic gave Stempeniu a chance to talk a bit more with Rachel, who was grave and somewhat reflective. Her lovely blue eyes gazed far, far into the distance, not at Stempeniu, and her ears heard him talking for a long, long time.

And talking was something Stempeniu could really do. He had the gift of the gab—that rascal! His words spun round and round a person, like the words of a demon, and he stared into the eyes.... The eyes? What am I saying? The heart. Deep, deep into the heart.

Stempeniu talked, and Rachel listened, and the noise of the wedding company was so overwhelming that no one could hear this conversation except for the last few words.

"So that's your Moyshe-Mendel?" Stempeniu asked her, glancing at a young man who was holding the lapel of a Jewish coat and arguing away at that lapel with body and soul, with might and main.

"That's him," replied Rachel, stepping aside as if offended.

Rachel, her feelings bruised, didn't even look towards the corner where the musicians were sitting. Stempeniu hung around her for a long time, but it didn't help. One can actually say that she got tired of him, sick and tired—of that Stempeniu with his arrogant eyes and his ways.... "Ugh! It's shameful, scandalous for a Jewish woman to be anywhere near him...."

Such were Rachel's thoughts as she walked back to the bride, ready to forget that there was such a person as Stempeniu. But... wait! What was that sudden commotion? Stempeniu was playing a sorrowful melody again, and the group was backing him up. Gone was the clamor, gone the uproar! Men fell to brooding, women held their tongues, boys and girls clambered up on the benches and tables—everyone wanted to hear Stempeniu.

Isaak-Naphtali leaned his head to one side, listening with a knowledgeable air. Dvosse-Malke, bound up in a silk cloth and holding a plate in her hand, stood transfixed where she was, and even the waiters with tucked-up coattails and the waitresses with turned-up skirts likewise remained where they were, spellbound, in the middle of the room. And Stempeniu's violin melted into such a plaintive, poignant melody that the entire company held its breath, dying, simply dying ... lifeless people!... Hearts filled, overflowed, tears came to the eyes. Jews sighed, Jews moaned, Jews wept. And Stempeniu?... Who cared about Stempeniu? No one saw him, no one saw any Stempeniu, no one saw any fiddle. They heard the sweet tones, the divine chant that filled the room.... And beautiful Rachel, who had never heard Stempeniu play before, stood and listened to the magical singing, to the rare sounds—and couldn't understand what was happening. Something pulled at her heart, something caressed her, but what it was—she didn't understand. She looked up to where the wondrous melodies were coming from, and her eyes met two wonderful black burning eyes gazing straight at her, piercing her through like two spears.... Rachel lowered her head and saw the wonderful black burning eyes, Rachel looked every which way—and kept seeing those wonderful black burning eyes....

AFTER THE WEDDING SUPPER

The wedding supper had been over for some time now, it was long past the "Hooray" melodies, past the presentation of wedding gifts, past the bride's "chastity dance"—the company was reveling, everyone tipped the band for a dance and did a cheerful jig. Yontel the slaughterer performed a kazatska, and opposite him the mother-in-law herself was letting go with lots of pluck and belly (pardon me!), and the entire crowd was clapping to accompany Yontel, who didn't even notice that he was dancing with a woman, and he squatted up and down like a daredevil, and opposite him, the mother-in-law was hippity-hopping with her arms akimbo, and grinning at Yontel, with a broad grin across her broad face like the moon at midmonth....

Things got even wilder after that. Men were dancing in just their (excuse the expression) breeches. Isaak-Naphtali had already removed his coat, he stood there in his broad, white shirtsleeves. They had nudged and noodled him until he finally agreed to take off his coat, and someone cocked a cap on his head down to his nose—and everyone laughed at him with drunken eyes, and his own son Moyshe-Mendel, Rachel's husband, dragged him by one sleeve into the round.

"Use your legs! Use your legs!" shouted Moyshe-Mendel, jumping up to the ceiling.

The musicians were already playing alone, without Stempeniu. They were totally letting go by now. One of the swollen-cheeked buck-toothed boys was leading. Shneyer-Meyer, the second fiddler, with the black tangle of hair, was dozing. Yokel the Bassist was asleep. Only the younger men were concertizing to beat the band, and most of all poor Mekhtshi the Drummer. He was thrashing away as if his life depended on it. His red hair hung down to the drum, and all you could see was his shoulders heaving and his bow legs stamping. And Stempeniu? Stempeniu was wandering among the young wives, and especially around Rachel.

"Mother-in-law, do let's go home " said Rachel to Dvosse-Malke, who stood there, watching Isaak-Naphtali in his white sleeves and his cap.

"C'mon, dear!" replied Dvosse-Malke. "Tomorrow's market day, we've got to get some rest. Just look at them carrying on!"

And Dvosse-Malke left with Rachel.

The edge of the dark-blue sky began turning lighter, more radiant. Dawn was coming. A rooster crowed. And ten others responded. From far, far away came the barking of a dog. All homes, even the farmhouses, were still shut. Only Hersh-Ber the slaughterer's light was on. Hersh-Ber always got up an hour before dawn to study the Talmud.

"Now, Rachel, wasn't Gnessi's daughter something? Did you get a load of her getup??"

But Rachel didn't answer. She was lost in her own thoughts. Who could tell what and whom she was thinking about?...

"Mother-in-law!" said Rachel all at once. "That was the first time I ever heard Stempeniu play."

"C'mon, child! The first time indeed!" replied her mother-in-law. "What about that evening at Leybtsi's place? And at Nekhemiah's home? And at Sarah's home? And at the rebbe's?"

"I don't recall," answered Rachel. "I only heard about him a lot, but I never saw him."

"Well, obviously.... At that time, you were just.... Well, what were you? A baby chick when Stempeniu played at the rebbe's daughter's wedding in Skvirre. Oh, was that a wedding! May the Good Lord bring such weddings to all my loved ones. What a wedding! Just imagine, I was expecting at the time, I was carrying Yossel, and I was, let me see, I was in my sixth—no, no, my *eighth* month.... Why, where ever are you going, Rachel? We're home, and you're wandering off to Gnessi's place! Goodness gracious me! Hahaha!"

"Oh dear," replied Rachel, peering all around. "A fine thing!! Really! Hahaha!"

And the two laughing women entered their home to lie down for a few hours, for tomorrow Mazepevke was having a huge market day, practically a county fair.

RACHEL CAN'T FALL ASLEEP

How awful! Rachel couldn't sleep! She tossed and turned, she covered herself and uncovered herself—but sleep wouldn't come! No matter how hard she tried not to think about him, about Stempeniu, I mean—he kept popping up in front of her, the devil only knows how and when! She squeezed her eyes shut as tight as she could—and saw his wonderful black burning eyes, which stared straight at her, beckoned to her, called to her.... "Oh, get rid of him!" she thought. "If only Moyshe-Mendel were here!" She opened her eyes and saw Stempeniu with his fiddle, and she thought she could still hear the rare and beautiful playing.... "Oh, what music, oh...! No wonder people tell such fantastic stories about him!" And Rachel remembered all the lovely tales she had heard about him in Skvirre, during her schooldays, when she was learning how to write from Mottl Shpraiz, the girl's scribe. Back then, her girl friends had told her stories about how Stempeniu had once taken a bride away from a groom, and the bride died of shame, and they set up a black wedding canopy by her grave. And once Stempeniu had gotten back at a girl for calling him a lecher.... And once Stempeniu had played at an aristocratic wedding, in a count's home. And the count's daughter, a great beauty, had fallen for him and had said: Come what may, even death itself, she just had to have Stempeniu.... And when the count heard this, he tried to talk Stempeniu into it, at first with threats, then cajolingly, and at last he promised him three whole villages if he would convert and take the daughter for his wife. But Stempeniu replied in French (he knew German and French) that even if the count offered him a torrent of ducats, he wouldn't take a single drop of baptismal water for love or money. (And that was why he was so greatly respected by all pious Jews, even the Rebbe.) And when the count's daughter heard what he said, she threw herself fully dressed into the river.... And there were so many wondrous tales that made your flesh crawl....

Rachel also recollected what her girl friends had told her about Stempeniu's having a bottle of "love potion." "Love, dove, heavens above!" thought Rachel, remembering all those pretty stories. "You can keep your love! My Moyshe-Mendel loves me without any potion. And do I love him? Do I love Moyshe-Mendel?"

And Rachel turned over, with her face to the wall, and thought hard about all these things. This was the first time she had ever had such a thought: "Oh, it's all a bunch of nonsense. What's this love-dove business anyway? I certainly don't hate him!"

And honestly, why should she hate him? Moyshe-Mendel wasn't bad-looking, thank goodness. A wee bit modern, he tucked his earlocks up out of sight, he read newspapers, he liked to drink a glass of wine, crack a joke, have some fun with young people—but he was a fine young man. True, he was a bit of a stranger to his wife, he hardly ever exchanged two words with her, he would mumble something and then zip off to synagogue or to the market. And he never sat down, to speak, to talk to his wife, just like that, for fun, the way people do. Not on your life, he was like a wild doe.

Before her marriage, Rachel would never have expected that, poor thing! When she got engaged, it seemed as if everyone envied her for her husband—what a wonderful man (he was so handsome)! There was no one like him in all the world! How happy she would be!... And now? Now she saw that all her girl friends were leading fine lives. One, who had moved to a large city with her husband, wrote her the most incredible letters. And another was already mistress of her own home. And even Hannah-Mirel, who had moved heaven and earth to get a husband and finally married a widower with five children—well, she was happy now too. And Rachel?... Ahh, she had nothing to boast about. Locked up all week like a bird in a cage. Eating, drinking, sleeping! Her father-in-law and mother-in-law wouldn't let her breathe: Rachel, Rachel, day and night. And Moyshe-Mendel with his ways, his spare words, as though she were some sort of—goodness knows what! Shush! Someone was knocking at the door. That might be Moyshe-Mendel. Her mother-in-law went to open.

"Moyshe-Mendel!"

"What's up?"

"Is that you, Moyshe-Mendel?" his mother asked.

"Oh, what dancing, goddamn it! Brrrr!" her son replied.

"What are you chattering about?" his mother went on. "Get undressed and go to bed!"

"Goddamn it! What drinking, that Beryl-Menashe, hahaha!"

"For goodness' sake, Moyshe-Mendel! What are you blabbering about?" Dvosse-Malke said to him, striking a match.

"Can't you see he's as drunk as a lord, mother-in-law?" said Rachel. "Light a candle over there, please, he'll break every bone in his body!"

"Hey, goddamn it, give me another glass!"

Jibbering to himself, Moyshe-Mendel collapsed on his bed and quickly fell asleep with a dreadful snore. Dvosse-Malke also went to sleep. Her little children had been sleeping for some time now. Every corner of the house was filled with hissing and whistling. Everyone slept soundly, only Rachel couldn't doze off. No matter how hard she strained, sleep just wouldn't come!... The moon shone in through a window, and a long white beam fell on the bed, where Moyshe-Mendel was sprawled with his face up, his mouth open, his eyes gaping, his neck twisted, and his adam's apple, a sharp knob, jutting out of his throat—he was hideous to look at.

115

Rachel didn't want to look—but look she did. Moyshe-Mendel had never seemed so ugly to her as now, on this night. And, willy-nilly, she compared him with someone else, with that rascal Stempeniu.... Was this the same Moyshe-Mendel as once? The bridegroom with his lovely white face, his sweet smile, with his merry eyes, his straight posture, with his gait, with his graceful manners, his sparkling jokes? Was this the same Moyshe-Mendel?...

And Rachel, willy-nilly, compared him once again with someone else, with Stempeniu....

Go away, go away, you dark thoughts, stop tormenting a Jewish woman!

THE VEILING LUNCH

The next morning, Hiene, the beadle's wife, came to tell Dvosse-Malke that the mother-in-law, the bridegroom, the bride, and all the in-laws were inviting them to the veiling lunch, the ceremonial meal at which the bride dons the *sheytel*, the marriage wig. Rachel had already put on her sheytel and she was all dressed up in the latest fashion (by Dovid Mekhanik, the ladies' tailor): a sky-blue frock with white lace trimming and very broad sleeves, which were being worn in Mazepevke, always a few years behind in the fashions. On her head, a blue silk openwork kerchief, revealing the entire wig and the braids.... But false braids. Rachel had put away her own blond hair long, long ago, concealed it forever, for all time! A few strings of pearls around her neck, on her white, lovely throat, a large golden necklace, a brooch, bracelets, rings, eardrops—all the Jewish jewelry, all the Jewish wealth.

Rachel, all decked out, in her room, where Moyshe-Mendel was still lying in the same position as last night, with his jutting adam's apple and his gaping mouth, and snoring endlessly.

"Oh, what a difference there is between the two Moyshe-Mendels, I mean, between Moyshe-Mendel, the man I was engaged to, and Moyshe-Mendel, the man I'm married to. *That* Moyshe-Mendel was so charming, his eyes glowed like candles, his voice was as sweet as honey, his gestures were all so pleasant, so

116

dear! And this Moyshe-Mendel? He's so long and skinny and round-shouldered and he's got a red beard sprouting. Where did he get that goat's beard?"

And, willy-nilly, she kept picturing that scoundrel who hadn't let her sleep all night long—what an awful thing! "It's my own fault," thought Rachel, "it's all my own fault. Imagine running into a calamity like Stempeniu! What sort of woman stops and talks to a musician? It's disgraceful. And what would people say if they saw me talking to him? It's lucky there was such a commotion. And what would Moyshe-Mendel have said?..."

And with a smile, Rachel walked over to Moyshe-Mendel's bed and leaned over him and spoke his name. Moyshe-Mendel opened his gray eyes and stared for a long time and couldn't fathom what he saw before him.

"Moyshe-Mendel!" said Rachel, bending over him fully. "Moyshe-Mendel! Don't you recognize me?! Goodness, the way you're looking at me! Don't you care for me like this?"

"Lemme alone, I wanna sleep!" And with these words, Moyshe-Mendel turned to the wall and burst into a ferocious snore.

"The mother-in-law and the happy couple and all the kith and kin would like you to come to the veiling meal!"

It was Hiene, the beadle's wife, calling out as she stuck her head in the door. But when she saw Rachel standing over her husband's head, she swiftly withdrew.

Rachel met the bride before she even donned her wig. The two friends hugged and kissed, and instantly launched into an ardent conversation, the way two young wives always do.

The company was gathering little by little, and the waiters and waitresses were covering the tables with all sorts of goodies: with cakes and preserves, with gingerbread, and almond bagels, and every kind of strudel. Yesterday's beadles and yesterday's paupers were already here. The father-in-law, Haym ben-Tsion, had washed his hair and donned a velvet cap, and the mother-in-law had already shouted herself hoarse, but she still kept managing and ordering, sending one person here, another there, and screaming with her last ounce of strength:

"You're driving me to my grave, God help me! You put a platter of cake and preserves where you ought to put a bottle of vodka and glasses! Oh, *veyz mir!* Oh, my heart, my heart! What's the use of all my sacrifices! What's the use of having a wedding! You spend a fortune, and in the end—what's the use! Not even the musicians are here! There's no way out but suicide!"

"Quiet! Silence!" yelled Haym ben-Tsion, the father-in-law. "Why are you making such a racket? You're not helping matters any! She does nothing and she shrieks! What are you shrieking for anyway? Haven't you ever married off a child before? Is this the first time? Just look at her, she's rattling! The whole town's invited, and all the relatives, and she just runs around and screeches! What's wrong with you anyway!"

"Who's screeching, you lunatic! Who's screeching?"

"I should know who's screeching? Why don't you tell me?!"

"I'm not screeching! *You*'re screeching."

"I'm screeching? Bullshit! It's the other way around!"

"You're screeching now, Haym ben-Tsion! What's come over you?"

"A grand good morning to the happy father-in-law and the mother-in-law, to the groom and the bride to all the kith and all the kin on both sides, and to all the dear friends. Now play a *vivat* for all you're worth!"

With this vociferous proclamation from Haykel the Jester, the musicians took up their instruments, and the wedding became a wedding again! The guests wiped their hands on their coattails, pushed up their sleeves, and after washing, they sat down at the table for the veiling lunch. And now Stempeniu took his violin and repeated all of yesterday's tricks with a few extras thrown in, plus two or three new pieces, while the audience gaped awestruck, in sheer ecstasy. All eyes were glued on him, on Stempeniu, only Rachel wouldn't look toward that corner—but still she saw him, but still she felt him watching her.... It was only when Stempeniu put down his violin and the company was in an uproar—it was only then that Rachel raised her blue eyes and saw...Stempeniu.

"What do you think of him?" the bride asked her after not saying a word the whole time.

"Who?" said Rachel innocently.

"Stempeniu! Isn't he a miracle-worker?"

Rachel didn't answer. She felt the blood rushing to her face. The bride noticed and asked:

"Are you hot, Rachel? Tell me, are you hot?"

"Yes, hot. Awfully hot. I'm going to step out for a minute to cool off," Rachel answered.

She left the table and at every step she encountered a servant, who gave her the right of way with great respect—not for her, but for her silken attire. Still, she couldn't get to the door that quickly. First of all, she would have to walk past the musicians, who were feasting their eyes on her, telling one another in their jargon: "Dig the groovy chick! Yummy-scrumptious!..."

And when her eyes met Stempeniu's, her heart began pounding, such as she had never felt it pound before. She blushed more furiously and she felt a dreadful heat in her face, like a person next to a burning house. On top of all her troubles, whom should she run into but the father-in-law, Haym ben-Tsion, almost by the door, and now a new turmoil started. Haym ben-Tsion was a pious man and he was terrified of women. The encounter was sudden. Haym ben-Tsion ought really to have backed away as is customary. But, the devil take it, he stepped to the right, and since Rachel was moving to the right, they nearly collided, missing each other by a gnat's eyelash. Haym ben-Tsion had an idea: He jumped to the left. Unfortunately, Rachel had the same idea and also swerved to the left. Haym Ben-Tsion realized he had to step to the right quickly, but by the time he shifted, Rachel was standing face to face with him, almost as if to spite him—and God knows how long they would have kept dancing like that, if, to their good fortune, the hoarse mother-in-law hadn't come lumbering over to argue with her husband in their normal way. Rachel used the opportunity to slip outside and cool off from the dreadful heat.

RACHEL'S BIOGRAPHY AND
HAIA-ETEL'S ROMANCE

But the outdoors was even hotter. It was a day in July. The sun stood at its zenith, roasting and broiling mercilessly. On the wooden or thatched roofs of Mazepevke, it poured out thousands of rays, that trembled and hovered, like the waves of a river. Schoolboys say: "The *Shekhinah* (Divine Presence) is resting."

Rachel stood facing the market. It was vast and deserted. The shops with red curtains were open, and the women sat on rectangular stools, knitting stockings at a fearful speed. Troughs of berries, cookies, shortbread stood by their sides, and a goat kept sneaking up with a hankering to cause trouble, only the women wouldn't let her. Far, far away, a pair of oxen were trudging along, dragging a huge wagon filled with sheaves of grain and sending up an enormous swirl of powder. Behind it walked a little peasant boy, barefoot, with a big, warm hat, a bag, and a long whip; and a dog was running after him, with a lolling tongue.

Rachel stood there, gazing at the humdrum scene, and compared it with her sky-blue silk dress, with the pearls, bracelets, eardrops, rings—and she felt alien to the surroundings, to the whole of nature, she felt betwixt and between, neither a market vendor nor a countess—simply a Jewish woman, a daughter of Israel, that was all, she had a husband, she lived with her in-laws, never doing a lick of work, and her husband was either in synagogue or at the market, walking about with his cane and cracking jokes.

Now, standing there, close to nature, Rachel, for the first time ever, began thinking about her life, about who she was, and a new thought passed through her mind, she was lacking something—she didn't know what, but something was lacking, something was missing....

Rachel was a simple Jewish woman, devoid of tricks or dodges. In a word, what we call a "daughter of Israel." Growing up among a lot of children, she was nothing special to her parents in Skvirre: "A daughter, so what? Let her grow up as best she can...." And so that she wouldn't wander about in front of them, and so that they might have one less child underfoot, they whisked her off to Hebrew school with her brothers. Then, when she got a bit older, they sent her to Mottl Shpraiz, the tutor for girls, and he taught her how to write. There, Rachel had her girl friends, of course, younger and older, but she liked hanging around the older girls, she liked hearing them tell stories, lovely, wondrous tales. And the girls, in turn, liked Rachel for her singing, her lovely singing.

"Sing for us, Rachel, darling! C'mon, sing! There are no boys around!"

Rachel was ashamed of singing in front of boys and adults, and her friends even told her it wasn't right to sing for big boys, a girl mustn't do that....

"C'mon, Rachel. Sing! Just look at her! She has to be coaxed!"

And Rachel obeyed the big girls and crooned a song, a Yiddish ditty, in her soft, delicate voice.

> *On the mountain stood a dove,*
> *And she so sadly did hum:*
> *Where oh where is my sweet love?*
> *To me he cannot come....*

Rachel sang the song with great feeling, as though she understood the word "love." The others, however—I mean the older girls—did seem to understand, for they would sigh and grieve and, occasionally, shed a tear....

They loved hearing Rachel sing these songs, and the one who enjoyed it most was Haia-Etel, a very beautiful girl, an orphan. She was not unusual. Her life story was that of many Jewish girls, and it can be reeled off as quickly as a blessing. Here it is:

Once, and not so long ago, there were two brothers in the town of Skvirre, one was named Aaron and the other Leyb. Aaron died while still young, and his wife died soon after, leaving their daughter Haia-Etel. Her uncle Leyb felt sorry for her and took her into his home along with her inheritance. But Uncle Leyb didn't act very decently towards the orphan, he kept the inheritance (some three thousand rubles supposedly) for himself and gave her the air (if you'll pardon the expression)—he married her off to a bigot, a philistine, the worst kind of scoundrel, who tormented the life out of her. And, while still young, only twenty-two, Haia-Etel passed away.

Now our Rachel was as close as could be to Haia-Etel, and they loved each other very much. One Sabbath afternoon, the two of them had been sitting together at a window, coiffured and wearing their Sabbath best, as is proper. Rachel, as usual, was singing her songs, and Haia-Etel was listening. The song went:

> *Ah, you're going away,*
> *Ah, you're going away,*
> *And you're leaving me behind!...*

"Rachel, my dear, Rachel my sweet!" said Haia-Etel. "Sing it again!"

"Again?" Rachel asked in surprise. "Well, I can start all over again, if you like."

Ah, you're going away,
Ah, you're going away,
And you're leaving mee bee-hiiind!...

All at once, Rachel saw the orphan cover her face with her hands, her shoulders were heaving. Rachel stopped singing when she heard her sob.

"Goodness gracious, Haia-Etel! You're crying!? Why in the world are you crying? What's wrong, tell me, Haia-Etel? Why are you crying so suddenly?"

"Oh, Rachel dear!" she answered with a sob. "Oh, Rachel dear. That song, that song of yours!"

"My song? What's the matter with it? Why is it making you cry like that?"

"Oh, Rachel, don't ask, don't ask a bitter heart! There's a fire burning in me! An infernal blaze, right here, can't you see!"

And Haia-Etel pointed at her own heart, and Rachel looked at her, amazed and confused.

"Why are you looking at me like that, Rachel? You don't understand, you can't feel what's in me. My heart is so heavy, I'm so miserable, so devastated, I have such awful troubles—I really have to tell you everything... everything!"

And Haia-Etel told Rachel a story, a sad story, an ordinary story, that occurs so frequently among Jews, but still a very sad story—about how her Uncle Leyb had treated her so hideously, and most of all, that wicked woman, her aunt, and if it weren't for their young son, Benjamin, she would have run away long ago or else thrown herself into the river. Benjamin was her only consolation in the world, they had grown up together, he was like a brother to her, a blood brother—but now he had gone away, leaving her with all her cares and woes, as though he were a stranger, a total stranger.

"I don't understand, Haia-Etel. Why would anyone be so grief-stricken if their very own brother had gone away, and he isn't even a real brother!"

"Oh, Rachel. You don't know how close I felt to him, how much a part of me he was, really, just like my own brother, even more than my own brother, I tell you! Whenever I saw Benjamin, there was a light in front of my eyes, and when he went away...."

"Benjamin *had* to go away, Haia-Etel. He got married!"

122

"Oh, Rachel darling, don't say that, I can't hear it. The word 'married' tears my heart out! When I hear someone say 'Benjamin got married,' then I don't feel like living anymore. You just don't know, Rachel. And I hope you never ever know anything like this.... Why are you looking at me like that? Benjamin promised, he swore he would marry me."

"But then why *didn't* he marry you, Haia-Etel?"

"You're like a child, Rachel. How can you ask? He probably wasn't destined for me. He was probably meant for *her!*"

"But he swore he'd marry *you.*"

"So what! He was getting ready to tell his father, he kept putting it off day after day. He was afraid of him—you know what Uncle Leyb is like—until they arranged the engagement with her. And when I tried to talk to him about it, he told me the wedding was still a long way off, he'd be able to talk to his father—and so the months went by and the years, until the day came, that awful day, the most wretched day in my life.... I was at the wedding myself, I saw everything with my own eyes, everything, I watched him put the ring on her finger, I heard him say the things a bridegroom has to say.... The cantor and choristers were singing, and Benjamin looked at the ground to avoid my eyes—but I know he saw me.... Oh, Rachel! How can I go on living? How can I endure it?"

"If that's the way he is, Haia-Etel, then he's a big liar and absolutely worthless."

"No, don't say that, Rachel. You don't know Benjamin. You don't know how wonderful he is, you don't know what a good heart he has!... It's all Uncle Leyb's fault—that monster! My father's blood upon his head, oh God, oh God!"

"Goodness, he's really gotten to you, Haia-Etel!"

"Gotten to me?! I'm dying, I'm at the end of my rope—and you say he's *gotten* to me!"

"Well, and what about *her,* Haia-Etel? Is she pretty?"

"Who?"

"Benjamin's wife."

Haia-Etel turned crimson at these words, and then pallid, and then all sorts of colors. Rachel couldn't understand why her friend didn't answer. But she did sense that she mustn't repeat the question. "She's probably uncomfortable, so she's not saying anything, she's upset, she doesn't want to talk about it...."

Some time later, Rachel saw her friend at a wedding, at Haia-

Etel's own wedding. She was a bride like all brides, she sat the way a bride ought to sit, kept silent, walked to the canopy, put her wig on the next day, had a wan face, a brooding look, she didn't seem cheerful.... But so what, it didn't matter: That's the way a bride has to be. What is she supposed to do? Dance a jig?...

Who could tell what was on her mind, in her heart? A Jewish woman's heart is a secret, a big secret. A box, a closed box, and it's not proper for any man to peek inside, it's not really very respectful....

AND ONCE AGAIN RACHEL

At Haia-Etel's wedding, Rachel wondered just what was going on in the bride's heart. Rachel didn't talk about this to anyone. But she was intelligent enough to realize—and her heart even sensed—that her friend was far from feeling her best as she sat there with her destined groom, a total stranger, while her own Benjamin was off somewhere with his wife. Rachel very much wanted to ask Haia-Etel if she had heard from Benjamin—how was he, had he written? But upon going to her and gazing into her wan face and hearing her sigh over and over again, Rachel didn't have the heart to bring him up.

We can imagine that this was the first time in her life that Rachel thought about such things. Perhaps one real fact in life can arouse a lot more thoughts and a lot more feelings than ten good books. Of course, Rachel was a simple Jewish girl, quite artless, but she wasn't stupid. Why shouldn't her native intelligence manage to grasp something? She certainly knew nothing of heroes, of novels, romances, but she did have a pure heart, a pure Jewish heart. So why shouldn't she be able to feel another person's sorrows, another person's sufferings? Haia-Etel and her Jewish romance caused Rachel to suddenly grow a few years older.

At the time, Rachel was also engaged to be married, and she heard so much praise about her fiancé Moyshe-Mendel and all his virtues that she considered herself the luckiest girl in the world.

"My oh my, aren't you lucky!" she heard on all sides.

"A treasure! A windfall! Isaak-Naphtali is a rich man, the finest man in Mazepevke, and he has a son, his only child, and what a boy! A jewel, I tell you!"

124

And Moyshe-Mendel really was a fine boy and could appeal to anyone. He was good, lively, he had a talmudic mind, he knew the Bible inside out. Furthermore, his penmanship was excellent, he had mastered several scripts, so that the whole town marveled at his writing, and even Mottl Shpraiz, the "girls' scribe" in Skvirre, saddled his red nose with a pair of spectacles, perused the bridegroom's handwriting with the eyes of a mayven, and admitted that the boy had a golden hand, and if he kept practicing until he got perfect, he would, God willing, be able to write.

Rachel seldom talked with her fiancé, for where was he and where was she? It's quite a way from Mazepevke to Skvirre, and all in all they met only once, and for only a couple of hours to boot, and in a whole bunch of people to boot, and with the groom-to-be in one room and the bride-to-be in another room—to boot. Still, they did exchange letters almost every week for a whole year, until the wedding. Admittedly, Mottl Shpraiz (why should we deny it?) played a large part in the correspondence. For since the boy's letters were in three languages—Hebrew, Russian, and German—Mottl Shpraiz had to make sure the bride was not put to shame. And in order to demonstrate quite plainly that any graduate of Mottl's school had something on the ball (which couldn't be said about other scribes), Mottl saw to it that the bride's letters contained a fourth language, French, or rather French characters, in which Mottl was utterly proficient. Altogether, one may say that the groom and the bride played their writing game throughout a year, and they stopped only when the real preparations began for the wedding.

The wedding went off like all Jewish weddings. The bride's side didn't act quite properly, they weren't quite genteel, rather Jewish.... And the groom's side pouted and chaffed a bit and called the father-in-law a pig behind his back, which he fully deserved. But so what, it didn't matter: They had a drink, as people do; they made up again; the bride took leave of all her near and dear; they accompanied her till just beyond the town; they hugged, they kissed; they wept; they were sending away a daughter—and she was being taken away, to live with her in-laws.

AND ONCE AGAIN RACHEL

There, with her in-laws, a new world began for Rachel. Everyone liked her instantly, the daughter-in-law, and the only daughter-in-law, and a lovely, intelligent daughter-in-law. And they doted on her, indulged her, they wouldn't allow a speck of dust on her chair. And the most doting of all was Dvosse-Malke, who was delirious at her good fortune and ready to lay down her life for Rachel. It was always "Rachel dear!" and "Rachel dear!" whenever there was a fat piece of meat, a juicy bone, a tasty morsel—always "Rachel dear!" No sooner would Rachel open her eyes in the morning than—aha!—the pitcher of chicory stood on the table. And Dvosse-Malke, who was actually a very busy person, a market woman—Dvosse-Malke would scurry about, making sure her daughter-in-law got everything the moment she needed it.

"Oh, please don't go to all this trouble, mother-in-law."

"No trouble at all. Drink, Rachel dear! Eat, Rachel dear!"

Another time, the mother-in-law came dashing home from the market up in arms, she burst into the kitchen, yelling at the hired help, cursing and scolding violently as though someone were murdering her.

"What's wrong, mother-in-law?" asked Rachel.

"I thought you were awake ages ago—and the milk is still standing there, boiling and boiling! Dammit, may the maid boil and steam! And I have to run around like a chicken without a head! The store's mobbed, God preserve us! And he, my dear husband, just stands there with his hands behind his back like some in-law at a wedding! I begged him to take home these two fresh bagels! In case you're hungry—eat them, Rachel darling, they're good bagels, I always get my bagels from Leytsikhe, I refuse to get them anywhere else, not for a king's ransom—May God help her, the poor thing, what a horrible time that drunkard of a husband gives her! How can such a monster exist on God's earth?!—I just don't understand it.... He's just an embarrassment to the father, may he rest in peace.... Yes, now what was I saying? Oh, I'm in such a dither! Wait, here she comes, our great beauty—the maid! Where've you been all day?!"

And out came a new series of screams and curses about Rachel's milk, about Rachel's chicory, about Rachel's breakfast—in other words, the whole house whirled around Rachel. Even the father-in-law, who was always preoccupied with himself and his business dealings, constantly looked in on her, asked after her.

All this wooing and worship were actually very unpleasant for Rachel and made her uncomfortable. And to tell the truth, Rachel wasn't as fond of them as they were fond of her.

When we say "they," we mean her father-in-law and mother-inlaw, of course. We're not including Moyshe-Mendel, the chief personage, for the relationship between the young people couldn't actually be called good or bad. They never talked very much with one another, and they really couldn't talk: A young man like Moyshe-Mendel can't just sit down at home, right smack in the middle of the day, and talk to his wife. And in the evening, if they did happen to be alone in a room, it never lasted for more than a minute. Either Isaak-Naphtali dropped in to see how they were, or else Dvosse-Malke brought in a pitcher, or a cup, or a glass, or a bowl.

"Just try it, Rachel dear, for curiosity's sake, and have a taste of these preserves."

"Goodness, mother-in-law. I've tasted these preserves a hundred times already!"

"C'mon, child, what are you talking about! You've never even laid eyes on these preserves!"

And Rachel had yet another taste of the preserves, which were already coming out of her ears.

"Gracious me, Rachel darling, you're just wasting away. How can you eat so little! I just don't see what keeps you alive! Goodness gracious me! If anyone from Skvirre sees you, they'll curse the dickens out of me! 'A fine mother-in-law! May she rot!' That's what they'll say! 'A fine way to feed a daughter-in-law! Hanging's too good for such a mother-in-law!' Please, just eat something for my sake!"

"Please don't, mother-in-law. I've had enough, really, I've had quite enough."

"Please, just as a favor to me, daughter. You can do a favor for your mother-in-law once in a while. Pretend I'm your mother! Just take a teensy bit, and don't be so mean to me!"

And Rachel choked down a teensy bit more, and she had more than enough, she was fed up with this life of hers, even though she knew they were loyal to her, completely devoted, and if she had wanted the blue of the sky, they would get it for her. Could there be any excuse? If Rachel had a wish, it had to come true!

However, a human being's not an ox, not a goose, content just to be well-fed. A human being can't get much pleasure from having people run after him all the time, everywhere, worshiping the very ground he treads on, always at his heels, eyeing his every last morsel, every last sip, standing over him when he sits down, sitting over him when he sleeps—in a word, clutching his entire life in their hands and not leaving anything up to him....

That was Rachel's dismal situation at the time this story takes place. Rachel didn't even have someone she could complain to. Her parents thought she was happy, and their letters to her were always full of pride, joy, and blessings to God for all He had done for them. And her letters to them were also filled with "blessings and success," with "joy and pleasure," with "Blessed Be His Name," and with "knock on wood," and they always ended with "happiness and joy," and "joyous hearts, *amen selah!*"

Deep in her heart, she bore a grudge against Moyshe-Mendel because he kept far away from her and acted kind of superior to her, not like her equal, as is the custom of a young Jewish man, a gem! He can't go down to his wife's level, it doesn't seem right to him, it's unpleasant.... But in his heart of hearts, Moyshe-Mendel didn't dislike her, on the contrary, he was devoted to her, very devoted, quite naively so, in fact. Once, Rachel was quite ill and spent a few days in bed. Moyshe-Mendel never left her side, he moaned, he worried, he exhausted his strength.

"The poor thing!" he said to his mother, and there were tears in his eyes. "We've got to call the doctor or the healer. I can't stand this, she's burning up! The poor thing!"

By the third day, Rachel got better. Moyshe-Mendel never left her side, and, sitting there, by her pillow, he now had a chance to talk a bit with his dear, lovely Rachel. To tell the truth, both of them wanted to talk. Moyshe-Mendel sat very close to her, so close that her lovely face, wrapped in a white cloth, was almost in his hands.... Rachel raised her blue eyes to Moyshe-Mendel and waited for him to say something. Moyshe-Mendel looked down. But when she turned her head towards the window, he looked at her, and when she looked at him, he turned his head towards the window. And so they kept glancing at each other for a long while without speaking. This was the first time after a whole year of marriage that the couple had a chance to talk in private, but they couldn't quite arrange it, they didn't know how to start. Rachel, being the woman, had the right to wait until he spoke, and

Moyshe-Mendel, being a fine young man, waited until *she* spoke—
and meanwhile, both kept silent, exchanging glances.

"What is it, Moyshe-Mendel?"

"What do you mean what is it?"

"Why are you staring?"

"Who's staring?"

"You're staring."

"I'm staring?"

"Well, who *is* staring?"

Rachel turned to the wall, and Moyshe-Mendel began chewing
on his beard, gazing at Rachel for a long, long time, and sighing,
until she turned her head and caught him gazing and sighing.

"What is it, Moyshe-Mendel?"

"What do you mean what is it?"

"Why are you sighing?"

"Who's sighing?"

"You're sighing."

"I'm sighing?"

"Well, who *is* sighing?"

And again they fell silent. Moyshe-Mendel moved even closer,
cleared his throat, and tried to begin:

"Listen, Rachel, about what you said—"

The door burst open and in ran Dvosse-Malke with a clamor:

"For goodness' sake! Didn't I *know* the turkeys would smash
my china?! He got a yen for turkeys—just like that! All at once! ...
How're you feeling, Rachel? You know what? I think you've got a
fever. I can tell. Didn't I warn you not to stand outdoors without a
scarf! Don't ever stand outdoors without a scarf! I sent for Kussiel
the healer again. Isaak-Naphtali went himself."

"Why bother, mother-in-law? It'll pass, I'm getting over it. I'm
going through a transition now."

"With you, everything's a transition. A fine transition! Come,
come, child, just listen to yourself! I'll have to sit down here for a
while...."

And Dvosse-Malke pushed a chair over to the bed and sat
down.

"You know what, Momma?" Moyshe-Mendel suddenly
exclaimed. "Why don't you go to the store? I'll sit with her."

And his eyes met Rachel's eyes, and he could read in them:
"Oh, Moyshe-Mendel, you've hit the nail on the head!"

"Are you kidding?!" replied Dvosse-Malke and moved closer to

129

the bed. "Go to the store?! What's the big loss? Those huge amounts I take in?! My worst enemies can have them! With all my heart! Listen, Moyshe-Mendel, why don't you go to my bedroom and take a nap on your Papa's bed! You haven't slept all night, you know!"

And that was how they lived, the happy but shackled couple, they had room and board, but never a moment to themselves, they were always under the wings of the good parents, the devoted parents-in-law. And neither the husband nor the wife grumbled, neither complained to the other. Moyshe-Mendel just kept on: He would look into a holy book, do a bit in his father's business, he had his buddies with whom he sometimes had a good time in the synagogue or the market. In a word, Moyshe-Mendel just kept living.

But Rachel didn't live at all. She ate and drank, she tasted her mother-in-law's preserves twenty times a day, never did a lick of work, never got together with other people, since Isaak-Napthali's daughter-in-law can't associate with "just anyone," and "just anyone" is not going to associate with Isaak-Napthali's daughter-in-law, for "just anyone" considers himself much finer, wealthier, and more genteel than Isaak-Naphtali, and Isaak-Naphtali considers himself wealthier and more genteel than all the householders in Mazepevke—and so time stretched on for Rachel, as in a prison: eating again, sleeping again, a cup of coffee again, a dear mother-in-law with preserves again, and so on and so on, a whole long year.

RACHEL SINGS SONGS

That was our Rachel's situation when we saw her at the wedding of Haym ben-Tsion's daughter, at the veiling lunch, standing outside by the door, gazing at the Mazepevke marketplace with its stores, market women, the wagon with the lumbering oxen and the peasant boy with the broad hat.

That was our lovely Rachel's situation at the time she first heard that entrancing music of Stempeniu's.

Rachel loved listening to music—oh, how she loved it! It had always given her so much pleasure! Whenever she heard someone singing or playing a new song, she instantly took it over and sang it in her lovely, mellow voice. her parents would beam with joy and say: "She's got a man's head. What bad luck that she was born a woman, otherwise—she would have set the world on fire...."

Her parents apparently did understand that there was some kind of ability in their daughter, something that nowadays we call "talent." But in those days, Rachel's parents assumed that her ability to take over and sing a tune was in her head because she had a man's head. Among us Jews, the head plays the most important role, more than all the two hundred forty-eight parts put together. A head, a fine little head! That's the crowning glory for us! But, be that as it may, Rachel sang like a free bird until fifteen or sixteen. Wherever she heard a cantorial piece, or a Hassidic chant, or a musician's melody, anything whatsoever, Rachel would sing it again in her own pure voice, which was a delight to hear.... But the moment she became engaged, her mother told her:

"Enough, daughter, no more twittering! You'll be living with your in-laws, and just imagine what kind of impression you'll make if you suddenly start chirping away! It's not respectable!"

Rachel, of course, understood that it wasn't proper, so she obeyed, and stopped singing.... But she didn't really stop altogether, for sometimes a crooning would burst from her of its own accord, out of habit, apparently, and how could she help it if the singing went on by itself?... When you see where the water's coming from, you can block it, but if you don't see, if you don't know—then what can you do?... However, not only when she was engaged, but even after the wedding, she would sometimes forget herself, forget what she was, and she would burst out singing as in the past, let herself go as she used to do when she was a girl. She would forget that her mother-in-law was in the room, listening to every word she sang:

> *Oh thee, oh right there,*
> *In that very spot,*
> *Two doves are standing, a pair!*
> *Cooing a lot, and kissing a lot,*
> *And how could they care?*
> *Cooing a lot, and kissing a lot....*

"Oh, goodness me! Oh, what am I doing? Rachel cried out

and pulled herself together upon catching sight of her mother-in-law.

"Now, now, it doesn't matter!" her mother-in-law calmed her down, pretending not to notice, sniffing and peering into a jar of preserves. "You know, Rachel, I'm worried the gooseberries won't turn out. I had the same rotten luck a year ago: eight quarts of preserves went bad on me...."

And needless to say, Rachel would never have sung in Moyshe-Mendel's presence for anything in the world: it would have been very silly and awfully unpleasant—opening her mouth right in front of her husband and singing....Perhaps Moyshe-Mendel wouldn't have minded, he might have been very interested. He had heard her crooning a few times and he knew that she had an angel's voice. But how would he have looked to himself if he suddenly sat down in his own home—and listened to his wife singing songs? A fine thing for a respectable young man! If he happened to hear her by chance—then okay....And it did happen, but very seldom. At such times, Moyshe-Mendel would stop, all ears, and then cough as though he were only just arriving, and enter the room as though nothing had happened....

Rachel spent an entire year like that, all alone, among good and loyal people, who were utterly devoted to her; and you can't say that her life was good, and you can't say that her life was bad. She felt alien with her relatives, solitary in her family, deserted among good, loyal people. Sitting morosely over her work, some piece of embroidery, Rachel would hum to herself out of habit, and all at once her heart would ache, and she would yearn for the place where she had spent her childhood.

Flying, flying,
The golden birds,
Over all the seas,
Say hello,
You golden birds,
To my mother dear!
Flying, flying,
The golden birds,
Over all the rivers,
Say hello,
You golden birds,
To my father dear....

Dvosse-Malke often liked to tiptoe in and eavesdrop on her singing daughter-in-law.

"What's wrong, Rachel, are you homesick?"

"Oh, no, mother-in-law....I'm just humming," answered Rachel, smiling and wiping her tears.

RACHEL RECEIVES THE GOOD LETTER

We left Rachel in the middle of the veiling lunch, standing by the door and staring at the huge marketplace of the town of Mazepevke. She was deep in her thoughts, which we spoke about earlier. However, her thoughts were quickly interrupted by our bold friend Stempeniu.

This fine fellow, who had an eye on Rachel, noticed her leaving the table. He waited a bit and then went out after her. Stopping by the door, he started a conversation about his town, Mazepevke, and her town, Skvirre. He knew her town very well, all its little bridges, all its fine sights, like the palm of his hand, as they say. And he also talked to her about the city of Yehupets, he had heard she'd been there once. Rachel only replied to every tenth word.

"How come," Stempeniu asked her, "how come nobody ever sees you takin' a walk, not even on *Shabbes* or holidays? You've been livin' here for almost a year, more'n a year, and no one ever sees you on Berditchev Street. You live so far away, at the end of town, I didn't even know you were here.... I only found out yesterday when I saw you.... I wanted to rap with you a little yesterday, but I couldn't.... You know what these Jewish towns are like. You start to talk, and soon everyone else is talkin' about you.... Listen, just go for a walk on Saturday afternoon on Berditchev Street.... The whole town's out there.... Positively, you hear? Positively, Saturday afternoon, on Berditchev Street!"

Rachel didn't have time to answer, because her devoted mother-in-law Dvosse-Malke had noticed she wasn't at the table. She went to look for her, and when she found her standing outside by the door with Stempeniu, she was a bit surprised at first: "Why is she suddenly standing there with him?" However, Stempeniu, who

133

was generally rather cunning and knew what to do in such cases, instantly turned to Dvosse-Malke:

"We're talking about the wedding, the rebbe's wedding in Skvirre.... Your daughter-in-law was still a child back then, when I played at the rebbe's wedding. She doesn't remember it at all...."

"Of course not. How is she supposed to remember?" Dvosse-Malke replied. "But I remember it very well. I was there with my husband, and we spent the night outdoors because the town was so jammed."

"Jammed?" Stempeniu went on. "I can tell you a lot more." And he launched into a lengthy conversation with Dvosse-Malke about different things, smooth-talking his way out of the predicament. And meanwhile, Rachel excused herself and went back indoors to the bride. We've already said that Stempeniu had a way with words, and we have to tell you about another quality of his: He could talk with elderly women, chatter glibly, wind them around his little finger—he had a tongue in his head, and he spoke like an angel. There's an old saying: "An educated witch is worse than a born witch." When it came to glibness, Stempeniu was a sage. He had been to a good school, as we shall see.

"He's got his nerve," Rachel thought to herself. "Ordering me to be on Berditchev Street on Saturday afternoon—positively! Positively? He won't have it any other way? What an idea! Only a musician could talk like that!"

These were the dark thoughts with which Rachel came back in to the wedding. And when the dear Holy Sabbath came, and her in-laws and also Moyshe-Mendel lay down for their naps to take a bit of Sabbath pleasure from their sweet sleep—which Jews have thought the world of since time immemorial—Rachel, as usual, sat down alone at the window and stared out into the street, humming a song to herself. There, on the street, as on every Sabbath, she saw girls with freshly washed hair, with blue ribbons in their braids, with red, yellow, green dresses, with gloves, and with shiny-new, squeaky shoes. They were going out for their "promenade" on Berditchev Street. They wanted to show off their red or blue ribbons, their red, yellow, green dresses. They wanted to have a far look, in passing, as is our custom, at the boys, at the handsome boys in cloth coats, long trousers, and with shiny vizors on their Sabbath caps. The girls would then modestly lower their eyes, and their cheeks would turn crimson with embarrassment, and their hearts.... In short, they were going to live it up!

Rachel knew all about it. Why shouldn't she? After all, she herself had once been a girl with red and blue ribbons in her braids, and she herself once went strolling down the promenade with a bunch of girls on a Sabbath afternoon. But now?

Rachel looked around. Everybody was fast asleep and snoring heartily. Everybody! She was the only one sitting there, as though among dead people, as though among real corpses. She leaned her head on her hands, deep in thought, and remembered an old song she used to sing when she was a girl:

All alone,
As lonesome as a stone,
No one to talk to,
Only myself alone,
As lonesome as a stone,
No one to talk to—

"Good Shabbes!"

Rachel lifted her head and saw—Stempeniu.

"I said: Good Shabbes!"

"What's this? What's he doing here?" Rachel was about to ask and move away from the window.

"A good Sabbath to you too!" she replied, turning as red as a beet.

"You didn't listen to me, you didn't go out to Berditchev Street....? I kept lookin' for you for nothin'.... Well, I.... that is to say.... Well, just read this!"

And Stempeniu handed Rachel a folded leaf of paper and quickly vanished from sight.

Rachel held the sheet of paper for a long, long time, not knowing what to do with it, not understanding what it was, what it meant.... Once her initial surprise was gone, she unfolded what turned out to be a large sheet of music paper, she saw huge letters, plain Yiddish words with a lot of mistakes:

My deerest angel in the sky, wen I saw your raydiant shape, both my eyes felt raydiant in a raydiant fire with my hart, burning with grate love for you my sole wich your hevenly eyes have with your raydiant shape drawn to you from the verry first, you are my life, the life of my hart my soul I cannot sleep I dream for you are the lite in the darkness in eyes I love you like my verry owne life for ever I wership the groun you wawk on I kiss your lovely eyes from farr away

Stempeniu

135

FROM THE PRINCESS BACK TO THE PRINCE

Now let's leave the princess, as we do in Jewish fairy-tales, and go back to the prince. We'll turn away from Rachel and talk about Stempeniu.

Granted, Stempeniu's letter, which is recorded above word for word, was not all that skillful. But what can you do? Stempeniu was certainly a hero, a handsome guy, a fine scoundrel, but he wasn't a writer. Go fight city hall! His father, Beryl the Bassist, may he rest in peace, saw that Stempeniu wanted to play music and refused to go to school for love or money, so Beryl decided to teach him his own trade. He had him try out all the instruments until the boy remained with the violin, and Beryl the Bassist, who had other musical children besides Stempeniu, actually said that Stempeniu had a streak of his grandfather, Shmulik the Trumpeter, who had personally know Paganini. Thus, by the age of twelve, Stempeniu could already man an instrument and play an entire wedding. That was why Beryl the Bassist loved him more than his other children, who went about in rags and tatters, or simply naked and barefoot. And even though Beryl was a martinet and used to pull Stempeniu's ear, or beat him, whip him, thrash him, break every bone in his body, the boy was nevertheless his favorite, his jewel, a gold mine for his old age. Beryl showed his son off to everyone, proudly saying, half in musician's lingo: "Just look, you bastards, my junior fiddler's gonna make bread for me in my old age. You can bet your bottom ruble."

However, Beryl the Bassist was not fated to have his beloved son with him in his old age. At fifteen, Stempeniu took off with three rubles in his pocket and an old broken fiddle under his arm, and he wandered though the world. He roamed and rambled everywhere, through so many towns and cities, with so many different bands. Stempeniu couldn't hold out anywhere for more than six months. He always had to keep moving, on and on: from Mazepevke to Stepevke, from Stepevke to Korets, from Korets to Balte, from Balte to Old Constantine, and from there to Berditchev, and on and on, until he hit Odessa. And from Odessa, he headed back—roving from shtetl to shtetl, where he could easily play, make a name for himself, enjoy his reputation. And that's what happened. Any place Stempeniu came to, the people had already heard of him. The Jews has found out that a man named

Stempeniu was vagabonding through the world, a man whose music was the end of the world. Which explains the stir caused by Stempeniu when he and his group reached that town. For of course, Stempeniu had his own group by the time he was eighteen, and they wandered about, playing only at certain weddings, rich ones. And so, in the course of time, Stempeniu beat all the other bands, for instance the Kanatop Musicians, who were quite renowned, the Smillers, the Vinitsers, the Sharagraders, and so many other famous groups that the world had been listening to.

Naturally Stempeniu didn't win any friends by taking all the plums from the other musicians, who cursed him roundly and wished him the worst. To his face, they patted him on the back; but in their hearts, they hated his guts. Every musician knew deep down that the moment Stempeniu picked up the fiddle, all the other musicians might as well go to bed.

Musicians, you must know, have always loved to exaggerate. They tell an endless wealth of fairy-tales, wondrous stories, legends. Dreadful exaggerations were heard everywhere about Stempeniu, and it was said that his violin came from Paganini himself. When people heart that Stempeniu would be coming with his band, the local musicians would naturally curse their hearts out at him, only to be outdone by their wives, whose curses would have curled the devil's hair.

"All year long, we go hungry, we starve, we borrow, we pawn, we eat our shoeleather, and what happens? The rich man has a wedding, and along comes a demon, the worst devil in the world, Stempeniu, and grabs the food from our mouths. May he rot in hell!..."

However, Stempeniu never had any real enemies. He was a good pal. When the wedding was over, he would get together with the local musicians and treat them to a lavish supper, the liquor flowed freely, they had a wild time, everybody got some money, and before Stempeniu left, he handed out presents to all the children. In a word, he was decent and respectable.

"You know," the musicians' wives said to one another afterwards. "You know, there's nothing more precious than a Jewish soul."

But most of all, Stempeniu found favor in the blue or black eyes of the musicians' daughters, the girls he got engaged to everywhere. And when he swore to a musician's daughter that he was madly in love with her, you could have believed him. For the time

137

being, he really was in love with her (musicians usually have beautiful daughters). But the instant Stempeniu left town, his great love was gone with the wind and the smoke. And coming to the next town, he promptly fell in love again with a local musician's daughter, he swore again that he was madly in love with her, that he worshiped the ground she walked on, that he couldn't live without her, he gave her presents when he said good-bye, drove away—and went through the same thing in the next town....

We can't say that most of these affairs turned out all right for the fiancées.... True, many of his beloveds quickly forgot all about Stempeniu and married some other musician. But a few of them, very stubborn girls, put so much faith in that scoundrel, really believing he would come back, if not today then tomorrow, if not tomorrow, then the day after—until they finally began languishing and perishing. While Stempeniu was in some darkened room, kissing a musician's daughter, any number of his brides were lying somewhere else face down, weeping over their rotten luck, their beloved had forgotten them, he had deserted them, never giving them a second thought....

These were the unhappy brides that Stempeniu left in nearly every town that he passed through with his band. But you can't win them all. Sometimes your luck doesn't hold out, and it's your turn to weep and wail. Stempeniu's luck ran out on him when he least expected it. He had to get married, though that was the last thing in the world he wanted to do!

STEMPENIU UNEXPECTEDLY GETS MARRIED

One day, Stempeniu and his band arrived in Mazepevke. They played for three weddings in a row together with the town musicians, who argued with him about their rights and swore that if he ignored them, they would take him apart bone by bone. And they would have done a nice job of it if Stempeniu, who had a good heart, hadn't been willing to join forces.

Since there were several days between weddings and Stempeniu had nothing to do in the meantime, he got to know the daughter of Shaike the Fiddler. She was a fine girl of about twenty-two, dark and fat, and he fell madly in love with her in his usual way: He kissed her, hugged her, caressed her, brought her presents, fondled her like a fiancé, and when the time came to leave, the dark-haired girl (Freydel was her name) told him not to delay any longer, but to sign the engagement contract right away, as is the custom. Stempeniu, not used to that sort of thing, shilly-shallied, tried to talk his way out of it, but even the Good Lord couldn't help him now. Freydel was as tough as nails, she grabbed him by the hand and wouldn't let go, and presto!—the betrothal party took place, God bless them! The musicians drank themselves silly toasting the famous bridegroom, and they celebrated three days straight in Shaike the Fiddler's home, until the dear bride-groom and all the dear guests drove off to the next town, and the town after that, and so on.

Needless to say, Stempeniu promptly forgot all about the wedding and the betrothal and the dark-haired girl, and he did business as usual, that is, he had his romances in every town, as he was used to doing. And so he went from town to town with his group, playing at weddings and having a great time! When all at once— Well, nothing lasts forever in this world! Everything comes to an end. And things came to an end for Stempeniu too. Lightning struck him, and thunder. A plague raged into his young life! Just listen to his misfortune:

He was playing at a wedding in some small shtetl, somewhere in the Ukraine, while romancing Hershke the Flutist's daughter (a rather attractive girl), whom he promised to marry—when in burst Mekhtshi the Drummer with the sleepy face. He motioned to Stempeniu and whispered to him:

"Hey, Stempeniu, there's a chick waitin' for you in that house."

"A chick? What chick?"

"A dark chick with green eyes."

And Stempeniu strode over to the house and saw the dark-haired girl, the fiddler's daughter, his fiancée Freydel!

"Why're you staring like that, Stempeniu? Don't you recognize me. Just get a load of him, peeping and eyeing me. It's me, Stempeniu, me: Freydel, your fiancée, Shaike the Fiddler's daughter."

"Ha! Yeah, I know. What'd you think? I know, I know! But how'd ya get here? Where ya comin' from?"

"How I got here? On my legs, Stempeniu, on my legs. I asked directions all the way. I just arrived at Hershke's place. Where am I coming from? From home."

"Well, what's happenin'? When did you leave home?"

"Happening? Nothing much, Stempeniu. No news. When did we leave home? Oh, about six or seven weeks ago. We've been everywhere! Every place we came to, we were told: 'He was here but he's already left.' We barely got on the right track.... Well, how are you, Stempeniu?"

"What?! Me? I'm all right. Why not! C'mon, Freydel, let's get away from here," he said to her, seeing that the musicians were starting to gather around them and stare at the dark girl with the black braids and the green eyes.

"Okay, let's go," Freydel replied.

And Stempeniu put on his jacket, picked up his cane, and went strolling through town with the dark-haired girl. He peered around to make sure no one was in earshot, and then he said to her more vehemently:

"Now, listen, what's this all about?"

"What do you mean: 'What's this all about?'"

"Well, why'd you come here?"

"Well, get a load of you, acting like you don't know, like you dropped dead or something!"

"Listen, Freydel," Stempeniu got more emotional. "Listen, Freydel. I don' like no one pullin' stunts like this on me! I asked you: 'What're ya doin' here?' And you start jivin' me!"

Freydel's green eyes flared up at Stempeniu and, tossing her long black braids, she snapped:

"What am I doing here, you wanna know? I've come for you, Stempeniu. At the betrothal party, you said you'd write in two weeks at the latest and let us know about the wedding date. We waited and waited for more than two months, and when we saw we wouldn't be hearing from you, we decided to go and track your ghost down ourselves, and we've been everywhere, to the ends of the earth, and it was only after lots and lots of trouble that God helped us and we—"

"Tell me, Freydel, who's 'we'? You keep saying 'we' went and 'we' came...."

"The two of us. Me and Mom."

"Your Mom?" cried Stempeniu, stopping dead in his tracks. "Your mother? What's she doin' here?"

"Stop screaming, Stempeniu! What'd you think? That I'd come alone? A girl doesn't travel alone. A fine thing! Imagine!"

"Yeah, but what does your old lady have to do with me?" asked Stempeniu, walking back with her.

"She's your future mother-in-law, Stempeniu. Your future mother-in-law. And later on, she's gonna be your present mother-in-law."

"Freydel, do you seriously intend to marry me?"

"And you didn't mean it seriously, Stempeniu?"

"It's off the wall!"

"What's off the wall!"

"Listen, gettin' hitched is the last thing in the world I wanna do."

Freydel halted for a minute and gazed into Stempeniu's eyes. Then she looked all round and finally spoke to Stempeniu very quietly:

"Just you listen to me, Stempeniu! Don't think you've met up with some dumb kid who doesn't know which side her bread is buttered on. I know you very well, Stempeniu! I know all about your carryings-on. You like getting engaged to a different girl every week, but it doesn't matter, you've sowed your wild oats, that's okay.... Basically you're all right, you've got a soft heart, you're a good-looking guy, one in a million, you're a wonderful fiddler and you can support a wife—that's why I want you and that's why I'm marrying you, on the spot! You can argue all you like, it's no use, you're wasting your time, Stempeniu, believe me. Now bend your head, I want to tell you a secret...."

And Freydel, the dark-haired girl, whispered a secret into Stempeniu's ear, and Stempeniu shuddered from head to foot. He stood there like a clay golem, in the middle of the road, unable to open his mouth, to utter a word. And then along came Mekhtshi the Drummer with his red hair, and he told Stempeniu that he was supposed to go to the town Rothschild to talk about a wedding. Stempeniu took leave of Freydel, nodding and sighing:

"I'll see you later, Freydel!"

"You're not kidding you'll see me later!" she replied, happily saying good-bye to her darling fiance Stempeniu.

All the people who saw Stempeniu at the wedding were astonished at his pale face and his absent look. It just wasn't the old Stempeniu, a better-looking corpse would have been buried posthaste! It was as though someone had whisked away his merriment, his ardor. Yes indeed, Stempeniu saw that his sweet life as a free bird was over, he was sticking his head in a yoke forever and always. Adieu, radiant summer evenings and long strolls outside of town with musicians' daughters! Adieu, long, delicious braids, undone hair, huge, black eyes! Adieu, silvery moon!...

Naturally, Stempeniu fought a bit, he struggled like a fish in a net, with his last strength, using any means he could, but it was about as useful as applying leeches to a corpse. Freydel and her mother stuck to him like those ghosts that come in a dream at night, dragging you off to face the music in the heavenly court of justice.... And he was scared to death of his future mother-in-law, who knotted up her black maw as though with a piece of string, but her face blazed as though she were all set to pounce on Stempeniu any minute like a ferocious cat and scratch both his eyes out—if it weren't for Freydel who kept holding her back.

"Leave him alone, Mama, you'll spoil everything. Just watch him, but don't say anything, keep your eye on him so he doesn't escape. It'll be all right, Mama, Stempeniu is mine, he's mine!..."

SAMSON PUTS HIS HEAD IN DELILAH'S LAP

Freydel put down her foot and got her way: She married Stempeniu according to the law of Moses and Israel, and once she got her hands on him, she really took him in hand. She got a little help from her Mama, who was finally seeing the proud and joyful day when she became a mother-in-law, and Stempeniu had a taste of hell and he was not disappointed. The newlyweds moved to Mazepevke, and Stempeniu settled down there with his band, a resident, in one place.

"It's over, Stempeniu, no more wandering around! Your traveling days are done, Stempeniu, done!" said Freydel to her husband, who was all hers now, and she did whatever she wanted to with him—or else!

After the wedding, another life began for Stempeniu, a brand-new life. He had been a spirited bachelor, but no sooner was he married and in Freydel's hands than he lost all his strength, all his courage, all his brilliance. At home, Stempeniu had no say whatsoever.

"Just remember, your business is the band and weddings.

What do you need money for, silly?" That's what Freydel would say, taking every last kopek he ever earned.

Freydel was the picture of avarice. She had grown up in a very poor family and had almost never set eyes on a kopek. As a girl, she hardly ever got a ribbon or a comb, and then only with bitter tears. She went barefoot till the age of fifteen, acted as nanny to the younger children, and got more than her share of slaps from her mother as well as her father, Shaike the Fiddler, who was a drinking man. She ate next to nothing, she dressed to match her bare feet and it was only on Purim that a few kopeks came her way, for delivering Purim presents to other people's homes. She would stash those kopeks deep in her bosom, so that her Mama wouldn't trick her out of them, and she slept with her hoard until Passover, when she bought herself a ribbon or a comb. And that was Freydel's life until she reached eighteen, when she suddenly grew into a tall, a lovely, a healthy girl—ready for marriage! When Freydel got engaged to Stempeniu, she herself didn't realize how lucky she was. Only her mother, who did realize it, argued away at her, setting her straight: She ought to know that her fiancé was making a mint, but that he was a rather frivolous sort, and he spent money like it grew on trees, she shouldn't let him get away with murder, she had to keep him under her thumb, the way her mama did with her papa, Shaike the Fiddler....

When Freydel married Stempeniu, she didn't forget her mother's advice; little by little, and cleverly, she taught her husband the meaning of the word "wife," she explained that a husband can have no secrets from his wife, a wife is not an outsider, she's not a mistress, no, she's his flesh and blood, she is him and he is her. In a word, he had to know, he had to *feel* that he had a wife....

When Freydel began running her own household and kept seeing new rubles that Stempeniu earned so often, she pounced on them like a starving man spotting food. But she didn't enjoy the money. Freydel was worried that they might be penniless from one day to the next, her husband might not earn money later on, God forbid. So she made herself a little pouch and began saving kopek after kopek.

"What are you hidin'?" asked Stempeniu, noticing her movements.

"Curiosity killed the cat. Don't get any gray hairs over it, Stempeniu!" Freydel answered with a smile, and kept doing what she had to, skimping, scrimping, scanting at the market, the store, the butcher's, serving just barely enough for lunch, often not eating or drinking enough, scraping together ruble after ruble. Gradually, when she had gotten together a tidy little sum, she started lending money on security and charging interest. The first time, it just happened, it was an accident, a neighbor had asked to borrow some money, and Freydel did her the favor. Why not? And then, when she saw that the money was growing, and that one ruble became two in the course of time, she began doing business with her small capital, until she simply became a "usurer" with all the trimmings and all the stuffings of this profession, which a lot of our rich people indulge in (this is just between you and me) and don't really dislike at all....

How peculiar! Where did Freydel get her lust for hoarding money? Not from her papa, Shaike the Fiddler, nor could she have seen the like among any of the renowned musicians. Where will you find anyone comparable to musicians, who never turn over a kopek and who spend money like water. Jewish musicians—especially in those days—were like Gypsies, a special tribe, with a special jargon, and with special ways of their own. They always had a good time, it was always Purim for them, life was merry, lively, they fiddled, frolicked, fooled around, worked, carried on, played wild pranks, talked about cheery things.... When they came home to their wives, they joked, gobbled up beans and dumplings or else tightened their belts, but they were always romping, dancing, frisking, going to bed hungry, borrowing money the next day, pawning their pillows, redeeming them and then pawning them all over again. The daughters of musicians were usually joyous and frivolous creatures themselves, there were no veils on their hair or their lives....In a word, the musicians lived in paradise, with all the virtues and faults of paradise....And in such an eden, who would ever dream of worrying about tomorrow?

Naturally, Freydel's papa was no tearful sort. Shaike the Fiddler was as poor as a synagogue mouse, but a jolly and jovial mouse, and whenever he earned a ruble he caroused it away in the twinkling of an eye, as they say. And Freydel's mama liked to live well, that is to say, eat well. They hardly had a shirt to their names, but as long as there was a pillow to be pawned they always ate. "All our good luck goes straight to our bellies....How does the old proverb go? 'It's better to deal with the baker than the doctor.' Eat, drink and be merry!" That's what she'd say, Freydel's mama, who was a spendthrift even for a musician's wife.

So how did Freydel get to be the way she was? Where did she get her stinginess? Perhaps it came from want, from always being penniless in her parents' home. Or maybe it was natural with her. Maybe a stingy soul had gone astray into the musician's family and been reincarnated as Freydel.

Whatever it was, Freydel made weird grimaces, sweated, and frothed even if she only *talked* about money.

All the musicians' wives were jealous of her. "What luck!" they said in chorus.

But there was one way in which God neglected Freydel: He gave her no children. And who knows, perhaps that too was why she was utterly devoted, body and soul, to money—because the finest pleasure, the joy of children, was denied her. Generally, we see that the wives whom God has not blessed with children are nasty women, they lack the goodness, the softness of their sex. Such women can love only themselves.

And that's the sort of woman Freydel was. But it can't be said that she hated Stempeniu. Why should she? A handsome man, a paragon, a rare violinist—one in a million, and—this was the nitty-gritty—a good provider, a gold mine!

"My Stempeniu," Freydel boasted to her friends, "my Stempeniu—when he plays a note on the strings, out comes a ruble, two notes and it's two rubles, three notes—and it's three rubles. You understand?"

As far as rubles went, Stempeniu was the very opposite: money meant nothing to him. He'd play at a wedding, stuff his pockets with cash, and—before you knew it, not a kopek was left. If he had something, he gave, he shared, he lent. If he had nothing, he borrowed. In this way, Stempeniu was an artist. All he cared about was the band—present something new, perform an operatic piece, contract for a wedding, do the wedding, playing as God commanded, so that Jews licked their fingers—it was no mere scraping.

There were two things that Stempeniu loved more than anything in the world: himself and the violin. He was busy with himself all the time: bedecking and bedizening himself, curling his hair—in a word, making himself a "bachelor," as Freydel so cuttingly put it, and he would then forget all about the violin.

But when he picked up his violin, he forgot all about himself and the rest of the world. If ever he was overcome with melancholy, he would take his violin, chain the door, and then play his

145

own fantasies for three or four hours at a time, he fiddled anything that drifted into his mind. Now he would pour himself out in a lament, so dolefully, so dismally, and softer and softer. And then he would suddenly lose his temper and play louder and louder, until all at once, something like a sigh tore from the depths of his heart, and the blaze went down a bit, and his anger died out, and soft melodies, dear, sweet songs, growing sadder and sadder, came pouring out endlessly, and then he would become a little cheerier, livelier....Of course, that didn't happen often, the mood didn't sweep him up all the time, but once he was lost in his violin, there was no possibility of yanking him away. Stempeniu's imagination seethed and settled like a source—the more, the fresher.

A person with feeling, with a soul, could not possibly have heard enough of this free music, which cannot be committed to paper. It sounded like an entreaty to the Lord of the Universe from a bitter heart, a prayer to God for mercy, for compassion, the sort of prayer that has to be, that must be accepted up there, at God's Throne....It is said that the Rebbe of Rizhin had his own orchestra, which played while he intoned the praises of Him Who Lives Eternally. That was truly a thought from a great man, an idea from a lofty poetic soul.

"Oh that bitch, Fat Kaile, may she drop dead, the dirty slob. She's paid me the interest for last week, and for this week she says she can't pay me till after Sabbath!"

That was the type of conversation with which Freydel welcomed Stempeniu when he came out of his room after playing, he was still ablaze, his black eyes were shining. That was the fire in his eyes that was so attractive. The fire would flare seldom, and when his eyes met Freydel's, the fire vanished.

When Stempeniu came home after playing a wedding, Freydel would greet him with a smile, fawning on him like a kitten:

"What do you need money for, Stempeniu?" Freydel would say, shaking out all his pockets. "What good is it? What don't you have? You've got everything you need, you're not hungry, God forbid, and you don't go naked, and when you need a couple of kopeks, don't I give them to you? Why don't you let me have the money? It'll be safe with me. Just give it to me. Give it to me!"

And Stempeniu stood there like a child being punished, and Freydel twisted him around her little finger, he was like putty in her hand. Ah! What's happened to you, Stempeniu? How can such a nobody like Freydel dance on your head, and you let her lead you around by the nose, like Samson putting his head into his beloved Delilah's lap?...Ugh! Stempeniu, what a shame, what a terrible shame!

ALL IS NOT LOST

Poor, poor Stempeniu!...

But it's not quite what you think. You don't have to feel all that sorry for our hero. He may not have had much say in his home and he certainly didn't wear the pants there. But to make up for it, he had his world, a world of his own, which had nothing whatsoever to do with Freydel. In his world, Stempeniu was a king, and, as we shall see, he was very happy there.

First of all, he spent half the day rehearsing, that is to say, playing the new numbers over and over again with the band; they would kid around, listen to the jester's quips, and laugh at Mekhtshi the Drummer, whom the jester liked to tease. Then they would tell one another stories about some wedding or other. For every Jewish wedding has its story. At one wedding, the bridegroom dug in his heels, and, come hell or high water, he refused to go to the wedding canopy until they paid out the dowry ruble by ruble, right then and there. At another place, the bride wept so much that she fainted dead away and they could barely revive her—and all the while the jester kept cracking jokes. At a third wedding, a fine thing happened: After the dinner, when it was time to dance—And the musicians burst out laughing, like cannonfire.

"What are you guys carrying on about? Just get a load of their tomfoolery!" Freydel shouted from her room.

"Don't let it bother you!" Stempeniu replied arrogantly. "Haven't I told you a hundred times to keep your nose out of our business!"

And at that moment, Stempeniu felt like the master of the house, a true sultan in his home.

The rest of the time Stempeniu spent dressing, grooming, caring for his clothes, polishing his boots to make them shine like mirrors, combing his hair so stylishly, curling his lovely, black curls, smoothing his white dickey, and then he picked up his cane, a cane with a small knob, a fig carved out of ivory, and he donned a broad, black cap with a shiny vizor pulled down to the eyes. Tilting his head so that the curls were spread on his shoulder, Stempeniu went and took a walk through the town. He had his friends here, whom he would meet, and strolling past the shops, he greeted the young wives, the shopkeepers. The women flushed, they remembered they had been girls once and they had known Stempeniu back then.... Those were the days....And now? Who thought about it now?...

But still, you can find such young wives nowadays, and especially girls who stand talking to Stempeniu for a long time at the door, talking, chatting about this and that, laughing....

Naturally such things can't just happen like that, a neighbor sees them and she goes and tells another, a third one, the rumor begins, and when Jewish tongues wag about you, you'll never hear the end of it.

"What's all this gossip about, Stempeniu? have you done it again?"

"Done what again, Freydel?"

"Done what again?!...How can you ask! Everyone's gossiping about you. We're the talk of the town."

"I don't know what you want from me, Freydel."

"What I want from you? I want you to change your old habits....It's about time! Wherever there's a young wife or girl in town, you have to get to know her and stop to talk to her for three whole hours—you just can't get your fill!"

"Oh? Are you possibly referring to the fact that I was talking to Esther?"

"Oh, of course, Esther, what could be wrong with talking to Esther?! What is she anyway, a holy saint or something?!"

"I was speaking to her about a business matter."

"You and your business matters....I know you, Stempeniu!"

"Well, you oughtta know about it. Her father wants to have the wedding in Yehupets, that's a crazy whim of his. Well, I ran into Esther, so I discussed the matter with her. Wouldn't it be a drag if I let a wedding like that slip away from me?"

"How did he ever hit upon Yehupets, the lunatic!" asked Freydel, and her green eyes lit up with the fire that always flashed in them whenever she sniffed money....

"How can you ask questions about a lunatic?" replied Stempeniu, escaping the matter unscathed.

And that's how matters were taken care of, that matter and all matters. Stempeniu had a sharp mind and he knew how to get around Freydel.

Out of town, when Stempeniu went traveling with his band, he was, of course, even more successful. There he had, as the saying goes, "a kosher pot and a kosher spoon"—he could do whatever he wanted to, and when Stempeniu came to some shtetl to play a wedding, he just didn't feel like leaving it anymore. There he had "matters" upon "matters," cheerful ones and dismal ones without end. In short, that was a special world for Stempeniu, his very own world, which Freydel was not allowed to enter for anything in the world, even though she very much wanted to. She actually tried to bribe Mekhtshi the Drummer, but it didn't work. Here, in his world, Stempeniu was a new man, totally different from the Stempeniu in Freydel's house.

STEMPENIU STARTS FALLING IN LOVE

In his own world, Rachel began playing an important role for him, the most important role in his life. We can believe him when he says that his letter to her, which we saw earlier, was quite serious and truthful, for he fell in love with Rachel the moment he set eyes on her at the wedding in Haym ben-Tsion's house.

Stempeniu didn't write the letter immediately. It took a few days for the fire that Rachel's blue eyes kindled in his heart to burn forth, blaze up until he couldn't hold back anymore, he locked himself up in his room, and there, where he wrote his music, and with the same pen and on the same lined music paper, he wrote that letter.

Stempeniu sweated a bit over the letter. Writing was a chore for him, he had never learned how to write anywhere, just on his own. So it was really no wonder that he had a hard time.

Stempeniu carried the letter around for a few days, he couldn't find a way of giving it to Rachel. Mekhtshi the Drummer was a good messenger for such letters when they were out of town, but here, with Freydel around, Mekhtshi was a dangerous postman to use. Stempeniu could hardly wait for the Sabbath, he got all dolled up like a young girl, he put on a high hat in the latest fashion of the times, and went out to Berditchev Road, as on every Sabbath, to take a walk, calculating that Rachel would probably be there. But he was wrong: All the young wives, all the girls were strolling about, sneaking glances at Stempeniu, smiling and turning crimson—they were all there, only Rachel wasn't there! The letter he had written gave him no peace. He felt drawn to her more and more strongly.

"I ought to try and go there, to the street where Isaak-Naphtali lives, maybe I'll find her...." Those were Stempeniu's thoughts, and so he slowly walked towards the window, where Rachel was sitting deep in her thoughts, singing that little song:

All alone,
As lonesome as a stone,
No one to talk to,
Only myself alone,
As lonesome as a stone,
No one to talk to—

At first, when she suddenly heard the "Good Shabbes" and saw Stempeniu in front of her, she thought it was a dream (she had already seen Stempeniu in several of her dreams....). But when she unfolded the small slip of music paper and read Stempeniu's letter, she stood up, looked through the window, and said to herself:

"He's lucky he went away. I would have played some music for him that he'd never forget! Oh, that Stempeniu!..."

She clutched the letter and was about to hurl it out the window, but then she faltered, read through it again, rolled it up the way you roll up a scroll, and put it in her pocket.

Rachel's anger kept getting bigger and stronger, she just wanted to see him alone and ask him privately: What was the meaning of this? What was he up to ? How dare he write her a note like that! Just who did he think he was anyway? And who did he think *she* was?...She began pondering ways of meeting him in some place where no one could overhear them, and she finally hit upon something.

A CORAL NECKLACE FROM FREYDEL

"Listen, mother-in-law, if it's not too expensive, I'd really like to have a necklace of coral beads. Good heavy coral."

"Well, how often have I told you: Just go over to Freydel and

150

pick out whatever your heart desires. If you like, we'll go right now. For my sake, she won't charge you much."

Our dark-haired Freydel, who lent money on interest and took security, mostly coral, had gradually, almost for fun, started dealing in the coral itself, on the side, she bought it very cheap from her debtors and then offered it much cheaper than any coral vendors, and her moonlighting grew and grew until she was actually doing business with all the dealers in Berditchev and Brody. Everyone in Mazepevke knew that you could get a decent string of coral from Freydel, Stempeniu's wife Freydel.

Miraculous! Where did Freydel get her sales talent, her way of dealing with the customers, her ability to talk them into buying? When Dvosse-Malke and her daughter-in-law stepped into her house, Freydel welcomed them with open arms:

"Hello, hello! How are you, Dvosse-Malke? You know, I've had my eye on you for a long time?"

"On me? How come, Freydel?"

"How come, you ask? Why, a year ago, you brought a gem into your home—and that was that! You should have come here with your daughter-in-law at some point and picked out something for her. Why, I tell you, Dvosse-Malke, it's a crying shame!"

"You're so right, Freydel darling, but it's not my fault. What can I do if my daughter-in-law doesn't want coral, no matter how much I beg her?"

"Now that's a new one on me! What do you mean she doesn't want coral? With you, she doesn't want, but with me she will want, don't worry!"

And Freydel quickly opened a huge green chest, and began pulling out one set of coral beads after another, placing them in front of the customers, talking all the while and uttering all sorts of good wishes and compliments like a true businesswoman.

"Just look, Dvosse-Malke, if you take my word for it, you'll have your daughter-in-law buy this string of beads, may you and I be as pure as these beads. Why they're pure Orleans beads! Just try them on, if you please, on your throat, that's right. Oh, I'm absolutely envious, they look so beautiful on your white throat! Wear them in good health and may God grant that your mother-in-law can buy five strings of such big pearls a year from now. Oh, how wonderfully they dress your face! Tell me, Dvosse-Malke, you're a jewelry mayven, what's your opinion? It should only happen to me, by God!"

151

With these words, Freydel pulled a mirror out of the chest and held it up in front of Rachel, Freydel's green eyes glittered with pride and joy, and she had worked up a sweat with all her talking and swearing and wishing.

"And is your Stempeniu working hard?" Dvosse-Malke asked, pointing to the room where rare and sweet sounds were coming from.

"Yes, he's playing," Freydel replied and began showing other strings of coral, all kinds, and meanwhile she and Dvosse-Malke got into a long conversation, which is what happens when two shopkeepers get together and talk shop.

Rachel sat on the side, not listening to their conversation. Rachel heard another conversation, another voice, other words, that could be heard from Stempeniu's violin, words that went straight to her heart, and she stood up only when the violin stopped playing and Stempeniu appeared in the doorway. Their eyes met and both he and she turned a fiery red....Stempeniu halted at the door, unsure of what to do next. And as she looked at him, Rachel told her mother-in-law that it was time to go home. Dvosse-Malke gasped and wrung her hands:

"Oh, for goodness' sake! Just look at how long we've been talking! Well, Freydel, what are you going to charge me for the beads. You can't ask too much from me, Freydel. You've got to be straight with me!"

"As straight as a ramrod! Listen, Dvosse-Malke, let me choke on the first food I eat if I tell you a lie! Sossi wanted to force eighteen rubles on me for the beads, may the Good Lord preserve me and my husband! What can I do? I hesitated—Sossi is Sossi, and you're Dvosse-Malke. I'll give them to you for fifteen rubles, and believe me, I swear on my grandmother's grave, I'm not earning a kopek on them, as God is my witness!"

"Well, fifteen is fifteen, I'll give you twelve, Freydel, twelve rubles in cash."

"Oh, the Lord preserve us, Dvosse-Malke, don't haggle!" shouted Freydel heatedly, grabbing Dvosse-Malke's hands as if they were about to dance a jig.

In that moment, Rachel and Stempeniu could quickly exchange a few words.

"I want to tell you something, Stempeniu."

"I want to tell you something too, Rachel."

"You already did tell me something."

"When?"

"In the letter."

"It wasn't much."

"It was too much."

"No, it wasn't even one one-hundredth."

"You're wrong."

"I swear by my life, I'm dying! Where can I meet you?"

"I don't know where we can meet."

"In the evening?"

"Where?"

"On Monastery Street."

"When?"

"Saturday night. You can go out on the other side to Monastery Garden."

"I can't, I won't."

"You have to, Rachel. Please, just come out for a minute! Be there, I'll wait for you, on Saturday night, for God's sake, Rachel...."

"I won't come."

"You will come, Rachel, you will come!..."

"Well, daughter," called Dvosse-Malke. "Come on, let's go home. We barely got it for fourteen rubles. Why, I didn't realize you were such an expert businesswoman, Freydel!"

"Oh, Dvosse-Malke, God preserve you, you're a hard bargainer, upon my word! Good day to you and stay well! Wear the necklace in the best of health! Use it in the best of health! May it last forever, and may you live even longer!"

"She can go on crutches, the bitch, the way she haggled me to death!" said Freydel to Stempeniu, closing the door behind them. "And that daughter-in-law, the white heifer, she just sits there and keeps her mouth shut. She looks about as good in that coral as a pig!..."

When Rachel came home with her coral necklace, her mother-in-law took her over to the father-in-law, smiling so happily as though she had won God knows what.

"What do you say to these beads, Isaak-Naphtali? A bargain, honestly, a fantastic bargain!"

Isaak-Naphtali went up to Rachel, took a hard look, like a real expert, sniffed, and then asked:

"What did you pay for them?"

"See if you can guess, you're a businessman, so to speak. Well, c'mon, try and guess," said Dvosse-Malke with a smile.

"I can't tell whether they were expensive or cheap."

"If I say it's a bargain, silly, then it's a bargain, a real steal! Believe me, I did enough dickering and haggling with that cheating bitch, that musician's wife, may she drop dead! Oh boy, can she ever bargain, she's a real market woman. The devil only knows where and when she go her training! And what a mouth she's got, she foams like boiling milk—I hope she kicks the bucket, that lousy bitch!... Well, cat got your tongue, Isaak-Naphtali? C'mon, let's hear your expert opinion, what do you think the coral should cost?"

"What this coral should cost?" repeated Isaak-Naphtali, stroking his beard. "Now, let's see, these beads should cost, about, well about—Wait, I'll tell you exactly how much, I don't want to make a mistake—a bargain, you say, a bargain? Well, if it's a bargain, then you paid no less than five and a half rubles, but it's worth a full seven."

"Asshole!" Dvosse-Malke shot out like a cannon, and Isaak-Naphtali quaked and stepped aside. "You asshole! You shithead! A coral necklace like this—five and a half rubles? You crazy idiot! A deaf mute wouldn't have said that in a year! Don't you have eyes in your head? Take a good look, you big moron!"

And Dvosse-Malke grabbed Rachel's hand, pulled her over to her father-in-law, pushed up Rachel's head, and showed Isaak-Naphtali the bargain, while spouting insults and curses. Poor Isaak-Naphtali sniffed and blinked, afraid to say a word. Until God took pity on him and in walked Moyshe-Mendel with his cane, he was coming from the marketplace—and now he began estimating the price of the beads on Rachel's lovely white throat and he guessed they must have cost in the neighborhood of three rubles.... Dvosse-Malke blazed up in such fury that she practically burst out crying like a little child, she was grief-stricken that no one understood what a big bargain she had gotten and perhaps she was heart-broken that Stempeniu's wife had so grossly deceived her.

"And you call yourself a businessman?!" she shouted at Moyshe-Mendel. "You're as big an expert as your father! Three rubles, sonny-boy? Why not less?!"

"Because they're not worth more, they're very plain beads. I've seen coral beads in my time, Mama. You can believe me, I've seen really valuable coral necklaces...."

All day long, the three of them argued and bickered about the coral necklace.

"You'd give me a lot more pleasure if you shot a bullet into my heart," screamed Dvosse-Malke, "rather than saying 'five and a half' to me! Okay, let her cheat me, the bitch. I hope she gets the plague—no one's ever cheated me!—Fine, I hope God strikes her dead, her and that Stempeniu of hers. But why pour salt into my wounds and say 'five and a half' to me? You and your goddamn 'five and a half'! I hope she gets five and a half dozen boils on her body and five and a half fevers in her liver! I swear, I'm going to get my money and my blood back from her, like from a dog's teeth! You can believe me! But how can you torment me with 'five and a half'!"

The whole scene was so unpleasant for our Rachel that she took the coral beads from her throat and hid them deep, deep down in a chest, intending never to wear them again as long as she lived. The thing that annoyed our Rachel most was that Moyshe-Mendel was so absorbed in fighting with his mother over the beads that he didn't even come over to Rachel as he should have done, as is right and proper, to say: "Wear them in good health." They had led her around by the hand all day and peered at her necklace as if inspecting a cow, everyone stepped over to her, pushed up her head, touched the beads—and ignored her completely.... Rachel, who was not nasty or bad-tempered by nature, was furious at everybody all day long, and especially at Moyshe-Mendel. This fine fellow thoroughly enjoyed his lunch and then trotted off to synagogue. And since there was a party there that evening to celebrate the completion of the study of a talmudic tractate, Moyshe-Mendel remained from after evening prayers until dawn, as he did quite often.

155

Rachel felt altogether ill and angry. Her face blazed like an infernal fire, her head was splitting, her ears were buzzing and whistling. She didn't understand what was wrong with her.... At suppertime, she couldn't eat a bite. Naturally, Dvosse-Malke nagged her to eat more, to drink more—but it was no use. Rachel went to her room with red eyes, quickly undressed, lay down in her bed, and then all at once, a flood of tears burst from her eyes—hot, burning tears, and so many, so many.

A HARD NIGHT

Why did Rachel weep? She didn't know why herself, and she didn't even feel she was weeping. For a long time, her heart had been heavy, very heavy, and suddenly it was soaked through, it overflowed, it poured out its tears. Rachel, as we've already said, felt that she was lonesome, that she was lacking something, that something was missing, but what it was she didn't know and couldn't know. Rachel knew perfectly well that her parents had married her off, gotten her off their backs. The term "off their backs" is enough to show how separated people get: children from parents and parents from children. The term "off their backs" can often be heard among us Jews, in almost every family. The term "off their backs" is a terrible shame, an insult to our entire nation, which boasts of being so compassionate.... Most of all, Rachel was annoyed by Moyshe-Mendel, by his behavior and his actions towards her. Rachel understood what part she played for her gem of a husband with her beauty and kindness, with her virtue and loyalty. Rachel saw what she meant to him....

And lately, Rachel had been especially upset, confused, bewildered. What she had endured with Stempeniu was no trifle. Rachel, pious Rachel, who had never swerved from her Jewish way of life by even a gnat's eyelash, who had never transgressed even the most insignificant rule of all the laws for Jewish women, Rachel, a Jewish wife immersed in the Yiddish Bible—thinking about another man, receiving a letter from him, meeting with him—and she didn't resist. On the contrary, she felt so drawn to him, not with a bad thought, God forbid, but just like that, to see him and hear him play the violin.

Oh, his music, his music! Rachel would have been willing to give up food and sleep forever so long as she could hear Stempeniu, hear him and...see him! His eyes, when they gazed they warmed, they caressed, they pampered.... Oh, his eyes!

Rachel grabbed her head with both hands and listened to her temples beating, her heart beating, and her soul yearned, yearned. She didn't know what was happening to her. She pulled the quilt up over her head and saw her old friend Haia-Etel, may she rest in peace. Rachel remembered that story of Haia-Etel and Benjamin, and a frost ran through her body. She pushed the quilt away and suddenly she heard a very familiar melody, a familiar sound of a familiar violin. Rachel thought she was imagining it, but the music came nearer and nearer; it was the kind of music they play to escort the in-laws home after a wedding. Rachel had already heard and recognized what was being played, she also realized that it was Stempeniu playing away on the violin, and she had no doubts that it was Stempeniu accompanying the in-laws home after the wedding dinner. But what was he doing there? There was no wedding on this street tonight and there were no in-laws here! What could it mean? But the drum and the cymbal came nearer and nearer. The whole band was playing with a vengeance, but more clearly than anything else she could hear Stempeniu's violin, for its sweet melody, its tender song were subduing all the other instruments.

Rachel couldn't lie still. She leaped out of bed, strode over to the window, opened it, and leaned way, way out.

Rachel hadn't seen such a night for a long time. The moon was strolling in the middle of the sky and it was surrounded by millions of stars—diamonds twinkling and glistening. The air was warm, soft, and fresh. No breeze whatsoever, so that the high poplars looming in the big Monastery Garden stood tall and erect like sentries on guard. No leaf stirred. But seldom, very seldom, a lovely scent of fragrant herbs came wafting from there, and it was very welcome in Mazepevke, which had a different smell during this day....

And this wonderful night was so fitting for our lovely Rachel, pure, virtuous, beautiful Rachel with her long, white throat, and the rich blond hair lying scattered upon it. (Ah, could Rachel have thought at such time that the moon and the author of this novel could see her own hair, without the marriage wig?) Her eyes were no less blue or pure than the pure, blue heavens, and her lovely, radiant face was no less beautiful than the lovely, radiant night.

But Rachel's thoughts were elsewhere: Her mind was where the strange music could be heard and her heart was where Stempeniu's violin was.

The musicians were playing so sadly, as though they had only just buried someone, put him in the ground. For us, a joyous occasion comes out as weeping, and fun and pleasure make us shed tears....Even gloomier was the music at midnight, when all the world was sound asleep and only a tiny group of Jews were celebrating with a dismal tune as they came home from the wedding dinner with lowered heads: What was it? Had parents gotten a child off their backs—please excuse me—taken care of a child, for goodness' sake—well, all right....In this quiet, lovely summer night, you could hear Stempeniu's violin more clearly than ever, it grieved the heart, it drew the soul, it sapped your life's blood—and Rachel stood half naked at the window, listening. She wanted to flee from there, close the window and flee, but she was shackled to the spot as if in irons, as if held by a magnet. She gazed and she listened so earnestly as though she weren't hearing his violin, as though she could hear him talking to her, pleading, begging, weeping....And not only Rachel was listening to those beautiful melodies from Stempeniu's violin in the radiant summer night: The moon and the stars, the soft, fresh air, all nature and all her creatures awoke from their slumber and got up for a moment to find out what the strange singing was at midnight, what those sounds were at midnight.

The nocturnal chorister, the tardy nightingale in Monastery garden, upon hearing that music, rolled up his sleeves and tried to show off his prowess as he likes to do; but now, in late summer, he couldn't sing more beautifully than Stempeniu's violin, for the poor bird had lost his voice at the end of spring, and all that remained was a screech, the kind that rises from a cantor's throat after the Days of Awe—if you'll forgive the blasphemous comparison....The rooster, that screamer, heard the playing of the musicians and, thinking it was already dawn, stepped down from his perch, flapped his wings, mumbled his morning prayers, let out his usual cockadoodledoo with a cantorial cantillation, and then went back to his rest, furious that he had been bothered for nothing....Even the dogs, the hounds, far away, on Monastery Street, at first began barking and howling, as is their custom, upon hearing the Jewish musicians in the middle of the night, and then they fell silent and looked for places to sleep. Even the cow,

158

Dvosse-Malke's chestnut cow, stopped chewing her cud near the house, perked up her ears, and let out a deep moan from her belly, like a sinful Jew. And the neighbor's two goats got so excited that they sprang up from the ground and changed places, menacing each other with their horns. In short, all things and creatures came alive, showing that they could hear the music in the warm silent, radiant, magical summer night.

At the same time, our virtuous Rachel was standing at the window as though shackled in irons. She stood there, riveted, wonderstruck, in utter confusion. "Oh, what a night! Oh God, what a night this is!" She stood there, absorbing it with all her senses. She swallowed mouthfuls of the fresh air. She was totally spellbound. She gazed at the blue sky and remembered those summer nights when she was a girl, sitting in front of the house, gazing up at the white moonbeams while playing jacks and singing that old song:

> *The moon is shining through the night,*
> *And Pearl is sitting by the door,*
> *Sighing and moaning through the night,*
> *Alas, her heart is so sore!*
> *Sighing and moaning through the night,*
> *Alas, her heart is so sore!*

She had sung the song in those bygone days, never understanding it, and now she did understand it, not fully, but she understood something and felt it. She felt that something was tugging at her, pulling her outside, into the open air. She felt hemmed in here, hot and ill, ill!...Rachel remembered another song that she used to sing as a girl, during summers, outside by the door.

> *I stand on the shore*
> *And I can't come to you,*
> *Oh you call me from afar—*
> *But I can't swim to you.*
> *Oh, you call me from afar,*
> *But I can't swim to you!*

"From afar?" But he was so close now! He was right there, Stempeniu, with his violin, his long hair, his black, burning, fiery eyes, which were always staring at her and warming her with their glow, with their fire. And at that moment, she yearned to be near him forever, to be near him and listen to him playing forever, and see his beautiful eyes forever.... But there was one thing Rachel didn't understand: How had he come here, Stempeniu, at midnight, with his violin?

How had Stempeniu come here with the in-laws? She simply couldn't understand, no matter how hard she thought about it. Rachel remembered that there had been a wedding somewhere near the synagogue. How had the in-laws gotten here? She understood the mystery only when she saw them very close by, almost at her house, the musicians and the in-laws. She solved the riddle only when she saw Stempeniu halting right at her house, right next to her window, and starting to play more freshly, more ardently. Now Rachel understood what Stempeniu had done: He had taken along the whole crew, all the in-laws, all the guests, from a dozen streets away, past her window, and for whom? At first, it was very pleasurable for her, and her heart was so joyful that it almost sprang from her breast. And willy-nilly, Rachel burst into such merry laughter that she was frightened by her own voice, she looked at herself standing there half-naked, her throat bare, without her marriage wig—and she hastily jumped away from the window, slammed it shut, and threw herself into the bed.

"Oh God, oh God!" thought Rachel. "The things you can do if you don't notice where you are! Standing naked in the middle of the night, at the window, in front of a crowd of men, thinking about such vain, silly things, having such ugly thoughts about someone like Stempeniu.... And Stempeniu—leading a whole congregation of Jews along a dozen streets—for what, for whom? It takes a lot of nerve to do a thing like that!... Where does he get such nerve?... I have to ask him. He has to stop doing that! He's making me miserable!... I have to have it out with him once and for all. What's that old saying: 'It's better to let off steam right away!'... He tells me a fairy-tale: Lovey-dovey! 'Very respectable I swear, Saturday night,' he says, 'on Monastery Street,' that's where he'll make his intentions clear.... I wish it were Saturday night already so I could hear what it's all about. Of course I'll go, why should I be scared? Scared of whom? Jews should only be scared of God!... It's a disaster, it's an evil spell.... There are good reasons why people tell all those stories.... But what does he want from me, what does he want? And who's to blame if not me? You mustn't give someone else even your little finger.... If Moyshe-Mendel were here now, I'd tell him everything. But where is he? Does he ever listen to me? What does he care if I'm miserable, if

I'm in agony?... Oh, I ought to pray. It's no good not praying!...

"For Thy Redemption I hope, oh Lord,
I hope, oh Lord, for Thy Redemption,
Oh Lord, for Thy Redemption I hope."

Rachel buried herself deep, deep into the pillows, covered herself up with the quilt so as not to hear the musicians, and prayed out loud: "For Thy Redemption I hope, oh Lord." But they came sneaking in through the window, the sweet songs of Stempeniu's violin, growing softer and fainter and farther away. And Rachel prayed:

"For Thy Redemption....
I hope... for Thy Redemption....
... I hope...."

And Rachel fell asleep.

Rachel fell asleep and she dreamt that Stempeniu was putting a string of coral around her neck.... on one side stood her father-in-law in his prayer shawl and prayer thongs, and Freydel was hitting and smacking him for all she was worth.... Moyshe-Mendel was dead-drunk, he was straddling a poker, making crazy faces, and Stempeniu was putting a string of coral around her neck.... On the other side stood Haia-Etel in her Sabbath best, decked out like a princess, smiling so joyously, so sweetly, and lighting many candles.

"What are you doing, Haia-Etel?" asked Rachel. "Why are you lighting so many candles?"

"How can you ask," Haia-Etel answered, laughing. "It's the Eve of Sabbath, it's time to light the candles and say the blessing!...."

Rachel looked at the candles burning brightly and shining, and Stempeniu was putting a string of coral around her neck.... He stood next to her, so close that she could hear him breathing. He stood there gazing straight into her eyes, warming her with his stare. Rachel was happy, she laughed and sang, and Stempeniu was putting a string of coral around her neck.

Suddenly, the candles went out. Haia-Etel and everyone and everything vanished. It was pitch-black and icy cold, like a cellar, like a grave.... The wind whistled and blasted, and a singing could be heard, a gloomy singing: a violin was playing, once again a familiar violin. Stempeniu's violin. Stempeniu himself wasn't there, but his violin could be heard, yet it was so sad, so gloomy, like the *ne'ilah,* the last prayer on Yom Kippur. And there was the sound of weeping and sobbing. It was Haia-Etel crying for her youth, which had sped by so quickly, like a dream, crying for her darling Benjamin, who had left her for someone else, forgetting Haia-Etel, forgetting....

"Oh, Mama!" screamed Rachel and woke up, turned over on her other side, fell asleep, and dreamt again, all kinds of dreams. She was bewildered all night long, and she thought she could feel Stempeniu next to her, putting a string of coral around her neck.... Then Haia-Etel returned with black candles, crying, mourning, reading prayers out loud: "Almighty Father in heaven, powerful God, Lord of all lords, King of all kings, who art only God from eternity to eternity! May our ardent prayers reach Thee and be granted by Thee. Hear the prayers of the pure souls who stand before Thy Throne of Glory and plead to Thee on our behalf and for the living on the earth, who are as full of sins as a pomegranate is full of seeds, and our forefathers...."

Haia-Etel spoke the prayers out loud. She wept, she grieved, she lamented—and she disappeared.

A FIRE IS KINDLED

In the town of Mazepevke, there is a monastery, which, they say, was built by Mazepa. A high, white stone wall surrounds the monastery on all four sides and occupies three-quarters of the town. On one side of the wall, there are shops in niches, and on the other side, deep cellars, where, they say, the highwaymen hid all their weapons, and where apples and all kinds of goods are now stored. The third side of the wall is overgrown with brambles and guarded by tall poplars and other trees, beyond the wall, in the big Monastery Garden. The fourth side of the wall is bare and smooth, crumbling in many spots and losing clay and bricks, so that for many years it's been in need of repair. Facing it there are houses and cabins, yards and patches, both Jewish and Christian, and the narrow street running between the bare wall of the monastery and the houses is called Monastery Street.

There, on Monastery Street, in a corner where the trees begin, our lovers had their first rendezvous: Rachel and Stempeniu.

Readers, who are used to "highly interesting" modern romances, have suffered enough from this novel, which has had no tearful scenes, no assignation. No one has shot himself, no one has poisoned himself, we have met no counts or marquis. We keep seeing only ordinary people, musicians and everyday Jewish women. These readers must be looking forward to Saturday night, they are waiting for a piquant and titillating scene on Monastery Street.... But I have to say in advance that their expectations are useless. There won't be any piquant and titillating scenes because our Rachel hasn't come here like a debauched woman hurrying to kiss her lover in the darkness, heaven forfend! Rachel only wanted to ask him how he, Stempeniu the Musician, had the nerve, the chutzpah, to write a letter to her, Isaak-Naphtali's daughter-in-law, Moyshe-mendel's wife, and such a letter to boot!...

"I have to give him a piece of my mind!" she thought to herself. "I have to make it clear to him once and for all! What's the old saying?—'It's better to let off steam right away....'"

This thought did not come to her suddenly. Rachel had had a whole week's time and even more, all day Saturday, to think it over and, oh me, oh my, what things she had thought in that one day! What a terrible struggle she had had with her temptation.... No, the word "Temptation" isn't proper here at all. How did she, a Jewish wife, who had never read novels and never known about romances, except for the story that her friend Haia-Etel had told her (may she rest in peace), the story we talked about earlier—how did Rachel come to feel temptation, love? Nonsense! If she were still unmarried, it would be different. She'd be—how can we put it?—a free bird, her hair still uncovered, an independent person. But she was a young wife, and an extremely pious wife at that, and of an excellent family! She was enraged at herself, a blazing fire, and she could find no rest. First she lay down on her bed, but then she felt all stirred up like a feverish invalid, who feels sick at heart and bored to death—he only wants to dash out into the world.... Rachel got up and went over to the *Tsene Rene*, the Yiddish Bible version for women. She opened up in the middle of Genesis and— how odd! Her eyes fixed on the verses: "And Dinah the daughter of Leah which she bare unto Jacob, went out to see the daughters of the land. And when Shechem the son of Hamor the Hivite... saw her, he took her, and lay with her, and defiled her. And his soul clave unto Dinah. Now the Bkhai writes 'Shechem talked her into it....'"

Rachel gazed at her *Tsene Rene,* which her mother-in-law had given her when she was still engaged, and little by little she began forgetting that she was sitting with the Bible, and her thoughts wafted over to him, to Stempeniu, to Monastery Street, under the trees, where he had promised to wait for her.... And no sooner did Stempeniu enter her thoughts than she felt drawn to him, like a magnet, and she didn't understand what was happening.

"I only want to ask him what he wants from me and why he's bothering me."

And now Rachel remembered her friend Haia-Etel, may she rest in peace, and the way she had suffered because of her Benjamin.... But Haia-Etel was related to Benjamin and she was only a girl, while she, Rachel, was a married woman, a "matron" (oh dear, what a harsh word for a Jewish woman). And he—who was he? A musician! What business did he have with her? Who did he think he was anyway writing letters to her! That no-account fiddler! That brazen good-for-nothing!

"Come hell or high water," she decided. "Come hell or high water, I have to tell him. Why should I be afraid of him? I'll meet him, I'll go over there, it won't matter—nobody'll see me. I'll just dash over for a minute, it's not far, it's just across the way...."

And Rachel looked though the open window into Monastery Street and saw the trees, the high poplars, standing proudly, and she heard the birds singing so beautifully from the garden. And her thoughts wafted over to the place where she would see him and talk to him privately, within an hour or even less. And she felt her heart pounding and struggling and (the truth, we have to tell the truth!) the minutes were long for her—she could hardly wait, if only it were night. Her father-in-law and her husband would come back from synagogue and perform the ceremony closing the Sabbath, her mother-in-law would change her clothes and start carrying on about the samovar and the borsht for the final Sabbath meal—and that's when Rachel would slip into her shawl and walk slowly, towards the door, step outside, just as if she were going for a stroll—who would take a second look at her? Until she came there, where.... oh, her body trembled, her cheeks burned, and her heart—oh, her heart! it practically leaped out of her body, and she felt more and more drawn to that place, and that was all she could think about. She saw nothing before her eyes, only the trees of Monastery Garden, only Stempeniu with his blazing eyes. She heard nothing, only the lovely singing of the birds in the garden, and that godlike playing of—Stempeniu. At this point, Rachel was totally absorbed in one thought—to get there, to Stempeniu, be there, with Stempeniu, and nothing in the world could have held her back....

THE FIRE BURNS AND THEN GOES OUT

And as for Stempeniu, no sooner was it night than he sent his band out to the *zmires,* the traditional pre-wedding party, where the girls get together with the bride and dance. Then he took the violin under his arm so that Freydel would think he was going to the wedding. But once he left the house, he handed the instrument to Makhtshi and then he sped to Monastery Street, and he paced up and down in the shade of the trees, stopping every minute to see if Rachel was coming, beautiful Rachel. He never doubted for an instant that she would come. His heart told him she would. He had seen it in her eyes when they had met that day, the day she was trying on the coral necklace.

And Stempeniu was not mistaken. Scarcely had fifteen minutes gone by when he caught sight of a woman across the street, floating towards him with a white shawl on her head. She was walking very quickly, glancing around on all sides. The white shawl was pulled down almost over her eyes, and her hands were trembling, her teeth chattering, her heart pounding—her entire body shaking. She took a hard look, she halted, she spotted Stempeniu and moved towards him, saying:

"How dare you, sir—let me ask you—"

"Don't use the polite form with me, Rachel, use the familiar form," replied Stempeniu, taking hold of both her hands and staring deep into her eyes. In his eyes, Rachel saw the same glow as in the stars that were gazing down from the dark-blue sky of the beautiful summer night.... All the Jews in Mazepevke were concluding the Sabbath, chanting the praises of the prophet Elijah, as was customary, sighing and brooding, worrying about work and business, wishing they could have the luck of the pious man who had met Elijah and greeted him and been greeted by him. The women of Mazepevke removed the veils from their heads, took off their Sabbath garments, their jewelry, and set about their everyday work. In a word, Mazepevke was busy ushering out the dear and holy Sabbath—and it never occurred to anyone that at this very moment, Rachel, the daughter-in-law of Dvosse-Malke, was standing with Stempeniu the Musician on Monastery Street, and that the two of them were talking about things that were anything but Jewish....

Only the blue heavens, the bright stars, which were peering down with their brilliance, only the high poplars in the monastery, only the nocturnal birds in the huge garden, calling to one another in their language—only they could hear and see what was happening; only they knew that on this lovely, magical night, under the monastery trees, in the Christian street—Rachel was standing right next to Stempeniu, in such a different state that she completely forgot who she was and what she was. Here, amid the lovely splendors of nature, Rachel felt as she had never felt in her life. The fear, which had stalked her all the way here, suddenly left her, and she felt as if she grown wings and were as free as a bird and could fly, fly.... Stempeniu moved closer to her and placed his hands on her shoulders. Rachel shuddered. She wanted to step away but, instead, she looked at Stempeniu, and tears rolled down from her radiant blue eyes.

"Why are you crying, Rachel?" asked Stempeniu, wiping her tears away with his hands.

"Ah, Stempeniu, I feel so good here, next to...you..." (she shifted to the familiar form) "next to you, Stempeniu! Why am I...? Why can't I be...?"

"Mine? Is that what you want to say? You *are* mine, Rachel, you *are* mine!"

"What do you mean I'm yours, Stempeniu? How can that be?"

"You're mine, my beloved, do you understand, because I'm yours forever, for all time, until the dark grave, I'm yours till death, my darling, my life!"

"Benjamin said the same thing, he swore—and then in the end...."

"Who's Benjamin?" asked Stempeniu, amazed, peering into Rachel's eyes the way you look at a child when it says something utterly silly. "Who are you talking about, my darling?"

"Benjamin, Haia-Etel's cousin. My friend Haia-Etel was an orphan and she had a cousin named Benjamin, and when they were very young, they swore they would get married, he promised her, he swore an oath on his holy word of honor—and in the end, oh, it was so ugly for her, poor Haia-Etel, she died a long time ago, God rest her soul, may she forgive me.... But she was crazy about Benjamin, she worshiped the ground he walked on. She told me so herself.... I can see her now, I can see her by the window, with me singing songs to her, and she's crying and she keeps saying: 'Oh, don't believe them, you mustn't believe what men tell you!...'"

Rachel told about her friend Haia-Etel the orphan, and Stempeniu kissed Rachel's hands, caressed her, looked into her eyes—and Rachel kept talking about Haia-Etel and how she passed away, how she went out like a candle, out of love for her dear Benjamin....

Haia-Etel had been dead for several years, but Rachel remembered her well. She often dreamt about her. Now she felt as if Haia-Etel were standing on the other side of the wall, wearing a shroud and gazing over at Rachel and beckoning to her, pointing at Stempeniu and shaking her head as though to say: "What are you doing?..."

"What's the use, Rachel my darling, what's the use of talking and remembering such things, especially at night? Just look at me with your bright, lovely eyes, oh the way they shine and glow like two beautiful diamo—"

Stempeniu hadn't even uttered the last word when Rachel wrested herself loose from his hands with such force that Stempeniu was terrified of her.

"For God's sake, Rachel, what's wrong?"

He tried to take hold of her again, but she wouldn't let him. She trembled and whispered: "Do you see her? She's over there! She's standing there!... She's looking at us, at us...."

"Who's standing there? Who's looking at us? What are you talking about, Rachel? My darling, come to me, take my hand...."

"Oh! Leave me alone, Stempeniu, leave me alone." She was using the polite form again. "Can't you see, something white is standing there? Oh, it's her, it's Haia-Etel! Haia-Etel!... Oh, leave me alone, leave me alone!... How dare you, how dare you!... Good night to you! Good night!..."

And Rachel vanished in the shade of the trees. Stempeniu saw only the ends of the white shawl fluttering in the wind, looking like two white pinions. That is how a good angel flees, that is how a good dream disappears....

Oh, you Jewish woman, you showed your virtue there and your purity. Oh, Jewish wife! You showed all your fidelity there, all your devotion!

Upon coming home, Rachel wanted to tell everyone, shout to everyone, where she had been and whom she had met. But she found the entire household sitting around a table with several guests, in front of a huge samovar, and they were all engrossed in talking shop, as Jews usually do, gathering somewhere on Saturday night when the Sabbath is over. After resting for twenty-four hours, you chat a little about business, about the next day's fair, and about various political matters.

"I'm not going to have a booth at the fair," said a fat little man with a dry-goods store. "The fairs can go to hell! I'm fed up with them! Troubles and headaches—that's all you can get out of a fair!"

"Why do you say that?" exclaimed Dvosse-Malke, her hands folded on her chest. "I don't understand why you're so down on fairs, Yudel. Just last week, Lord preserve us, you made a bundle— may it happen to all Jews. Why, you were raking in money all day long!"

"All you talk about is raking in money!" cried Isaak-Naphtali, not looking at his wife as he worked the beads on an abacus.

"And I wouldn't want a worse fair than last Sunday," cried Moyshe-Mendel, checking the accounts. "How can you deny it? I don't understand."

"That's the point," said Yudel, "you just don't want to believe anyone else. When you see ten peasants crowding in and practically carrying away my booth, you call that 'raking in money' and you start resenting it."

"You know what, Yudel?" exclaimed a cross-eyed young man. "Why don't we forget about the county fair. Tomorrow is another day, and we'll have our fill of it then. Let's talk about something else."

And they began talking about important matters: citrons for the Feast of Tabernacles, synagogue problems, and of course war. Everyone talked, everyone smoked, the samovar boiled and steamed and the house was filled with fumes. The oven was hot: borsht and goose breasts were cooking for the last Sabbath meal.

"Where've you been, Rachel?" Dvosse-Malke asked her daughter-in-law.

"Right there...on Monastery Street."

"What's it like outside? Nice weather? God preserve the weather for all fairs.... What's wrong, dear, you're so pale, do you have a headache? Maybe you should lie down a bit."

At these words, everyone turned around and looked at Rachel's wan face, and it was unanimously decided that she was groggy from the samovar's fumes. Rachel went to her room to lie down, and now the company began talking about fumes and how fumes were no laughing matter, they might seem like nothing, why, they were only smoke—but they could kill a person just like that. And one man related that once, in his grandfather's home—may he rest in peace—the entire household was practically wiped out by fumes. And someone else told a lovely story about how his uncle's entire family was practically poisoned by a kind of fish known as a "sea eel," and they were just barely saved from death. Another man told a very lovely story about a demon, a poltergeist, a wandering ghost, and so on and on...until they began talking about death.

"Whatever people talk about, in the end they talk about death!" someone exclaimed.

"'Elijah the Prophet'—we ought to have a look—'Elijah of Tishbi'—what's my wife doing?—'Elijah of Gilead.'..." Moyshe-Mendel suddenly murmured, while singing the "Elijahs" of the Sabbath night. He got up from the table and went to look in on Rachel.

RACHEL GOES BACK TO
THE STRAIGHT AND NARROW PATH

"Help! Help!" the company heard a shout from the side room, and they all dashed in and saw Rachel stretched out on the bed, her head thrown back, and Moyshe-Mendel standing next to her, scared out of his wits.

"What's wrong? What's happening? Fainted? Water! Hurry!"

"Water! Water!" everyone shouted and no one moved.

"Oh, godamn it all!" screamed Dvosse-Malke and got a dipper of water, took a mouthful, and sprayed it on Rachel's face, which was as dead as a tomb.

"Get the doctor!" screamed Moyshe-Mendel in a strange voice.

"The doctor! The doctor!" they all screamed, looking at one another.

"Tie her hands with a handkerchief and squeeze her nose!"

"Her nose! Her nose!" they all screamed and stood where they were.

"That's right, Dvosse-Malke, harder, harder!" the guests spurred her on as she worked with might and main, rubbing, squeezing, pouring water, pulling eyelids—until finally they revived Rachel from her faint and got her to sit up. Rachel looked around groggily and then asked: "Where am I? I'm so hot. so hot!..."

"Move away, everybody, give her air!" said Dvosse-Malke and sent the whole company into the living room, while she and Moyshe-Mendel stayed with Rachel, whose eyes were fixed on Moyshe-Mendel.

"What's wrong, daughter, what happened?" the mother-in-law asked.

"What is it, Rachel?" asked Moyshe-Mendel, leaning over her.

"Please ask your mother to leave," Rachel answered softly.

"Mama, please step outside for a moment," said Moyshe-Mendel. He accompanied his mother out of the room and then returned to Rachel's bed.

"Tell me what's wrong," Moyshe-Mendel asked her for the first time with deep love.

"Oh, Moyshe-Mendel, swear you won't tell anybody.... Swear it'll remain our secret.... Promise you'll forgive me for what I've done to you.... If Haia-Etel, Lord rest her soul, hadn't warned me.... Oh, if it hadn't been for Haia-Etel.... Oh, Moyshe-Mendel, my darling!"

"Just listen to what you're saying, Rachel. You're raving! What do you mean, Haia-Etel?"

"My friend Haia-Etel, may she rest in peace. Haia-Etel the orphan, she's been in the True World for a long time. I've dreamt about her several times. But today, now.... Ah, Moyshe-Mendel, bend over to me, nearer, nearer.... That's right, I'm scared.... I'm sorry for what I've done, oh, how sorry I am!"

And Rachel moved closer to Moyshe-Mendel until she was lying in his arms. The room was dark. Only a single ray of light entered from the door to the living room, and Rachel and Moyshe-Mendel could hardly see each other. Their eyes met and a

170

tiny fire kindled in them, the kind of fire you see when people fall happily in love for the first time, when the heart and not the tongue does all the talking, when people converse with their eyes and not their lips.

"Tell me, Moyshe-Mendel my darling, do you really care for me?"

"How can you ask?" Moyshe-Mendel replied. "You're right in my heart like a—I don't know like what...."

Moyshe-Mendel had no other way of expressing his love for Rachel. But we can believe that he meant it with all his heart, seriously—and perhaps more seriously than the fine fellow who has a greater knack for uttering his feelings in words.

But let's leave them, the happy couple, there in the half-darkened room, where, a year after the wedding, they had their first chance to have a heart-to-heart talk, as they sat there like doves. Things that had been hidden deep down for an entire year suddenly came to the surface like trees on water.

Once Rachel felt a little better, Moyshe-Mendel sat next to her, softly crooning the "Elijahs" under his breath.

"Elijah the Prophet ... Elijah of Tishbi ... Elijah of Gilead ...."

And Rachel said to him:

"I want to ask you to do something for me, Moyshe-Mendel. Promise you'll do it."

"Well? What is it? Tell me, Rachel, I'll do anything you want me to."

"I think we've lived with your family long enough. You're no longer a student, we've got a little money tucked away, thank goodness—why don't we move to a big city, Yehupets. Once I'm there, among my friends and relatives, and with you—I'll feel as fine as ever. We'll be alone. It's time we stopped living off your family, honestly, I'm so sick and tired of it that I can't enjoy anything. We're like strangers with your family, absolute strangers...."

Moyshe-Mendel sat there, gazing in surprise at Rachel. Then he began rocking and swaying like before, singing his "Elijahs."

"Okay, very good, 'angry man,' it's fine with me. 'Elijah the Prophet'...this very week!"

"You'll do it for me, Moyshe-Mendel, won't you?" Rachel said to him with deep love. "We'll be on our own, I'll have my own household, and I'll take care of you like the apple of my eye. Ah, Moyshe-Mendel, you're usually so absent-minded that you never say a kind word! But today you're so different, so different...."

"Elijah the Prophet...." crooned Moyshe-Mendel softly, "Elijah of Tishbi... Elijah of Gilead...."

And in the living room, the men were having a different kind of conversation: they were trying to figure out why Isaak-Naphtali's daughter-in-law had suddenly fainted. One man said it was an evil eye, another concluded the opposite, she'd been caught in a draft, and the third one, an elderly Jew with married children, had his own explanation:

"Believe me, I've got three daughters-in-law, I know a thing or two about such matters, I tell you, she's having 'whims.' Isaak-Naphtali, get set for cakes and vodka or a circumcision. Mazel-tov, Dvosse-Malke! Your daughter-in-law—well, well, she'll be all right! Why are you so embarrassed, Dvosse-Malke? Don't worry, it's per-fectly kosher.... Jews do it all the time...."

Dvosse-Malke was simply melting with delight, she'd been anxiously looking forward to this for a long time.

"Well, well!" she said, pretending to be annoyed. "Cut it out— you and your jokes! I'd better see how the borsht is doing. It's tak-ing longer than usual!..."

A YEAR LATER

"A dull story!" says the reader, apparently quite dissatisfied, for he's been raised on those modern romances, where people hang them-selves and drown themselves, poison themselves and shoot them-selves, or where a heder teacher becomes a count, a serving maid becomes a princess, and a *belfer* (school assistant) becomes—a dragon. Now can I help it if we have no counts or princesses? We have only ordinary Jewish men and women, Jewish girls and Jewish musicians.... But why bother with justifications? By now, the reader can say what he likes. I've brought him this far, and he'll certainly go further with me, he'll want to know what happens in the end and what becomes of Rachel, and what becomes of Stempeniu.

We will now skip a year (what is one year in a human life?) and we will visit Isaak-Naphtali's home for the dinner concluding the Sabbath. And there we find the same people as a year ago, and hear the same conversations as a year ago, with not a hair changed.

And everyone keeps talking about the fair, business, profits, children—until the conversation turns to Moyshe-Mendel and Rachel, who live in Yehupets now.

"Dvosse-Malke, show us the letter from the kids in Yehupets," Isaak-Naphtali cried to his wife. "Here, read it Yudel."

"Let him read it!" said Yudel, pointing to the cross-eyed young man.

The cross-eyed man took the letter and read it fluently; the salutation was in Hebrew:

> Peace and all good wishes to my beloved Father, the wise, learned, enlightened, and eminent gentleman, the highly esteemed Lord Isaak-Naphtali, son of Moses-Joseph, may he rest in peace. And to my highly honored and pious Mother—

"Stop that!" they all shouted. "Stop that! That's all rhetoric, for God's sake, kid stuff, it's their foolishness! Read the rest, on the other side!"

The cross-eyed man turned the letter over and continued reading its mixture of Yiddish, Hebrew and Russian:

> And since you have asked me, Dear Father, to tell you about business and commerce here in Yehupets, I must inform you—

"Oh, so that's what it means!" the company cried happily. "Keep reading, go on!"

> I must inform you that dry goods do particularly well here as does haberdashery, though haberdashery does not do as well as dry goods. And groceries likewise do not do badly, no worse than in Mazepevke. Woolens are worth their weight in gold. Sugar, flour, and bran are also a business here, they are exported, and Jews earn tidy sums thereby. In short, Yehupets is a blessed land, the city itself is enormous and worth a visit. It is altogether another world here in Yehupets, you can meet Jews here of whom you would never have dreamt that they were Jews. Paper is also a business here, everything is business here. And Jews frequent the stock exchange, buying and selling all kinds of stocks, and brokers earn money galore.
>
> And my beloved spouse Rachel sends you all her fondest greetings. She writes to you herself below. May the Good Lord grant that we hear good news from you—amen. I must also inform you that the store which I rented is located right on Alexandrovsky Street, and the money I take in is not at all bad, praised be the Lord. My beloved spouse Rachel, long may she live, has already mastered the trade and can already talk to the customers. But I go and buy at

the fairs myself. I have credit with merchants in Moscow and Lodz. Dealing with Moscow is not difficult, Moscow sells with a conscience and likes Jewish clients. Even when a businessman goes bankrupt, Moscow helps him out and will not let him fall.

Dwellings are extremely expensive here. For two alcoves and a kitchen— one hundred seventy-five rubles a year, not including wood and water, and everything costs a fortune here. Jews are mostly agents and brokers and there are an enormous number of these Jewish agents and brokers here, and a Jew can thereby earn a respectable ruble. In short, Yehupets is a place to earn one's living. May God give us health and strength and grant that we hear the same from you, which I wish you, I your son, who wishes you peace and happiness in your lives,

Moyshe-Mendel

son of the highly esteemed Isaak-Naphtali of Mazepevke.

My very best to my dear uncle and my dear aunt with all their offspring and their household.

My very best to Reb Yudel with all his offspring and his household.

My very best to the highly esteemed Reb Simkhe-Hersh with all his offspring and his household.

My very best to the highly esteemed Reb Dov-Ber with all his offspring and his household.

My very best to Stisye-Beyle with all her offspring and her household.

Rachel's letter followed, in a Germanicized Yiddish:

I too send greetings to my highly esteemed father-in-law and my dear mother-in-law. I hope you are well. I am in good health, may God preserve me. Also my Yossele greets you and thanks his dear grandmother for the blouse many times. He promises you that God will give life for that and, God willing, in three or four years he will begin going to heder and, God willing, he will learn eagerly and, God willing, he will be a good Jew, may God grant him a long life, amen. Dear father-in-law, if you could make Yossele a skullcap and a pair of woolen socks, I would be very thankful, for I am very busy in the store, and I do not want to hire a nurse for Yossele, it would not be right. I have only taken on a girl and I pay her four rubles out of my household money, she looks after the baby and pastures the cow—you should see the cow I bought! She gives a whole gallon of milk, excellent milk, and I get cheese and butter from her, thank the Lord. But my dear Moyshe-Mendel has suddenly started hating dairy products. Give him a good talking-to, please, he doesn't take care of himself at all! Yossele is bawling his head off now, the poor thing wants to eat—may I hunger in his place! I will conclude my letter, please send heartiest greetings to all our friends and relatives and please write to us, God willing, and I remain your devoted and well-wishing daughter-in-law, Rachel.

"Well," said Fat Beryl. "My own children should do no worse!"

"You're sinning, Dvosse-Malke, you're sinning!" said Yudel. "I swear, you're sinning!"

"Of course, thank the Good Lord, they're all doing well—knock on wood. But I miss her so much—I can't forget her, Yudel, I can't forget her."

And Dvosse-Malke started listing all her daughter-in-law's virtues and all her manners and showed him why she couldn't forget her. Everyone talked, they talked about Yehupets and about business in Yehupets. Then they poured themselves drinks, they toasted, *l'chaim,* holding the cups for a long time, and they wished one another all the luck in the world, and glad tidings for all Jews and salvations and consolations. But then the borsht came to the table, spreading a marvelous fragrance through the house, and the company became merry. They were absorbed in their conversations and forgot all about Moyshe-Mendel and Rachel and the city of Yehupets and all of them together.

STEMPENIU HAS A TRUE TASTE OF HELL

But one person could not forget beautiful Rachel. The reader can guess that we are talking about Stempeniu.

Yes indeed, Stempeniu. Who can possibly depict his great sorrows? Who can feel his heart and grasp his great chagrin?

"How awful!" thought Stempeniu. "How miserable!" thought Stempeniu. "She didn't even remember me, she didn't even say a word, she didn't dash off two lines to me, for politeness' sake: 'So long, I'm leaving!' Dammit, it's awful."

Never had anything like this happened to Stempeniu, although any number and all kinds of things had indeed happened to him, and once—some pretty awful things that ended pretty badly, as we mentioned earlier. Yet he would never have dreamt of such a setback, such a rebuff as he'd gotten from Rachel. Stempeniu, who was so respected in the rabbi's court that even the rabbi's daughters joked around with him. Stempeniu, who was so doted upon by Countess Brerzerzko and all the Polish noblemen that they sent out their carriages for him and spoke French to him—Stempeniu should get a rebuke, and such an awful one at that, from a simple Jewish woman!?"

"I really miss her!" Stempeniu admitted to his band "I really and truly miss her and I'd go after her in Yehupets, if it weren't for... if it weren't for...." Stempeniu looked around on all sides, and the musicians knew *whom* he was looking for.

The musicians all loved Stempeniu, they simply adored him, they would have gone through hell and high water for him. And as much as they loved Stempeniu, they despised Freydel. They couldn't stand her greed, her stinginess, her foul temper.

"Before he got hitched up," the musicians said to one another, "he didn't give a shit about money, you could get a ruble from him, or even three, or four, and never have to pay him back. But ever since that filthy bitch got her claws into him, he's never got a kopek of his own, no matter what he does. Remember those great dinners we used to have with him and the trips we used to go on! Now, everything's lousy, we ain't got nothin', our bellies swell up like mountains, and we starve our guts out. Not a crust of bread all year long, and all we do is sit around lookin' forward to the weddin' season. You'd think that just for politeness' sake she'd offer a guy a cup of tea occasionally, and maybe even have us over for a meal—may she rot in hell, the bitch!"

"Believe you me, there are times when I feel I'm about to croak from hunger, but I wouldn't eat a crumb of that bitch's bread for any amount of gold in the world!"

"How can he live with her, that snake, that pig!? I would've fed her poison a long time ago or strung her up, I swear on my mother's grave!"

"Oh, Stempeniu, you're up shit's creek and you've been sold down the river!"

That's the way his band spoke about him. They knew all about his problems, they felt his sorrows, even though he never spoke about them to the other musicians.

If Freydel was in the market or busy with her wares and clients, then things were fine: Stempeniu treated the band to cigarettes, they sat around, they kidded around, they exchanged stories about the past, and they rolled cigarettes like there was no tomorrow. But then, in flounced Freydel, everyone was turned off, and they started leaving one by one.

"For God's sake, it's as smoky as a tavern here!" said Freydel,

176

snorting and peering at the packet of tobacco, which was running low. "Smoking like chimneys, it's disgusting! My head's already aching from the fumes! You'll be the death of me! You think there's something virtuous about smoking so much, Stempeniu? Listen to me, Stempeniu darling, stop smoking. Believe me, it'll ruin your health!"

"You don't give a shit about my health, Freydel! Just admit that your heart bleeds for the money I spend on cigarettes! Why put on an act?"

"How can you say such a thing! Who's putting on an act? I only care about his health and he says I'm putting on an act! What a morning! I've haggled my lungs out, I've bargained and dickered, I've eaten my heart out, I didn't take in a kopek, and I've been cursed out like a maid, like a maid, I've been humiliated, I've been trampled on like a piece of dirt—and my corals just lie there and rot!..."

"I'd really like to know, Freydel my dear, why you hustle so much and why you're such a tightwad! Do you have a mob of starvin' kids to feed?"

"Get a load of him, the poor shmuck! You should cut your tongue out, that's what you should do! Maybe I carry everything off to my mama, huh, Stempeniu? Or maybe I eat it up myself, I'm such a glutton, right, such a drunkard, right—the whole world oughta watch out for me—huh, Stempeniu? C'mon, look me in the eye, Stempeniu! Huh?"

"Did I say you ate anything up? It's the other way around, I'm only sayin'—"

"You're saying, you're saying—how should I know what you're saying, huh, Stempeniu? You should curse God for saddling you with a spendthrift like me, a spendthrift who turns one kopek into two and thinks about you day and night. C'mon, just tell me, what are you lacking, what don't you have? Cat got your tongue? Why, I'd love to know: What would've become of you and your fiddle if it weren't for me, Stempeniu, if you didn't have me for a wife?"

"Oh, for God's sake!"

"Oh, for God's sake!? You've already forgotten the way you looked at the wedding—not a shirt to your name, not a single sock without a hole in it, no pillow, no pillowcase, nothing and less than nothing, and you were earning chunks of gold—where did it all go to?"

"Am I supposed to tell you what I did with my earnings when I was a bachelor?"

"Ah, that's the trouble with you, Stempeniu, that's your problem! You can't stand hearing the truth about yourself, and you complain if a woman works her fingers to the bone for you, drudges, labors, goes through agony, doesn't even allow herself a crust of bread, and leads a horrible life, and all for whose sake? For him! All for his sake, and do you know for what good deeds? He's sure to put up a golden tombstone for me—oh God in heaven, oh God, oh God!"

"What'd I do to you? Who's doing anything to you?"

"What should you do to me? You've done enough to me already! You robbed me of the best years of my life! You took a young child, an innocent girl, you pulled all that sweet talk on me, you promised me golden mountains, oh, what cock-and-bull stories you told me, you liar! If only I'd never met you! I'd have a man worthy of me and I'd never have become Stempeniu's wife—what luck, what marvelous luck I've had!!"

"Well, are you sorry we got hitched, Freydel? There's a rabbi in Mazepevke and a river, which means we can get divorced—"

"What? Is that what you're after? So the cat's out of the bag! You think I don't know that's what you want? You wanna get rid of me! I'm in your way! What did I ever do to deserve this, Stempeniu? I ask you, for God's sake, tell me what did I do to deserve this? I wanna know too!"

"Oh," replied Stempeniu, waving his hand, he went to his room and took the violin down from the wall.

The violin—that was his comfort, his only friend in the world. With the violin, he could forget his troubles, remember his youth, his freedom, which he had lost forever, forever! So many different people were evoked by the singing of his violin; so many lovely, happy, radiant, images of the past came to him when he began to play; they appeared—and vanished!...

Among all the past images, one image touched him more than any other, an image he could not forget: the dear and lovely image of Rachel, her bright face, her blue eyes, her long lashes, her white throat, and her sweet, good smile for which he would have given anything, anything in the world!

Stempeniu played and played; he played on and on, so that Rachel's ghost would not disappear as always. He only wanted to see her ghost. Even thinking about her was so dear to him, so dear.

Stempeniu played as he had never played before. One can say that in his playing he reached the highest possible level. Anyone who didn't hear him play at that time did not hear anything good.

That's the kind of joy we feel when a bird sings in its cage: The bird is dreaming of green leaves, gorgeous blossoms, open air, a free world, an open world, a great, wide world, and it feels like singing to pour out its bitter heart—and it sings, it weeps, it pours out everything it feels! And we feel joy and delight, we have true pleasure.

"I really miss her so much!" Stempeniu said for the hundredth time to his band. "I miss her like she was my flesh and blood, and I'd go after her in Yehupets if it weren't for...."

And Stempeniu looked around on all sides and saw Freydel dickering with a customer over corals, silk cloths, woolen yarn.

Our Freydel had gradually rigged up a whole shop in her house and had become a genuine businesswoman, on a par with all the other storekeepers in Mazepevke.

Very frequently, she was visited by her mother, Fat Zipporah. Her mother said Shaike missed his daughter very much and had sent his wife to see how Freydel was. But Freydel knew she was lying, there wasn't a crust of bread in her parents' home and her mother had come here to put an end to her fast, to get a bit out of life, to make her stomach stop growling.

"You know what, daughter? Why don't you make those butter rolls, you know, the kind I used to make, pleated and nicely dried out. They're so healthy with a cup of chicory, and with a nice load of butter they're absolute heaven. And for breakfast, fry some goose cracklings with an onion. Papa's always loved that, if you remember that far back. Food is the best medicine."

And Zipporah licked her lips and thought up a new breakfast every day, a new lunch and a new snack and a new dinner—and it can't be said that Freydel was very happy about it. The first week, she more or less put up with it, but the second week, she began getting huffy with her mother, and her mother got huffy with her, until they had an awful fight and they let out all their anger on Stempeniu when he tried to butt in and make peace between his wife and his mother-in-law.

"Mind your own business!" shouted Freydel. "And don't worry, I won't give my mama your legacy. Don't worry, Stempeniu!"

"A fine son-in-law!" said Zipporah with a jab of her tongue. "An ox has a long tongue, but it can't blow a shofar! Decent people treat a mother-in-law like a mother. He can see how my darling daughter treats me! How does the saying go: 'Blow your nose and smear your face'—and he won't even wiggle his tongue! Some man you are, you fiddle-strummer! I just don't understand why he doesn't get fed up with it, Lord in heaven! And what my daughter has to boast about—I'll never know. If you're lucky, then even a bull will have a calf. I've seen creatures like you, I have! Your father-in-law was once a fine fiddler like you, Stempeniu, but he turned out to be a big nothing. What's that old saying? 'A new broom sweeps clean.' You can't get angry at me, Stempeniu, I'm just telling you the plain truth, and even though every dog's the master in his own kennel, I'm not exactly an outsider, you know, I'm your mother-in-law, after all, and if you're going to dine with the devil then you'd better use a long spoon...."

And Zipporah unleashed her tongue and talked a blue streak, as was her custom when she let go. But Stempeniu didn't hear her out. He picked up his violin as he always did when he was in a bad mood—and he forgot all about his wife and his mother-in-law and all his problems. And he only saw Rachel with her blue eyes....

"I miss her, I really and truly miss her!" Stempeniu brooded and tried to think of some way of going to her, of seeing her again, somehow, somewhere....

Idle thoughts! He didn't realize that he would soon be done with his song, that his days were almost gone, he didn't see that his black curls would keep thinning out, that his fiery eyes were gradually losing their glow, that creases were emerging on his white forehead.

Foolish strong man! Don't forget yourself. Can't you see your Delilah, your wife Freydel, at your side? Your Delilah has rocked you, has lulled you in her lap, softly shorn away your long hair and taken away your strength, all your strength, as the other Delilah did to Samson.... You've got one comfort left in the world—Your violin.

Play, Stempeniu, play your violin! Play, and we will listen...

INTRODUCTION TO
THE NIGHTINGALE

Sholem-Aleykhem wrote *Yosele Solovey*—translated here as *The Nightingale* ("solovey" means "nightingale")—in 1886 as the second novel of a projected trilogy about the lives of Jewish performing artists.*

It was first published in 1889, when he included it in the second volume of his *Yidishe Folksbibliotek,* a Yiddish literary journal he had established to advance the cause of a new kind of Yiddish literature.

Yosele, the protagonist of *The Nightingale,* son of a small-town cantor, grows up singing with his father in the synagogue and listening to his father's stories of the great traveling cantors. Apprenticed to one of these great cantors, he travels with him to other towns and cities, where he is highly acclaimed by the public.

Before Yosele leaves his village, he and Esther, his childhood friend, neighbor, and devoted sweetheart, vow wordlessly to marry. But Yosele is tricked into marrying a wealthy young widow, Perele-the-Lady, instead. Esther hears of his marriage and is brokenhearted. She reluctantly agrees to marry a wealthy widower, a moneylender, who is despised by the people in the community. Yosele arrives at the height of Esther's wedding celebration and becomes severely ill. When his wife arrives, he becomes deranged.

Unlike the heroes and heroines of fairy tales, they do not live happily ever after. The realities of the Jewish world, with its arranged marriages, parental authority, the need for a good dowry in order for a girl to make a good match—the grinding poverty—all are pictured in *The Nightingale,* alongside the romantic love story and the freedom, excitement, and glamour of the life of the artist.

As Anita Norich puts it in *Prooftexts* ("Portraits of the Artist in Three Novels by Sholem Aleichem," September 1984: 237-251:

> Yosele Solovey's ending is out of all proportion to what precedes, but Sholem Aleichem makes its meaning clear: the characters have been destroyed by the conflicts between their desires and social possibilities and norms.

The selection below from *The Nightingale* (translated by Aliza Shevrin) comprises three chapters from about the middle of the novel, describing how Yosele is entrapped by Perele, "the lady." It is preceded by an introduction in the form of a letter to Sholem-Aleykhem's wife, here translated for the first time by the editors of this anthology.

---

*Stempenyu, the first novel in the trilogy, appeared a year earlier (1888) in the first volume of the *Folksbibliotek;* it is about a Jewish *klezmer* (musician), a violinist; it appears in its entirety, in translation, in this anthology.

Dear Precious Friend!

My second Yiddish novel, *Yosele Solovey,* I bring to you as a gift today, on the day of your birth. I hope that this gift will please you, not because I can convince myself that it has all the virtues. I know myself quite well that I have not entirely followed grandfather Reb Mendele's rule that "a work one must polish and polish" for two reasons, first, time doesn't permit. One is, after all, no more than a sinful human being, alas, and in the end only a half a writer, that is to say, half tradesman and half writer, as is the case with Jews. One must have in mind the world also, not just the world to come. And secondly we are after all, just between us, young people, human beings that never have any time, everything in a hurry, catch as catch can, always afraid that we shouldn't, God forbid, miss something...So then what? Because I feel that you know that as far as it was possible for me, I worked and took pains with my Yosele till God helped me and I lived to see that he has at least somewhat the appearance of a living personage.

Accept then please, dear friend, this gift of mine just as it is, and may it serve to mark how much I love you and treasure you.

> Your best true and loyal friend,
> The Author.
> **Kiev, 26 December 1889.**

182

FROM

The Nightingale

XVIII

PERELE THE LADY IS ABOUT TO LEAVE THE TOWN OF
STRISHTCH BUT REMAINS ON ACCOUNT OF YOSELE

Between Yampele and Makarevka, exactly midway, one finds a certain town, Strishtch by name, which is renowned for its old families, their descendants, cabalists, simple ordinary people and poor folk who go about, each with a copy of his family tree attesting to the remarkable fact that he is the grandchild of his grandfather and hence is entitled to a coin or two. What those Jews lived on is hard to say, if you should ask a Strishtcher how he managed, he would answer, "Just like this, as you see"—and he believed he had fully answered your question. Their principal occupation was brokering, a stranger would be astounded by the multitude of middlemen: grain brokers, moneylenders, real estate and employment agents, would-be cantorial impresarios. Almost every Strishtcher was a middleman. There were plenty of idlers too and all kinds of societies—a Mishnah Society for religious study, a Psalms Society for devotions, a Shomrim L'boker Society for alerting the community to danger, and other societies, seemingly without number. You could also find several large synagogues, small prayerhouses, a home or two where little more than the required ten men gathered for worship, a bathhouse, and two cemeteries, an old one and a new one, and they were thinking of buying land for a third.

You could count the wealthy people on one hand, they were called "the Strishtcher Aktziznikes." Apparently this name stuck with them when they bribed their way out of Aktziz. The brothers Aktziznikes were famous, not so much for their philanthropy as for their great wealth. "They are as rich as Korach," is what they said of them in Strishtch. "They live like royalty but don't give so much as a groschen to anyone. The blessed God apportions to this one everything and to the other nothing...." Nevertheless when one of the brothers died, all the shops were closed and the whole town mourned Reb Moshe-Wolf the Aktzizniker, as was fitting when the richest man in town dies. Reb Moshe-Wolf died childless and left almost his entire fortune to his two younger brothers, Meir-Hersh and Pesach-Leib. He also left a tidy sum to his third wife, the young bride he had brought from Bardichev a few years before his death. People said that this young widow had managed to salt away some two hundred thousand rubles, which, so the story ran, she was planning to take with her to Bardichev, where she would find a young man to marry, not another old codger like Moshe-Wolf. But at that very moment Yosele Solovey came upon the scene, and Moshe-Wolf's young widow, Perele the Lady, stayed on.

She was called Perele the Lady in Strishtch because she was almost the only one who dressed like a princess, drove about in a carriage, kept a dog, and played the pianoforte. While Moshe-Wolf was still sitting *shiva* for his second wife they were already whispering in Strishtch that he would now marry a young, modern woman, and why not? Money he had—he could allow himself anything he desired. The townspeople hit it right: Moshe-Wolf, after observing the appropriate thirty days of mourning, drove off to Bardichev (where else?) and soon brought back with him a "lady." As long as Strishtch had been a town, a woman had never kept a dog or played the pianoforte. The first time they heard her play, people crowded into her street and exclaimed, "My! A woman who's a musician!" and gossip began to fly about the dog and the piano. From that time on, "The Lady" or "Perele the Lady" stuck with her. People rubbed their hands together in anticipation of collecting some extra money from her—"After all, a Lady! It would be beneath her dignity to bargain. Of course she'll give a donation. People like that love to do such things!" But they quickly saw that they had fooled themselves from start to finish. Perele the Lady, who had grown up in Bardichev, a trading center, could bargain better than all the Strishtcher fish-wives, and she hated giving a donation even more than her husband did. "Of course you have to know how to tinkle away on the piano," the Strishtch wives said sarcastically. "Of course you have to act like a grande dame in order to push us around!" Or "Perele, may you be well! Give us some bread. Pretend you're giving it to your dog."

While he was still in Makarevka, Yosele had been invited to perform for Shabbos in Strishtch. He had turned up his nose at the invitation, not wanting to waste his time in such a place, a town known mainly for its poor people. Moreover he had planned to make a short visit to Kashperev and from there go home to Mazepevka. The traveling was becoming tedious; he was forever on the road, far from home. He was even thinking of writing a few words home (it had been so long since he had written!) when in came Gedalye, cursed be his name, and with his doubletalk he persuaded Yosele that it was far better to stop first at Strishtch to chant the Sabbath and from there go on to Mazepevka, in order to avoid Kashperev, saying in his usual elliptical way, "Because Kashperev is so hospitable to cantors, may it burn to the ground three times over, may it be cursed!" So reasoned Gedalye, and so it was decided, without objection.

In Strishtch for Shabbos, Yosele the Nightingale and his company presented the town with a service that threw it into an uproar. People besieged the inn where Yosele was staying in order to get a look at the Mazepevka Nightingale, if only from a distance. Among those who were curious to see Yosele was Reb Moshe-Wolf's young widow, Perele the Lady, who had heard him sing and came home from the synagogue in a state of excitement, disquieted, quite agitated. "I am so eager to see his face," Perele the Lady said to those close to her. Saturday afternoon she put on her silk outfit, adorned herself with her most expensive jewelry—pearls, diamonds, and other precious gems—and promenaded through town with her personal maid, making sure to stroll right past the inn where Yosele and his company happened to be lodged. It was summertime and the windows were open; leaning on his elbows at one of the windows, with a silver-bordered, gold-embroidered yarmulke on his head, was Yosele the Nightingale. His hair worn in the turned-under Russian peasant style, fell over his shoulders; his face was pale, and his smiling eyes, large and shining, gazed out from under full brows. Around him stood the choirboys, mocking and laughing at the town of Strishtch and its people.

"What do you make of this 'Trishtch?'" joked the boys among themselves. "This town is at the bottom of the heap!"

"Who is that young woman dripping with jewels from head to toe?" asked Yosele, scrutinizing Perele the Lady as her large eyes met his. Perele was not a bad-looking woman, still young, with a round figure, a fair complexion like a fresh pastry, a full chin, and a fleshy neck hung with large pearls. Her fingers were adorned with rings, her wrists with bracelets and bangles, her neck with

185

many-stranded necklaces, her figure expensively attired in silk and velvet in the latest Bardichever fashion. Strutting like a peahen, she made sure to pass the inn several times, each time catching a glimpse of Yosele. When she came home Perele felt her heart stirring with passion.

Even while Moshe-Wolf was alive she had decided that if she were left a widow, she would take a young man who would be handsome and fair-haired. Since Moshe-Wolf was old and infirm, she had certainly expected to be left a widow. He had married her only for her beauty. The marriage contract for over a hundred thousand left her well provided for. He had promised to make her happy for a hundred and twenty years and not to forget her in his will. Perele was still a very young girl then, but like all Bardichever girls, she loved to dress up, follow the latest fads, while always keeping an eye open for a rich husband. Naturally, when Moshe-Wolf came calling, he didn't make her heart skip a beat, but the hundred thousand rubles and his carriage and his fine furniture so turned her head that it seemed the right thing to do. There was, however, one thing she could not abide and that was the name of Strishtch—"What kind of name is Strishtch! A fine name! Feh—disgusting...!" Perele brooded, and it rankled her. But Moshe-Wolf did her a great favor; right after the wedding he took ill, lingered several years, and finally died, liberating Perele the Lady. Nonetheless she conducted herself as a devoted wife, as a Jewish daughter, should: she sat *shiva,* observed the required thirty-day mourning period, and then, together with her maid, Leah'tzi, packed her clothes and prepared to leave. As you would expect, she was besieged by matchmakers from all over pressing upon her favorable matches, but Perele the Lady wouldn't hear of it—she wanted no part of that dull Strishtch and couldn't wait to be out of it. She had already written to her parents that after Shabbos, God willing, she would be coming home to Bardichev. But as it turned out, she remained in Strishtch. And on account of Yosele the Nightingale!

"What do you think of this Yosele?" Perele the Lady asked Leah'tzi, her maid, as they were strolling by the inn, casting a glance in that direction.

"What can I say?" answered Leah'tzi. "He's surely as handsome as the morning star, just like that Solomon, the character in the romances—tall, well built, and golden-haired."

Leah'tzi the maid loved to read romances, the first page of

which always carried the inscription "A Most Interesting Novel, Reprinting Forbidden." Leah'tzi would read the romances aloud to Perele the Lady while Moshe-Wolf was lying ill. Even though Perele ridiculed her for her silly stories, she nevertheless enjoyed them. Perele had brought this maid with her from Bardichev. Her duties consisted solely of dressing her mistress, strolling with her, and making sure to be always at her side; she was also her only confidante and, like her, looked forward with all her heart to her master's early demise, although they were both ashamed to say so openly. They understood each other implicitly and were both eager to go home.

Even though Leah'tzi was no beauty and had a pockmarked face, she had a fiancé in Bardichev. His name was Levi-Mottel and he was in the "tobacco business," meaning that he sold cigarettes. No matter what others thought of him—he might have been an old, pimply bachelor with ugly red hair—in her eyes he looked like an "angel, tall, well built," and that was why she was "in love" with him, exactly as described in those "romances" she read. Leah'tzi loved her betrothed and was faithful to him, entirely devoted. She sent Levi-Mottel every last ruble she could scrape together; she didn't allow herself so much as an extra dress, a shawl, or boots. "I have to send it off to Levi-Mottel, who really needs the money!" In return Levi-Mottel sent her appreciative letters every week, one the identical twin of the other, as if born of the same mother.

"And I greet you," Levi-Mottel would write every week, "and I thank you, my dear, for the gift and I've had new boots and galoshes made and I beg you to write how your health is and if your master is still alive and I am, thank God, well and there is no work; cigarette rollers are not cheap and there's no work and I'm not making any money and send me, my dear bride, money for a new suit and the other suit is old already and write me how your health is and if your master is still living."

These letters were to Leah'tzi the most precious things in the world. She lived with the satisfaction that Levi-Mottel was dressing well with her money and was wearing her suit and her boots and galoshes.

"Fool, fool!" Perele the Lady would say to her. "Foolish girl! He'll end up putting a fancy headstone on your grave, that fiancé of yours! Don't you see?"

Leah'tzi had no reply to that; she had her mind made up. She counted the minutes, the seconds, until she would finally go home to Bardichev and stand under the wedding canopy with Levi-Mottel. "Who cares what she says, the madam, or what she thinks! If I could show her what is in my heart, then she would know not to make fun of such things...."

But the time came when Perele the Lady would speak differently; the time would come when she would discover that "True love is not a servant," as Leah'tzi used to say, "whom you can dismiss with a wave of the hand," as Perele had once thought. After coming home from her stroll, Perele flung herself into an armchair, summoned Leah'tzi, and asked her to feel her brow.

"You have a headache, madam? What shall we do?"

"A headache, you say? It's my heart, silly goose, it's my heart that's aching. I'm beside myself, I'm burning up, I'm in pain, I'm fainting, and you say that!"

"What's the matter then, madam? Tell me, so I'll know too."

"Oy vey, Leah'tzi, what can I tell you? It's awful, it's the end of me! There's a fire burning right here, in my heart! From the first moment I heard him singing and ever since I laid eyes on him I feel it's the end of me!" Perele the Lady wept from great heartache. Leah'tzi stood by in deep thought, trying to figure out what might be done. As she was not given to subtleties, she didn't have to think long.

"Do you know what, madam? Listen to me. You're a free woman now, thank God, and a rich one too—would that I had your worries. Now, listen to me. Grab him and marry him!"

Perele the Lady almost leaped from her armchair, greatly excited, and burst out laughing, tears in her eyes. "Foolish girl! What do you mean, 'grab him'? Doesn't he have a say in it too?"

"So what are you afraid of? That maybe he won't want you? Is that it? You think you're ugly? Or that you are, God forbid, common? Or that you're a widow? Some problem! A lot of women would love to be in your place! Or maybe it's a sin for you to take a young boy? Even a lunatic wouldn't say that! What is it, then? The wonderful life you had with your husband? Wasted three and a half years in this God-forsaken Strishtch. The great joys you had here? Seems to me, living in the same house with a sick man, you've earned your reward. No one knows how somebody else's shoe pinches, and you don't owe anybody an explanation!"

"Ach, Leah'tzi! My soul! My heart!" Perele the Lady said and threw herself into Leah'tzi's arms.

In a big pond one finds all sorts of fish; in a city like Bardichev one found all sorts of people. Perele the Lady's origins were not of the highest: her father, Meir Zeitchik, was what we used to call a speculator. He was ready to buy whatever was for sale but never had any permanent business of his own. Should an old plant, a factory, a house to be repossessed, an estate, or a broken-down shack come on the market anywhere, Meir Zeitchik was ready to buy. If someone discarded an old carriage or old furniture, Meir Zeitchik was on the spot to make an offer, just so long as he could make a ruble on the deal. You could find anything at Meir Zeitchik's, whatever your heart desired. Is it iron? There's iron. Brass? There's brass. Feathers? There's feathers. If it's everything you want—there's everything, everything! He never had any capital of his own but always managed with other people's money. As with most merchants, business was sometimes good and sometimes bad. All in all, he led the life of a tolerably successful businessman, borrowing here, grabbing there, giving a little, taking a little—managing!

Although Meir Zeitchik raised his children to be good Jews, he never thought of educating them or teaching them to play the piano and other such worldly things, as Jews do nowadays. Meir said, "For my daughters a dowry is all I need. What good is all that other nonsense?" As luck would have it, he had bought up a pianoforte, quite cheaply, from one of the gentry who was selling out and leaving town. Try as he might, he couldn't find a customer for the piano, and it remained unsold for quite a while, covered with a sheet, till one day it occurred to Meir: "Here's a piano. Perele's growing up. She's as pretty as a picture. Why shouldn't she learn to plunk on the piano? Anything can happen these days. Maybe it can help her to get a finer husband. What do you say, Malke, ha?" Meir's wife, Malke, agreed to it. The only problem left was where to find a teacher for Perele who wouldn't cost too much.

With time Perele learned how to play, exhibiting a real talent for the piano, even though, when it came to other matters, she was shallow-minded and not too bright. Her piano playing caused quite a stir in Meir's neighborhood. "They know how to play the *piano* over there!" the neighbors said. For that reason Perele gained more respect in the house. While her younger sisters were busy with housework, Perele would sit idly by, her hands folded, or would dress up in her Shabbos best and go out strolling, acting as if the middle of the week were the Sabbath. Everyone had to wait on her hand and foot, treating her with respect. "Imagine, she knows how to play the piano—that's really something!" Even Meir and Malke fussed over her, while Perele looked down on them all condescendingly, counting herself their better. To strangers the Zeitchikes, as Meir and Malke were called in town, bragged constantly of their Perele's playing.

"Play a little something for us on the pianoforte, Perele," they would ask when a stranger visited, and they beamed with pride as she did so. "Perele can play the piano!"

But later, when Perele was a little older, her piano playing became a liability. She wasn't just another girl; she had to dress elegantly, had to have a pretty hat, a parasol, gloves, and all the other accessories that a "mamselle" requires. And didn't she have to attend the theater? How would it look if a girl who play piano failed to go to the theater? But that was nothing compared to what her parents went through when it came time to arrange a match. Only then did they discover how much the piano had cost them. The bridegrooms they could afford Perele spat at; and the ones she desired, alas, they could not possibly afford because the bridegrooms Perele wanted demanded big money. Meir and Malke realized how God manages His world! Their daughter treated them badly, not at all like a cultured mamselle who plays piano but like a common Bardichev girl who can talk back to her mother and father. God knows what they would have done with her if the match from Strishtch hadn't materialized—such a happy, fortunate match! Meir raised his hands to God and said, *"Boruch sh'ptarni*—Thank God I'm rid of her," swearing never again to keep a piano in the house.

Although her parents sent their daughter to Strishtch in fine style, they did not receive from her a single groschen in return, although she wrote them happy enough letters. Once there, she did not provide them with so much as the worth of a glass of water. She did not behave at all decently toward her family.

That's the kind of "madam" Perele the Lady was.

XIX

A NEW CHARACTER IS INTRODUCED—BERL-ISAAC IS HIS NAME—AND YOSELE RIDES IN A CARRIAGE

The rich man is lucky in all things. It's not enough that he is rich and can afford any luxury he wants, he is also always surrounded by a multitude of hangers-on who are willing to serve him for nothing, hoping they will gain some favor by doing so. The rich, attended by so many hangers-on, come to believe they are entitled to be waited upon—they must be worth it—and as a result they look down on these followers, as befits a master looking down on his slaves. That describes the kind of rich people the Aktziznikes of Strichtch were. Each of the three brothers had clustering about him his little clique of Jews, his followers—meaning his unpaid servants. Each hanger-on strove to be closer to his benefactor. If that benefactor showed the least preference for one, the others would redouble their efforts, turn themselves inside out, groveling in the dirt. One of the most dedicated and persistent hangers-on of Moshe-Wolf's, may he have a bright Paradise, was a certain Berl-Isaac. Who this Berl-Isaac was and what he did was hard to say exactly, because he had no particular occupation, he hung around Moshe-Wolf, made himself useful, and in that way scratched out a living. He was, in fact, distantly related to Moshe-Wolf, but he knew Moshe-Wolf wouldn't want to be reminded of it, so he set aside his kinship. What did it matter if he was or wasn't a relative, so long as Moshe-Wolf was rich.

Berl-Isaac had a way of walking slowly, looking sideways at people, speaking softly, suavely, sparing words, not being forward, as others were, and always turning up exactly when and where he was needed. For these reasons he gained Moshe-Wolf's favor more than anyone else in his household. If it ever happened that he was called to account and berated, Berl-Isaac would accept it, tuck it away in his pocket, and—sha!—quiet! "All rich people are like that," Berl-Isaac would say afterward. "Sometimes they have to get mad, so you have to let them get it out of their systems."

The entire time that Moshe-Wolf lay ill Berl-Isaac never left the courtyard; like a loyal dog, he guarded the house, on the alert,

191

sniffing out and checking into everything quietly, walking slowly and inspecting every little corner. He had been told my Moshe-Wolf's two brothers to inform them immediately should Moshe-Wolf's condition worsen, God forbid. After all, he was old and sick and had no children; they weren't about to trust his young wife.... Berl-Isaac was quick to understand; he didn't need to have any diagrams drawn for him, and he did what he was told. When Moshe-Wolf was at the point of death, both brothers were already in the house. As expected, Berl-Isaac didn't neglect his duties. After Moshe-Wolf died, Berl-Isaac remained on. When the master is dead the mistress becomes rich. Isn't that the way it is?

The entire time of sitting *shiva* and the following thirty days of mourning Berl-Isaac was always to be found in the courtyard, not leaving his post for a moment in case he was needed. But Perele the Lady had little need of him. Every Strishtcher person was revolting to her, despised and loathsome. Leah'tzi the maid hated him as well. "That young man," she would say, "with his quiet talk and his sideways glances, makes me sick just looking at him. I can't stand him!" Berl-Isaac was fully aware of this, and he tried in every way he could to placate her, to find her soft spot. "If not today, then tomorrow"—thus he consoled himself. "The time will come—*Preyde koza doh voza*, as the Russian saying goes—'The goat will come to the cart'"—and the time did come. That Shabbos evening, after Perele the Lady had bared her soul to her maid, Leah'tzi came upon Berl-Isaac as he was walking about the courtyard, dressed for the Sabbath, a kerchief around his neck, softly humming a tune, as is the custom on Sabbath evening.

"When were you figuring to leave?" Berl-Isaac said, sidling up to Leah'tzi, glancing at her slyly.

"Leave?" Leah'tzi answered, irritated as usual. "You're all ready for us to leave!"

"What, then? Not done packing yet?" he asked, his face crinkled with an ingratiating smile.

"What packing?" Leah'tzi said angrily. "He can't wait, can he? There are more important things than that! Listen to me, Berl-Isaac! You're pretty sure of yourself. I know you. I'm going to tell you something, but first you have to swear by your wife and children that it will remain between us."

Berl-Isaac's face, which till then had been smiling, turned earnest. Bit by bit Leah'tzi disclosed the whole story and again made him swear that no one else would know of this. Berl-Isaac heard her out, thought a moment, his squinting eyes darting about, and said to Leah'tzi, "Trust me. It's done. Tonight after the Havdalah service, he's here."

"Remember now, Berl-Isaac, you swore by your wife and children to keep it a secret."

"A secret, a secret!" Berl-Isaac echoed and slowly went off to the inn where Yosele and his choir were lodged.

The negotiations that took place between Berl-Isaac and Gedalye Bass were highly diplomatic. They were very cautious with each other, sparring like two veteran boxers, until they had worked out a mutually acceptable plan.

First Gedalye saw to it that without knowing the real reason, Yosele would agree to meet Perele the Lady. "There's this rich woman, they call her Perele the Lady," Gedalye said Saturday night after Havdalah, "who really wants to meet you. She knows all the big cantors and loves singing and she herself plays the piano. It wouldn't hurt to go visit her." Yosele obeyed him. He and Gedalye went over to Perele's home, where they beheld a large, brightly lit house with richly furnished rooms elegantly decorated with velvet divans, soft armchairs, crystal and bronze chandeliers, dizzyingly tall mirrors, flower vases, and all kinds of pictures in gold frames.

Upon seeing all this for the first time in his life, Yosele's head began to spin. "If you play your cards right," Gedalye whispered in his ear, "all this can be yours." Yosele stared at Gedalye in amazement. It finally dawned on him that his visit had been arranged with a match in mind. Yosele was ready to make an about-face and take off; he felt like sinking into the earth out of fright and embarrassment. "Run, Yosele, run away!" he said to himself. "Run as fast as your feet can carry you! Run home, run away as far away as you can get, the sooner the better!" But it was too late. Approaching him was Perele the Lady, an attractive young woman dipped in gold and heavily bejeweled. As he took in this "Lady," Esther came into his thoughts—the devoted Esther whom he would soon be seeing, God willing. He had to laugh to himself when he compared Perele to Esther. "Could I? Could I do such a thing? Could I exchange Esther for this one? How can you compare them? No comparison!" Perele the Lady gave him her hand, a small, white, cold hand, and he felt that cold little hand scorch his flesh. A mist seemed to settle over his eyes, his ears were ringing, his head felt as if it were splitting open—he was lost.

For almost the first time in his life Yosele heard piano playing.

He had heard it from a distance many times, but to be sitting so close to a beautiful woman as she played, her small, white fingers seeming to draw from the instrument such soft sounds, such tender melodies—that he could never have imagined. The room was soon filled with beautiful sounds, and Perele became even more charming in his eyes than before. As always happened with him, things quickly took on an entirely changed aspect: the house was transformed into a palace and Perele into a princess; in a state of ecstasy he arrived to the sound of miraculous, divine music that melted his heart, caressed his soul, renewed his vitality. He passionately desired to join her; he longed to blend his voice with the sounds of the piano. Yosele the Nightingale began to sing, following the same rhythm, the music pouring from his throat, his rare, accomplished voice forming such sweet, tender melodies that Perele the Lady stopped playing to listen to him sing. But Yosele insisted she keep on playing. As she accompanied him, his exquisite voice poured forth sublime supernatural sounds like a nightingale's.

Gedalye Bass, who was reclining in a comfortable easy chair off to the side, had not heard such singing from Yosele as he heard that Saturday night at Perele the Lady's. Even Gedalye's corrupt soul, which understood only money, was elevated, sublimely satisfied, as he heard Yosele singing. Nevertheless he reasoned it would be wiser for him to return to the inn and leave Yosele alone. Leah'tzi the maid had with great condescension served him a glass of tea on a silver tray, but Gedalye refused the tea, muttering that he had to be off, and slipped out.

Not till midnight, when he was getting ready to return to the inn, did Yosele look around and realize that Gedalye was gone. Perele, Yosele, and Leah'tzi enjoyed a laugh together, and it was decided that they would wake the coachman and have the carriage hitched up. But waking the coachman proved unnecessary; coachman and carriage were already in attendance at the door. Just outside the door Berl-Isaac was nodding off. Leah'tzi looked at his half-asleep face and said to him, "So you're the one who made sure the carriage was ready, Reb Berl-Isaac, eh? You really are something!"

"So, what do you think, Leah'tzi, is he mine?" Perele the Lady later asked her maid, standing almost naked and then flinging herself onto the bed.

"Of course!" Leah'tzi answered, covering her mistress with a soft satin blanket. "Of course! Couldn't you tell by his sparkling eyes that he's completely smitten?"

"Leah'tzi, dear heart, dear soul!" Perele exclaimed, embracing the maid and pressing her tightly to her heart.

And Yosele Solovey, sprawled out in the comfortable carriage taking him from Perele's to the inn, felt a new life beginning for him, and Perele's visage appeared before his eyes. He forgot where he was; he could think only one thing—to visit again tomorrow, again to see Perele and again to hear her play. Another thought also flew through his mind: he imagined seeing before him the two hundred thousand rubles Gedalye had mentioned in passing...a plan was forming in his head. He pictures himself driving into Mazepevke in a carriage drawn by four spirited horses. The town stops dead, sees him, and is stunned. His father runs out to greet him. "Welcome home, Yosele!" Yosele takes out a bundle of bills and says to his father, "Here, Father—ten thousand, twenty thousand—forget about being a cantor, it's high time!"

And Esther? At that moment Yosele forgot there was an Esther who had been waiting for him so long, and when he did think of her he dismissed the question forming in his mind, "Why am I so troubled?"

XX

HE FALLS INTO THE NET AND REALIZES IT TOO LATE

It had been much harder to persuade Yosele to visit Perele that first time than it was to have him sign the betrothal agreement and then stand under the wedding canopy with her. Gedalye Bass made all the arrangements with the rabbis, cantors, and synagogue officials. He himself did the running around, the organizing, and making the preparations for the wedding. Naturally, Berl-Isaac, his partner, helped out. It was a considerable task Gedalye took upon himself. He also had to battle with Perele's two brothers-in-law, the Aktziznikes. They absolutely opposed the match, adamantly vow-

195

ing that, come what may, blood would flow in the streets before they would allow such a disgrace to take place in Strishtch. "Let her go, for all we care, to Bardichev," they said, "and throw herself at whomever she pleases. We won't allow such a humiliation of our dead brother, whose body isn't yet cold in the grave. What is going on? What kind of wantonness is this?"

Gedalye was not silent. He had the ability, with his half sentences, to dissuade anyone. He convinced them that it was an honor rather than a humiliation, God forbid, for their brother, may his soul rest in peace. Who knew into whose hands such a rich woman with so much money might fall these days? Yosele was, first of all, a properly brought-up son of a respectable father; he came from a long line of rabbis, and this very day two rabbis and three rabbinical assistants could be counted in the family. And second of all, he didn't need her money, he had money enough of his own. It was no small matter, the way Yosele could spin gold; a ruble was as dear to him as his own eyes! Gedalye, one can say, knew how to handle these Strishtcher snobs. Along the way he found out that the Aktziznikes had a grievance against the widow, something about a partnership entered into with a rich landowner. Gedalye set to work and persuaded her to give the brothers the contract—who needed it! This rankled Perele, but she reluctantly gave it up, and on the third day after signing the betrothal agreement, they were married; afterward the guests returned to wherever they had come from. Gedalye paid off his choir and returned home with a sackful, more than enough money to marry off his daughter and some to put away for the future. All in all, it had worked out well for him.

Gedalye Bass had been worrying that Yosele's voice was beginning to lose its pure timbre. He might even lose it altogether because he was at the age when the voice undergoes changes, and until he would establish his mature voice, a year or two could go by. Now, Gedalye figured, he can have the voice of a hyena or sing like a fish for all I care, I won't waste any tears over it. Still, he parted from Yosele as from his own child, wishing him a long life of honor and riches with his wife and no further need ever to chant on the pulpit as long as he lived.

And Perele the Lady clung to Yosele, not leaving his side for so much as a second. Leah'tzi, humming a song, packed the bags for the trip. Her heart was trembling with anticipation, because in a few days she would be with her Levi-Mottel. Berl-Isaac helped her pack, ran errands, did odd jobs, and worked hard, as if he belonged to Perele. "Nothing is ever lost on the rich," Berl-Isaac reasoned. "I maintain 'The goat will come to the cart.'" But, alas, this time Berl-Isaac had made a grave miscalculation. When the time came to take leave, Perele the Lady didn't so much as spit in his hand. Like a plaintive kitten, like a timid wretch, Berl-Isaac stood by, his head to the side, grinning obsequiously, trying to be of service, waiting on everyone hand and foot, a pitiful expression on his face, and wishing them "Go in good health! Go in good health!" But in his heart a raging fire was burning. That bitch, that cheap tramp—may she break her neck on the way, God in heaven!—"Go in good health! Go in good health!" Berl-Isaac said for the last time, doffing his cap and bending over double while his thoughts went to the roll of bills Gedalye had given him as his share of the matchmaking money, which warmed his bosom and comforted him like a priceless possession.

And so our three heroes—Perele, Yosele, and Leah'tzi the maid—sat in a large, comfortable coach drawn by four horses as they rode from Strishtch to Bardichev with happy hearts. Leah'tzi pretended to sleep so as not to appear to be looking at how her mistress was hanging on Yosele's neck and how they were laughing and kissing each other, acting like lovebirds. That I've lived to see such a sight! Leah'tzi said to herself. The grass hasn't even grown on the other one's grave, his soul hasn't even reached the Other World yet, and already she's hanging on a new one! And how she ran after him—my God! Couldn't she wait a little? And she got herself a cantor, hee-hee-hee! If my Levi-Mottel were here, he would get a good laugh out of this! What these rich folks will do!

My mistress is also a good one with her sweet talk—"My soul, my heart, my love"—so long as it pays off. I lay out her clothes—dear God, may I have half of them. Does she ever say, "Share a little bit of my luxury, take a pair of stockings for yourself, for appearance's sake, or a shirt or an old dress, whatever you want"? Does she ever say, "Here, Leah'tzi, have a little something to remember me by"? Not a chance! Would anyone else in my place have put up with it? Anyone else would have broken her bones, not so much as a shred would have been left. For all I care, let her burn with her whole fortune, with all her *shmattes*. As for me, may God help me get home safely and start planning to get married.

These musings filled Leah'tzi's head as Perele and Yosele were kissing, embracing, and fondling each other. And the horses drew

197

the coach with its three passengers onward, leaving behind fields and forests, villages and small towns.

Not one of them noticed how time was passing. All three were preoccupied with their own thoughts, all had their own fantasies, their own gratifications. Perele had never been as happy as she was at that moment, traveling with her handsome "hero," her "angel." He was hers, hers! The very thought that such a "hero," whom one reads about meeting only in romances, that such an "angel" was hers, made her head spin, intoxicated her, and delivered her into a sweet, blissful sleep.

And Yosele?

Later on, when Yosele the Nightingale would come to his senses and look around at where he found himself, he would swear that he absolutely could not remember what had happened to him since first meeting Perele. When, where, and how he had married Perele the Lady—he could not for the life of him recall. He could remember only a thick fog settling around him, gold coins, diamonds and gems glittering before his eyes. Stretching out invitingly before him were several bright, happy, festive days. People were waiting upon him as if he were a prince. The princess, Perele, was sitting at his side, not leaving him for a moment, hanging on his neck, kissing him, fondling him. "Yosele, Yosele, my sweetheart, my soul, my hero, my angel!" And his head was spinning, spinning. He had felt as if he were in a cloud—confused, dazed—in a connubial Garden of Eden, in heaven itself, redolent with all manner of spices, where wine and oil flow and almonds grow, where birds sing and people go about without a care. And he is singing beautifully and sweetly and will do so forever. Perele is playing the piano and he is singing and the whole world resounds with voices, with music. He can go on forever this way, without a care, in this Garden of Eden, just singing and singing....

The journey from Strishtch to Bardichev in the comfortable carriage, the air so sweet and fragrant, with Perele close by him, seemed to Yosele like a delightful dream. He didn't want to take into account where he was going or why; he simply wanted the dream to last forever. But here on earth, where life lasts but a minute, a mere second, a dream cannot last forever. A dream must come to an end; the time must come to wake up, there is no use in wishing otherwise.... And when he did wake up and begin to look around at where he was, like a drunkard waking up sober after a drinking bout, he wondered what he had done. God in heaven, he thought. What am I doing here?

He saw around him a sprawling city, dingy, bleak, muddy. Men and women streamed through the streets. Coachmen shouted, shopkeepers hawked their wares, fishwives cursed. The stench of the mud was so strong that one had to cover one's nose. Where had he landed? In Bardichev. The coach had come to a halt in front of a dirty, square outer wall, and after passing though a dark alley with mud-covered steps, they came to a house. Yosele saw standing before him a tall, thin, wrinkled man wearing a cap and, alongside of him, a short, fat woman wearing a large bow under her chin and a headband on her forehead. The tall man greeted him, kissed him, and the fat woman spoke to him with the familiar "du," congratulating him, and both stood back to look him over. These were his in-laws. Perele had informed them by letter that she was bringing home a fine inheritance and an even finer husband. Something to celebrate! Joyous occasion! Their daughter had come back, thank God, thank God! Her late husband's death excepted, may every Jewish girl have her good fortune!...

All of Perele's parents' friends gathered to give a mazel-tov and to inspect Yosele, staring at him constantly. He looked all around him like a small boy who had just been brought to *cheder* for the first time. He was trembling, and everything appeared new and strange. He looked at his bride, at Perele, and she wasn't at all the same Perele as in Strishtch but an altogether different woman! There she had possessed infinite charm for him, there her eyes had had a different life to them, there she had spoken to him in a different way. The former Perele seemed to have vanished and another one had appeared before his eyes. Then there was the little matter of living in Bardichev! He wasn't used to this kind of life, to their talk, to the customs. Everything, everything was alien. He felt utterly out of place. What was he doing here and what on earth had brought him here? What did he have in common with Meir Zeitchik and what did he care about his business? What significance did Perele's loans and banknotes and interest rates and all her other dealings have for him? Perele, upon arriving home, had quickly become involved in investing her money profitably. All he wanted was to be free. Ach, God Almighty! He had not realized before marrying Perele that he would wind up stuck in this hell, among total strangers, never seeing the light of day, not to mention singing or playing piano.

199

Yosele would wake up in the morning, drink his coffee, and look out the window—dark, dreary, muddy—may God protect him! Then he would listen to a long harangue about business, again business, again percentages, again money. After lunch Perele would go shopping with her mother, cheating the salespeople and hunting out bargains. Yosele looked on astonished, listening to Perele talk to the women in their own slang, swearing and scolding like an experienced fishwife. Day and night an unholy racket, swearing and cursing. Perele quarreled with her sisters, screaming at them, trading insults. Her mother and father always took her side—after all, she was the aristocrat in the family! More and more Yosele somberly recognized his wife for what she was. Observing her as she quaked over a groschen and noting all her unflattering, unpleasant gestures, he thought to himself, Is this the Perele I imagined to be so refined and gentle, so decent, so beloved? Now look at her! He tried again to talk to her about his previous plans—to travel abroad, to study, sing, perform. She would have none of it! "You want to be a cantor?" she cooed, putting her arms around his neck. "What good will that do you, silly fool? Just wait a little and I'll invest my money properly, and then we'll both be able to travel in style to the spas, to the vineyards, for the 'cure'— you know, where all the rich people go, silly. And you're talking about being a cantor, studying, singing! Feh, dear heart, forget it, my sweet life, forget it and let me kiss your bright eyes and your wonderful golden hair, my angel, my wonderful hero!"

As time went on Yosele realized what he had done, that he had placed himself in bondage, fettered himself forever, for always. Like a bird locked in a cage, he tried thrashing about to free himself, and saw it was no use struggling. All those sweet dreams he had once dreamed were now vanishing like mist. Gone were those golden, precious fantasies of his, blown away like smoke, and in their place came other fantasies, other thoughts. Gone were the sweet sounds of yesterday, gone were the beautiful images he once saw before him! The carriage, his homecoming to Mazepevka, the wonderment of his acquaintances and good friends, the joy he would give his father—gone, gone! Other images took their place, another kind of life. In place of that former sweet-smelling Garden of Eden now stood before him the dreadful Bardichev mud. In place of palaces, a dreary house with dreary people. In place of singing, talk day and night of trade, percentages, profit, money, costs. In place of a comely wife, a vulgar woman who was always hanging on his neck, hugging and kissing him, not allowing him to leave her side. And everything was so commonplace! So ordinary! He was bored, the world and his life were tiresome, stultifying. Behind his back he could hear them talking about him—"That's him, Yosele, the one who married the rich widow....," and it pierced him to the quick. When he looked at Perele he was reminded of Esther, and he began to fully comprehend the fact that he had committed a grievous mistake, that he had ruined his life, that he had behaved badly toward Esther, toward his father, and toward himself. He sank into a depressed, distraught frame of mind.

"Yosele, my soul, my sweetheart, my dear little nightingale," his wife, Perele, said to him when they were alone, she playing with his long, thick hair, "what's the matter? Why are you so distracted? You go around looking so preoccupied and pensive. Tell me, what do you need? Don't I deserve to know the truth? What's the matter? Are you tired of me? Bored?"

Bored? Yosele thought. Bored to death! But he restrained himself, gritted his teeth, and told her a big lie. "Bored with you? God forbid! What can you mean, 'bored' with you?" And as he said these words, his thoughts, his mind, his heart, and all his feelings were far away in Mazepevka.

201

INTRODUCTION TO

WANDERING STARS

Blondzhende Shtern (Wandering Stars) is the third of Sholem-Aleykhem's novels about Jewish performing artists.*

The first one, *Stempenyu*, dealt with a Jewish musician; the second, *Yosele Solovey (Yosele Nightingale* [translated as *The Nightingale*]), dealt with the world of the Jewish singer. The one selected from below, translated as *Wandering Star*, deals with Yiddish actors, with the world of the Yiddish theater.

At the beginning of the novel two families in the little Jewish town of Holeneshti, in Bessarabia, find their children gone one fine morning; the cantor's daughter and the rich man's son have vanished. It is only in the following chapters that Sholem-Aleykhem backtracks to show us how these two handsome young people have run off—why and with whom.

The rest of this long (in its abridged English translation by Frances Butwin it runs to 312 pages) novel takes us on an odyssey stretching from Holeneshti to Bucharest, Lemberg, Vienna, London, and, finally, to New York. In it we follow the careers, the ups and downs, of the two "blondzhende shtern" from Holeneshti, Reyzl and Leybl, two star-crossed lovers, who, while they develop their brilliant careers independently, yearn always for each other.

The very night they run away from Holeneshti they are unhappily separated from each other. Leybl, after some struggle and much wandering, becomes a celebrated Yiddish actor; Reyzl, a famous concert singer.

The reader follows Leybl's story mainly. In the end, the lovers overcome all kinds of obstacles to become reunited in New York.

Or do they?

It depends on which version you read, for Sholem-Aleykhem wrote two different endings to *Wandering Star***: one for the so-called American version (it began its publication in serial form in Warsaw newspapers in

---

*According to Dan Miron in his *Encyclopedia Judaica* article on Sholem-Aleykhem, it is his longest novel; other evidence suggests that *Der Blutiker Shpas (The Bloody Hoax)* may be somewhat longer: *Wandering Star* is 731 pages in the Yiddish 1914 Warsaw Yubileum Oysgabe; it appears in abridged form in Frances Butwin's English translation.

**"Wandering," by the way, does not convey exactly the same meaning as the Yiddish word *blondzhend*. The Yiddish word *blondzhen* really means to wander or blunder about because one has lost one's way, is lost. There is no single English word which can convey that meaning, at least none we can think of. In English, one can use the word "wander" to mean "roam purposely, at will, because one wants to." In Yiddish, *blondzhen* never means that. But since we cannot find an exact equivalent in English, "wander" will have to do. Also the original Yiddish title, *Blondzhende Shtern*, is in the plural; literally translated, the English title should be *Wandering Stars*, rather than *Wandering Star*.

1909 and completed its publication in 1911 in a New York newspaper), and another for the Russian translation in book form which appeared in 1913 (even before it appeared in Yiddish in book form).

The American version ends happily; the Russian one tragically. In a letter to the famous Yiddish literary critic, Sh. Niger, in 1912, Sholem-Aleykhem wrote that he wanted no one to see the American ending and that he would change it. But in another place Sholem-Aleykhem tells us he can't stand anything but a happy ending. You will have to read the Russian in order to savor the tragic ending: it doesn't exist in Yiddish (or English, for that matter).

In one place, Sholem-Aleykhem says the following about his three novels about Jewish artists:

> Whoever reads my second Yiddish novel will discern that my second hero, Yosele Solovey, stands, in many ways, much higher than Stempenyu (the hero of his first novel about Jewish artists). And the third hero, the true poet who is still in my thoughts for my third Yiddish novel *(Wandering Star)*, must, of course, stand on an even higher level than Yosele.

Whether he actually realized this ambition for *Wandering Star* is hard to say. He himself seemed to think so. In 1909 he wrote to a friend, "I ... felt the need to end my trilogy with the third novel following *Stempenyu* and *Yosele Solovey*, as I once promised to do.... There I said that my third 'hero' would be a higher type, a more refined soul...."

It is at any rate, as Anita Norich says, the novel with the most "extended social panorama" of the three.

Sholem-Aleykhem loved the theater. As his daughter put it in her biography of him: "My father's heart was in the theater" (Waife-Goldberg, 209). Because of his great genius for natural dialogue, many critics felt that his talent was more suited to the writing of plays than to the writing of novels, stories, and monologues. As a matter of fact, one of his earliest attempts at writing was a play called *Yakhnehoz*, published in 1894. And he did have one brief success in the theatre during his lifetime: in 1905 one of his plays, *Scattered and Dispersed* (originally only a story written in dramatic form) was performed at the Warsaw State Summer Theater in Russian (Yiddish theater being banned in Russia at the time). In a letter to his daughter, Tissa, he wrote of that performance:

> What shall I tell you about yesterday's triumph? I myself have participated on occasion in crazy ovations for beloved artists. But I have not seen anything like this, even in my literary fantasies. After the first act I was literally strewn with flowers. Then after every act I had to come out to receive repeated curtain calls. During the fourth act the audience simply went wild, applauding every phrase that had any bearing on the subject of the play. As the last curtain came down, hats began to fly in the air, and an enormous elemental force moved toward me, as if to swallow me up. For a moment I thought the roof would come down.... Good God what would have hap-

pened if it had been possible to play it in Yiddish? My fate and your future (I am referring to my progeny) are closely bound with the Jewish theater. (151-2)

In 1919 his dramatized version of the Tevye stories was performed in New York with Maurice Schwarz as Tevye. His stage version of *The Bloody Hoax* was performed in 1920 as *Shver tsu zayn a yid* by Muni Weissenfreund (later Paul Muni) in a production by Maurice Schwartz.

But he never really was able to succeed with this medium. And his greatest, bitterest failure came in 1906 when he came to New York to a great welcome and reception and was hailed in the newspapers as "the Jewish Mark Twain." He came with high hopes of gaining a great success in the New York Yiddish theater. He gave one play to the great Jacob Adler to perform, and a second to the equally prominent Yiddish actor/impresario of the time, Boris Tomashefsky. Both theaters had to close their doors after less than two weeks of performances. His attempt at success on the then booming New York Yiddish stage had been a dismal failure. A disappointed man, he returned to Europe.

His failure with the Yiddish theater in New York in 1906 is not a little reflected in his treatment of the Yiddish theatrical scene in New York at the end of *Wandering Star.*

In the beginning of the book, Reyzl and Leybl are sitting close together, in love, talking and looking at the night sky. Reyzl says, "Look, the stars are falling." Leybl laughs, and says "with gentle condescension: 'Don't be frightened Reyzl. It's natural for them to fall. Stars always seem to be falling. But they don't really fall; they wander .'"

What follows are the first four chapters of the novel that set the stage for our *blondzhende shtern,* our wandering stars, the two stage-struck shtetl lovers, Reyzl and Leybl, later to be known to admiring European and American audiences as Roza Spivak and Leo Rafalesko.

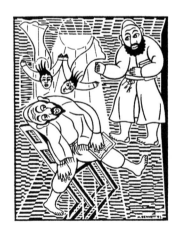

FROM

Wandering Star

1. "THE BIRD HAS FLOWN"

Early one Sunday morning, toward the end of summer, Leah, the Cantor's wife, awoke before anyone else, looked out the window, saw it was broad daylight, and exclaimed to herself, "A plague on me. Market-day and I'm still sleeping." Quickly she dressed, splashed cold water over her fingernails, swallowed down the morning prayer in one gulp, and snatching her basket, set off for the market place in such haste as though God knew what bargains lay in wait for her.

Outside the heat of the day smote her like a blast from an oven. Though it was early, the little Bessarabian town of Holeneshti already sweltered in the sun. At the market place Leah felt like a fish that has been tossed back into a cool stream. Here was no ordinary market. It was more like a fair. The peasants had brought to town their finest dairy products, vegetables and fruit—and everything a bargain! Huge melons and green cucumbers were practically given away. As for onions and garlic and other greens— no use asking. Leah bought everything, a little here and a little there, and soon her basket bulged. And then, at the last moment, the Lord sent her a bargain to crown all bargains—a mess of fish. Leah hadn't dreamed of shopping for fish, but they fell right into her lap. Actually, to call these fish was a presumption. Minnows, mere heads and tails—eat and spit—but the price! She'd be ashamed to tell anyone. Yes, this had been her lucky day at the market. Out of the single ruble she had brought with her there still remained a good bit of change.

Well, if that was the case, she must buy the Cantor a present— ten freshly laid eggs to make into ten eggnogs. "The High Holidays are coming and Isreal must be in good voice. Did you ever hear such a thing? And some candy for Reizel. What a sweet tooth that child has."

Fondly she thought of her daughter. Then, lest the thought appear a boast before the Lord, she added under her breath, "May all the harm meant for her fall on my head."

And the Cantor's wife darted in and out of the booths and stalls, appraising, bargaining, choosing, until the rest of the ruble had melted like snow in her hands. Only then did she start for home.

Nearing the house, she heard a series of trills, *Mi-i-i bo-a-ash va-mi-i ba-maim.*

It was the familiar, beloved voice of her husband which had rung in her ears for so long and of which she never grew weary. Israel was preparing a new version of the *Rosh-Hashono* prayer. "And we will declare the might..." Her Israel was not one of those renowned cantors whose names had spread all over the world. But in his own town of Holeneshti he was renowned enough. You may be sure the town wouldn't exchange him for one of those new-fangled city cantors or let go of him for a million. But that was beside the point. If Israel the Cantor hadn't managed to teach on the side, they would never have made ends meet. Luckily, besides being a cantor, he was also a fine Biblical scholar and a master of the Holy Tongue, and the Lord had also blessed him with a talent for penmanship. He had a round dozen youngsters in her *cheder* from the best homes in town, Rapalovich's son among them. Two such sources of income were not to be sneezed at. Still, it often happened that both occupations didn't bring in enough to provide for the Sabbath. Never mind, they hadn't starved yet.

As she put down her heavy basket and wiped the sweat off her face, Leah wondered why her daughter Reizel didn't come running to meet her. Usually, when she came home from market, Reizel ran out of the door, her face shining and her long braids swinging behind her. "What did you bring me, Mother?" she would call, as she burrowed into the basket for sweets.

"Wait, wait," the mother would stop her. "The river isn't on fire. First we have to put on a pot of chicory for your father. Did you ever see such a thing?"

But today nobody ran out to meet her. The basket stood untouched where she had set it. Except for the Cantor's warbling, which now rose to a crescendo, the house was strangely quiet. Reizel must still be sleeping, thought Leah, and busied herself about the stove. As she worked, she muttered under her breath:

"May night's darkness descend on my head. The morning half gone and she's still in bed. There's a girl for you. Any minute the boys will begin to arrive and she'll be running around half-naked. She thinks she's a small child. Israel, Israel!" She raised her voice. "He doesn't hear me. Just listen how he's letting himself go this morning. Dear God in Heaven, a person would think he expects to have his pockets stuffed with gold for his singing. And, instead, Reizel goes around in broken shoes. May the harm intended for her come down on my head. How long will that girl sleep? I'll have to go wake her. Have you ever seen such a thing?"

And Leah went up to the curtain that divided the room in half, lifted a corner with the tips on her fingers, and peered in. She looked at the bed, then at the window, and remained standing stock-still. She felt as though a heavy millstone had turned over in her breast. She screamed to her husband. "Israel!"

He stopped in the middle of a high note.

"Leah, what is it?"

"Where's Reizel?"

What do you mean, where's Reizel? Isn't she sleeping?"

Half an hour later the news had spread through the town. The Cantor's daughter had disappeared.

People began streaming through the house. "What's the news" "Is she gone?" "Where did she go?" "How did it happen?" Questions and answers flew back and forth. The Cantor alone said nothing. He stood in the middle of the room like a stone image, staring at the people who came and went. People touched their foreheads with their fingers, meaning, "The poor man has gone out of his mind."

Leah didn't stay home. Followed by a crowd of other women, she ran distraught through the town, wringing her hands and crying, "Reizel, my daughter, my treasure." They looked into alleys and gardens, they combed the bank of the river, they crossed the bridge, they hunted through the cemetery. Reizel was nowhere to be found.

At last the women brought Leah home half-fainting with terror and grief. The house was overflowing with people. Someone had rolled up the curtain that divided the room, and Reizel's bed stood exposed to view. It hadn't been slept in, and the window was wide open. A couple of the town's wags winked at each other.

"So the bird has flown from its nest."

207

The good people of Holeneshti weren't above making a jest of another's misfortune.

In those days every little Jewish town, no matter how poor, boasted its own Croesus, known as Rothschild.

The Rothschild of Holeneshti was Ben Rapalovich.

To go into detail about the extent of his wealth is superfluous. Suffice it to say that every day of the week Rapalovich's table seated no less than twenty-odd souls. Aside from sons and daughters, sons-in-law and daughters-in law, and grandchildren, all of them with well-nourished bodies, red cheeks, and fat jowls, there was his mother, an ancient crone whose head shook in a perpetual "No, no," the wet nurse, a good-looking young wench with rosy cheeks, and a certain young fellow, a distant relation, whom Rapalovich employed as his secretary and cashier.

At the head of the long board, like a king surveying his subjects, sat Ben Rapalovich himself, a typical Bessarabian Jew, with a comfortable paunch and an exuberant beard which refused to lie down like a proper beard but radiated in every direction from his dark, glistening face.

When the Rapaloviches sat down to a meal, their laughter and talk, the scraping of chairs, and the rattle of dishes and silver were deafening. But Rapalovich refused to be distracted by a small thing like noise. When he ate, he ate, and what went on around him was no concern of his. One thing at a time was his motto. He himself had little to say, but he didn't mind others talking. Only once in a long while, when the noise got really out of hand, he would pound on the table and shout, "Quiet, you bastards. Look down into your prayer books and attend to what you're reciting." Which meant, "Look into your plates and watch what you're eating."

For Ben Rapalovich spoke in a shrouded language of double meanings. To him a horse was a "fellow," money was "crockery," a wife was "an affliction," a son was a *"kaddish,"* a daughter was a "blister." Bread was "yarn," a house was "an attic," an alcove "a cell," and so on. An entire dictionary could have been complied of his speech.

In the least conspicuous place at the table, among the little children, sat his wife Beilka, a frail little woman, silent and unobtrusive. Each time you saw her you were struck with fresh wonder. How did this tiny crumb of a woman bring forth such a boisterous brood? And yet, as is often the case, this tiny woman carried on her frail shoulders the burden of the entire household. She was everywhere at once and her head ached for everyone. Long ago she had given up her position of honor to the aged grandmother. She seemed to have no wants or desires of her own. Her whole life was bound up in her children.

The old grandmother, whose head shook with palsy, seemed to have been created for the express purpose of reminding the others of the last stages of man. She had lost all her senses but one—a sharp eye. It was she who first noticed that the youngest of the brood, Leibel, was missing from the family board.

Her sharp eye scanned the long table and her voice quavered. "Where's Leibel today?"

Everyone hushed and looked around. It was true Leibel was missing. Though the Rapalovich clan was so large, it had never before happened that one of its members stayed away from a meal.

Peremptorily the head of the house issued a command.

"Let the young lamb be fetched from the pasture." Which meant, "Bring the boy home from *cheder.*"

At once a messenger was dispatched to the home of Israel the Cantor.

The family was on its last course, fresh melons and hot chestnuts, when the messenger returned with the astounding news that Leibel hadn't appeared at *cheder* that day. And he added another bit of information. The Cantor's only daughter, Reizel, had vanished during the night, no one knew where.

It was as though a bombshell had exploded in their midst. Too shocked for speech, the family stared at each other in silence. If a thought had occurred to anyone, he kept it to himself. Only the old grandmother, accustomed to speaking her mind, said, "Take a look into the cash drawer. I could swear I saw Leibel prowling there last night."

Rapalovich shrugged. Old people had strange whims. Nevertheless, he nodded to the cashier and that worthy bestirred himself and went up to the cash drawer. He unlocked it and leaped back, shouting, "Master, the money is gone."

At these words, a cry was heard at the end of the table and a small figure crumpled down in a faint.

It was the silent, unobrusive, frail little Beilka.

The town of Holeneshti seethed like a vat. Here was a scandal for you—two scandals rolled into one. A young couple had disappeared, and such an oddly assorted couple, the poor Cantor's daughter and the son of the wealthiest man in town.

209

Shopkeepers locked up their shops, teachers dismissed their pupils, workers laid down their tools, housewives forsook their pots and pans, the whole population poured out into the streets and overflowed the market place. Men, women, and children gathered in knots to air the scandal.

Rumors and conjectures began making the rounds. If one person reported something, a second capped it with something else; a third interrupted to say both storytellers were nothing but dumb oxen. Now the way he heard it.... But before he could begin, a fourth remarked that the third man knew less than the dead. Wait until he told them *his* story—a long, fanciful tale citing example and precedent for this and that detail....

Then a newcomer joined the group, a red-headed fellow with dim eyes, and put forth a ridiculous query. "Listen, my friends, let me ask you a question. How does it happen that the two birds have flown on the same night that the Yiddish theater packed up and left town?"

"Listen to him, what's one thing got to do with the other?'"

"It seems to me one thing has plenty to do with the other."

"Your brain's addled with the heat. Go jump in the river."

The crowd burst out laughing and the red-headed one put on an injured air.

"Cackle till you burst. If you're so wise, let me put another question to you. What were the actors doing last week at Israel the Cantor's house? If you don't believe they were there, take a walk to the Candor's and ask him."

"And pour more salt on his wounds? Not us."

"Then stop babbling foolishness and let me tall you what the actors were doing there. It seems they found out the Cantor had a pretty daughter who could also sing, and knowing he was a poor man, they asked him to let them take her into the theater and make an actress of her. Well, friends, is that to your taste?"

"It tastes good enough. But how do you account for Rapalovich's young son?"

"There you've got me. My head's been splitting all day trying to figure that out. Is it possible Rapalovich's son was in love with the girl? How could that young whippersnapper get into such a fix? Should I say the Cantor put the girl up to something? We know Israel too well for that. Then was it his wife? There might be something in that. No telling what a woman will do."

"Hush, children, the Governor rides," called out one of the

wags, pointing to the police chief who just then flew by in a shiny carriage hung with bells, and drawn by a pair of white horses which the crowd at once recognized as "Rapalovich's steeds." Next to the police chief huddled Yechiel the Musician, who had played for every performance of the Yiddish theater.

At sight of the carriage and horses and Yechiel's pale, frightened face, the stock of the red-headed one with the dim eyes soared sky-high. The listeners drew closer to him as he unfolded his story. Now his words not only had taste; they assumed the substance of truth.

With this clue to the disappearance of the young couple, let us leave the good people of Holeneshti to sharpen their wits on the new evidence, and turn back a short time to the day when the Yiddish theater arrived for its first visit since Holeneshti became a town and Bessarabia a province.

2. A STRANGER ARRIVES

Earlier that summer a stranger had arrived in Holeneshti. His appearance alone caused a mild stir. On his head was a battered derby, in his hands an imitation-leather suitcase. He was short and homely but his eyes were shrewd and his face was clean-shaven from top to bottom.

When the stranger announced that he had come to engage a hall for a Yiddish theater, the mild stir turned to an uproar. People came running from all over town to gape at him.

The inhabitants of Holeneshti had never seen a live actor. What was the theater? Did you eat it with a fork or a spoon? Did you sprinkle sugar or salt over it?

Sizing up the town and its inhabitants with one glance of his shrewd little eyes, the stranger pushed the derby back on his head, and said, in a curiously rasping voice, "I can see by the looks of things that our ancestor Adam never observed the Sabbath here."

A simple statement, it seems, yet it caused so much merriment, the stranger had to gape in his turn. When the guffaws had died down, he spoke again, this time earnestly.

"Friends, I've come a long way and my stomach is rumbling with hunger. Can anyone tell me where I can quiet its rumble?'

An ordinary request, you might think, and yet this, too, was received with high glee. The street rang with fresh peals of laughter.

The stranger appeared hurt at this levity. "I'm not joking. In plain words, where can I tie on the feed bag?"

That capped it. The crowd seemed to have been seized by a collective cramp. They doubled over and, holding their sides, rocked back and forth with unsuppressible laughter.

Within half an hour the whole town was repeating, "Where can I tie on the feed bag?"

"What a *schlimazl,*" they chortled, and wiped the tears from their eyes.

The *schlimazl* presently found what he had been seeking, a hostelry that served food. Not a pretentious place, but it would do.

Having dispatched a juicy herring and washed it down with a glass of native wine, our worthy drew a cigarette from his breast pocket, lit it, and addressed himself to the landlady, a presentable woman of gipsy complexion named Necha. He began peppering her with questions. Where was her husband, or was she a widow? Or perhaps a divorcee? The landlady found it hard to keep a straight face, and turned away from the *schlimazl.* Whereupon the *schlimazl* slung his cane over his arm, tipped his worn derby over one eye, and, putting his hands in his pockets, went strolling through the town. As he walked, he kept his eyes peeled for a likely place to set up the theater.

He was not alone in his rambles. At his heels trotted a ragged but enthusiastic mob of small urchins, newly won devotees of the Yiddish theater. And at last the stranger stopped before a huge, empty structure covered with a tin roof, in a big courtyard which also stood enpty.

"When God created the world in six days, He must have set this barn aside for the Yiddish theater," the stranger exclaimed, and walked into the yard.

It was Rapalovich's yard and barn he had stumbled upon.

Holeneshti didn't have to wait long for the Yiddish theater. As soon as the *schlimazl* had rented Rapalovich's barn, he dispatched the following letter:

My dear friend, Albert,

I am writing to report that I am now in Holeneshti a town in Bessarabia, as big as a yawn but chock full of people who devour cornmeal mush and guzzle wine as though it were water, but they will run to the theater as though the devil were behind them. And I have hired a hall that would do London proud, and it has a stage so big you could ride a sleigh and a team of horses through it, with a tin roof so a drop of rain can't squeeze in. The owner of this theater is named Rapalovich. He is stuffed with money like a sack with grain, still he wanted a down payment but I told him to cool his heels the money I said would come in the mail any day. And I found a lodging place. I'm not bragging but I can't complain either the landlady is a juicy little morsel it's eat drink and enjoy yourself and everything on credit. Don't let the grass grow under your feet but send me the decorations and playbills and pawn everything and bring the company down. If you sit around on your ass any longer we'll all starve to death and to get an engagement here is as easy as eating a *rossel fleisch* is for Hotzmach and speaking of Hotzmach, tell him to stop making eyes at the prima donna he'd better take care of Ethel Dvora first and will you please be so kind as to go over to my lodging I left a briefcase with some censored plays under my bed and send me the playbills without fail and don't get into a huff because I am not sending a wire all I have to my name is twenty kopeks.

Your friend who sends kind greetings to everyone,

Sholom Meyer

In a few days Sholom Meyer received the following reply:

Honored friend, Sholom Meyer,

A curse on you, why did you have to borrow fifteen rubles from Braindele Kozak and tell her to charge it to my account do I have accounts with her you bastard you know how much we all love Braindele that tightwad the way she trembles over every groschen as for the decorations and props you mentioned in your letter either you're playing dumb or you've gone mad you know very well that the props have been pawned long ago and where will I get the money to get them out of hock when I can't get an engagement here for love or money and I won't throw my own savings down the drain to stuff other people's gizzards they were too hard to come by in the first place. Unless they all sign a contract as Jacob signed for Rachel without any mention of profits or shares everybody wants to be a full partner how do you like that? Hotzmach my partner too! He'll never lived to see the day though he keeps threatening he will run off and start a company of his own let him run till he drops dead where will he get the props and the scripts and who will support his cast may he rot ten feet under ground. I am sending you the playbills and I want you to hire the hall for nine performances and a benefit and listen you thief what's the idea of babbling about twenty kopeks to your name are you too proud to

213

pawn your watch the way I did everybody is willing to make me the scapegoat everything is on my shoulders everybody wants the leading part and
when it comes to shelling out money nobody home. Listen this is my last
try if Bessarabia works out fine if not you can all go to the devil I am
going to Rumania to collect a new troupe that will make man and God
rejoice, meanwhile get everything ready but don't run up any bills we are
coming Friday evening and Saturday night we have a rehearsal and Sunday
we start performing and listen let me tell you that your censored plays
have been on the trash pile for a long time and I get letters from all over
the world with guarantees of engagements but I have turned them all
down because first I will run through Bessarabi and then we will see.

With kindest regards and best wishes from your friend and director,

Albert Shchupak

3. THE HOLENESHTI PUBLIC

Drunkards who hadn't tasted the bitter drop in months, starvelings
who had long been denied a bite to eat, couldn't have thrown
themselves on food and wine more avidly than the people of
Holeneshti threw themselves on the Yiddish theater.

Opening night found not only Rapalovich's courtyard but the
whole street in front of his house overflowing with people. The
crowd was so thick, you couldn't have thrown an apple among
them. But not everybody was prepared to go in. In the first place,
tickets cost money and money was a scarce commodity in Holeneshti. In the second place, theater wasn't everybody's dish. It was
well enough for young folks, for women and children to watch the
antics of comedians. But older men, respectable citizens, some of
them greybeards with daughters old enough to be led under the
marriage canopy, would have nothing to do with such frivolity.
Still, even these solid citizens were not exempt from the plague of
mankind, curiosity. Where is it written, they argued, that a man
shouldn't take a look from outside through a chink in the wall at
what is going on in the theater?

Against such chink-in-the-wall spectators the management hit
on a remedy, a water-sprinkler from which gushed a cold stream of

water. This method worked more efficiently than a squad of police and it was cheaper.

Its inventor was none other than our acquaintance Sholom Meyer, the *schlimazl*. What his function in the theater was is hard to explain. He was nothing and at the same time everything—bookkeeper, cashier, scene-shifter, ticket seller, and prompter. And when necessary he turned actor. To call him an accomplished artist would be exaggerating. But he was better than that, a hard worker, as faithful to his master as a dog, as Shchupak the director was well aware.

Most important of all, from the viewpoint of the public, Sholom Meyer was in charge of passes, candidates for which were plentiful in Holeneshti.

First and foremost was the Rapalovich clan, some twenty-odd souls. Rapalovich could afford to pay the price of admission many times over, but why should a man pay to enter his own barn? As the doors of the theater were flung open, Rapalovich, followed by his children and grandchildren, the cashier and wet nurse and other hangers-on, marched in and filled the first rows. When Sholom Meyer asked for tickets, Ben Rapalovich looked him up and down and said in a loud voice, "Take those sawed-off stumps of yours out of my sight before I pound you into cornmeal mush."

Sholom Meyer immediately discovered that he was needed elsewhere. And there were others who demanded passes. Take Yechiel the Musician. Who would have thought that a mere fiddler would boast such a large family? And what about the other members of the orchestra? And the wig-maker? And the carpenter, the smith, the tailor, the shoemaker? All had wives and children. And that juicy morsel of a landlady. Was she to blame that she had two younger sisters and a mother as deaf as a post? Enough that she supported them with food and lodging. Was she obliged to buy theater tickets for them, too? And Simon David the teamster and Chaim-Bear the porter, who had helped cart the scenery from the train. Let Albert the director gnash his teeth and tear his hair, let him fall in an apoplectic fit and drop dead altogether. Whoever had passes coming to him managed to get them. And if someone walked in without even a pass—well, let him come in.

You must never argue with the public.

Not the entire audience came in free. Many paid their last hard-earned ruble for a ticket, borrowed from friends, or pawned their last trinket or heirloom. When your children begged and pleaded and wept to go, you had to have a heart of stone to refuse them.

But what could you do when you had no money at all, no one to borrow from and nothing to pawn?

Into this last category fell Israel the Cantor. The income from both of his occupations didn't provide for luxuries like theater tickets. Reizel pleaded as hard as the other young people in town to be allowed to go, and Leah racked her brains for a way. Let the gossips wag their tongues, let them say she spoiled her only child, raised her on sweets and confections. Reizel must go to the theater.

And Leah found a way. Since Rapalovich's son Leibel was her husband's pupil, and since the entertainment was to take place in Rapalovich's barn, both the pot and the spoon were kosher. The whole thing was made to order. First she broached the subject to Israel, who would have nothing to do with it. His pride wouldn't allow him to speak to young Leibel. But where her child was concerned, Leah the Cantor's wife was willing to swallow her pride. As Leibel was about to leave the *cheder* that day, she drew him aside.

"Leibel, I have a favor to ask of you."

Leibel flushed and stared at his teacher's wife. A favor of him?

When he heard her request, his cheeks grew even redder. He was quite willing, he said, to speak to his mother, who would speak to his father, who would speak to his mother, who would ask his father.... Leibl stopped in confusion. But the meaning was plain. He would do it. Here Leibel's grave blue eyes met Reizel's dancing black ones, which seemed to say. "You're wonderful, Leibel. I know you can do it. If you only want me to go to the theater, I know I will go."

That same afternoon Leibel brought back the answer. He had spoken to his mother, who had spoken to his father, who said that if Reizel came to their house that evening she could go to the theater with them.

Reizel's face became radiant. She threw herself at her mother, hugged and kissed her, and, humming a dance tune, began whirling her mother around. Leah pushed her away, laughing.

"Have you gone out of your mind, child? Better hurry and get washed and dressed. Then I will braid your hair for you. After all, you're going out among people tonight. Have you ever seen such a thing?"

That evening Leah herself ecorted Reizel to the Rapalovichs' and entrusted her daughter to Beilka's care.

"You know she's my one and only child, the apple of my eye."

Beilka looked at the young girl and what she saw seemed to meet with her approval. "Don't worry," she promised, "I'll watch over her as though she were one of my own."

Left alone at the Rapaloviches', Reizel felt uneasy at first. She was surrounded by so many strangers, who all seemed to devour her with their eyes. And the questions they asked her, each one separately and all together. "How old are you?" "What is your name?" "Where do you live?"

And all those eyes. They wouldn't stop boring through her.

Her own eyes were drawn to everything. Reizel had never, in her wildest dreams, beheld such a house. Such a multitude of rooms, so much furniture, so many tables, chairs, beds, mirrors, and knick-knacks, and the supper table set with such a profusion of dishes. Such bowls of fruit, so many different kinds of perserves. And the noise, the clatter, the talk, the laughter. So that's what being rich meant.

Reizel had known that her father's pupil Leibel was the son of the richest man in town. But just what that meant had never been clear to her. That it was good to be rich and bad to be poor she had heard from her mother not once, but a thousand times. "Pawn your empty purse and become rich." "Luck always favors the rich." "The rich are even welcome in the next world." Until now these proverbs had been empty of meaning. Now she sat at a sumptuously laden table surrounded by gay, carefree faces. For the first time in her life she felt a twinge of envy. Then her eyes met a pair of grave blue eyes, the only familiar eyes there. They seemed to be saying, "Are you happy with us? I am so glad you are happy." Her heart stirred and she felt an unaccustomed delicious warmth steal through her limbs.

4. THE CURTAIN RISES

The theater was filled long before starting time. Who wanted to take a chance on being late? Late arrivals had to sit in each other's laps, and the last to come in stood squeezed in the aisles or flattened against the walls. They felt greatly put upon; they had paid good, hard cash for seats, and where were they? Low grumbles were heard, then louder complaints, then a hue and cry. At the peak of the hubbub Sholom Meyer, resourceful as always, gave the musicians a signal to start up a tune. Hearing music, the audience thought the curtain was about to go up, settled down as best it could, and quiet descended.

But the music stopped and the curtain remained drawn. From behind it came shouts and curses, the sound of running feet, furniture being moved, hammers pounding. The audience became restive, children wriggled in their seats, pounded on the floor, and clamored loudly for the show to begin.

Among the young people eagerly waiting for the curtain to rise was a young couple, a boy with fair hair and blue-grey eyes and a vivacious dark-eyed girl with dimpled cheeks. They sat close together, oblivious of everyone around them, who were equally oblivious of them. Who had eyes for Rapalovich's young son and the Cantor's girl with the curtain before them?

This was the first time Leibel and Reizel found themselves so close to each other. They had seen each other other often enough at her father's *cheder,* but there Leibel had to keep his eyes on his books. And Reizel's mother, Leah, was strict. She wouldn't let her go near any of the pupils. "A girl," she would say, "has no business with boys. For a girl is a girl and boys are boys. Did you ever see such a thing?"

Leah wouldn't even allow Reizel to sing when the boys were at their studies. And Reizel loved to sing better than anything in the world. Sometimes she forgot her mother's prohibition and a melody burst from her lips. When that happened the boys stopped their reading and listened with bated breath. And later, at home, more than one of them remembered and sighed and dreamed of the teacher's daughter.

For Leibel it had been more than a passing sigh or a dream. Reizel's face and voice haunted him at all times. More than once, in the *Gemorah* held in front of him he saw not the fine print of the text but Reizel's vivid face.

Many times he had sought excuses to linger behind the others to speak to Reizel only to have that mother of hers come between them. On her part, Reizel, too, had stolen glances at her father's pupils, seeking out Leibel among them. Not because he was the wealthy Rapalovich's son, which had meant little to her, but because of what her father had said about him, that he had a good head on him, and a fine voice. Israel was no mean judge of those two abilities.

Leah, of course, interpreted this in her way. "Why not? It's a rich man's luck to have gifted children. Have you ever seen such a thing?"

Now Reizel and Leibel sat close to each other on a single bench. Leibel could feel her nearness: he thought he could hear her heart beat. Or was it his own heart pounding? He wanted to say something to make her eyes sparkle and her dimples come out. But his throat felt too tight. Reizel wanted to speak, too, but couldn't think of anything to say. So they looked at each other wordlessly.

All at once they realized how fast time had flown, for now the lights went out one by one. Voices whispered on all sides.

"Oooooh."

"It's as dark as in Egypt during the plagues."

"Ow, My foot."

"Whose fault is that? You have a sore foot, so leave it at home."

"Be quiet. *Shah.* Let it be quiet."

"The devil with you—be quiet yourself."

The audience drew a long breath, shivered, and was still. Leibel didn't know how it had happened, but all at once Reizel's hand, a warm, soft hand, was clasped in his own. He gave it a light squeeze, as though to say, "Happy?" And she replied with a soft pressure which meant, "Very."

The curtain had risen.

For the people of Holeneshti the theater was a bit of luck which had dropped down on them from the clear sky. But for Rapalovich's son and the Cantor's daughter it was more. It was sheer heaven. It was a return to the legendary Garden of Eden. Night after night they went there, occupied the best seats, and beheld the wonders unfolding before them.

A new world had opened up for them in which people disguised their features, dressed in peculiar garb, strutted about, spoke strange words, danced and sang, and acted out scenes which evoked gales of laughter or melted you in tears.

Who were these people? Were they ordinary human beings?

Impossible. They weren't mortals such as you and I, but spirits and demons, or else angels from heaven. Their every gesture and movement, the way they walked forward or stepped back or even stood still was a marvel. They must be bewitched, along with everything around them. From the moment the curtain went up, Reizel and Leibel fell under a magic spell, forsaking the earth for a region of spirits and fairies, demons and angels.

However, when the curtain went down, the magic vanished, the demons and angels gone into thin air. Leibel and Reizel returned to their ordinary selves in the ordinary workaday world. From the top-most pinnacle of heaven they had plunged back to earth. Stunned, they comforted themselves with the thought that the curtain would go up again; again the next night they would soar into heaven.

All the young fellows in Holeneshti envied Leibel because it was in his father's yard that this splendor took place. And all the girls in town were dazzled by Reizel's good fortune in her sudden elevation to the seats of the mighty.

And Reizel's mother, Leah, wasn't above boasting about it. What if she had found favor in the eyes of the rich? Didn't a child like Reizel deserve it?

Still, lest people jump to the wrong conclusions, Leah was careful to explain how it had all come about. "How did my child fall in among the Rapaloviches? Wait, I will tell you. I happened to run into Beilka Rapalovich at the market one day. 'Good morning,' says she. 'A good day to you,' say I. 'And how are you and yours?' she asks. 'God be thanked, and how goes it with you?' 'Don't ask,' she tells me. 'There's bedlam at my house. Some kind of theater has come to town, and they set it up in our barn. You can imagine the excitement among my boys and girls. And how is *your* daughter? I've been hearing fine things about her.' 'Thanks,' I tell her. 'It could be worse.' 'Why,' she says, 'don't you send her over to my house?' 'And what would she do there?' I say. 'She'll get acquainted with my girls, go along to the theater with them. Why not?' 'Thanks,' I tell her, 'I'll ask Reizel. If she's willing to go, I'll certainly send her.'"

A lie, every word of it. But what won't a mother do for her child? Leah found further occasion to drop remarks in front of the neighbors.

"Reizel, what did you have for supper at the Rapaloviches last night?"

"Reizel, what time are you going to the Rapaloviches tonight?"

Or later: "If they ask you for supper again, don't turn them down. No use being bashful. Did you ever see such a thing?"

When the performance was over, the audience made a rush for the doors. Earlier everyone had wanted to be the first to enter; now everyone wanted to be the first to leave. Leibel and Reizel were almost carried out in the press of the crowd.

Outside the night was fragrant and balmy, a semi-tropical Bessarabian night, velvety-black, pierced with stars and lit by a red harvest moon. The day had cooled off and the thick dust had settled, making it possible to breathe again. The cool breeze carried odors of ripening grain, melons, apples, and pears.

The Jews of Holeneshti walked home from the theater, not sedately, with polite leave-takings like big-city theater-goers, but yelling and gesticulating. In such a crowd everyone feels duty-bound to impart to the next person what he had seen and heard, in a shrill voice, with inflections and gestures. Everyone is convinced that what *he* saw and heard no one else saw or heard. One repeats a joke several times over for emphasis; another imitates the comedian; a third hums snatches of a song. Children tumble under the grown-ups' feet, laughing and shrieking and crying. Young people gather in clumps or loiter in pairs, reluctant to go home. But there is nowhere to go after the theater, and soon the town is quiet again. At home everyone says his prayers, blows out the lamp, and the town sleeps.

In the small house on God's Street where Israel the Cantor lived, a smoky lamp burned late. The Cantor and his wife were waiting for their daughter's return.

Israel, a distinguished-looking man with a silky black beard, sat in his night clothes and skullcap, fanning himself and intoning the bedtime prayer. Leah, enveloped in a voluminous white gown that threw into sharp relief her swarthy face and snapping black eyes, sat on her bed, her figure casting a grotesque shadow on the whitewashed wall.

The moment Reizel entered the door, Leah pounced on her What sort of "comedy" had the actors put on tonight? Which of their friends was there? What did she eat at the Rapaloviches?

Reizel hardly heard what her mother was saying. Her face was aflame with excitement, her heart was filled to bursting, and there was a rapt, faraway look in her eyes. In her ears still rang the voices of the actors declaiming their lines, the strains of the orchestra and the laughter of the Rapalovich clan. Loudest of all echoed Leibel's whisper: "Will you come again tomorrow?"

"Yes, I will come. How can you ask?" She had not spoken, but answered him as always with a pressure of her hand.

Later, as Reizel snuggled down into her pillow, she shut her eyes, and gave herself up to dreams which carried her far off from God's Street, back to her newly found Garden of Eden, to the world of the theater.

V

The Three Great Novels/Characters

TEVYE, MENAKHEM-MENDL, AND *MOTL-PEYSI-DEM-KHAZNS*

Sholem-Aleykhem surrounded by characters from his Tevye stories.

INTRODUCTION TO
TEVYE THE DAIRYMAN

Sholem-Aleykhem wrote the Tevye stories between the years 1894 and 1916. They were first published together, in the form of a "novel," in 1911 in Warsaw (not including, of course, the episodes written at a later date), a complete edition not appearing until 1918 in New York.

There is some controversy among some critics/scholars as to whether *Tevye the Dairyman* can rightly be called a novel. Hillel Halkin thinks it can; Dan Miron thinks not. At any rate, whether the series of episodes centering around Tevye and his daughters, written and published over the course of twenty-three years, can be called a novel or a series of "mythic" stories, we will leave to the *talmide-khakhomim* to figure out.

But one thing I think all the critics and scholars, as well as general readers, can agree on, and that is that *Tevye the Dairyman* is Sholem-Aleykhem's greatest work.

Why that is so is not so easy to say. The answer lies in the combination of the character of Sholem-Aleykhem's Tevye, the character of Tevye's daughters, and the plight of the Jews trapped in the Russian Empire of the time, so subtly refracted in the Tevye stories. Sholem-Aleykhem is known as a great humorist, but as we read these Tevye stories, we witness one tragic situation after another. Wherein lies the humor? It derives, of course, from Tevye's beautiful humanity and grace in the face of all his troubles, his way of talking, his inimical "quotations," his way of dealing with his wife and others—these always provoke a smile, sometimes even a laugh. But, all in all, what's there to laugh?

In the stories, Tevye speaks of seven daughters. The Tevye cycle contains stories about only five of his daughters (Tsaytl, Hodl, Khave, Shprintse, and Beylke). A sixth daughter, Taybl, is mentioned in the Shprintse story, but there is no story about her, nor is there one about the seventh daughter, who remains unnamed.

This translation of *Tevye the Dairyman* is the first to include every part of the original, including the short preface ("I Am Not Worthy") as well as the little "header" preceding the first story, "The Grand Prize," and a summary and the final paragraph of the last episode, *"Vekhalaklakoys" ("Slippery Places").*

Miriam Katz, the translator of the Tevye stories presented below, tells us the following:

As a young man in New York my father worked on the staff of the Yiddish Newspaper *Der Tog (The Day)*. It was to this newspaper that Sholom Aleichem contributed some of his last stories, from the time of his arrival in the USA from Europe in 1914, at the beginning of World War I, and up to his death in 1916.

The long, narrow slips of tinted paper on which Sholom Aleichem wrote, with tiny curlicues scribbled on the margins, fascinated my father. He subsequently treasured them, so great was his admiration and respect for the great Jewish writer. I remember the look of those manuscripts from my childhood.

Such were the memories and thoughts that prompted me to undertake the translation of this book from the Yiddish into English....

It is an interesting exercise to compare the highly successful *Fiddler on the Roof* with the original, *Tevye the Dairyman,* on which it is, loosely, based.

What follows are Sholem-Aleykhem's introduction ("I Am Not Worthy") and all eight of the Tevye stories (the last one being represented by a summary and its final paragraph). *Tevye the Dairyman* is all here in Miriam Katz's inspired and accurate translation.

It is, of course, Sholem-Aleykhem's masterpiece.

"I bought you a cow then for fifty rubles, it would have been a steal at fifty-five. What if it did drop dead three days later? It was not my fault: didn't the other cow I bought you also kick the bucket?"

I Am Not Worthy

With all respect to my very dear friend Reb Sholom Aleichem, God grant you health and a good living together with your wife and children, let great pleasure be yours wherever you go, amen!

"I am not worthy!" So I must say using the words our forefather Jacob said—in the Sabbath section of the Torah—when he set out against Esau, begging your pardon... If this is not quite right, I beg you, Mr. Sholom Aleichem, not to hold it against me, I am a simple man. You, of course, know more than I do—that goes without saying. Alas, a person coarsens in a village: who has time to look into a book or learn a portion of the Torah with Rashi's commentaries, or anything else? It's a lucky thing that when summer arrives the rich people from Yehupetz come to Boiberik to their summer homes, their *dachas,* so that one is likely to meet an enlightened person sometimes, to hear a good word. Believe me, the remembrance of those days when you sat near me in the woods listening to my foolish yarns is dearer to my heart than any amount of money! I don't understand how I found so much favor in your eyes that you should take up with such an insignificant person and even write letters to me and, above all, put my name into a book, serve me to the world as a dainty dish, just as if I were I don't know who, so I may well say: *"I am not worthy!"* True, I am really a good friend of yours, let God help me to a hundredth part of what I wish you! You saw, I am sure, how well I served you back in the good old days when you lived in the big *dacha*—do you remember? I bought you a cow then for fifty rubles, it would have been a steal at fifty-five. What if it did drop dead three days later? It was not my fault at all: didn't the other cow I gave you also kick the bucket? You know very well yourself how hard I took this, I absolutely lost my head then! I tried my very hardest to get you the best of everything, so help me God, and you, too, if he so wills, in the coming year. He should, as they say, *"make our days the same as in olden times."* And let God help me make a living and be

healthy, and my horse—begging your pardon—should be healthy, and my cows should give enough milk for me to go on serving you with my cheese and butter in the best possible manner, you and all the rich people from Yehupetz, God grant them success in their undertakings, all good things and happiness. And the same to you for the trouble you take, for bothering yourself on my account, for the honor you are paying me with your book, I can only repeat: *"I am not worthy!"* With what have I earned such an honor—that a world of people should suddenly become aware that on the other side of Boiberik, near Anatovka, there lives a Jew named Tevye the Dairyman? But you probably know what you are doing, I don't have to teach you wisdom, you know how to write, and in all other matters I trust your noble nature and am sure that you will see to it in Yehupetz that this book brings me, too, some benefit. It really would come in handy now: the Lord be willing, we shall soon have to think of a match for a daughter, and if He grants, maybe even for two daughters at once. Meanwhile remain in good health and be happy always, as your friend Tevye wishes you from the bottom of his heart.

Tevye

Oh, Yes! I almost forgot! When the book is ready and you are prepared to send me some money, please send it to Anatovka, care of the local slaughterer. I observe two memorial days there, one in the autumn, just before the Russian *Pokrov,* and the other around the Russian New Year. These days I spend in the *shtetl.* Ordinary letters you may send directly to me in Boiberik, addressing them: *Peredat gospodinu Tevelu molochnaho yevrei**.

1895

---

*To be forwarded to Mister Tevel the milky Jew (incorrect Russian).—*Tr.*

The Grand Prize

A wonderful narrative describing how Tevye the Dairyman, a poor man burdened with a large family, was suddenly, out of the blue, made happy through a miraculous event worthy of being written up in a book. It is presented as told by Tevye himself, word for word .

"Who raiseth up the poor out of the dust, And lifteth up the needy out of the dunghill..."
Psalms, 113:7

If you are destined to win a grand prize, Mr. Sholom Aleichem, it comes right home to you. As it is said in the Psalms, when it moves your way it comes in a rush! Cleverness or skill have nothing to do with it. But if, God forbid, it goes the other way—you may talk yourself blue in the face and it will be of as much use as last winter's snow. Over a bad horse, they say, neither wisdom nor advice can prevail. A man toils, struggles, gets so exhausted he is ready to lay himself down and die! Then all of a sudden, no one knows from what and from where, luck descends on him from all sides. As the Torah says, *"Relief and deliverance will come to the Jews."* It means that while his soul is still in his body, while the blood still pulses through his veins, a Jew should never lose hope. From my own experience I know how the Almighty led me to my present livelihood. How did it happen that I started selling cheese and butter all of a sudden, when my grandmother's granny never dealt in dairy foods? It will be worth your while to hear the whole story from beginning to end. I'll sit down here next to you on the grass and let my horse graze meanwhile, for, as it is said, *"the soul of everything that lives"*—a horse is also one of God's creatures.

Well, it was around *Shabuoth* time—I don't want to tell any lies, it might have been a week or two before *Shabuoth*, or maybe even a few weeks after. Don't forget that little by little, to be pre-

229

cise, a year of Sundays has already gone by since then, that is, exactly nine years or ten, or maybe a bit more.

In those days I was not the same person I am now. That is, I was the same Tevye, but different. As they say, the same old woman but under a different veil. I was then—may this never happen to you—as poor as poor can be, although, to tell the truth, I am by far no rich man today. You and I together should this summer earn what I would need to be as rich as Brodsky, but as compared to those days I am today a well-to-do man with my own horse and wagon, with a couple of, knock on wood, milch cows and another cow that is due to calve any day now. It would be a sin to complain, we have cheese and butter and fresh cream every day, all earned with our own labor, we all work, nobody is idle. My wife, bless her, milks the cows, the children carry the jugs and churn the butter, while I myself, as you see, drive to the market early every morning and call at every Boiberik *dacha*. I get to meet this person, that person, all the important people from Yehupetz, I chat a while with them and this makes me feel that I am also worth something in the world, that I am, as they say, no "lame tailor". To say nothing of the Sabbath; I'm really a king then, I look into a Jewish book, I read the weekly portion of the Torah, a bit of *Targum*, some of the Psalms, *Perek*, this, that, and something else; looking at me, Mr. Sholom Aleichem, you probably think: "Eh, this Tevye really amounts to something!..."

But what was it I began to tell you? Oh, yes, so at that time, I was, with God's help, a bitterly poor man, starving to death—such a fate shouldn't befall others—with my wife and children three times a day not counting supper. I toiled like a mule, hauling logs from the woods to load into box-cars at the railway station for, it's a disgrace to say, two *zlotys** a day, and this not every day, either. Go and support such a houseful of eaters, God bless them, and also, begging your pardon, my boarder, the horse, who wanted to know nothing of Rashi's commentaries but had to munch fodder every day without any excuse at all!

So what does God do? It is He, after all, who feeds and nurtures us, He rules this little world in a wise and orderly manner. Seeing how I struggle for a piece of bread, He says to me: "You think, Tevye, that it's already the end of the world, that the sky has

---

*A Polish monetary unit equivalent to less than half of a U.S. dollar.—*Tr.*

fallen down on you? Pooh, you are a big fool! Just wait, you'll see how, when God so wills, your luck will about-face and a bright light will shine in all the nooks and crannies." Like in the High Holiday hymn describing the Day of Judgment: *"Who will be raised and who flung down"*—who will ride and who go on foot. The principle of this is faith—a Jew must hope, only hope and have confidence. What if you do suffer meanwhile? After all, that is why we are Jews, as it is written: *"Thou hast chosen us"* — it is not for nothing that the whole world is envious of us. Why am I telling you this? I am telling you what God did for me, really *"miracles and wonders,"* you must hear it.

"And there came the day." One summer evening I was driving my empty wagon home through the woods. My head was bowed, my heart was heavy. The horse, poor thing, could barely move its legs. "Crawl, *shlimazl,* get lost together with me! Since you are Tevye's excuse for a horse you must know what it means to fast all of a long summer day!" There was silence all around me, every crack of my whip echoed and re-echoed in the woods. The sun was setting, the day was dying. The shadows of the trees became longer and longer—as long as the Jewish exile. As the dusk thickened, a great gloom settled in my heart. Various thoughts flitted through my mind, images of people long dead came towards me. Then I remembered my home, woe is me! The house is dark and bleak, the children, bless them, are naked and barefoot, waiting, poor things, for their *Tateh,* their father the *shlimazl,* hoping he will bring them a fresh loaf of bread or maybe even a white roll. And she, my old woman, is grumbling, as women are wont to do: "Children I had to bear him, a whole seven, take and throw them—God shouldn't punish me for my words—alive into the river!" Nice hearing such words, eh? A man is no more than flesh and blood—the stomach cannot be filled with words. You snatch a bite of herring and then you yearn for tea, but with tea you must have sugar, and sugar, they say, is in Brodsky's refineries. "For the piece of bread I go without," says my wife, God bless her, "my innards will excuse me, but without a glass of tea in the morning I am a dead woman—the baby sucks all the juices out of me the whole night long!"

Meantime, one is, after all, something of a Jew; *Minhah,* the afternoon prayer, is no goat, it won't run away, but pray one must. Then just imagine what kind of praying it was then, just as I stood up to say *Shmin-esra,* the horse, as bad luck would have it, bolted and I had to run after the wagon, holding on to the reins and chanting: *"God of Abraham, God of Isaac, God of Jacob"*—truly a fine way to chant *Shmin-esra!* And to make it worse, I was then just in the right mood to pray with zest, from the bottom of my heart, hoping that it might, perhaps, lift the load from my soul.

Well, to make a long story short, here I was running along behind the wagon and chanting *Shmin-esra* loudly, as if I were in the cantor's pulpit in the synagogue: *"Thou sustaineth the living with loving kindness,"* and *"keeping Thy covenant even with those who sleep in the earth."* Oh, thought I, not only the dead lie in the dust... Oh, how we suffer! Not, of course, those rich people from Yehupetz who spend a whole summer at their *dachas* in Boiberik, eating and drinking and basking in luxury. Oh, God Almighty, what have I done to merit this kind of life? Am I worse than other people? Help, dear God! *"Look upon our afflictions"*—just look upon us how we toil, put an end to the wrong suffered by the wretched poor, for who, if not You, will take care of us? *"Heal us, O Lord"*—send us the medicines, the ailments we already have. *"Bless us"*—bless this year for us, O Lord our God, with every kind of crop, with corn and wheat and barley; although, thinking it over, what will I, *shlimazl* that I am, get out of it? What difference does it make to my nag—begging your pardon—whether oats are dear or cheap? But shame on me, you don't question God, and a Jew, especially, must take everything as being for his good and say: *"And this, too, is for the best"*—probably God wills it so...

"And for slanderers let there be no hope"—I went on chanting; the slanderers and the 'ristocrats who say there is no God in the world will be put to shame when they get *there*. They'll pay for their blasphemy, and with interest, because He is one who *"breaketh His enemies"*—a good payer, with Him you play no games, with Him you are humble, you implore him, you cry out to Him: *"Merciful Father"*, dear, kind Father! *"Hear our voices"*—listen to us. *"Have mercy upon us"*, have pity on my wife and children, they, poor things, are hungry! *"Deign Thou..."*—have compassion for your beloved Children of Israel, as you once did in the Holy Temple, when the Priests and the Levites... Just then—stop! The horse suddenly stopped and stood stock-still. Hastily I rolled off the last piece of *Shminesra* and then raised my eyes: two very strange creatures were coming towards me out of the forest. They were either disguised, or strangely dressed.

Bandits—flashed through my mind, but I immediately thought

better of that. Pooh, Tevye, aren't you a fool? Just reflect, you've been driving through this forest for so many years, both in the daytime and at night, why should you suddenly think of bandits today? "Giddy-up!" I shouted to my horse, took heart and treated it to a few lashes of the whip, making believe I hadn't noticed anything.

"Reb Jew, my good man, listen!" cried one of the creatures in a female voice, beckoning to me with a kerchief. "Do please stop for a moment, wait a while, don't run away, we won't do you any harm!"

Oho, an evil spirit! was my thought, but I soon told myself: You ass! Why all of a sudden devils and demons?

So I stopped the horse. Now I took a good look at the creature: females, the older one wearing a silken kerchief over her head, the younger one wearing a wig*. Their faces were flaming red and covered with beads of sweat.

"Good evening, well met!" said I very loudly, trying to look cheerful. "What do you wish? If you want to buy something I have nothing but a bellyache I wish on all my enemies, a weekful of heart pains, a head dizzy from worries, dry aches and wet anguish, troubles and misery wholesale and retail!"

"Shush, shush," they cried. "Just see how his tongue has loosened! When you hook a Jew with one word beware of your life! We don't want to buy anything at all, we only wanted to ask you whether you know the way to Boiberik?"

"To Boiberik," I exclaimed, forcing myself to laugh, "it's just as if you'd asked me whether I knew that my name was Tevye."

"Oh, so your name is Tevye? A good evening to you, Reb Tevye! We can't see what's so funny? We're strangers, from Yehupetz, we live on a *dacha* in Boiberik," they said. "We went out for a short walk early this morning, but lost our way in the woods, and have been wandering around in circles ever since and couldn't find the right way. We heard someone singing, so at first we thought, God forbid, it was a bandit. But when we got closer and saw that you were, thank God, a Jew, our hearts felt a little lighter. Now you understand?"

"Ha-ha-ha! A fine bandit!" said I, "Did you ever hear the story of the Jewish highwayman who attacked a passer-by and asked him for a pinch of snuff? If you wish I can tell it to you."

---

*Orthodox married women wear wigs.—*Tr.*

233

"Two very strange creatures were coming towards me out of the forest."

"The story leave for another time," they said. "Better show us the way to Boiberik."

"To Boiberik," I repeated. "Why, this is the right way. Even if you don't want it to, this road will take you directly into Boiberik."

"So why didn't you say so at once, why the silence?"

"Should I have shouted, or what?"

"In that case," they said, "you know, perhaps, how far it is to Boiberik?"

"It's not far," I answered, "only a few versts*, that is, something like five, six or seven, and maybe even all of eight versts."

"Eight versts!" exclaimed both women at once, wringing their hands and almost weeping. "Do you realize what you are saying? It's no trifle—eight versts!"

"Well," said I, "what can I do about it? If it were in my power I'd have made the distance a little shorter. A person must try everything in the world. On the road it happens that you have to crawl uphill through mud, and it is the Sabbath eve, to boot, the rain is lashing your face, your hands are numb with cold, your heart is faint with hunger, and—cr-ra-ash! An axle breaks."

"You're talking like a ninny," they said to me, "you are out of your mind! Telling us old wives' tales, stories from the *Arabian Nights?* We haven't the strength to take another step. Except for a glass of coffee and a butter roll, we haven't had a morsel of food all day, and here you come along with your yarns!"

"Oh, if that's the case," said I, "then it's another thing. As they say, you don't dance before you eat. The taste of hunger I understand very well, you don't have to explain... I probably haven't as much as seen any coffee or butter rolls for well over a year." As I spoke, a glass of steaming coffee with milk and a fresh butter roll appeared before my mind's eye, and other goodies, too. Oh, you *shlimazl*, I thought to myself, so you have actually been raised on coffee and butter rolls? A hunk of bread with a piece of herring isn't good enough for you? But the Tempter, Heaven preserve us, spites me with visions of coffee and of rolls! I smell coffee and taste a butter roll, fresh, delicious, soul-enlivening!

"You know what, Reb Tevye?" said the women. "It would be a good idea, since we are standing here, for us to climb into your wagon and for you to take the trouble to drive us home to Boiberik. What do you think of that?"

---

*An old Russian unit of linear measure equal to 3,500 ft.; 8 versts is 5.5 miles.—*TR.*

"A fine notion," said I, "here I'm coming *from* Boiberik while you have to go *to* Boiberik! So what's the solution?"

"Well, so what," they said, "don't you know what to do? A wise man would turn his wagon around and drive back to Boiberik. Don't worry, Reb Tevye, rest assured that when, God willing, you get us home safely we should have as many afflictions as what you'll lose on this transaction."

They're speaking gibberish to me, thought I, obscure language, most unusual! Into my head came corpses, witches, pranksters, evil spirits. You blockhead, son of a woodpecker, I told myself, why are you standing there like a stump? Jump onto your wagon, show your horse the whip and make yourself scarce! Meanwhile, however, in spite of myself, I unintentionally let out:

"Get into the wagon!"

The women didn't have to be asked twice. They climbed in, I seated myself on the box, about-faced the shafts and gave my horse a taste of the whip—one, two, three, giddy-up! But who, what, where? The animal wouldn't budge, go and cut it in two!

Well, I thought, now I understand what kind of women these are. It was no good wind that drove me to stop all of a sudden and be drawn into a conversation with women!

You must understand: on the one hand, there was the forest with its silence and gloom, on the other, these two creatures in the guise of women... My imagination ran wild. I recalled the story told about a carter who was once driving all alone through a forest. He suddenly saw a bag of oats lying in the road. He jumped off his dray and lifted the bag—it was so heavy that he all but ruptured himself before he managed to heave it onto the dray. Then he continued on his way. After a verst or so he took a look at the bag of oats—no bag, no oats. Instead there was a goat in his dray, a bearded goat. He tried to touch it but the creature stuck out a tongue a yard long, let out an eery, mad peal of laughter and vanished into thin air!

"Why aren't we moving?" asked the women.

"Why we aren't moving? You see, don't you," said I, "that the horse is not in the mood."

"So use your whip—you have one, haven't you?"

"Thanks a lot for the advice, it's a good thing you reminded me, but the trouble is that this animal has no fear of such things. He is as used to the whip as I am to poverty," said I, trying to joke, but meanwhile shaking as if in a fever.

To make a long story short, I poured out the bitterness of my heart on the poor beast until, with God's help, it bestirred itself *"and they went out of Refidim"*—we drove away along the road through the forest. A new thought entered my head as we jogged along: Oh, Tevye, are you an ass! *"If thou hast begun to fall"*—a pauper you were and a pauper you'll stay! Look, God has sent you an encounter that happens once in a hundred years, so why don't you settle beforehand on a payment for your services? You should know what they will give you. According to justice, conscience, humaneness, law and I don't know what else there is no sin in earning something out of such an affair. Really, why not get a lick of a bone since it has come your way? Stop your horse, you ox, and tell them, so and so, *"I will serve thee for Rachel thy daughter"*—if I receive such and such a sum from you, well and good, if not— I must ask you, begging your pardon, to get off my wagon! But then I thought again: You really are an ox, Tevye! Don't you know that a bearskin can't be sold in the forest, or, as the peasant says: *Sche nye poimav a vzhe skube,* that is, you haven't caught it yet and are already skinning it!

"Why don't we move a little faster?" asked the women, poking my back.

"What's your great hurry? Nothing good ever comes of haste," I answered, glancing at my passengers out of the corner of an eye: women, seemingly, ordinary women, one with a silken kerchief on her head, the other with a wig. They sat there looking at each other and whispering.

"Have we still far to go?" they asked.

"Most certainly no farther than from here," I answered. "Soon we'll go downhill, then uphill; after that downhill and uphill again, and only after that will come the big uphill stretch and then the road will take us right into Boiberik..."

"A piece of *shlimazl!*" said one women to the other.

"A lingering ailment," remarked the other one.

"The last straw!" exclaimed the first one.

"Looks crazy to me!" rejoined the second one.

Of course I must be crazy, thought I, since I let myself be hoodwinked!

"Where, for instance, my dear ladies, would you like to be dropped off?" I asked.

"What do you mean—dropped off?"

"It's just an expression drivers use," I answered. "In our lingo it means, 'Where do you wish me to take you when we get to Boiberik, God willing, in good health,' as people say, it's better to ask twice than to blunder once."

"Oh, so that's what you mean? Then please drive us to the green *dacha* that stands by the river on the other side of the forest. Do you know where it is?"

"Why shouldn't I know," said I, "I'm at home in Boiberik. I should have as many thousand rubles as the number of logs I've hauled to that *dacha*. Only last summer I delivered two loads of wood there at once. A rich man lived there, a millionaire from Yehupetz who must be worth at least a hundred thousand rubles, or even two hundred thousand!"

"He lives there this year, too," said the women, whispering to each other and tittering.

"Oh, so it is likely that you are some kin of his?" I asked. "Then it might not be a bad idea if you would kindly take the trouble to put in a good word for me, do me a good turn—there might be something for me to do, some kind of a job. I know a young man, Israel is his name, he lived near our *shtetl*... he was just a nobody. Well, now he's gone up high, nobody knows how, he's become a big shot, earns twenty rubles a week, or even forty—I don't know! Some people have luck! Or, for instance, what does our *shokhet's* son-in-law lack? What would have happened to him if he hadn't gone away to Yehupetz? True, he did have a real hard time during the first few years, he almost starved to death. But his troubles are over now—the same should happen to me. He sends money home already and wants to bring over his wife and children, but he has no residence permit*. So how come *he* lives there? He has plenty of troubles, I can tell you that... Well, I always say that if you live long enough you are bound to get somewhere. Here is the river, and here is the big *dacha!*" With these words I drove dashingly right up to the porch.

Our appearance cause a great uproar! What joyous exclamations and questions!

"Oh, oh, Granny!" "Mother!" "Auntie!" "Our lost ones have returned!" "Congratulations!" "But where were you?" "A whole day, we were worried sick!" "We sent post-riders in all directions."

---

*In tsarist Russia Jews had to live within the Pale of Settlement in small towns. Special residence permits were needed for living in larger towns and cities—*Tr.*

"We thought, who knows what might have happened. Wolves, or maybe bandits, God forbid!" "So what's the story?"

"It's a fine story, really: we got lost in the woods and wandered far away, ten versts maybe. Suddenly there appeared a Jew. What kind of Jew?... A *shlimazl,* with a horse and wagon... Had trouble persuading him."

"Of all the horrible nightmares! All alone, with no guide?" "What an adventure, what an ordeal! We must say a prayer for deliverance from danger!"

Soon lamps were brought out to the porch, the table was set, and they began to bring out hot samovars, tea-glasses, sugar, preserves, dainty pastries, fresh-smelling butter rolls, followed by all kinds of food, the most expensive sorts, broths twinkling with fat, roasts and goose, the best wines and cordials.

I stood outside, observing from a distance how, knock on wood, these Yehupetz rich folk ate and drank, no harm should befall them. It's worth pawning your last shirt, I thought, only to become a rich man! What fell to the ground from this table would be enough, I thought, to last my children a whole week until Saturday. Oh, kind, true God, You are a long-bearing Lord, a great God and a good God, merciful and just, why is it that You give one everything, the other nothing? One has butter-rolls, the other—the plagues of Egypt. Then I had another thought: Eh, but you are a great fool, Tevye, upon my word. Do you want to tell *Him* how to rule the world? Since *He* wills it so, then so it must be; if it had to be otherwise, it would have been otherwise. But why shouldn't things actually be otherwise? The answer is: *"We were slaves..."* That's why we are Jews, the Chosen Ones of this world. A Jew must live with faith and confidence; he must believe, firstly, that there is a God in the world, and he must trust in the Eternal One, trust that, God willing, things will get better.

"Where is that man?" I heard somebody ask. "Has he already left, the *shlimazl?*"

"God forbid!" I raised my voice from the distance. "How could I leave without saying goodbye? *Sholom aleichem,* a good evening to you, *'God bless the sitters,'* eat in good health, and welcome!"

"Come over here, why are you standing out there in the dark," they said. "Let us at least have a look at you, see your face. Perhaps you'll take a drop of vodka?"

"A drop of vodka? Ah," said I, "who refuses to take a drop of

"The table was set, and they began to bring out hot samovars, tea-glasses, sugar, preserves...roasts and goose, the best wines and cordials."

240

vodka? As the Good Book says: *'What is for health and what is for death,'* which means, as Rashi explains, that God is God and vodka is vodka. *Lehayim!"* said I and emptied the glass. "May God keep you wealthy and happy. Jews should always be Jews, God should grant them health and strength to endure their troubles."

"What is your name?" asked the rich man, the *gvir* himself, a fine-looking man wearing a skullcap. "Where do you come from, where do you live, how do you make a living? Are you married? Do you have any children and how many?"

"Children? It would be a sin to complain," said I, "for if each one of them is worth a million, as my Golda wants to convince me, then I'm richer than the richest man in Yehupetz. The trouble is that poor is not rich, crooked is not straight, as the Book says: *'Who has made a distinction between the sacred and the profane,'* meaning that he is merry who has the *mezumen.* However, it is the Brodskys who have the money, while I have daughters. And from girls, as they say, the head twirls. But no matter, God is our Father. He rules, that is, He sits up above and we struggle down below. One toils, hauls wood—what else is there to do? As the *Gemara* says: 'If you can't have a meat dish then a herring is a good fish.' The whole trouble is the eating. As my grandmother, God rest her soul, used to say: 'If the mouth weren't so bold, the head would be crowned with gold.' Please excuse me, but there is nothing straighter than a crooked ladder and nothing crookeder than a straight word, especially when you down some vodka on an empty stomach."

"Let the man have something to eat!" ordered the *gvir,* and at once there appeared on the table all kinds of food: fish and meat, roasts, quarters of fowls, and no end of gizzards and livers.

"Will you have something to eat?" they asked. "Then go wash your hands."

"A sick man you ask, a healthy one you give," I said. "But thank you anyhow. A drop of vodka—that's all right, but to sit down to such a feast while out there, at home, my wife and children, God bless them... If it were your kind will to..."

In short, they must have understood what I meant, for they began to load my wagon, each one carrying something separately: this one a white loaf, that one some fish, another one a roast, this one a quarter of a fowl, that one tea and sugar, a third one a pot of drawn fat, a fourth—a jar of jam.

"These things," they told me "you'll take home as a gift to

your wife and children. Now tell us what we should pay you for the trouble you took on our account."

"What an idea—I should tell you! As much as your kind nature wills, that much you will pay me. We won't haggle," I said, "a gold piece less, a gold piece more, as they say. A pauper can't become any poorer."

"No, we want to hear from you yourself, Reb Tevye! Don't be afraid," they said, "for this, God forbid, we won't chop your head off."

What does one do in such a case, I thought. It's a plight: if I say "a ruble" when perhaps they might give me two!.. If I say "two rubles" I'm afraid they might look at me as if I were crazy: what is there to pay two rubles for?

But at this point my tongue slipped, and before I knew it I cried out: "A trey!!!"

This made the whole company laugh so loudly that I thought the earth would swallow me.

"Please excuse me if I've said the wrong thing," I said. "A horse goes on four legs and sometimes stumbles, so what can you expect of a man with one tongue?"

The merriment went up a pitch, they actually held their sides with laughter.

"Let there be an end to your laughter!" cried the *gvir* and took a big purse out of his inner pocket, and from the purse he pulled out—how much do you think? A tenner, a note as red as fire, I'm telling you the truth, as both of us live and breathe! And then he said:

"This you have from me, and you, children, give from your pockets as much as you think you should."

In short, what can I say? Five-ruble, three-ruble and one ruble notes began to fly onto the table. My limbs trembled so that I thought I'd faint.

"Well, what are you standing there for?" asked the *gvir*. "Take up the few rubles from the table and go home in good health to your wife and children."

"God bless you," said I, "and reward you many times over, you should have tenfold, a hundredfold as much as you have, and all good things and great happiness!" With these words I raked up the money with both hands, without counting, and crammed it into all my pockets.

"Good night," I said, "a good future and good health to you, and great happiness to you and your children and your children's children."

As I turned to go to my wagon the *gvirte,* the rich man's wife, she of the silken kerchief, called me back:

"Wait a moment, Reb Tevye. From me you shall receive a special gift if, God willing, you come here tomorrow morning. I have a dun-colored cow, it used to be a wonderful milker, gave twenty-four glasses of milk. Somebody cast a 'good' eye on it and now it no longer milks—that is, you can milk it, but no milk comes out..."

"A long life to you," said I, "don't trouble yourself, with us your cow will both be milked and give milk. My old woman, God bless her, is so clever that she shreds noodles from nothing, with five fingers makes gruel, celebrates the Sabbath out of miracles and puts the children to bed with slaps... Don't be angry with me, please excuse me, I beg your pardon, perhaps I let my tongue run away with me. A good night, health and joy be yours forever." With these words I went out into the yard.

I looked for my horse—woe is me, a misfortune, a calamity! I searched here and there and everywhere— *"the child is not,"* there is no horse!

Well, Tevye, I thought to myself, you've been had!

And then there came to my mind a fine story I once read in a book: a company of "evil brethren" once caught an honest Jew, a Hasid, when he was away from home, and lured him to an out-of-the-way palace where they wined him and dined him. Suddenly they all disappeared, and he was left all alone with a female who soon turned into a wild beast that quickly became a cat, and the cat—a dragon. Look out, Tevye, I said to myself, maybe you are being duped?!

"Why are you fumbling out there, what are you grumbling about?" somebody asked me.

"Why am I fumbling!? Woe is me that I live in this world," I answered, "my horse is gone."

"Your horse," they answered, "is in the stable, just take the trouble to go over there, into the stable."

I went into the stable, and what did I see? Yes, truly, as I am a Jew! My nag was faring quite well, standing among the *gvir's* horses, its jaws immersed in oats, chewing with great gusto!

"Listen here, my sage," I said to the horse, "it's time we went home. One shouldn't go for food so greedily. An extra bite may cause great harm."

In short, I finally managed to talk the horse, begging your pardon, into letting me harness it, and then I set out for home in a lively, merry mood, chanting *"Almighty Lord"* as if I were tipsy. The horse, too, had undergone a great change, had grown, as it were, a new skin. It no longer waited for a lash from the whip, it ran as smoothly as a psalm.

It was a bit latish when we got home, but I woke up my wife with a happy shout.

"Happy holiday, *mazl-tov*, congratulations, Golda!"

"A black and desolate *mazl-tov* to you," she answered. "what's put you into such a festive humor, my dear bread-winner? Are you returning from a wedding or a circumcision celebration, my gold-spinner?"

"A wedding and a circumcision rolled into one! Just you wait, my wife, I'll show you a treasure," said I, "but first wake up the children, let them, poor things, also partake of the Yehupetz dainties."

"Either you are insane, crazy or deranged, or out of your mind. You talk like a madman, God have mercy on us!" So spoke my wife and dealt me out the whole chapter of curses as a woman usually does.

"A woman," said I, "is always a woman. It was not for nothing that King Solomon said that among his thousand wives he couldn't find a single level-headed one. It is indeed a lucky thing, upon my word, that it is no longer the fashion to have a lot of wives," and I went outside to my wagon and brought in and put out on the table all the goodies that had been packed up for me.

When my crew saw the loaves and rolls, when they caught a sniff of the meat, they pounced on the food like a pack of hungry wolves, poor things. Their hands trembled as they snatched the food, but their jaws worked unerringly. As the Book says: *"And they did eat"*—and Rashi explains: they crackled like locusts. Tears came to my eyes.

"So tell us," said my spouse, "who gave a meal for the poor, or was it just a feast, and why are you so proud of yourself?"

"Have patience, Golda, you'll learn everything in good time. But first blow up the samovar, then we'll all sit down around the table and drink tea in proper style. A man lives only once, not twice, especially now when we already have a cow of our own that gives twenty-four glasses of milk; tomorrow, God willing, I'll bring the cow home. Now, Golda," said I, pulling out the whole pack of money, "try and guess how much money we have here!"

I took a look at my wife—she was as pale as death, couldn't utter a word.

"God be with you, Golda darling," I exclaimed, "what's scared you so? Maybe you are afraid that I stole this money or held up someone? You ought to be ashamed of yourself! You've been Tevye's wife for such a long time, how can you think such things? You little fool, this is *kosher* money, earned honestly by my own wit and toil. I saved two souls from great danger, if not for me, God knows that would have happened to them!"

In short, I told her the whole story from beginning to end: how God had led me by the hand. After that we both began to count the money over and over—it was exactly twice eighteen* and one extra, so there we had a bundle of thirty-seven rubles! My wife burst into tears.

"Why are you crying, silly woman?" I asked.

"How should I not cry when the tears flow?" she answered. "When the heart is full the eyes overflow. So help me God—my heart told me that you would return with good tidings. I can't remember when Grandmother Tzeitl, may she rest in peace, last appeared to me in a dream. I was lying asleep and suddenly I dreamed I saw a brimful pail of milk. Grandmother Tzeitl was carrying this pail, covered with her apron to shield it from the evil eye, and the children were wailing, 'Mama, a sip of mi-i-ilk!'"

"Don't gobble up the noodles before the Sabbath, dear heart," said I, "let Grandmother Tzeitl abide in bright paradise, I don't know whether we'll be the richer for that. However, if God could perform the miracle that brought us a cow, He will probably see to it that the cow is a real cow... Let us better put our heads together, Golda my heart, and decide what to do with the money."

"By all means," said Golda, "what do you plan to do with so much, knock on wood, money?"

"With the greatest pleasure," said I. "But what do *you* think we might do with such a big, knock on wood, sum?"

So when we both began to think, to plan, to rack our brains, to consider all kinds of businesses. What didn't we buy and sell

---

*Eighteen—a good-luck number . — *Tr.*

that night! We bought a pair of horses and soon sold them at a profit; we opened a grocery store in Boiberik, sold out the stock and soon opened a dry-goods shop; we bargained for a piece of forest-land, took a few rubles for the option and backed off; we tried to buy the Anatovka meat tax concession*, made some money and decided to become money-lenders.

"My enemies should be so mad!" at last cried my wife. "You want to squander the few *groszy*** and have nothing left but a whip-handle?"

"What then? Do you think it's better to deal in grain and go bankrupt? Isn't it enough that the world is being beggared through wheat? Go and hear what's doing in Odessa!"

"What do I care about Odessa?" replied Golda. "My forefathers never set foot there and neither will my children as long as I am alive and my feet carry me."

"Then what do you want?" I asked her.

"What I want? I want you to stop playing the fool and talking nonsense."

"Of course," said I, "you're the wise one now; as they say, rubles give rise to thoughts, so if you are *maybe* going to get rich you are surely *already* wise. It's always so!"

Well, we quarreled and made it up several times, and at last we decided to buy, in addition to the cow we are getting for nothing, a real milch cow.

You probably want to ask me: why a cow and not a horse? So I'll answer: why a horse and not a cow? Boiberik is a place where all the wealthy Yehupetzers rent *dachas* for the summer, and since they are refined folk accustomed to having everything delivered ready-made to them, to be put straight into their mouths—firewood, meat, eggs, chickens, onions, pepper, parsley—then why shouldn't someone undertake to bring them cheese and butter and cream and so on? Seeing as the Yehupetzers are fond of food and their money is, you might say, a bastard, a good profit could be made from such a business. The main thing is to deliver good merchandise, and such wares as mine you wouldn't find even in Yehupetz. Both of us together should receive as many blessings as

---

*A special tax on *kosher* meat levied by the tsarist government. The right to collect it was granted to a concessionaire, a wealthy person who extorted the money from the Jewish population, making life especially hard for the poor.—*Tr.*

**A polish monetary unit equal to 1/100 zloty.—*Tr.*

the number of times important people, Gentiles, have implored me to bring them fresh dairy products: "We've heard, Tevye," they would say, "that you are an honest man, even though you are a scabby Jew." Do you think you'll get such a compliment from Jews? My enemies should waste away for as long as I'd have to wait for it! From our pettifoggers you don't get a good word. The only thing they know is to peer into someone else's pot. Seeing that Tevye has an extra cow and a new wagon they begin to rack their brains: from where and from what? Maybe this Tevye deals in counterfeit money? Or runs a still on the quiet?

Ha-ha-ha! Go on, brotherkins, rack your brains in good health! is what I think to myself.

I don't know whether you'll believe me, but you are almost the first person I've told the whole story to, just as it happened...

However, it seems to me that I've already talked a little too much. Please don't hold it against me, but we've both got to go about our own affairs, or, as the Bible says, *"Every crow to its own kind"*—to each his own. You to your books, I to my pots and jugs. But one request I will make: don't write me into one of your books, and if you do, then at least don't mention my real name... I wish you health and may everything always go well with you.

1894

247

Tevye, Golda, their seven daughters, and the cow.

The Soap Bubble

"There are many thoughts in a man's heart"—that's what it says, doesn't it, in our sacred Torah? I don't have to explain it to you, Reb Sholom Aleichem. In plain Yiddish we have a saying: "The best horse needs a whip, the wisest man—advice." Who do I mean? Myself, that's who, for had I had the sense to consult a good friend and tell him everything, I would surely not have gotten myself into such a pretty mess. *"Life and death issue from thine own lips"*—when God wishes to punish a man, He takes away his reason. How many times have I told myself: Just think, Tevye, you blockhead, people say that you aren't altogether a fool, how come you let yourself be taken in, and so stupidly? What would you have lost from the earnings—knock on wood—you make with your little dairy business that has won such a good reputation everywhere, in Boiberik, in Yehupetz, and far and wide? How fine and how sweet it would have been right now if your *mezumen* was lying quietly in a chest, safely hidden, without a human soul being aware of it! For who cares, I ask you, whether Tevye has any money or not? Indeed! Was the world much interested in Tevye when he lay sunken—such a fate shouldn't befall others—nine cubits deep in the ground, dying of hunger three times a day with his wife and children? Only later, when God took notice of Tevye and changed his luck all of a sudden, when Tevye somehow or other managed to build up a little business, when he began to save up a few rubles, only then did the world take heed, and plain Tevye became Reb Tevye—no kidding! Plenty of good friends appeared; as it is written in the Book: *"He is beloved by everyone"*—when God gives a spoonful, people offer bucketfuls. Each and everyone came along with his advice: this one said a dry-goods shop, that one—a grocery, this one—a house, an estate, landed property, another one said wheat, this one—timber, that one—auctioneering...

Brotherkins!" I told them. "Leave me alone! You are widely mistaken: you apparently think I am Brodsky. We should all have as much as I need to make up three hundred rubles, even two hundred, or even a hundred and fifty! Another's property is easy to count; it seems to glitter like gold, but when one comes up close it's only a brass button."

In short, may Heaven preserve them, our petty folk did finally put a "good" eye on me! God sent me a relative—such close kin that I couldn't have told him from a hole in the wall! Menachem-Mendel was his name, a rolling stone, a flighty gadabout, a twister, a good-for-nothing, may he never rest! He hooked on to me and turned my head with his fantasies, his castles-in-the-air. So you may well ask me: *"Wherefore did it come to pass?"* how did I, Tevye, fall in with Menachem-Mendel? The only justification I have is the passage from the *Haggadah* that says:... *"Slaves we were....,"* meaning so it was ordained. Here's the story.

I went to Yehupetz once at the beginning of winter with my bit of merchandise—over twenty pounds of fresh butter from butterland, a couple of bags of beautiful cottage cheese—gold and silver, we should both wish ourselves no worse! As you understand, I sold off my goods immediately, didn't leave myself a lick; I didn't even get to visit all of my summer customers, the Boiberik summer people who look forward to my coming as if I were the Messiah. And no wonder—they get sick and tired of your Yehupetz dealers who can by no means supply them with such goods as Tevye's. I don't have to tell you—as the prophet says: *"Let another praise thee."* Good merchandise is its own praise.

Well, I sold out all my wares, threw my horse a little hay and went for a stroll in the city. *"Man is born of dust and to dust he returneth"*—a man is no more than mortal, so he wants to take a look at the world, catch a breath of air, look at the rarities Yehupetz displays in its windows, as if saying: "With your eyes—as much as you like, but with your hands—don't you dare!"

Standing in front of a large window behind which there lay piles of gold half-imperials*, silver rubles and no end of all kinds of paper money I thought: God Almighty! If I had but a tenth part of what I see here what would I have to ask from God and who would be equal to me? First of all I'd find a match for my eldest daughter, give her a dowry of five hundred rubles in addition to bride-gifts, clothing and wedding expenses; my horse and wagon and the cows I would sell and move to the city, buy myself a seat by the Eastern

---

*A gold coin in the former Russian Empire. — *Tr.*

wall in the synagogue, and for my wife, God bless her, a few strings of pearls, and I would give out alms like the finest householder. I would see to it that the Temple got a new tin roof instead of standing, as it does now, roofless, ready to cave in any minute. I would set up a *Talmud-Torah* for the children and a hospital, as in all decent towns, so that poor people shouldn't have to huddle on the bare ground in the prayer-house, and I would immediately get rid of that brazen Yankel, the trustee of the burial society, and put an end to his guzzling vodka and chicken livers at the community's expense!

"*Sholom Aleichem,* Reb Tevye!" somebody called to me from behind my back. "How are you?"

I turned around and took a look—I could have sworn I knew his face! *"Aleichem Sholom,"* I answered, "where do you hail from?"

"From where? From Kasrilovka," he answered, "I'm a kinsman of yours, your wife Golda's own third cousin once removed."

"Hold on," said I, "aren't you a son-in-law of Boruch-Hirsch, Leah-Dvosya's husband?"

"Right you are," said he, "I am Boruch-Hirsch Leah-Dvosya's son-in-law, and my wife's name is Sheine-Sheindl, Boruch-Hirsch Leah-Dvosya's daughter, so now you already know me."

"Just a moment," said I, "your mother-in-law's grandmother, Sarah-Yenta, and my wife's aunt Frumeh-Zlata were, I seem to remember, first cousins, and if I am not mistaken, you are Boruch-Hirsch Leah Dvosya's middle son-in-law, but I've forgotten what your name is, its slipped my mind somehow. What is your real name?"

"I am called," said he, "Menachem-Mendel Boruch-Hirsch Leah-Dvosya's, that's what they call me at home, in Kasrilovka."

"In that case, my dear Menachem-Mendel," said I to him, "I owe you an altogether different sort of greeting! Come, tell me, my precious Menachem-Mendel, what are you doing here, how are your mother-in-law and your father-in-law, long life to them? How is your health, how is your business getting along?"

"Eh," said he, "my health is, thank God, not bad, I live; but my business affairs aren't so good at present,"

"God will help you," said I, glancing at his threadbare clothes and worn-out shoes. "No matter, God will help you, things will probably get better. As the Book says, *'All is vanity',* money, I say, is round, today it rolls this way, tomorrow that way, the main thing is to go on living. What is most important is hope, a Jew must go

"This one said a dry-goods shop, that one—a grocery, that one—a house, an estate…another said wheat, this one—timber…."

on hoping. What if you do suffer? After all, that's what we Jews are in this world for. As they say, if you're a soldier you must smell gunpowder. *'Man is likened to a broken pot'*—the whole world," said I, "is a dream. Better tell me, Menachem-Mendel, my good man, how you come to be here, all of a sudden, in Yehupetz?"

"What do you mean," he asked, "how I come to be here? I've been here already, little by little, for something like a year and a half."

"So you," said I, "are a local, a real Yehupetz resident?"

"Sh-sh-sh!!!" he exclaimed, glancing around in all directions, "don't shout so loudly, Reb Tevye; I do live here, but that's between you and me."

I stood there looking at him as if he were crazy, "You're a fugitive," said I, "and hiding yourself in the middle of the marketplace?"

"Don't ask," said he, "Reb Tevye, that's the way it is. You, apparently, have no idea of the Yehupetz laws and customs... Come, I'll explain, so you'll understand how one can both *be* and *not be* a local resident." And he gave me a whole song and dance on the subject of how a person struggles for his life in Yehupetz.

"Listen to me, Menachem-Mendel, come with me to the village for one day," said I, "your bones, at least, will get a little rest. You'll be our guest, and a most welcome one, my old woman will be overjoyed."

In short, I talked him into coming with me. When we arrived—what jubilation! A guest! An own third cousin! No small matter, for blood, as they say, is thicker than water. My wife began to shower our guest with questions: what was new in Kasrilovka? How was Uncle Boruch-Hirsch? What was Aunt Leah-Dvosya doing? Uncle Yosl-Menashe? Aunt Dobrish? And how were their children getting along? Who had died? Who had gotten married? Who was divorced? Who had given birth and who was expecting?

"Of what use, my dear wife," said I, "are someone else's weddings or circumcisions to you? You'd better see to it that we have something to put into our mouths. *'All who are hungry enter and be fed'*—before eating one doesn't feel like dancing. If it's a borsht—well and good, if not—no matter, let it be *knishes* or *kreplakh,* stuffed or empty dumplings, or maybe even *blintzes* with cheese, or *vertutti*—anything you have, but make it quick."

Well, so we washed our hands and had a good meal, as you say: *"They ate"* and Rashi explains: "As God bade them."

253

"Eat, Menachem-Mendel," I urged him, "anyhow, as King David said, it is a *'vanity of vanities.'* It's a foolish world and a false one, while, as my grandmother Nehameh of blessed memory used to say—she was a clever old woman, wondrously wise—it's in the bowl that health and pleasure are to be sought."

My poor guest—his hands even trembled—couldn't find enough words to praise my wife's cookery. He swore by all that was sacred that he couldn't remember when he had eaten such a wonderful dairy meal, such delicious *knishes* and *vertutti.*

"Don't be silly," said I, "if you'd had a taste of her bakery, or noodle pudding—you would then learn the meaning of Paradise on earth!"

Well, after we'd eaten and said our benedictions, the talk turned to what was uppermost in our minds; he spoke of his affairs, I—of this and that and another; he talked about his deals, told us stories about Odessa and Yehupetz, said that about ten times already he had been *na konye i pid konyom*—riding a horse and thrown from the horse—rich today, poor tomorrow, rich again and again a poor man. He dealt in some kind of stuff I had never in my life heard of, absurd and crazy sounding: *hos* and *bes,* shares-shmares, Potivilov, Maltzev-shmaltzev, the devil knows what they are, and the crazy figures he named, ten thousand, twenty thousand— money like firewood!

"I'll tell you the truth, Menachem-Mendel," said I, "from what you tell me of the ins and outs of your business I see it calls for real skill and know-how. But there's one thing I can't understand: since I am acquainted with your good lady it puzzles me greatly that she permits you to fly around so and doesn't come after you riding a broomstick!"

"Eh," said he with a sigh, "don't remind me of that, Reb Tevye, I get enough from her as it is, both cold and hot. You should only hear what she writes me, then you would say that I am a saintly man. But this," he went on, "is a small matter, you expect a wife to nag you to death. There is a much worse thing: I have, you must understand, a dear mother-in-law! I don't have to tell you—you know her yourself!"

"So with you," I say, "it's as the Bible says: *'The flocks were ringstraked, speckled and grisled',* which means a boil on a boil and a blister on the boil?"

"Yes, Reb Tevye," said he, "you've got it right; the boil is a boil, but the blister, oh, the blister is worse than the boil!"

Well, so we went on chatting until late at night. I was already quite dizzy from his yarns, from his crazy stories of the thousands of rubles that fly up and down, of Brodsky's wealth…All night long I dreamed of Yehupetz…. half-imperials…Brodsky… Menachem Mendel and his mother-in-law. Only in the morning did he get down to brass tacks; what, then? "Since," he said, "with us in Yehupetz cash has for some time now become preferable, while nobody cares a hoot for merchandise, therefore," said he, "you have a chance, Reb Tevye, to snatch yourself a goodly sum and at the same time literally save me, bring me back to life from the dead."

"Childish talk," said I to him, "you must think that I have the Yehupetz kind of money, half-imperials? You little fool," said I, "what I lack to be as rich as Brodsky we might both of us wish we could earn before Passover."

"Yes," said he, "that I know. But do you think a large sum is necessary for this? If you gave me a hundred today," he said, "I would turn it into two hundred in three-four days, into three hundred, six hundred, seven hundred and why not even a whole thousand?"

"It is quite possible," said I, "that it's as our Book says: *'The profit is great but it's far from my pocket!'* But what's the use of such talk? It's all very fine when there's something to invest—but when there is no hundred rubles it follows that *'alone you come in and alone you go out'* or as Rashi explains, when you plant a sickness you reap a fever."

"Eh, come on," said he, "I'm sure you can find a hundred rubles, Reb Tevye. With your business, your name, knock on wood!"

"What's in a name?" said I. "A name, naturally, is a good thing. But what of that? I remain with my name, while the money is all Brodsky's. If you want to know precisely, I'll tell you that I have all in all barely a hundred rubles, but I have eighteen holes to patch with this sum: first, to marry off a daughter…"

"Just listen to him," said he, "that's just the last to fit your shoe! Because when, Reb Tevye, will you have another such opportunity to invest one hundred and take out, God willing, enough for marrying off children, and for something else, too?"

And he went into a new three-hour-long harangue to let me understand how he makes three rubles out of one, and from three—ten. First of all, he said, you invest a hundred rubles and then you order ten somethings—I've already forgotten what they're called—to be bought for you; then you wait a few days until its price goes up. Then you send off a telegram somewhere with an order to sell, and with the money, to buy twice as much; then the price goes up again and you dispatch another telegram; this goes on until the hundred becomes two hundred, the two hundred—four hundred, the four—eight, the eight—sixteen hundred, real *"miracles and wonders"*! There are people, he said, in Yehupetz, who just recently walked around barefoot, they were brokers, messengers, servants, today they live in their own brick houses, their wives complain of stomach ailments and go abroad for treatment. They themselves dash around in Yehupetz on rubber wheels—hoity-toity, they don't recognize people any more!

Well, why drag out the story? He got me hooked. Who knows, I thought, maybe he was sent to me by fate? After all, I do hear that people find their luck in Yehupetz with the aid of their five fingers—am I any worse than they? He doesn't seem to be a liar who thinks up such songs out of his head. What if my luck really does, thought I, take a turn in the right direction and Tevye becomes something of a person in his old age at least? Really, when will the end come to my struggles, my exhaustive drudgery? Day in and day out again the horse and wagon, and again cheese and butter. It's time, Tevye, to take a rest, I told myself, to become a somebody, to go to the prayer house, to look into a sacred book. But what if, God forbid, things should go wrong, that is, fall buttered side down? Better not to think of that!

"Well? What do you think?" I asked my old woman. "How do you like his plan, Golda?"

"What can I say?" she replied, "I know that Menachem-Mendel is not, God forbid, just anybody, he won't hoodwink you. He does not come from any tailors or cobblers! His father is a very upright person, and he had a grandfather who was really a jewel: he sat day and night studying the Torah, even after he went blind. And Grandmother Tzeitl, may she rest in peace, was also no simple woman,"

"It's a fable about *Hanukkah* lights in the summer," said I, "we're talking business, and here she comes along with her grandmother Tzeitl who baked honey-cakes, and with her grandfather who lost his soul in a wine-glass... A woman is always a woman. It's not for nothing that King Solomon traveled the world over and couldn't find a woman with a rivet in her head."

In short, we agreed to set up a partnership: I invest the money

256

and Menachem-Mendel his wits, and whatever God sent us we would divide half and half.

"Believe me, Reb Tevye," he said, "I'll make a fine deal for you, God willing, as fine as fine can be, and with God's help will bring you money and money and more money!"

"Amen, the same to you," said I, "from your mouth into God's ears. But there is one thing I don't understand: how does the cat get over the water? I am here, you are there; money is a delicate material, see? Don't take offense, but as our Forefather Abraham said: *'If you sow with tears you shall reap with joy'*—it is better to make sure beforehand than to weep afterwards."

"Oh," said he to me, "maybe you want us to sign a paper? With the greatest pleasure!"

"Shush," said I, "if you look at it another way, it comes to the same thing: it's either or; if you want to kill me, of what use will a piece of paper be to me? As it is written in the Talmud: *'The thief is not the mouse, but the mousehole'* — it isn't the note that pays but the man, and if I already hang by one foot let me hang by both."

"You may believe me," he said, "Reb Tevye, I swear to you on my most holy word of honor, so help me God, I haven't the slightest intention of duping you, God forbid; everything will be aboveboard and honest. God willing, we'll divide everything equally, half and half, share and share alike, a hundred for me, a hundred for you, two hundred for me, two hundred for you, three hundred for me, three hundred for you, four hundred for me, four hundred for you, a thousand for me, a thousand for you."

Well, so I got out my few rubles, counted them over three times—my hands trembled as I counted—called my old woman to be a witness, made it clear once more what blood money this was and gave it to Menachem-Mendel; I sewed it up into his breast pocket so it shouldn't, God forbid, be stolen on the way, and we decided that no later than next Saturday week he would, without fail, write me a full account of our affairs. We took hearty leave of each other, embraced and kissed each other as is usual among relatives.

When I was alone all sorts of sweet thoughts passed through my mind, all kinds of daydreams, so pleasant that I wished they would never end. I saw a large, tin-roofed house in the middle of town, a real mansion with sheds and stables and stalls, with large and small chambers, with pantries full of good things, and I saw the mistress of the house jingling her keys as she flitted from room

257

to room—and she was my wife Golda, but unrecognizable: her face has changed, it has become the face of a wealthy woman, with a double chin and pearls strung around her neck; she gives herself airs and curses the maids vehemently; my children go around in their best clothes doing nothing. The yard is flocked with chickens, geese and ducks. Inside the house everything is bright, a fire flickers in the oven, supper is cooking and the samovar is puffing as it boils merrily! At the head of the table sits the master of the house, Tevye, that is. He is wearing a houserobe and a skullcap, around him sit the most prominent men of the town fawning on him, cringing before him: "If you please, Reb Tevye, no offense meant, Reb Tevye..."

"Oh," thought I, "money—the devil take your fathers and forefathers!"

"Whom are you cursing so?" asked my Golda.

"Nobody, I was merely thinking, daydreaming, seeing visions—ah, hopeless things... Tell me, Golda my love," said I, "do you know what he deals in, this relative of yours, Menachem-Mendel?"

"What I dreamed the other night and last night and this whole year should fall on the heads of my enemies! You sat up with the man a day and a night talking and talking and talking, and then you come to me and ask me what he deals in! You made up some sort of an agreement with him, didn't you?"

"Yes," said I, "we did make up something, but what it is I don't know, not for the life of me! There's nothing, you see, to get hold of; however, one thing has nothing to do with the other, don't you worry, my dear wife, my heart tells me that everything will turn out well and we, with God's help, so it seems to me, will earn money, and lots of it—so say 'Amen' and cook supper!"

Well, a week went by, and then another, and still another—no letters from my partner! I was beside myself, I lost my head and didn't know what to think. It can't be, thought I, that he should simply forget to write a letter; he knows quite well how anxiously we await it here. But then again another thought struck me: what will I do to him if he, for instance, skims the entire cream for himself and tells me that we haven't earned anything yet! Go tell him he's a so-and-so!? But it can't be, I told myself, how is it possible? I treat a man as I would a close and dear relative, I should only have what I wish for him, so how can he play such a trick on me? Then another thought struck me: the devil take the profit, let it be

258

his, *"Deliverance and protection will come from the Lord"*—may God save my investment from harm! A chill ran through my body.

You old fool, I said to myself, you already prepared a purse, you dunce! For the hundred rubles you could have brought yourself a pair of horses the likes of which your ancestors never owned and exchanged your wagon for a spring-hung britzka!

"Tevye, why don't you think of something!" cried my wife.

"What do you mean—I don't think? My head is bursting from thinking," said I, "and you say I don't think!"

"Something must have happened to him on the way," said she. "Either he was waylaid by robbers and cleaned out from head to toe, or he fell sick on the way, or, God forbid, maybe even died."

"What else, dear heart, will you think up?" I asked her. "Suddenly robbers out of the blue!" But I myself thought: Who knows what could happen to a man on the road?

"You, my wife, always have to think the very worst!"

"Well," said she, "he comes from that kind of a family. His mother, may she be our defender in Heaven, died not long ago, still a young woman; he had three sisters, so one of them died in her girlhood, the other one did get married, but caught a cold in the bath-house and died, while the third one lost her mind right after her first confinement, lingered on for some time and then died."

"All life ends in death," said I, "we'll all be dead some day, Golda. A man is like a carpenter: a carpenter lives and lives and dies, and a man lives and dies."

In short, we decided that I should go to Yehupetz. A bit of my stock-in-trade had accumulated by this time, a shopful of cheese and butter and cream, all of prime quality. We harnessed the horse and, as Rashi says: *"They journeyed from Sukos."* On to Yehupetz!

As I drove along, despondent, of course, heavy-hearted, as you may well imagine, all alone in the woods, all sorts of notions and thoughts entered my mind.

Now won't it be a fine thing, I thought, if when I arrive and start asking about my man I hear: "Menachem-Mendel? Oho-ho! That one is in clover, has his own brick house, drives around in carriages, is not to be recognized at all!" So I pluck up courage and go directly to his house. "Whoa!" somebody exclaims at the entrance and gives me a hard shove with an elbow. "Don't push so, man, this is no place for pushing." "I am," I say, "a kinsman, my wife is his third cousin once removed." *"Mazl-tov,"* he answers, "a great pleasure; however, it won't hurt you to wait here by the door

259

a while..." It dawns on me that the doorman should be tipped... As they say, *"What goes up must come down"*—meaning that the wheels won't turn if the axle isn't greased. And that the wheels won't turn if the axle isn't greased. And then I go straight upstairs to Menachem-Mendel and say: "A good morning to you, Reb Menachem-Mendel!" Who? What? *"There is no speech, there are no words.* "He doesn't recognize me at all! "What do you want?" he asks. I almost faint.

"What does this mean, Mister, you no longer recognize relatives? I am Tevye."

"Oh," says he, "Tevye? The name seems familiar..."

"Then maybe," say I, "my wife's *blintzes* are also familiar to you, remind yourself of her *knishes,* dumplings and *vertutti!*"

Then quite different thoughts come to my mind: here I come in to Menachem-Mendel and he gives me a most hearty welcome, "A guest! A guest! Sit down, Reb Tevye, how are you, how is your wife? I've been looking forward to your arrival, I want to settle our accounts." And then he takes and pours me a hatful of gold coins. "This," he says, "is the profit, and the principal stays in the business; whatever we earn we'll divide in half, share and share alike, a hundred for me, a hundred for you, two hundred for me, two hundred for you, three hundred for me, three hundred for you, four hundred for me, four hundred for you." So thinking I get a bit drowsy and don't notice that my nag has strayed from the road; the cart catches on a tree, and I get such a jolt from behind that sparks fly from my eyes. It's a good thing, say I to myself, that at least no axle broke, thank God.

Well, at last I got to Yehupetz. First of all I sold off my goods very quickly, as I usually do, and then I went about looking for my partner.

I wander around for an hour, two, and three, but *"the lad is gone"*—I can't find him! I begin stopping people, asking them whether they'd heard of or seen a man with the lovely name of Menachem-Mendel? "If," they say, "his name is Menachem-Mendel you should look for him with a candle; this isn't enough," they say, "there are lots of Menachem-Mendels in the world." "You probably mean his family name?" say I, "Let me know as much evil, with you together, if, all told, he isn't called—at home, in Kasrilovka—by his mother-in-law's name alone, that is,

Menachem-Mendel Leah-Dvosya's. What's more, his father-in-law, already a very old man, is also called by her name—Boruch-Hirsch Leah-Dvosya's, and even she herself, Leah-Dvosya, that is, is known as Leah-Dvosya Boruch-Hirsch Leah-Dvosya's. Do you understand now?"

"We understand," they say, "but all this is still not enough; what is his business, what does he do, your Menachem-Mendel?"

"What is his business? He does business here with half-imperial gold pieces, some sore of *'bess-mess'*, Potivilov, sends telegrams someplace—to Petersburg, to Warsaw," I explain.

"Oh!" they cry and rock with laughter. "Do you mean the Menachem-Mendel who sells last year's snow? Go, if you please, down over there—to the other side of the street; that's where lots of hares run around, and yours among them."

The more one lives, the more one eats, think I to myself, so now it's hares!? Last year's snow!?

So I crossed to the other side. There were so many people there, may no evil befall them, as at a fair; the crowd was so dense that I barely pushed myself through. People ran around like madmen, one this way, the other that way, bumping into each other, a real Bedlam with everyone talking, screaming, waving their hands: "Potivilov..." "Done, done!" "Caught you at your word!" "Shoved in a down payment... it'll scratch..." "You owe me brokerage..." "You're a rat... you'll get your head smashed..." "Spit in his face..." "Just look—a real kill!" "A fine speculator..." "Bankrupt!" "Flunkey!" "A curse on you and your ancestors!" Now slaps were about to fly in earnest.

"Jacob fled," I muttered to myself, "run away, Tevye, or you'll catch a few slaps yourself!"

Well, well, I reflected, God is a Father, Shmuel-Shmelki is his servitor, Yehupetz is a city and Menachem-Mendel is a breadwinner! So this is the spot where people catch fortunes, half-imperials? This Bedlam is what they call doing business? Alas and alack, Tevye, with your commercial deals!

To make a long story short, when I stopped in front of a great big show-window displaying all kinds of trousers I suddenly saw, reflected in the glass, my lost partner. When I looked at him my heart missed a beat, I felt faint. If I have an enemy anywhere, or if you have one, let us both live to see them looking the way

261

"When I looked at him, my heart missed a beat, I felt faint."

Menachem-Mendel looked! A coat? Boots? And his face—why, my God, healthier-looking corpses are laid to rest.

Well, Tevye, now you are really done for, I thought to myself, you can say goodbye to your little nest egg, as they say: There is neither bear nor forest—neither stock nor money, nothing but troubles...

He, evidently, was also greatly embarrassed, because we both stopped as if frozen and couldn't utter a word; we only looked right into each other's eyes, as roosters do, as if to say: "Both of us are hapless unfortunates, we might as well take up our sacks and go begging from house to house!"

"Reb Tevye," he said in a low voice, barely managing to speak, choking with tears, "Reb Tevye! Without luck one shouldn't be born at all... rather than such a life... be hanged... drawn and quartered!" And not another word could he utter.

"Of course," I said to him, "for this deed of yours, Menachem-Mendel, you deserve to be laid out right here in the middle of Yehupetz and flogged until you see grandmother Tzeitl in the other world. Just think what you've gone and done! You've taken an entire household of living people, innocent, unhappy people, and cut their throats without a knife! Oh God, how will I come home now to my wife and children? Come on, tell me yourself, you murderer, robber, cutthroat!"

"It's true," said he, leaning against a wall, "it's true, Reb Tevye, so help me God..."

"Gehenna, you fool," said I, "Gehenna is too good for you!"

"All true, Reb Tevye," said he, "all true, so help me God; rather than such a life, such a life, Reb Tevye..." and he hung his head.

I stood there looking at him, the *shlimazl,* as he was leaning against the wall, his head bent, his hat awry, and every sigh and every groan tore at my heart.

"Although," said I "if we look at it another way, then it becomes quite clear that maybe you are also innocent; let us examine the matter from all sides: did you do this with malice aforethought? But it would be foolish to think so, you were my partner on equal share-and-share alike terms; I put in the money, you put in your brains, woe is me! Your intention was for the best, for life and not for death, as the saying goes. Oh, so it turned out to be a soap bubble? It was probably not ordained; as it is said; *'Don't rejoice today because tomorrow...'* Man proposes and God disposes. Look, you little fool, take my bit of business—it's a solvent busi-

263

ness; still, as I say, since it was then so ordained, Heaven preserve us, last autumn one of my cows—it shouldn't happen to you—lay down and died; it could have brought in a bargain—fifty rubles if sold for *treif* meat; directly after that a red heifer fell, I wouldn't have considered taking even twenty rubles for it—well, so what can you do, wits won't help. If you're out of luck you're lost!

"I won't even ask you where my money is," I said. "I understand very well where it went, my blood money, woe is me! It's in a sacred place, in last year's snow. And whose fault is it if not mine? I let myself be talked into reaching out for easy money, stuff and nonsense... Money, brother, must be toiled for, slaved for, worked to the bone for! You deserve a good thrashing, Tevye, you do! But of what use is my crying now? As the Book says: *'The maiden screamed'*—scream yourself blue! Wit and remorse—these two things always come too late. It wasn't fated that Tevye should become a rich man. As Ivan says: *Nye bulo u Mikiti hroshi i nye budye*—no money had Mikita and none will he have. Evidently that's God's will. *'The Lord giveth and the Lord taketh away,'* Rashi explains. Come, brother," said I, "we'll take a few drops of vodka!"

And so, Mr. Sholom Aleichem, all my dreams turned out to be a soap bubble! Do you think I took it to heart and grieved over the loss of my money? May I be as free from evil! We know what the Good Book says: *"The silver and the gold are mine"*—money is mud! The main thing is man, that is, that a person should be a real human being. But what did grieve me? My lost dream. I wanted, oh, how I wanted to be a rich man at least for a while. But is wisdom of any use in this? *"Perforce you must live,"* says the proverb—with groans you live and with groans you wear out a pair of boots. You, Tevye, says God, should keep your mind on cheese and butter and not on daydreams. But faith, hope? The more troubles, the more faith, the poorer one is the greater are his hopes. From this it follows...

But it seems to me that I've talked too much today. It's time to think of my business. As they say, each one has his own scourges.

Fare you well, be healthy and happy always!

1895

264

Today's Children

You said "today's children"? *I have raised children*—you bring them into the world, sacrifice yourself for them, toil day and night, and for what? You think maybe it'll come out right this way or maybe that way, according to your own notions and means. I can't compare with Brodsky, of course, but neither am I just anybody, believe me: we don't come, as my wife, bless her, says, from tailors or cobblers, so I reckoned that I'd draw winning numbers with my daughters. Why? Firstly, God blessed me with good-looking girls, and a pretty face, as you say, is half a dowry. Secondly, I am now, with God's help, no longer the Tevye of former times, so I can aim for the finest match even in Yehupetz—what will you say to that? Yes, but there is a God in the world, a Merciful Father who shows his great miracles and makes me hot and cold, tosses me up and down. So he says to me: "Tevye, don't talk yourself into any foolishness and let the world go on as it does!" Just listen to what can happen in our big world, and who gets all the luck. Tevye the *shlimazl!*

To make a long story short—you probably remember what happened to me, may this never happen to you, the story with my kinsman Menachem-Mendel, may his name and remembrance be erased, our fine deal in Yehupetz with the half-imperials and the "Potivilov" shares, such a year on my enemies! How I grieved then! I thought this was the end, no more Tevye, no more dairy business!

"What a fool you are," my old woman said one day, "stop your worrying, nothing good will come of it! You'll only eat your heart out. Look at it as if you'd been waylaid by highwaymen and robbed clean. Better take a walk to Anatovka, go see Leizer-Wolf the butcher, he is very anxious, he says, to see you."

"What does he need me for? If he is thinking of that dun-colored cow of ours," said I, "he may as well take a big stick and beat the idea out of his head."

265

"Why so?" she asked. "Is it the milk you get from her, or the cheese and butter?"

"It's not that," said I, "it's the idea in general. It would be a sin to give such a cow away to be slaughtered; 'A pity for living things,' says our Holy Torah."

"Oh, stop it, Tevye! The whole world knows that you are a bookish man. Listen to me, your wife," said she, "and go and visit Leizer-Wolf. Every Thursday when our Tzeitl goes to his butcher shop for meat he pesters her: 'Tell your father he should come and see me. I have some important business to discuss with him.'"

In short, once in a while a man must mind his wife, mustn't he? So, thinking it over, I let myself be talked into going to Leizer-Wolf in Anatovka, a walk of about three versts. I came to his place, but he wasn't at home. "Where is he?" I asked a snub-nosed woman who was flitting about the house.

"He's in the slaughterhouse," she answered, "they're slaughtering an ox there since early morning. He should soon be home."

I wandered around Leizer-Wolf's home admiring its fittings. A household, knock on wood, after my own heart; a cupboard full of copperware, couldn't be bought with a hundred and fifty rubles, a samovar, another samovar, a brass tray, another tray from Warsaw, a pair of silver candlesticks, large and small gilded goblets and cups, a cast-iron *Hanukkah* lamp, and many other things, all kinds of trinkets without end.

God Almighty! I thought, I should only live to see my children, bless them, have so many fine things! What a lucky man the butcher is! It's not enough that he is so rich, so he has to have only two children of his own, already married off, and be a widower into the bargain!

At last the door opened and in stomped Leizer-Wolf, hurling curses at the *shokhet's* head. The slaughterer had ruined him, he had rejected an ox as big as an oak-tree, declared it *treif* over a mere trifle, found a pinhead blemish on a lung, may the Evil One catch him!

"Good day, Reb Tevye," he said, "why is it so hard to get you to come here? How do you do?"

"I do and I do and get nowhere. As the Book says: *'I want not your honey and want not your sting'*—neither money, nor health, nor life and soul."

"It's a sin to talk so, Reb Tevye," said he, "as compared to what you once were you are today, knock on wood, a rich man."

266

"We should both have what I still need to be as rich as you think I am. But no matter, *'Ascacurdeh demaskanteh desnubnoseh defercloseh**, as it is written in the *Gemara,*" said I, thinking: more fool you, butcher-boy, if there's such a *Gemara* in the world!

"You're always ready with the *Gemara,*" said Leizer-Wolf. "You are lucky, Reb Tevye, to be skilled in reading the tiny letters. But how do knowledge and learning concern us? Let us better talk of our business. Sit down, Reb Tevye." As he said this he shouted: "Let there be tea!" And as if by magic the snub-nosed woman suddenly sprang from somewhere, snatched up the samovar as the devil snatched the *melamed,* and vanished into the kitchen.

"Now," said he to me, "when we are alone, eye to eye, we can talk business. For some time already I've wanted to have a talk with you, Reb Tevye, and I've asked you many times, through your daughter, to take the trouble... See, I've cast an eye..."

"I know," said I, "that you've cast an eye, but your efforts are all in vain, it won't go, Reb Leizer-Wolf."

"Why so?" he asked and looked at me as if scared.

"Because," said I, "I can afford to wait a while, the river hasn't caught on fire yet."

"Why should you wait when we can come to an agreement at once?" he asked.

"That," said I, "is firstly. And secondly, I'm sorry for the poor creature. *A pity for living things!*"

"Just look at him, how he takes on!" laughed Leizer-Wolf. "If somebody heard you he would swear that she was your only one! It seems to me, Reb Tevye, that you have knock on wood, plenty of them!"

"So let them be," said I, "and let whoever envies me have none."

"Envies you?" he asked in surprise. "Who speaks of envy? Quite the opposite, just because they are so fine I want... You understand? Don't forget, Reb Tevye, what favors you may get out of it!"

"Oh, of course, of course," said I, "your favors can turn a head to stone. You won't grudge a piece of ice in the winter, that we've known for a long time."

"Eh," said he in a honey-sweet voice, "why do you compare, Reb Tevye, then with now? Things were somewhat different *then,*

---

*Words without meaning —abracadabra. —*Tr.*

267

and *now* they're different again. Now we're becoming sort of kin, aren't we?"

"What kinship are you talking about?" I asked.

"Ordinary—in-laws!"

"What do you mean, Reb Leizer-Wolf, what are we talking about?"

"No, you tell me, Reb Tevye, what we are talking about."

"What do you mean," said I, "we're talking about my dun-colored cow that you want to buy!"

"Ha-ha-ha!!" Leizer-Wolf rolled with laughter. "A fine piece of cow, and dun-colored to boot, ha-ha-ha!!!"

"But then what did you mean, Reb Leizer-Wolf? Go ahead, tell me, so I'll laugh too."

"It's about your daughter, your Tzeitl, we've been talking all the time! You know, of course, Reb Tevye, it shouldn't happen to you, that I'm a widower. I thought the matter over and decided that there was no need for me to look for luck among strangers, have dealings with matchmakers, with the devil knows whom, when here we are both on the spot. I know *you* and you know *me,* I like the girl herself, too—I see her every Thursday in my shop, I've spoken with her a few times, she's a nice, quiet girl. As for me, you see for yourself that I'm no poor man, I have my own house, a couple of stores, a few hides up in the attic and some money in the chest as well; what need is there, Reb Tevye, to make difficulties for each other, to play games with each other? Let's just shake hands on it, one-two-three, do you get me or not?"

In short, when he had had his say I sat there speechless, as one who suddenly receives upsetting news. My first thought was: Leizer-Wolf... Tzeitl... He has children her age... But soon I stopped myself: Just imagine, such luck! Such a lucky thing for her! She'll have anything she wants! Well, what if he is a bit tight-fisted? In our times this is supposed to be the greatest virtue: *"Man's closest friend is he himself."* When you're good for others you're bad for yourself. His only real drawback is that he is a bit common. Well, all right, not everyone can be a scholar. There are plenty of rich men, fine men, in Anatovka, in Mazepovka, and even in Yehupetz who can't tell a cross from an *alef.* Still, since it is so ordained, let me have as good a year as the respect they draw from the world. As the Book says: *"You can't build without a foundation,"* which means that learning lies in a strong-box while wisdom is in the purse.

"Well, Reb Tevye," said he, "why are you silent?"

"Should I yell?" I asked, pretending to hesitate. "This, Reb Leizer-Wolf, is a matter that calls for reflection. It's no joke, she's my first-born child."

"On the other hand," said he, "just because she's your first-born you will be able to marry off a second daughter, too, and later on a third, you get me?"

"Amen, the same to you!" said I. "There's no big deal in marrying off a child, let God only send each her predestined one."

"Oh, no, Reb Tevye," said he, "I mean something altogether different, for, thank God, you don't have to worry about a dowry for your Tzeitl—everything a girl needs for her wedding, clothing and so on, I take upon myself, and something will find its way into your purse, too..."

"Fie, shame on you!" I cried. "You're talking, begging your pardon, as if you were in your butcher shop! What do you mean—into my purse? Fie! My Tzeitl is not the sort of girl, God forbid, that I should have to sell for money, fie, fie!!"

"If you say 'fie'—let it be 'fie'," said he, "I meant for the best, but if you say 'fie' let it be 'fie.' If it suits you it suits me! The main thing is that it should be as soon as possible, I need a mistress in the house, you get me?"

"I won't raise any objections, but my spouse has to be talked with," said I, "in such matters she takes the lead. It's no trifle. As Rashi says, *'Rachel weeps for her sons'* the mother covers everything. Then she herself, Tzeitl, should also be asked. As they say, all the in-laws were taken to the wedding but the bridegroom was left at home!"

"Nonsense," said he, "you shouldn't ask—you should *tell*, Reb Tevye. Go home and tell them what is what and set up the wedding canopy—a couple of words and drink a toast to wet the deal!"

"Don't speak that way, Reb Leizer-Wolf, a girl is no widow, God forbid."

"Naturally," said he, "a girl is a girl, not a widow, and for that reason everything must be settled beforehand—clothing, this, that and other matters. Meanwhile, Reb Tevye, let's take a few drops to warm ourselves, what do you say?"

"With pleasure," said I, "why not? As the saying goes, Adam is a man and vodka is vodka. We have a *Gemara* in which it is written..." And I rattled off a *"Gemara,"* a sheer invention, something from the *Song of Songs* and from the *Song of the Kid.*

Well, so we imbibed the bitter drops, as God bade us. Meanwhile the snub-nosed woman brought in the samovar and we fixed ourselves a couple of glasses of punch. The time passed merrily, we congratulated each other, talked, babbled about the match, mentioned this and that and again the match.

"Do you know, Reb Leizer-Wolf, what a gem she is?"

"I know," he said, "believe me, I know. If I hadn't known I wouldn't have spoken at all!"

Both of us spoke at the same time. I shouted: "A gem, a diamond! You should only know how to take good care of her, not to show the butcher in you..."

And he: "Don't worry, Reb Tevye, what she will eat at my table on weekdays she never had in your house on holidays..."

"Come on," said I, "food is not all that important. The rich man doesn't eat gold coins, nor the poor man—stones. You are a coarse person, so you won't be able to appreciate her housewifery, her *hallah*-baking, her fish, Reb Leizer-Wolf, her fish! It's a real privilege..."

To this he said: "Reb Tevye, you are, excuse me, already played out, you don't know people, you don't know me..."

"You put gold on one scale and Tzeitl on the other and they'll balance!" I shouted. "Listen, Reb Leizer-Wolf, even if you had your two hundred thousand you wouldn't be worth the heel of her foot anyhow!"

"Believe me, Reb Tevye, you are a great fool, even though you are older than I am!.."

In short, we must have yelled at each other in this manner for quite a while and we drank ourselves tipsy, so when I came home it was already late in the night and my feet felt as if they were shackled.

My wife, bless her, immediately guessed that I was soused and gave me a good dressing down.

"Hush, Golda, don't scold," I said quite cheerfully, almost ready to dance a jig, "stop shouting, dearest one, we should be congratulated!"

"On what joyous event?" she asked. "For having sold the dun-colored cow, poor thing, to Leizer-Wolf?"

"Worse!"

"Exchanged it for another cow? Hoodwinked poor Leizer-Wolf?"

"Still worse!"

"Come on, say something, just see how a word has to be squeezed out of him!" she shouted angrily.

"*Mazl-tov* to you, Golda," I repeated, "we must both be congratulated, our Tzeitl is betrothed!"

"In that case you're really good and drunk and no joke! You must've had quite a glassful somewhere!"

"I had a few drops of vodka with Leizer-Wolf, and he and I also drank a few glasses of punch, but I'm still in my right mind," I said. "Know, brother Golda, that our Tzeitl has become engaged, in a lucky hour, to Leizer-Wolf himself!"

And I told her the whole story from beginning to end; how, and why, and when, everything we had talked about, without missing the slightest detail.

"Listen, Tevye," said my wife, "God should always help me wherever I go—my heart told me that it wasn't for nothing that Leizer-Wolf summoned you! But I was afraid to think about it, afraid it might, God forbid, all come to naught. I thank Thee, my dear God, my kind and faithful Father, only let it all be in a good hour, an auspicious hour, and may she grow old with him in honor and riches, because Frumeh-Soreh, may she rest in peace, didn't have too good a life with him. She was, may she forgive me, an embittered woman, couldn't get along with anyone, not at all like our Tzeitl, a long life to her. I thank Thee, thank Thee, dear God!.. Well, Tevye, what did I tell you, you noodlehead? Does a person have to worry? When it's destined, it comes straight home to you..."

"Quite true, there's a proverb that clearly says..."

"What do I need your proverbs for," she said, "we have to think about getting ready for the wedding now. First of all, make a list for Leizer-Wolf of everything Tzeitl will need for her wedding; she hasn't even a stitch of underthings, not even a pair of stockings, you tell him. Then—clothes. She needs a silken gown for the wedding, a woolen dress for summer, another for winter, a couple of cotton house-dresses, petticoats, and I want her to have two coats: a cat-pelt burnoose for weekdays and a good one, with ruffles, for the Sabbath; then—hook-up boots on high heels, shoes, a corset, gloves, handkerchiefs, an umbrella and all the other things a girl must have in these times."

"How come, Golda darling," I asked, "that you know about all this nonsense?"

"Why not?" she retorted, "didn't I live among people? Or perhaps I never saw, when I lived at home in Kasrilovka, how people dressed? You let me talk everything over with him; Leizer-Wolf is a wealthy man, he won't like to be bothered by the whole world. If you eat pork, let the fat at least run down your beard."

To make a long story short, we talked in this way until daybreak.

"Well, my wife," I said at last, "go and put together the bits of cheese and butter you have and I'll set out for Boiberik. All is well and good, but the business can't be put aside, as the Book says: *'Man's soul belongs to God,'* meaning that his body is on earth."

It was still dark when I hitched my horse and wagon and set off for Boiberik. When I arrived at the marketplace in Boiberik—oh, my! Can there be a secret among Jews? Everybody already knew everything and congratulations were showered on me from all sides.

"*Mazl-tov*, Reb Tevye! When, God willing, is the wedding?"

"The same to you," said I, "it's as the saying goes: the father hasn't been born yet but his son has already grown up on the roof."

"Nonsense, Tevye, you'll have to stand us a drink; knock on wood, such luck, you've struck it rich—a gold mine!"

"The gold can give out, what remains is a hole in the ground!"

However, not wanting to be a swine and begrudge my friends a treat, I said: "As soon as I get through with all my Yehupetz customers I'll stand you some drinks and eats, we'll have a fling, and that'll be that, which means *'merriment and enjoyment'*—even beggars may celebrate!"

I got through with my business very quickly, as I usually do, and then treated a bunch of good friends to a few drinks. We wished each other luck, as is proper among people, and I set off for home in a lively mood, half-seas over. The sun shone hotly on this fine summer day, but the shadows of the trees protected me from the heat on both sides, and the scent of the pines was as balm to the soul. I stretched out like a lord in my wagon and let the horse have the reins; plod along, old friend, I said, you know the way home yourself. As we trundled along I raised my voice in song; I was in such a festive mood that I sang the tunes sung on the High Holidays from *Rosh Hashono* to *Yom Kippur*. Lying on my back, I looked up into the sky, while my thoughts were here on earth. The Heavens, I thought, are for God, while the Earth he gave to the *Children of Adam*, they should bash their heads against walls, fight as the cats do for great "luxuries," fight for being appointed *gabeh,* for honors and seniority in reading the Torah and lessons from the *Prophets* in the synagogue... *"The dead cannot praise God..."* People don't understand how they should praise God for the favors He confers on them... But we, poor folk, when we have one good day we thank and praise the Lord and say *"A'ave"*— I love Him, for He hearkens to my voice and my pleas, He inclines His ear to me when poverty and afflictions surround me on all sides. Here a cow suddenly lies down and dies, then a devil brings along a relative, a *shlimazl,* a Menachem-Mendel from Yehupetz who takes my last ruble, and I already think that I am done for, this is the end of the world, there is no truth on earth. What does God do? He sends Leizer-Wolf the idea to take my Tzeitl as she stands, without a dowry, and therefore I will double my praises to You, dear God, for having looked at Tevye and come to his aid. Let me have proud pleasure from my child, when I come to visit her, God willing, and see her as the mistress of a wealthy home, all found for her, closets full of linen, well-stocked pantries with Passover chicken fat and preserves, coops full of chickens, geese and ducks...

Suddenly my horse made a dash downhill, and before I knew it I found myself lying on the ground amidst all the empty crocks and pots and the wagon on top of me! With difficulty and pain I managed to crawl out from under the wagon and get to my feet, bruised and half-dead. My wrath I vented on the poor horse. "Damn you," I shouted, "may the earth swallow you! Who asked you, *shlimazl,* to show that you can run downhill? You almost made a cripple of me, you *Asmodeus."* I gave it to him good and hard—as much as he could take. The poor animal evidently understood his mischief had gone too far: he stood with his head hanging low as if ready to be milked.

"The Evil One take you," said I and uprighted the wagon, picked up all the pots and crocks, and continued on my way.

It's a bad omen, I said to myself, hoping no new misfortune had happened at home...

Yes, *"So it was."* I drove along for about two versts and was already near home when I noticed somebody walking towards me in the middle of the road—a woman. I got a little closer—Tzeitl! I don't know why, but my heart felt as if it were sinking. I jumped off the wagon: "Tzeitl, is it you? What are you doing here?"

She fell on my neck, weeping loudly. "God be with you, daughter," said I, "why are crying?"

"Oh," she answered, "Father, *Tateh!*" Her face was bathed in tears.

The light went out of my eyes and my heart contracted painfully.

"What is it, daughter, what's happened to you? I asked and put my arms around her, stroking and kissing her. But she went on crying: "Father, dear Father, kind Father, I'll eat only one piece of bread in three days, have compassion for my youth!" And again she was choked with tears, couldn't utter another word.

Woe is me, I thought, I see where the land lies. It was an ill wind that took me to Boiberik!

"Silly little girl," I said, stroking her head, "why should you cry? It's either one or the other—no is no. Nobody, God forbid, is going to force you against your will. We thought it was for your good, we meant it for the best. But if your heart is not in it—what can be done? It probably wasn't ordained..."

"Oh, thank you, dear Father," she cried, "a long life to you." And once again she fell on my neck and started weeping, shedding tears.

"Listen, let there already be an end to this weeping," said I, "even eating meat dumplings can become tiresome! Get into the wagon and let's go home, your mother will be thinking God knows what!"

So we both got into the wagon and I began to calm her down with talk. I told her that we had the best of intentions; God knows the truth, all we wanted was to shield our child from misery. Well, it's come to nothing—evidently, such was God's will.

"It wasn't fated, daughter," I said, "that you should become the mistress of a wealthy home, and that we should reap a little joy in our old age, harnessed as we are, one might say, day and night to a wheelbarrow, not a good moment, only poverty and misery, bad luck over and over again!"

"Oh, *Tateh,*" she cried and again began to shed tears. "I'll go out and be a servant, I'll carry clay, I'll dig ditches!.."

"Why are you weeping, foolish girl," said I to her. "Am I reproaching you? Do I have any grievance against you? I'm in a dark and bitter mood, so I'm simply pouring out my heart, I'm talking to Him, to the Almighty, telling Him how He deals with me. He is a merciful Father, He pities me, but shows His power over me—He shouldn't punish me for my words—He settles accounts with me, and what can I do? Shout for help?"

I told her that probably things were meant to be so. He is up high above us, while we are down here, deep, deep in the ground, so we must say that He is right and His judgment is right, because if we look at it otherwise then I am nothing but a great fool. Why am I shouting, making such a racket? I am a tiny worm, I said, that wriggles down here on earth, so small that the slightest breeze, if God so wishes, could destroy me in an instant. Now do I have to make a stand with my foolish wits and try to tell Him how He should rule His little world? Probably, since He orders it to be so, it must be so; of what good are complaints? In our Holy Books it is written, said I, that forty days before a child is conceived in its mother's womb an angel comes along and announces: "The daughter of so-and-so will marry so-and-so!!" Let Tevye's daughter marry a Getzel, son of a Zorach, and Leizer-Wolf the butcher go elsewhere to find his mate; what is due to him won't run away, while you, said I, God should send your predestined one, only he should be a worthy man, and the sooner the better. Let His will be done, and I hope your mother doesn't yell too much, but I'll get enough from her anyhow!

Finally, we got home. I unharnessed the horse and then sat down on the grass near the house to try and think up what to tell my wife, to invent a tale from the *Arabian Nights,* so as to avoid trouble.

Evening was approaching. The sun was setting, frogs were croaking in the distance, the horse, hobbled, was munching grass, the cows, just returned from pasture, were standing over their mangers, waiting to be milked. All around me was the smell of grass—a true Garden of Eden! So I sat meditating and thinking how cleverly the Almighty had created this little world of His, so that each creature, from a human being to a cow, should earn its bread, nothing is for free! You, cow, if you wish to eat—let yourself be milked, yield milk, support a man and his wife and children. You, little horse, if you want to munch—trot back and forth to Boiberik, day in, day out, with the pots and crocks. The same goes for you, Man. If you want a piece of bread—go and toil, milk the cows, run around with the jugs and pitchers, churn butter, make cheese, harness the horse and drag yourself early every morning to Boiberik to the *dachas,* bow and scrape before the rich Yehupetzers, ingratiate yourself with them, smile at them, see to it that they are satisfied. God forbid you should injure their pride! Still, there remains the question: *"Mah nishtano?"* —where is it written that Tevye must slave for them, get up at the break of day, when God himself is still asleep, and for what? So that they should have fresh cheese and butter for their morning coffee? Where is it written that I must wear myself out working for a thin gruel, a *kulesh* of groats, while they, those rich Yehupetzers, rest their bones at their dachas, don't lift a finger for themselves and eat roast ducklings, good *knishes, blintzes* and *vertutti?* Am I not a Jew like they are? In all fairness, why shouldn't Tevye spend at least one summer at a *dacha?* Ah, but where will the cheese and butter come from? Who will milk the cows?.. Why, they, the Yehupetz rich, that's who!.. This crazy notion made me burst out laughing. As the saying goes, if God listened to fools, the world would have another face.

"Good evening, Reb Tevye!" someone greeted me. Turning around, I saw an acquaintance, Motl Kamzoil, a young tailor from Anatovka.

"Welcome! Mention the Messiah and see who comes!" said I. "Sit down, Motl, on God's good earth. What's brought you here all of a sudden?"

"What's brought me here? My feet!" he answered and sat down near me on the grass, looking towards the barn where my girls were flitting back and forth with the pots and jugs.

"It's already quite some time since I've wanted to come and see you, Reb Tevye," he said, "but I never seem to have the time: you finish one piece of work and take another. I now work for myself; there is, thank God, enough work, all of us tailors have as many orders as we can manage: it's been a summer of weddings. Berel Fonfach is having a wedding, Yosel Sheigetz is having a wedding, Mendel Zayika is having a wedding, Yankel Piskach is having a wedding, Moishe Gorgel is having a wedding, Meir Krapiva is having a wedding, Chaim Loshak is having a wedding and even the widow Trehubikha is getting ready for a wedding."

"The whole world," said I, "is celebrating weddings, I am the only exception; apparently, I am not worthy in God's eyes."

"No," said he, looking towards the place where the girls were. "You are mistaken, Reb Tevye. If you wished, you could also be getting ready for a wedding, it depends only on you..."

"How come?" I asked. "Maybe you mean a match for my Tzeitl?"

"A perfect fit!"

"Is it at least a worthy match?" I asked, thinking meanwhile: won't it be a fine thing if he means Leizer-Wolf the butcher!

"Cut and sewn to measure!" he retorted in tailors' talk, still looking off to where the girls were.

"From where, for instance," I asked him, "is this match of yours, from what parts? If he smells of a butcher shop I want to hear and see nothing of him!"

"God forbid," he answered, "by no means does he even begin to smell of a butcher shop. You know him very well, Reb Tevye!"

"Is this really a straight thing?" I asked.

"And how," said he, "straight! Straighter than straight! It is, as they say, merry, cheerful and lively—cut just right and sewn expertly!"

"So who is the man, tell me?" I asked.

"Who is the man?" repeated Motl, his eyes still on the barn. "The man is, Reb Tevye... you must understand—it is I myself."

No sooner had he said these words than I jumped to my feet as if scalded, and he after me, and so we stood face to face like ruffled-up roosters.

"Either you've gone crazy, or just simply lost your mind! You are the matchmaker, the in-law and the bridegroom all in one, that is, a whole wedding with your own musicians! I've never," said I, "heard anywhere that a young man should be his own matchmaker!"

"As regards what you say, Reb Tevye, about me being crazy—let all our enemies go crazy. I still have, you may believe me, all my wits about me. One doesn't have to be crazy to want to marry your Tzeitl. For example, Leizer-Wolf, who is the richest man in our town, also wanted to take her, even without a dowry...Do you think it's a secret? The whole *shtetl* already knows it! And as for your saying that I have come alone, without a matchmaker—you simply amaze me, Reb Tevye! After all, you are a man who knows something of the world. But why beat about the bush? This is the story: your daughter Tzeitl and I pledged our troth more than a year ago."

If someone had stabbed me to the heart I would have felt much better than when I heard these words: first of all, how comes he, Motl the Tailor, to be Tevye's son-in-law? Secondly, what kind of talk is this: they had pledged their troth, given each other their word to marry? And what about me? So I said to him:

"Cut and sewn to measure!" he retorted in tailor's talk.

"Don't I have some say where it concerns my child, or nobody asks me at all?"

"God forbid!" cried Motl. "that's just the reason why I came to have a talk with you, for I heard that Leizer-Wolf had proposed a match, and I have loved your daughter for over a year already."

"So if Tevye has a daughter named Tzeitl and your name is Motl Kamzoil and you are a tailor, then what can you have against her that you should dislike her?" I asked.

"No," said he, "that's not what I mean, I mean an altogether different thing. I wanted to tell you that I have been in love with your daughter for more than a year and that your daughter loves me and that we have pledged our word to each other to marry. I've wanted to come and talk the matter over with you several times, but have been putting it off for later, until I lay a few rubles aside to buy a sewing machine, and after that get myself decently clothed, since nowadays any self-respecting young man has to have two suits and several good shirts."

"Oh, get lost with your childish reasoning!" I shouted at him. "What will you do after the wedding, throw your teeth up into the rafters, or maybe feed your wife with shirts?"

"Eh, I really am surprised at you, Reb Tevye, that you should say such things! I mean, it seems to me that when you got married you owned no brick mansion, and yet... One thing or another—whatever happens to the Children of Israel will happen to Reb Israel. After all, I am a bit of a craftsman, too."

To make a long story short—he talked me into giving my consent. After all, why kid ourselves—how do all Jewish children get married? If one were to look at these things too closely, people of our class would never get married at all.

Only one thing troubled me, and I couldn't for the life of me understand it: what did it mean—they had given their word to each other? They themselves! What has the world come to? A boy meets a girl and says to her: "Let's get engaged, give each other our word to get married." That's simply wanton behavior!

However, when I took a look at my Motl, as he stood there with his head bowed, like a sinner, I saw that he was in full earnest, not trying any trickery, and then I had second thoughts. Let's look at the matter in another way. Why am I putting on such airs? Am I of such noble descent—Reb Tzotsele's grandson—or am I giving my daughter such a great dowry, or a splendid outfit? Alas! Yes, Motl Kamzoil is really a tailor, but he is a fine young man,

279

hard-working, can earn his wife's bread, and an honest boy, too, so what have I against him? Tevye, I told myself, raise no foolish objections, and say, as it is written in the Good Book: *"I have forgiven you"*—I wish you happiness!

Yes, but what's to be done about my old woman? She'll make such a scene! How can I reconcile her to this match?

"You know what, Motl?" I said to the young suitor, "You go back home, I'll fix up things here meanwhile, have a talk with this one, that one. As it is written in The Book of Esther, *'The drinking was according to law'*—everything must be considered. And tomorrow, God willing, if you haven't changed your mind, we'll probably see each other."

"Change my mind?" he shouted. "Me change my mind? I shouldn't live to leave this spot, I should turn into a stone, a bone!"

"What's the use of swearing to me," said I, "when I believe you without your oath? Go in good health, and a good night to you, and may you have pleasant dreams."

I went to bed, too, but sleep wouldn't come; my head was almost splitting as I devised one plan after another, until at last I hit on the right one. What was this plan? Listen and you'll hear what Tevye can think up!

Around midnight, when the whole house was fast asleep, one snoring, another whistling, I suddenly started yelling at the top of my voice: "Help! Help! Help!!!" Naturally, my screams woke the whole family, first of all—Golda...

"God be with you, Tevye," she says, shaking me, "wake up, what's going on, why are you screaming?"

I open my eyes, pretend to be looking around on all sides, and exclaim, as if terrified: "Where is she?"

"Where is who—whom are you looking for?"

"Frumeh-Soreh," I answer, "Frumeh-Soreh, Leizer-Wolf's wife, was standing here just now..."

"You must be out of your head with a fever, Tevye, God save you!" exclaims my wife. "Leizer-Wolf's Frumeh-Soreh, may she rest in peace, passed over to the other world long ago."

"Yes," say I, "I know that she died, but still she stood right here just now by my bed and spoke to me, she grasped me by the throat and wanted to strangle me!

"God save you. Tevye, what are you babbling about?" says my

wife. "You saw a dream—spit three times and tell me the dream, and I'll interpret it for you as a good omen."

Long may you live, Golda," say I, "for having woken me up, otherwise I might have died on the spot from fright. Give me a drink of water and I'll tell you my dream. Only I must implore you, Golda, not to be frightened and think God knows what, because it stands written in our Holy Books that only three parts of a dream may sometimes come true, while all the rest is nonsense, falsehood...

"First of all," I said, "I dreamed that we were having a celebration, I don't know whether it was a betrothal party or a wedding. There were many people, both men and women, the rabbi and the *shokhet*, and musicians, too... Meanwhile, the door opens and in comes your Grandmother Tzeitl, may she rest in peace..."

Upon hearing about Grandmother Tzeitl, my wife went pale as a sheet and cried:

"What was her face like and what was she wearing?!"

"A face she had," I said, "I would wish on all our enemies, yellow as wax, and she was wearing, naturally, a white shroud. *'Mazl-tov! Mazl-tov!'* she said to me. 'I am happy that you have chosen for your Tzeitl, who carries my name, such a fine and decent bridegroom, his name is Motl Kamzoil. He was named after my Uncle Mordecai, and although he is a tailor, he is an honest boy...'"

"Where does a tailor come into our family?" asked Golda. "There are *melameds* in our family, cantors, blacksmiths, gravediggers, and just poor people, but, God forbid, nary a tailor nor cobbler!"

"Don't you interrupt me, Golda," said I, "probably your Grandmother Tzeitl knows better than you do... Upon hearing such congratulations from Grandmother Tzeitl, I said to her: 'Why do you say, Granny, that Tzeitl's betrothed is called Motl and that he is a tailor when actually his name is Leizer-Wolf and he is a butcher?'

"'Oh, no,' said Grandmother Tzeitl once more, 'no, Tevye, your Tzeitl's bridegroom is Motl, he is a tailor and with him she'll live to a ripe old age, God willing, in honor and riches...'

"'All right, Granny,' said I to her, 'but what is to be done about Leizer-Wolf? I gave him my word only yesterday!..'

"No sooner had I uttered these last words than Grandmother

281

Tzeitl vanished and in her place there appeared Leizer-Wolf's Frumeh-Soreh and addressed me in the following manner: 'Reb Tevye! I have always held you to be an honest man, a learned and virtuous man. But how comes it,' said she, 'that you should do such a thing, that you should want your daughter Tzeitl to be my heiress, to live in my house, keep my keys, put on my coat, wear my jewelry, my pearls?'

"'It isn't my fault,' said I, 'your Leizer-Wolf wanted it that way...'

"'Leizer-Wolf?' she screamed. 'Leizer-Wolf will come to a bad end, and your Tzeitl... A pity, Reb Tevye, on your daughter; she won't live with him for more than three weeks, I'll come to her at night and take her by the throat like this...' And with these words she began to strangle me, so that if you hadn't woken me up I would already have been far, far away..."

"Tfu, tfu, tfu!" spat out my wife three times. "May it fall into the river, may it sink into the earth, may it crawl into attics, may it rest in the forest, but it shouldn't harm us and our children! A wild and evil dream, may it fall on the butcher's head and on his hands and feet! He isn't worth Motl Kamzoil's littlest fingernail, even though Motl is a tailor, because if he was named after Uncle Mordecai he is most certainly not a born tailor. And since Grandmother, may she rest in peace, has taken the trouble to come back from the other world to congratulate us, we must say that this is probably for the best and it is just as it should be, in a lucky hour. *Amen Selah!*"

To make a long story short I tell you that I must have been stronger than iron that night if I didn't die of laughter lying there under my blanket... *"Praised by He who did not create me a woman"*—a woman is always a woman...

Next day, of course, we celebrated their betrothal, and soon after that, the wedding—almost at one stroke. The young couple now live quite contentedly: he plies his trade, goes around in Boiberik from *dacha* to *dacha* picking up work, she is busy day and night with the cooking and baking, washing and cleaning and fetching water from the well, and they barely make enough for bread; if I didn't bring them some dairy food from time to time, or a few *groszy*, things wouldn't have been at all good; but go talk to her; she says—knock on wood—that she is as happy as can be, only her Motl should be in good health.

So go and argue with today's children! It's like I told you at the beginning—*"I have raised children."* You work your fingers to the bone for them, bash your head against the wall, but *"they haven't obeyed me"*—they insist that they know better. No, say what you will, but today's children are too clever!

But I'm afraid I've tried your patience this time more than ever before. Don't hold it against me, live in good health always.

1899

"Before I knew it, I found myself lying on the ground amidst all the empty crocks and pots, and the wagon on top of me."

Hodel

You are surprised, Mr. Sholom Aleichem, that Tevye hasn't been seen in such a long time? You say he has greatly changed, his hair has gone gray? Why, if you only knew what troubles, what heartache this Tevye has been having lately! As it is written: *"Man is born of dust, and to dust he returneth"*—man is weaker than a fly and stronger than iron... A real character out of a book, that's me! Wherever some pestilence, some misfortune or trouble crops up— it never dares miss me! Why is this so, can you tell me? Maybe it is because I am a trusting person and take everyone at his word? Tevye forgets what our wise men have warned us of thousands of times: *"Believe him but keep an eye on him,"* which in plain language means: "Don't trust a dog." But what can I do, I ask you, if such is my nature?

As you know, I am a great optimist and never lodge any complaints with the Eternal One. Whatever He ordains is good—for even if one did try to complain, would it be of any use? Since we say: *"My soul is for Thee and my body is Thine,"* then what does man know and what is he worth? I always argue with her, with my old woman: "Golda," I say, "you're sinning! We have a *midrash...*"

"What's your *midrash* to me," she says, "we have a daughter of a marriageable age, and after this daughter there come, knock on wood, another two daughters, and after these two—another one, let no evil eye fall on them!"

"Pshaw, Golda, that's nonsense," say I. "This, too, was foreseen by our wise men. There's a *midrash* for this that says..."

But she won't let me talk: "Daughters, grownup daughters, are of themselves a good *midrash!*" Go argue with a woman!

So you see that I have, knock on wood, a choice of merchandise, real good wares, I can't complain—one girl is prettier than the other. It isn't for me to praise my own children, but I hear what the world says: "Beauties!" And the prettiest is the second one, Hodel is her name, she is next after Tzeitl, the one who fell in love with a tailor, if you remember, and so cooked her own goose. As for looks—this second daughter of mine, Hodel, I mean—what shall I say? She is, as it is written in our sacred Book of Esther, *"of beautiful form and fair to look upon"*—shines like gold! Besides, as bad luck would have it, she has to have a head, too, reads and writes Yiddish and Russian, and as for books—she swallows them whole! You may well ask: what is there in common between Tevye's daughter and books, when her father deals in cheese and butter? That's just what I ask them, the fine young men, I mean, who haven't got a pair of pants, begging your pardon, they can call their own, but they have an urge to study. As we say in the *Haggadah:* *"We are all sages"*—everybody wants to learn, everybody wants to study. Go ask them: study what? Why? Goats should know as much about jumping into a neighbor's garden! Why, they aren't even permitted to enroll anywhere! Hands off!—shoo, away from the butter, kitty!

But you should see *how* they study! And who? Children of workmen—of tailors, of cobblers—so help me God!

Off they go to Yehupetz, or to Odessa, "lodge" in garrets, eat plagues and wash them down with fevers, for months on end don't as much as look a piece of meat in the eye, six of them pool their money to buy one loaf and a herring and—heigh-ho, make merry, paupers!...

In short, one such boy landed in our corner of the world, not far from here; I used to know his father, he was a cigarette-maker, as poor as poor can be. If our great sage Reb Jochanan Hasendler was not ashamed to sew boots, there is nothing wrong with having a father who rolls cigarettes.

One thing, however, troubles me: why should a poor man be so anxious to learn, to study? True, the devil didn't catch him, he has a good head on his shoulders, a very good head. His name is Perchik—"little pepper," but we translated it into Yiddish as Feferl—peppercorn. He really does look like a pepper, you should see him: a wizened, black and homely creature, but chock-full of brains, and with a tongue—real brimstone!

Well, here is what happened one day as I was driving home from Boiberik. I'd sold my wares, a full transport of cheese and butter and cream and various greens. Sitting in my wagon I lost myself, as I often do, in thoughts of heavenly things, of this and that, of the rich people from Yehupetz who had it so good, knock

285

on wood, so good, and of Tevye the *shlimazl* and his little horse who both slaved throughout life, and so on.

It was summertime, the sun was hot, the flies were biting, and the world all around me was a delight, vast and open. I felt like getting up and flying, or stretching out and swimming!..

Meanwhile, I looked around and saw a lad striding on foot through the sand, carrying a bundle under his arm, sweating and out of breath.

"'*Rise, Yokel, son of Flekel!*'" I cried to him. "Here, come along, I'll give you a lift, my wagon is empty. How is it written in our Book? '*If you see the ass belonging to a friend of yours lying under its burden you shall not pass it by*'—all the more so a human being." So he laughs and climbs into my wagon.

"From where, for instance," I ask him, "does a young man pace?"

"From Yehupetz."

"What had a lad like you to do in Yehupetz?"

"A lad like me is taking examinations."

"And what profession," I ask, "may a lad like you be studying for?"

"A lad like me," he says, "isn't sure himself yet what he is studying for."

"If that is the case," say I, "why does a lad like you trouble his head in vain?"

"Don't you worry, Reb Tevye," retorts he, "such a lad as I knows what he is doing."

"Since you know who *I* am," I say, "then why not tell me, for instance, who *you* are?"

"Who am I? I am a human being."

"I see," say I, "that you're not a horse! I mean, *whose* are you?"

"Whose should I be? I am God's."

"That I know—that you are God's" I say. "It is written in our Books, '*All living things are His.*' what I mean is from whom do you stem; are you one of ours, or maybe from Lithuania?"

"I *stem*," says he, "from our forefather Adam, but I *come* from this neighborhood, you know me."

"So who is your father, come on, tell me!"

"My father," says he, "was called Perchik."

"Phoo," I spit in annoyance, "did you have to torture me so long? So you are the son of Perchik the cigarette-maker?"

286

"So I am the son of Perchik the cigarette-maker," he admits.

"And you study," I say, "in the 'classes'?"

"And I study," says he, "in the 'classes'."

"All right," say I, *Adam* is a man and *'tzipur'* is a bird, but tell me, my jewel, what, for instance, do you live on?"

"I live on what I eat."

"Aha," say I, "that's good; so what do you eat?"

"Anything I can get."

"I understand, you're not finicky: if there is something to eat you eat, if not—you bite your lip and go to bed hungry. But this is all worthwhile—as long as you can study in your 'classes'. You think you're equal to the rich boys of Yehupetz? As the verse goes: *'All are beloved, all are chosen.'*"

And I went on talking to him in this manner, giving him chapter and verse.

But you have another guess coming if you think he listened meekly: "They won't live to see the day I equal myself with them, those rich Yehupetz brats! To hell with them!"

"It seems to me that you really have it in for those rich people! I'm afraid they must have divided your father's inheritance among themselves!"

"Let me tell you that I and you and all of us possibly have a large share in *their* inheritance," said he.

"You know what—let your enemies speak for you. I notice only one thing: you are not a pampered young man and your tongue needs no sharpening; if you have the time, come over to my house this evening, we'll talk a little and you'll have supper with us."

Of course, I didn't have to repeat my invitation; he arrived in the evening, right on the dot—when the borsht was already on the table and the dairy *knishes* were frying in the oven.

"If you wish," I said to him, "wash your hands and say grace, if not—you can eat unwashed—I'm not God's steward, I won't be beaten in the other world for your sins."

As I talked to him I felt that somehow I was attracted to this little man; just what it was I don't know myself, but drawn to him I was. I like people with whom one can exchange a few words, sometimes a proverb, sometimes a *midrash,* or discuss heavenly things, this, that, and another—that's the kind of person Tevye is.

From that day on my young man began to drop in almost

every evening. He had a few private pupils, so as soon as he had finished with his lessons, he would come over to me to relax and enjoy himself a little. You can imagine what he got for his lessons if our wealthiest man is used to paying no more than three rubles a month, and the teacher has to, moreover, help him with his paperwork—read telegrams, write addressees and even run errands sometimes. And why not? As it is written: *"With heart and soul"*— if you eat bread you should know for what. He was lucky, though, that he ate with us most of the time, and for this he gave lessons to my daughters; as the Book says: *"Eye for eye"*—a slap for a slap.

In this manner he became like a member of our family. The children would ply him with glasses of milk, while my old woman took care that he should always have a clean shirt and a pair of darned socks. That was when we changed his name to Feferl—the Yiddish word for the Russian *perchik;* it may truly be said that the whole family came to love him as if he were our own kin, for by nature, I'll let you know, he is really a fine person, nothing underhand about him: *"Mine is yours, yours is mine."*

There was only one thing I didn't like about him: his disappearances. All of a sudden he would up and go, and—*"The child vanished"*—no more Feferl! "Where have you been, my dear songbird?" He's as mute as a fish.

I don't know about you, but I hate a person with secrets. What I like is, as they say, to *talk* and to *tell*. But one must give him his due: once he did start talking it was *"who by fire, who by water will be destroyed"*—fire and water! What a tongue—Heaven preserve us! He spoke *"against the Lord and against His anointed, let us break their bands asunder."* The most important thing, of course, was breaking the bands. Such wild ideas he had, absurd, crazy plans, everything topsy-turvy, upside-down! For instance, a rich man, according to his crazy notions, is worthless, while a poor man, quite the opposite, is the real goods, and if he is a workman he tops the stack, because he works with his own hands, and that's what is most important.

"Still," I said, "that doesn't come up to money."

This made him furious and he tried to convince me that money was the root of all evil on earth. Money, he said, is the source of all the falseness in the world, and everything that goes on is not fair, and because of money injustice reigns over the world. And he cited me thousands of arguments and examples that made no sense to me at all...

"It comes out," I said, "that, according to your crazy reasoning, the fact that my cow is milked and my horse draws loads is also not fair?" Such and other tricky questions I asked him, bringing him up short at every step, as Tevye can! But my Feferl also knows how to argue—and does he know! I wish God hadn't granted him such skill!

If Feferl had anything on his heart he immediately came out with it. We were sitting outside my house one evening, discussing all the aspects of these matters—it's called philosophy. Suddenly he remarked, Feferl, that is: "You know what, Reb Tevye? You have very bright daughters!"

"Really, I thank you for the news, they have whom to take after," was my retort.

"One of them," he went on. "the eldest one, is very sensible, a human being in the full sense of the word."

"That I know without your telling me," said I, "the fruit doesn't fall far from the tree."

That's what I said to him, but my heart, naturally, melted with pleasure, for what father, I ask you, doesn't like to hear his children praised? How was I to foresee that this praise would grow into a fiery emotion, Heaven protect us?

Well, *"And it was night and it became day"*—the time was between day and night. I was driving along in Boiberik from *dacha* to *dacha* when somebody stopped me. I took a look—it was Ephraim the Matchmaker. This Ephraim, you must know, is a matchmaker like any other matchmaker; that is, he arranges matches. Upon seeing me in Boiberik he, Ephraim I mean, stopped me, saying:

"Excuse me, Reb Tevye, there is something I have to tell you."

"My pleasure, only let it be a good thing," I said and stopped my horse.

"You, Reb Tevye, have a daughter!" he said.

"I have," said I, "seven daughters, God bless them."

"I know," said he, "that you have seven; I have seven myself."

"So we have," said I, "a total of fourteen daughters."

"All right," he went on, "let's finish with the joking. What I have to tell you is this: I am, as you know, a matchmaker, and I have a match for you, a young man who is something special from special-land! Top quality!"

"And what," asked I, "do you call something special, top quality? If he is a tailor, a cobbler, or a *melamed*, then let him stay where he

289

"And for this he gave lessons to my daughters."

is, and for me, as it is written, *'freedom and deliverance will come from another'*—I'll find my equal somewhere else, as the *Midrash* says."

"Eh, Reb Tevye, you're starting on your *midrashim?* Before talking with you one has to tighten his belt! You shower the world with *midrashim.* Better hear out what a match Ephraim the Matchmaker wants to offer you; you just listen and keep quiet." And with this he began to read me his bill of sale.

What can I say? Something really out of the ordinary. In the first place, he comes from a good family, he's no upstart without kith or kin; this, you should know, is the main thing for me, since I am no nobody myself: in my family there are all kinds of people—*"spotted, striped, and speckled,"* as it stands in the Bible; we have just plain people, we have workers and we have men of property... Then, the young man is a scholar who is well-versed in the fine little letters. With me this is no small matter because I hate an ignoramus as I hate pork! To me an unlettered man is a thousand times worse than a rowdy; as far as I'm concerned you may go around without a cap, or even upside-down, but if you know what Rashi says you are already one of mine! That's the kind of person Tevye is!

"Then," went on Ephraim, "this man is rich, chock-full of money, he drives in a carriage drawn by a pair of fiery steeds—you even see the smoke!"

Well, thought I to myself, that isn't a bad thing, either. Better a rich man than a pauper. As it is written. *"Poverty is fitting for Israel."* God himself hates a pauper, otherwise a poor man wouldn't be poor.

"Well," asked I, "what else?"

"What else? He wants to become related to you—he's so eager, he's almost dead! That is, it's not exactly you he has in mind, he's dying to marry your daughter, he wants to marry a beauty, that's what he wants...."

"Oh, that's the way it is?" said I. "Let him go on wanting. But who is he, this rarity of yours—a bachelor, a widower, a divorcee, a black year?"

"He is a bachelor," said Ephraim, "although not so young, but a bachelor."

"And what," I asked, "is his holy name?"

That the matchmaker wouldn't tell me, go take and roast him alive!

"Bring her," said he, "to Boiberik, then I'll tell you."

291

"What do you mean—I should bring her? You can bring a horse to the fair, or a cow to be sold!"

Well, matchmakers, you know, can persuade a wall. We fixed a date: after next Saturday I would bring her, God willing, to Boiberik.

All kind of sweet thoughts came into my mind. I already imagined my Hodel driving in a carriage drawn by a pair of fiery steeds, and the whole world envying me, not so much because of the carriage and horses, as because of the benefits I bring the world through my rich daughter; I help the fallen with loans through my rich daughter; I help the fallen with loans without interest—I let this one have twenty-five rubles, that one fifty, another one a hundred; as you say, other people have souls, too.

So I meditated, driving home towards evening, giving the horse the whip and talking horse-language: "Horsie," I said, "giddy-up, giddy-up, hey, now just make with the legs a little faster, then you'll get your portion of oats sooner; as the Bible says: *'Without food there's no learning'*—if you don't grease the axles the wheels won't turn."

As I was talking in this manner to my horse I noticed two people coming out of the woods—a man and a woman, apparently. They were walking close to each other, talking very earnestly. Who could they be, I thought as I peered at them through the fiery rays of the setting sun. I could swear that it was Feferl! With whom was he strolling, the *shlimazl*, so late? I shielded my eyes with my hand and looked closer: who was the female? Eh, doesn't she look like Hodel? Yes indeed, as I live—it's Hodel! So this is how they study grammar and read books? Oh, Tevye, aren't you a fool! With such thoughts I stopped my horse and called out to the young people:

"A good evening to you, and what's the latest news about war? How come you're here all of a sudden? Whom are you waiting for? The day that's gone by?"

Upon hearing such a greeting my young couple stopped— *"Neither in Heaven nor on Earth"*—which means neither here nor there, shamefaced and blushing.

They stood so for a few minutes without uttering a word, their eyes downcast; then they raised their eyes and began to look at me, and I at them, and they at each other.

"Well," said I, "you're looking at me as if you hadn't seen me for a long time. It seems to me that I'm the selfsame Tevye as before. Not changed a hair."

292

I spoke to them half in anger, half in jest. At last my daughter Hodel, her face redder than before, said:

"Father, we should be congratulated."

"*Mazl-tov* to you," said I, "with good luck may you live. What's the celebration? Did you find a treasure in the woods? Or maybe you've just had a narrow escape from a great danger?"

"We should be congratulated," said Feferl, "we are betrothed."

"What do you mean," asked I, "by 'betrothed'?"

"Don't you know what 'betrothed' means?" he asked. "Betrothed means that I am engaged to marry her and she is engaged to marry me."

Speaking so, Feferl looked right into my eyes. But I also looked straight into *his* eyes, and I said:

"When was your betrothal-party? Any why didn't you invite me to the joyous event? I'm something of a relative, am I not?"

You understand, I joked with them, but worms were eating me, preying on my soul. But no matter, Tevye is not a woman, Tevye likes to hear out things to the end...

"I don't understand," said I, "a match without a matchmaker, without a marriage contract?"

"What do we need matchmakers for?" he, Feferl, asked. "We've been engaged for a long time already."

"Really? Divine miracles! So why did you keep quiet about it until now?"

"Why should we shout?" he asked. "We wouldn't have told you today, either, if not for the fact that we'll soon be parting, so we've decided that before this happens we must get married..."

This, as you understand, upset me greatly. *"The water reached up to the neck"*—I was hurt to the quick. His saying that they were engaged—well, that I could endure—how is it written? *"A'ave"*—love—he wants her, she wants him. But marriage? What words, "We must get married!" Gibberish!

It seemed that the bridegroom-to-be understood that I'd become a bit unhinged, so he said:

"See, Reb Tevye, this is how things stand: I have to go away from here."

"When are you leaving?"

"Very soon."

"Where, for instance, are you going?"

"This," said he, " I can't tell you, it's a secret..."

You hear? It's a secret! How do you like that?! Along comes a

Feferl, a small, dark, homely creature, presents himself as a bridegroom, wants to marry my daughter, is about to leave and won't say where to! Isn't it galling!?

"All right, a secret is a secret," said I; "everything is a secret with you. Only let me understand this, brother: you, after all, are a man of honor and are immersed in humaneness from head to toe. So how does it figure with you that you should all of a sudden out of the blue, take Tevye's daughter and turn her into a grass widow? This is what you call honor? Humaneness? I'm lucky that you haven't robbed me or set my house on fire..."

"Father!" exclaimed my daughter Hodel, "you just can't imagine how happy we are, he and I, that we've let out our secret to you. It's a load off our hearts. Come, Father, let's kiss each other."

Without more ado both of them embraced me, she on one side, he on the other, and they started kissing me and hugging me, and I them, and, evidently out of great zeal, the two of them began to kiss each other! A spectacle, I tell you, a real theater!

"Maybe it's already enough," said I, "of kissing? It's time to talk of practical matters."

"What practical matters?"

"A dowry," said I, "clothing, wedding expenses, this, that, and the other..."

"We need nothing," said they, "neither this, nor that, nor the other."

"Then what is it you do need?"

"We need," they said, "only the wedding ceremony."

Did you ever hear the like?

Well, in short, my words had as much weight with them as last year's snow, they had their wedding! Of course, you understand that it wasn't at all the sort of wedding that suited Tevye. What a wedding!.. A very quiet ceremony—woe is me!

Moreover, there was my wife, too—as one says, a blister on a boil! She nagged me, pestered me to tell her the reason for such a harum-scarum, hasty wedding. Go explain a fire to a woman! So I had to invent a maudlin story about an inheritance, a rich aunt in Yehupetz, all lies, all for the sake of peace.

On the same day, that is, a few hours after this fine wedding, I hitched up my horse and wagon and the three of us got in—that is, I myself, my daughter and he, the new-fledged son-in-law of mine, and we went to the railway station in Boiberik. Sitting in my wagon I glanced stealthily at the couple and thought to myself:

what a great God we have and how wondrously He rules this world of His! What strange, absurd beings He has created! Here you have a young couple just from under the wedding canopy: he is going away, the devil knows where, but she is staying behind— and not a single tear do you see, for appearance's sake at least! But no matter, Tevye is not a woman, Tevye has time, he can wait and see what the outcome will be...

Well, I saw a couple of young men, fine fellows with worn-out boots who came to the train to say goodbye to my song-bird. One of them was dressed like a peasant, I beg your pardon, with his shirt hanging out over his trousers; a whispered conversation took place between him and my son-in-law.

Look at that, Tevye, I said to myself, maybe you've gotten mixed up with a gang of horse-thieves, purse-snatchers, lock-breakers, or counterfeiters?..

Driving home from Boiberik with Hodel I couldn't keep these thoughts to myself. She burst out laughing and tried to convince me that these were very fine young men, honest, extremely honest, men whose entire lives were dedicated to the welfare of others, who didn't think of themselves at all.

"The one with the shirt," said she, "comes from a most respectable family, he left his wealthy parents in Yehupetz and won't take a broken *grosz* from them."

"Really? Actually a very fine young man, as I live!" said I. "In addition to the shirt hanging out over his pants and his long hair, if God should help him to acquire an accordion, or a dog to run after him—that, indeed, would be most extremely charming!"

With such talk I was getting even with her, and with him, too, pouring out the bitterness of my heart, that is, on the poor girl....

And she? Nothing! *"Esther held her peace."* Makes as if she doesn't understand.

I say: "Feferl." She comes out with: "For the common weal, workers..." A hopeless thing!

"What's the use," said I, "of your 'common weal' and your workers if everything is a secret with you? There is a proverb that says: Where there's a secret there's thievery... So tell me, daughter, why did he leave—Feferl, I mean—and where did he go?"

"Anything else," said she, "but not this. You'd better not ask about it. Believe me, when the time comes you'll know everything. God willing, you'll hear, and perhaps very soon, many things, much good news!"

"Amen," said I, "let it be from your lips to God's ear. But our enemies should know as much of health as I have even an inkling of what is going on here with you and what the play-acting means!"

"That's just the trouble—you won't understand."

"Why so? Is it so hard to understand? It seems to me that I understand more difficult things."

"This cannot be understood," said she, "with the mind alone. It must be felt, felt with the heart..."

That is how my daughter Hodel spoke to me, and while she talked, her face flamed and her eyes burned. Heaven preserve these daughters of mine! When they get involved in something, it's with mind and heart, with body and soul!

In short, I'll tell you that a week went by, two, three, four, five, six and seven weeks— *"Neither voice nor money"*—no letters, no messages.

"Feferl is lost!" As I said this, I glanced at my Hodel: there was not a drop of blood in her face, poor girl, and she went about the house looking for something to do, trying, apparently, to drown her grief in work. Still, she never even as much as mentioned his name! Hush, quiet, just as if there had never even been a Feferl in the world!

However, one day, when I came home, my Hodel's eyes were swollen from tears. I started to ask questions and found out that not long ago she had had a visitor—a long-haired *shlimazl*, who had spoken in secret to her. Aha, thought I, that must be the fellow who left his rich parents and wears his shirt over his pants... So without more ado I called my Hodel out into the yard and asked her bluntly:

"Tell me, daughter, have you already heard from him?"

"Yes."

"Where is he then, your predestined one?"

"He is," says she, "far away."

"What is he doing?"

"He's in prison!"

"In prison?"

"In prison."

"Where is he in prison? Why is he in prison?"

No answer. She looks me straight in the face and keeps quiet.

"Only tell me, daughter mine," said I, "as I understand, he is in prison not for robbery; in that case, since he is no thief and no swindler, I don't understand why he is in prison, for what good deeds?"

She was silent. *"Esther held her peace."* Well, thought I, you don't want to tell me—don't; he is your affliction, not mine. Serves him right! But inside, in my heart, I carried a pain. I am, after all, a father; doesn't it say in our prayers: *"As a father pities his children"*—a father is always a father.

Well, the evening of *Hashono Rabo* came. On a holiday it's my custom to take a rest, and my horse, too, rests. As the Torah says, *"Thou shalt rest from thy labors and so shall thy wife and thy ass..."* Besides, there is not much to do in Boiberik: it needs no more than one blow of the *shophar* to make all the *dachniki,* the summer people, scatter like mice during a famine, and Boiberik becomes a waste. At such times I like to be at home, to sit outdoors on the *prizba**. This is the best time for me. The days are gifts. The sun is no longer as hot as a lime kiln, it caresses you softly, a pleasure to the soul. The forest is still green, the pines still exude their pungent scent, and it seems to me that the forest takes on a festive look, that it is god's own tabernacle, his *sukkah;* this, I think, is where God celebrates *Sukkoth*—here, not in the cities where there is such a tumult, with people rushing back and forth, panting for breath, all for the sake of a piece of bread, and all one hears is money, money, and money!..

This night of *Hashono Rabo* was truly like Paradise: the sky was blue, the stars twinkled and blinked as if they were human eyes. Once in a while a star would shoot by, as an arrow flies from a bow, leaving for an instant a green streak—a falling star, somebody's luck had fallen. There are as many lucks as there are stars in the sky... Jewish luck... I hope it isn't my bad luck, was my thought, and this brought to mind Hodel. During the last few days she had become brighter, livelier, and looked altogether different. Somebody must have brought her a letter from him, from her *shlimazl.* I'd have liked to know what he wrote, but I didn't want to ask. She said nothing, so I kept quiet, too: Tevye is not a woman, Tevye can wait...

As I sat thinking about Hodel, she herself came out and sat down by my side on the *prizba*. Glancing around, she turned to me and said, in a low voice:

---

*A mound, or ledge, of earth banked against the outer walls of peasant houses (Ukrainian). — *Tr.*

297

"Do you hear, *Tateh?* I have to tell you something: today I am going to say goodbye to you... forever."

She said these words almost in a whisper, I could hardly hear her; her look was so strange—I'll never forget it. Meanwhile a thought flitted through my mind: She wants to drown herself!

Why did I think of drowning? Because—may this never happen to us—not long ago a Jewish girl, she lived not far from us, fell in love with a peasant boy and because of this boy... You understand already.... These troubles affected her mother so that she took sick and died, and her father spent everything he had and became a pauper. The peasant boy changed his mind and married somebody else. So she, the girl, I mean, went to the river, threw herself into the water and drowned...

"What do you mean," I asked, "that you are going to say goodbye forever?" As I spoke I looked at the ground, so that she shouldn't see how upset I was.

"It means," said she, "that early tomorrow morning I am going away and we'll never see each other again... Never..."

Upon hearing these words I felt a little better. Thank God for this at least—it might be worse, while better has no limit.

"Where, for instance are you going—if I might have the honor of knowing?" I asked.

"I'm going," said she, "to him."

"To him? So where is he now?"

"For the time being," she said, "he is still in prison; but soon he will be deported."

"So you're going, you mean, to say goodbye to him?" I asked, playing the fool.

"No," she answered, "I'm following him out there."

"Out there?.. Where is this 'out there,' what is the name of the place?"

"We don't know yet exactly what the place is called, but it is very far," she said, "far and full of terrible dangers."

That's what my Hodel told me, and it seemed to me that she spoke with elation, with great pride, just as if he'd accomplished something so important that he should be awarded a medal weighing at least thirty pounds!.. How was I to answer her? For such things a father gets angry with his child, hands out a couple of slaps or gives the child a good dressing down! However, Tevye is not a woman. To my way of thinking anger raises the devil. So I retorted, as I usually do, with a passage from the Bible:

298

"I see, my daughter, it is as the Bible says, *'Therefore shalt thou abandon...'* Because of a Feferl you're abandoning your father and mother and are going away to nobody knows where, somewhere out in a desolate place, on the shore, evidently, of the frozen sea where Alexander the Great sailed and got lost and was stranded on a distant island among savages, as I once read in a story-book..."

I spoke half in jest and half in anger, and all the time my heart wept. But Tevye is not a woman, Tevye restrains himself. Neither did she, Hodel, lose face: she answered me word for word, quietly, thoughtfully. Tevye's daughters can talk.

Although my head was bowed and my eyes were closed, yet it seemed to me that I saw her, Hodel, that is; I saw that her face was just like the moon, pale and lusterless, and her voice sounded muffled and it trembled... Should I fall on her neck, plead with her, implore her not to go? But I know that it won't help. Oh, these daughters of mine! If they fall in love, it's with soul and body, with heart and mind!

Well, we sat out there on the *prizba* for a long time, maybe all night. We were silent most of the time, and when we did speak it was almost not speech—half-words... She spoke and I spoke. I asked her only one thing: where did anyone hear of a girl marrying a fellow just in order to be able to follow him to the devil knows where!?

To this her answer was: "With *him* I don't care—I'll go anywhere, even to the devil knows where!"

I tried to explain to her how foolish this was. So she answered me that I would never be able to understand it. I told her a story about a hen that had hatched ducklings; no sooner did they gain the use of their legs than they took to the water, while the poor hen stood clucking on the shore.

"What," asked I, "will you say to that, daughter dear?'

"What," asked she, "can I say? It's a pity on the hen, but because the hen clucks should the ducklings not swim?.."

Can you understand such talk? Tevye's daughter utters no empty words...

Meanwhile time did not stand still. Dawn was already breaking. Inside the house my old woman grumbled. She had already sent for us several times, saying it was high time to go to bed; seeing that this was of no use, she stuck her head out of the window and said to me, with her usual benediction: "Tevye, what's got into you?!"

"In my heart I was like a boiling samovar, but I showed nothing."

"Let there be silence, Golda," said I, "as the Bible says, *"Why the uproar?.."* You must have forgotten that it is *Hashono Rabo* tonight? On *Hashono Rabo* our fates are sealed for the coming year, so on *Hashono Rabo* we stay up all night. Now you just do what I tell you, Golda: please kindle the fire in the samovar and let us have tea; meanwhile I'll go and hitch up the horse. I'm taking Hodel to the station."

And then, as my custom is, I made up a new cock-and-bull story about Hodel going to Yehupetz, and from there still further, all on account of that business, the legacy, and it might be that she would stay there over the winter, and maybe even over a winter and summer and another winter. Therefore, said I, we have to give her some food for the journey, some linen, a dress, a few pillows, pillowcases, this, that, and another.

As I ordered my womenfolk around, I told them there should be no weeping, for it was *Hashono Rabo.*

"There is an explicit law against weeping on *Hashono Rabo!*" I said,.

Well, they minded me as a cat minds, and there was plenty of crying, and when the time of parting came there was such an uproar, such weeping—the mother, the children, and even she herself, Hodel, particularly when she was saying goodbye to my eldest daughter, Tzeitl. (She and her husband, Motl Kamzoil, always spend the holidays with us.) Both sisters fell on each other's necks—we could barely tear them apart...

I was the only one who didn't break down—I was as firm as steel and iron. I mean, that's just a saying, "steel and iron"; in my heart I was like a boiling samovar, but I showed nothing—fie! Tevye is, after all, not a woman!..

We didn't talk at all on the way to Boiberik, but when we were already near the station I asked her, for the last time, to tell me what, actually, he had done, her Feferl?

"Every thing," said I, "must have some sort of taste."

At this she flared up and swore by all the holiest oaths in the world that he was absolutely innocent of any crime, pure as fine gold.

"He is a man," she said, "who cares nothing about himself. All he did was for the good of others, for the good of the world, above all for the toilers, the working people..."—so be a sage and try to guess what that means!

"He worries about the world?" I asked her. "Then why doesn't the world worry about him if he is such a fine fellow? But please give him my regards, this Alexander the Great of yours. Tell him that I rely on his honor, for he is a man of honor and I trust that he won't deceive my daughter and will write a letter once in a while to her old father..."

You think that as I spoke she didn't fall on my neck and begin to cry?

"Let us say goodbye," she said. "Farewell, *Tateh,* God knows when we will see each other again!"

At this I finally broke down myself... I remembered this very Hodel when she was a baby... a little child... I carried her in my arms... in my arms...

Please excuse me, Mr. Sholom Aleichem, that I... like an old woman... Oh, if you only knew what a daughter Hodel was... what a daughter... You should see the letters she writes... A godsend, this Hodel! She... deep, deep in my heart... deep, deep, I haven't the words to express what I feel...

You know what, Mr. Sholom Aleichem? Let us better talk of more cheerful things: what's the latest news about the cholera in Odessa?..

1904

302

Chava

"Give thanks to the Lord, for He is good"—whichever way God leads is good. That is, it should be good, for try and become a sage and make things better! Take me—I wanted to be clever, I interpreted Bible verses this way and that way and saw that it was of no use, so I gave it up as a hopeless job and told myself: Tevye, you're a fool! You won't overturn the world. The Almighty gave us *"the pain of bringing up children,"* which means the sorrows inflicted by children should be looked upon as blessings. For instance, my eldest daughter Tzeitl fell in love with the tailor Motl Kamzoil, so have I anything against him? True, he is a simple soul, not very well versed in the fine little letters, I mean, but what can be done? The whole world can't be educated, can it? But he is honest and hard-working, he works, poor man, by the sweat of his brow. They already have, you should only see, a houseful—knock on wood— of bare-bellied young ones, and both of them struggle *"in honor and in riches,"* as the saying goes. But talk with her, she'll tell you that everything is, knock on wood, fine with her, it can't be better. The only trouble is that there isn't enough food…There you have, so to say, round number one.

Well, and about the second daughter, I mean Hodel, I don't have to tell you, you already know. With her I gambled and lost, lost her forever! God alone knows whether my eyes will ever behold her again, unless we meet in the next world, in a hundred and twenty years… Whenever I speak of her, of Hodel, I still can't take it, it's the end of my life! Forget her, you say? How can one forget a living person? Especially such a child as Hodel? You should only see the letters she writes to me—your heart would melt! She writes that they are doing quite well out there. He sits in prison and she earns a living. She washes clothes and reads books and visits him every week; she hopes, she says, that the pot will boil over here, in our parts, the sun will rise and everything will brighten, and then he and many others like him will be released, and after that, she says, they will all begin their real work and turn the world upside-down. Well? How do you like that? Fine, isn't it?..

Yes, so what does the Almighty do? He is, after all, *"a gracious and merciful Lord,"* so He says to me: "Just you wait, Tevye, I will bring something to pass that'll make you forget all your former troubles..."

And sure enough—this is a story worth hearing. I wouldn't tell it to another person, because the pain is great and the shame is still greater! Only, as it is written in our Book: *"Shall I conceal it from Abraham?"*—I have no secrets from you. Whatever I have on my mind I tell you. But there is one request I want to make: let it remain between the two of us. I tell you once more: the pain is great, but the shame, the shame is still greater!

Well, as it stands in the *Perek: "The Holy One, blessed be He, wished to purify a soul"*—God decided to do Tevye a favor, so he went and blessed him with seven female children, daughters, that is, all of them lovely, clever, and beautiful, fresh and healthy—pine trees, I tell you! Oh, if only they had been ugly and ill-tempered it might have been better for them and healthier for me. Now, I ask you, what is the use of a good horse if it is kept in a stable? What's the good of having beautiful daughters when you're stuck away with them out in a hole where they see no live people except Ivan Poperilo, the headman of the village, or the clerk Fedka Galagan, a tall Gentile fellow with a mane of hair and high boots, and the Russian priest, may his name and his memory be blotted out. I just can't bear to hear his name—not because I am a Jew and he is a Christian priest. On the contrary, we have been well acquainted for many years. That is, we don't visit each other to have a talk, nor, of course, do we wish each other a happy holiday; but, no matter, when we meet we say good morning, a good year, what's new in the world? I hate to get involved in long conversations with him, because they are sure to turn into a discussion: your God, our God. But I don't let him go on—I interrupt with an aphorism and tell him that we have a certain verse in the Bible... So he interrupts me and says that he knows all these verses as well as I do, and perhaps even better, and he begins to recite our Holy Bible in Hebrew to me, with his Gentile pronunciation: *"Bereshit bara alokim"**—every time, every time the same thing. So I interrupt him again and

---

* *"In the beginning God created...",* the opening words of Genesis (Hebrew).—*Tr.*

304

tell him that we have a *Midrash*... "The *Midrash*," he says, "is called the *Tal-mud*," and he hates the *Tal-mud* for the *Tal-mud* is sheer trickery... So of course I get good and angry and start laying out anything that comes to my mind. Do you think he cares? Not at all! He looks at me and laughs, combing his beard with his fingers all the while. There is nothing more maddening in the world than the silence of a person you are shouting at, calling all manner of foul names—and not getting a word back! You are boiling, your bile is rising, while he just sits and smiles! At that time I couldn't understand it, but now I know what that smile meant...

Well, as I was coming home towards evening one day whom should I see standing near my house but the clerk Fedka, talking to my third daughter, Chava, the one who comes after Hodel. Upon seeing me the fellow about-faced, took off his cap to me and left. So I asked Chava:

"What was Fedka doing here?"

"Nothing," she answered.,

"What do you mean by nothing?" I asked.

"We were just talking."

"What's there for you to talk with Fedka about?"

"We've known each other for a long time."

"I congratulate you on your acquaintanceship! A wonderful friend—Fedka!" cried I.

"Do you know him then?" she asked. "Do you know who he is?"

"Who he is—that I don't know," said I, "I haven't seen his family register, however, I do understand that he probably stems from the greatest celebrities: his father must have been either a cowherd, or a watchman, or simply a drunkard."

To this she, Chava, that is, answered: "What his father was I don't know, to me all people are equal; but that he himself is no ordinary person—that I know for sure."

"And namely what sort of man may he be? Let me hear."

"I'd tell you," said she, "but you won't understand. Fedka—he is a second Gorky."

"A second Gorky? Then who was the first Gorky?"

"Gorky," she answered, "is almost the greatest man in the world today."

"Where does he live." I asked, "this sage of yours, what is his business and what kind of sermons does he preach?"

"Gorky," said my daughter, "is a famous writer, an author, a

305

man who creates books, a wonderful, rare, honest person. He also comes from the common folk, he had no schooling at all but is self-educated. Here is his portrait," she said, taking a small picture out of a pocket and showing it to me.

"So this is he, your saintly man, Reb Gorky? I could swear that I've seen him somewhere," I said, "either at the railway station carrying sacks or in the woods hauling logs."

"So in your opinion," said she, "it's a fault if a man toiled with his own hands? Don't you yourself work hard? And don't we work hard?'

"Yes, yes," said I, "you are quite right. In our Law it says: *'When thou eatest the labor of thine own hands'*—if you don't work, you won't eat... Still, I cannot understand what Fedka was doing here. It would give me greater pleasure if you were acquainted with him at a distance; you mustn't forget *'Whence thou camest and whither thou goest'*—who you are and who he is."

Her answer to this was: "God created all men equal."

"Yes, yes, God created Adam our forefather in his own likeness, but we shouldn't forget that each one of us must seek his equal, as it is written: *'From each according to his means...'*"

"Amazing!" cried she. "For everything you have a quotation! Maybe you can also find one explaining why people divided themselves up into Jews and Gentiles, into lords and slaves, into nobility and beggars?"

"Tut-tut-tut, daughter!" said I. "It seems to me that you've gone too far — strayed, as they say, into the *'sixth millennium'.*"

I explained to her that this had been the way of the world since *"before the six days of Creation."*

So she asked: "Why should that be the way of the world?"

I answered: "Because that is how God created His world."

"Why did God create His world so?"

"Eh," said I, "if we started asking questions—why this and why that—*'there would be no end to it,'* it would be a tale without an end."

"God gave us reason," she said, "so that we should ask questions."

"We have a custom," said I, "that when a hen begins to crow like a rooster it is immediately taken to the slaughterer; as we say in the benediction: *'Who gave the rooster the ability to discern between day and night...'*"

"Maybe we've already had enough yammering out there?!"

shouted my Golda from the house. "The borsht," she said, "has been standing on the table for an hour already, but he's still singing Sabbath hymns!"

"Here we have another holiday!" said I. "It's not for nothing that our wise men said: *'Seven idle words hath a golem'*—a woman contains nine measures of speech. We're discussing important matters and she comes along with her milk borsht!"

"The milk borsht," said she, "may be just as important as all your 'important matters.'"

"Congratulations! Here we have a new philosopher, directly from under the oven! It isn't enough that my daughters have become enlightened—now Tevye's wife has begun to fly though the chimney up into the sky!"

"Talking of the sky," said Golda, "may the earth swallow you!"

How do you like, for example, such a welcome on an empty stomach?

To make it short, let us leave the prince and turn to the princess—I mean the priest, may his name and memory be forgotten!

One evening I was driving homeward with my empty jugs and crocks; just as I was coming into the village I met the priest coming from the opposite direction in his iron-coated britzka, proudly driving the horses himself, his well-combed beard flowing in the wind. May the ill luck from this encounter fall on your head, I thought to myself.

"Good evening!" said he. "Don't you recognize me, or what?"

"It's a sign that you'll soon become rich," said I to him, taking off my cap and intending to continue on my way.

"Wait a while, Tevel," said he. "What's the great hurry? I have a few words to say to you."

"Oh," said I, "if it's something good—very well, and if it isn't—keep it for another time."

"What do you mean by another time?" he asked.

"Another time means when the Messiah comes."

"But the Messiah," said he, "has come already."

"That I have heard from you before, and not once; better tell me, Father, something new."

"That's just what I mean to tell you," said he. "I want to have a talk with you about you yourself, that is, about your daughter."

This sent a pang through my heart: what had he to do with my daughter?

307

"My daughters," said I, "are, God forbid, not the kind of girls you have to speak for, they can stand up for themselves."

"But this," said he, "is a matter of which she herself cannot talk, another must speak for her, because it is a most important matter, her future depends on it."

"Whose concern is the future of my child?" I asked. "It seems to me that since we are speaking of futures I am a father to my child for a hundred and twenty years, isn't that so?"

"True," said he, "you are a father to your child. However, you are blind to her needs. Your child is reaching out for another world, but you don't understand her, or else you don't want to understand her!"

"Whether I don't understand her or don't want to understand her is another matter," said I. "This we can have a little talk about. But what has it got to do with you, Father?"

"It has quite a lot to do with me, for she is now under my care," he answered, looking me straight in the eye and combing his flowing beard with his fingers.

This jolted me, to be sure: "Who? My child is under *your* care? What right have you?" cried I, feeling my temper flaring up.

"Don't get so worked up, Tevel!" said he with a cold-blooded smile. "Slow down. You know that I am no enemy, God forbid, of yours, even though you are a Jew. You know that I respect Jews, that my heart bleeds for them, for their obstinacy, for their stubborn refusal to understand what is meant for their own good."

"Don't you talk to me of our own good, Father," said I, "for every word I now hear from you is like a drop of deadly poison, like a bullet piercing my heart. If you are, as you say, such a good friend of mine, I ask only one favor of you: leave my daughter alone..."

"You are a foolish man," he retorted. "Nothing bad, God forbid, will happen to your daughter. She will be happy—she is going to marry a fine man, I should live such a life."

"Amen!" said I, forcing myself to laugh, while my heart was a burning Gehenna. "And who may he be, this bridegroom, if I might have the honor of knowing?"

"You must know him" said the priest; "he is a fine and honest young man, and pretty well educated, although self-taught, and he loves your daughter and wants to marry her, but he can't, for he is not a Jew."

Fedka! was my instant thought, and I felt my head swimming;

a cold sweat broke out all over my body, I could barely keep my seat in the wagon. But I wouldn't let him see anything—he won't live to see the day! So I picked up the reins, gave the horse a few lashes and took off without a goodbye— *"departed like Moses."*

When I got home—oh, everything was topsy-turvy! The children were crying with their faces buried in pillows, weeping loudly, Golda was more dead than alive... I looked around for Chava—where is Chava? No Chava!

I knew better—woe is me—than to ask about her. I was beset by the torments of the grave, and a flame of anger burned in me, I don't know against whom... I felt like giving myself a beating... I started yelling at the children and let out the bitterness of my heart on my wife.

I couldn't find a place for myself, so I went out to the stall to feed the horse and found him standing with a leg twisted over the far side of his tough. I grabbed a stick and began laying into the poor beast as if bent on skinning him and breaking all his bones: "May you burn alive, *shlimazl!* May you starve to death—not a single oat grain will you get from me! Troubles, if you like, you may have, and anguish, blows and plagues!.."

Shouting so at the horse, I soon caught myself thinking: *A pity for living things"*—for a poor innocent beast—what do I have against him? I sifted a little chopped straw into the manger and promised the horse that I would show him, God willing, the letter "hay"* in my prayer-book on the Sabbath.

Then I went back into the house, lay down, and buried my head in the pillow. I felt as if my chest had been cut open, my head was splitting from thinking, from trying to understand, to grasp the real meaning of all this. *"How have I sinned and what is my transgression"*—how have I, Tevye, sinned more than the rest of the world that I am punished more than all the Jews? Oh, Almighty God, Lord of the Universe! *"Who are we and what is our life?"* Who am I that you always have me in mind, and never permit any blight, trouble or misfortune to pass me by?!

So ran my thoughts, and I felt as if I were lying on live coals; then I heard my poor wife groaning and sighing—my heart bled for her.

"Golda," I asked, "are you asleep?"

"No," she answered. "What then?"

---

*The name of the first letter of the word "hay" in Hebrew.—*Tr.*

309

"Nothing," said I, "we've got ourselves into a nice hole. Maybe you have some idea of what's to be done?"

"You ask me for advice," said she, "woe is me... A child gets up in the morning, strong and healthy, gets dressed and embraces me and begins to kiss me, hug me and bursts into tears, but says nothing. I thought that she—God forbid—had lost her mind! So I ask her: 'What's the matter with you, daughter?' She doesn't say a word and runs out into the yard to see to the cows and disappears. I wait an hour, I wait two hours, three hours—where is Chava? No Chava! So I tell the children to run over the priest's house for a minute..."

"How did you know, Golda, that she was there?"

"Alas and alack! Don't I have eyes? Or maybe I am not her mother?"

"If you have eyes and if you are her mother," said I, "then why didn't you say anything, why didn't you tell me?"

"Tell you? When are you at home? And when I do tell you something—do you listen to me? When a person tells you something you immediately answer with a quotation; you've drummed my head full of quotations and that's how you get by..."

That is what she, Golda, said to me, and I heard her weeping in the darkness... She is partly right, thought I, because what does a woman understand? It pained my heart to hear her groaning and weeping. So I said to her:

"Look, Golda, you are angry at me because I have a quotation for everything; well, even this I must answer with a quotation. It is written in our Book: *'As a father has mercy on his children!'*—a father loves his child. Why doesn't the passage read: *'As a mother has mercy on her children'*—that a mother loves her child? Because a mother is not a father; a father can speak differently to a child. Just wait, tomorrow, God willing, I'll see her."

"God grant," said she, "that you will be able to see her, and him, too. He is not a bad man, even though he is a priest; he does have compassion for people. You implore him, fall to his feet, perhaps he'll have mercy."

"Who, the priest, may his name be accursed!? I should stoop to the priest? Are you crazy or have you lost your mind? *'Do not open your mouth to Satan,'*" said I, "my enemies won't live to hear of such things!"

"Ah, you see! There you go again!" exclaimed Golda.

"What did you think? That I should let myself be led by a woman? That I would live according to your female reason?"

310

We spent the whole night talking in this manner. At the first crow of the cock I got up, said my prayers, picked up my whip and set off straight for the priest's house. As you say, a woman is only a woman, but where else should I have gone? Into the grave?

When I entered the priest's yard his hounds gave me a splendid welcome and wanted to "fix" my cloak and taste the calves of my Jewish legs, to see whether they were good for their canine teeth... It was my good luck that I had taken my whip along; with its aid I made them understand the Hebrew quotation, *"Not a dog shall bark"*—or, as it goes in Ukrainian, *Nekhai sobaka darom nye breshet*—don't let a dog bark in vain.

The barking and the uproar brought the priest and his wife out into the yard. With difficulty they managed to drive off the merry pack, and then they invited me into the house, receiving me as an honored guest—they even wanted to put on the samovar for me. I said that the samovar was not necessary, that I had something I wanted to talk about with the priest eye-to-eye. He guessed what I meant and winked at his spouse to please shut the door from the other side.

I came straight to the point without any preamble: let him first tell me whether he believed in God...Then let him tell me whether he felt what it meant to part a father from a child he loved. Next, let him tell me what, to his mind, was a good deed and what was a sin? And another thing I wanted him to make clear to me: what does he think of a man who sneaks into another man's house and wants to change everything in it—move the chairs, the tables and beds?

Of course he was bewildered: "Tevel, you are a clever man, and here you come and hurl so many questions at me at once, and you want me to answer them all at one go. Wait a while and I'll answer all your questions, from first to last."

"No," said I, "my dear Father, you'll never answer these questions. Do you know why? Because I know all your thoughts beforehand. Better give me an answer to this: May I still hope to see my child again or not?"

At this he jumped to his feet: "What do you mean—see her again? Nothing will happen to your daughter, quite the opposite!"

"I know," said I, "I know you want to make her happy! That's not what I'm speaking about. I want to know where my child is, and whether I can see her?"

"Anything you want," said he, "but that—no."

311

"Tevel, you are a clever man, and here you come and hurl so many questions at me at once."

"That's the way to talk," said I, "short and sweet and right to the point! Goodbye now, and may God repay you many times over!"

When I got home I found my Golda lying in bed all bunched up like a ball of black thread; her eyes had already run out of tears. I said to her: "Get up, my wife, take off your shoes and let us sit down on the floor and mourn our child for seven days, as God has commanded. *'The Lord hath given and the Lord hath taken away.'* We are not the first and we are not the last. Let it seem to us that we never had any Chava, or that she has left us, like Hodel who went off beyond the *'mountains of darkness'* and God alone knows whether we will ever see her again…The Almighty is a merciful God, He knows what He does!…"

With such talk I poured out the bitterness of my heart, feeling that tears were choking me, like a bone struck in my throat. But Tevye is not a woman, Tevye can restrain himself! That, of course, is only in a manner of speaking, because, first of all—the shame! And secondly, how can I restrain myself when I've lost a living child, especially such a child, a diamond embedded deep in both my own and her mother's hearts, almost more precious to us than all the other children, I don't know why. Perhaps it is because she had been very sickly as a little child, had suffered *"all the troubles of the world."* We used to sit up with her whole nights, several times we snatched her, literally snatched, out of the clutches of death, breathed life into her, as one would breathe on a tiny, trampled chick, because if God so wishes He makes the dead come to life again, as we say in a *hallel: "I shall not die but I shall live"*—if it is not ordained that you should die, you don't die…And maybe it is because she was a good and faithful child, she always loved us both with all her heart and soul. So I ask: how could it happen that she should cause us such grief? The answer is that, firstly, such was our luck. I don't know about you, but I believe in Providence; and secondly, it was some kind of witchcraft! You may laugh at me, but I must tell you that I am not so benightedly foolish as to believe in gnomes, elves, *domoviks*, spooks and other such nonsense. But I do believe in witchcraft, for what could it have been but witchcraft? Just hear me out and you will also say the same thing.…

In short, as our Holy Books say, *"Perforce you must live"*—a

---

*A goblin, or brownie that was, according to superstition, supposed to live in every house (from the Russian word *dom*—house). — *Tr.*

313

human being does not take his own life—these are no idle words. There are no wounds that don't heal, and no trouble that is not forgotten with time. That is, one doesn't actually forget, but what can be done? *"Man is likened to a beast"*—a man must toil, suffer, labor to exhaustion for his piece of bread. So all of us got down to work, my wife and the children with the jugs and jars, I with my horse and wagon, and *"the world continued in its course"*—the world does not stand still. I told my family that Chava was *"never to be mentioned nor thought of"*—no more Chava! Blotted out for good! Then I got together some fresh dairy products and set off for Boiberik to my customers.

In Boiberik my customers welcomed me most enthusiastically: "How are you, Reb Tevye, why haven't we seen you such a long time?"

"How should I be," I answered. *"'We renew our days as of old'*—I'm the same *shlimazl* I always was, one of my cows has dropped dead."

"Why is it," they asked, "that all these miracles happen to you?" Then all of them and each one separately wanted to know what kind of cow I had lost, how much it cost me, and how many other cows I had left. Laughing merrily, they joked and made fun of me, a poor man, a *shlimazl*, as is the custom of rich people when they have just had a good meal, are in a cheerful mood, everything is fine and green outdoors, the weather is balmy—just right for a nice snooze. But Tevye is a person who can take a joke: not for the life of me would I have let them know what my feelings really were!

Having sold all my goods, I set off for home with my empty crocks and jars. Driving through the woods, I slackened the reins and let the horse go on slowly, so that he might stealthily crop a tuft of grass now and then. Losing myself in meditations, I let my imagination run away with me, thinking of life and of death, of this world and of the next, of what the world actually was, why a man lived, and similar things—all in order not to let myself think of Chava. But as if in spite, namely she, Chava, crept into my mind. Here she comes towards me, tall stately, beautiful and fresh as a pine tree, or as she was in early childhood, a tiny, sickly, almost lifeless little baby nestling in my arms, her head dropping over my shoulder. "What do you want, Chaveleh? Bread soaked in milk? A sip of milk?.."

For a while I forgot what she had done and my heart went out to her, my soul ached with longing for her. Then I remembered, and anger flared up in my breast against her, against him, against the whole world and against myself for not being able to blot out her memory, tear her out of my soul. Why can't I do it? Doesn't she deserve it? Was it for this Tevye had to be a Jew among Jews? Did he toil and suffer, root the ground, and raise children only for them to be torn away by force, to fall away as a pine cone falls from its tree, and to be carried away by the wind and by smoke? For instance, I thought, a tree, say, an oak, grows in the forest; then someone comes along with an axe and chops off a branch, another branch and another branch—what is the tree without its branches, alas? Better go, lummox, and chop down the whole tree and put an end to it! Why should an oak stand bare in the forest!..

As these thoughts flitted through my mind, my horse suddenly came to a standstill. What was the matter? I looked up and saw— Chava! The same Chava as before, hadn't changed a bit, not even her clothes were different!

My first impulse was to spring to the ground and embrace her, kiss her... But I was held back by a second thought: Tevye, what are you, a woman? I gave the reins a tug and cried to the horse: "Giddy-up, *shlimazl!*"—and pulled to the right. But Chava also went to the right, waving her hand to me, as if to say: "Stand still a while, I have to tell you something."

Something seemed to snap in me, something tugged at my heart, my limbs went weak and I all but jumped off the wagon! But I held myself in check and pulled the reins, making the horse turn left—Chava also moved left, looking at me wildly, her face deathly pale... What shall I do? I thought to myself. Shall I stop or drive ahead? Before I could look around she was already holding the horse by the bridle and crying: *"Tateh!* I'll sooner die than let you move from this spot! I beg you, please hear me out first, *Tateh*-Father!.."

Eh, thought I, you mean to take me by force? Oh, no, my dear! If that is what you mean—it's a sign that you don't know your father... And I began to lay into the poor beast for all it was worth. The horse lunged ahead obediently, turning its head backwards and twitching its ears.

"Giddap," I told the horse, "*'Judge not the vessel but its contents'*—don't look, my clever one, where you shouldn't." But do you think that I myself didn't want to turn my head and look back, to have at least a glimpse of the spot where she remained

"But Chava also went to the right, waving her hand to me."

standing? But no, Tevye is not a woman, Tevye knows how to deal with smoldering Satan...

Well, I don't want to waste your time with too long a story. If it was ordained that I should suffer the torments of the damned after death, I must surely have atoned for all my sins already. I know the taste of Gehenna and of purgatory, and of all the other tortures that are described in our Holy Books—ask me and I'll tell you!

All the rest of the way home it seemed to me that she was running after the wagon and crying: "Hear me out, *Tateh*-Father!" A thought crossed my mind: Tevye, you are taking too much upon yourself! What harm will it do if you stop for a while and hear what she has to say? Maybe she has something to say that you should know? Maybe, who knows, she has changed her mind and wants to cone back? Maybe she suffers in her life with him and wants you to help her escape from a living hell?.. Maybe, maybe and maybe and many another maybe flitted through my mind; again I saw her as a child and was reminded of the passage: *"As a father has mercy on his children..."*—a father can have no bad children, and I blamed myself and said that I *"do not deserve to be pitied,"* that I am unworthy of walking upon the earth!

So what? Why all this fretting and fuming, you stubborn madman? Turn your wagon back, you brute, and make it up with her, she is your own child, not another's! Strange thoughts crept into my head: What is the meaning of Jew and non-Jew?.. And why did God create Jews and non-Jews?.. And since He did create Jews and non-Jews, why should they be so isolated from each other, hate each other, just as if this one is from God and that one is not from God?.. I was sorry that I was not as learned as others in holy and in secular books, where I might have found the true justification for this...

In order to break up this train of thought I began to chant: *"Blessed are they who dwell in Thy house, and they shall continue to praise Thee...",* saying *Minhah,* the afternoon prayer, as God bade us.

But what good was this praying, this chanting, when inside, in my heart, an entirely different melody was playing: "Cha-va! cha-va! Cha-va!" The louder I chanted *"Blessed..."* the louder became the "Chava" tune, and the more I tried to forget her, the clearer was her image in my eyes, and it seemed to me that I could hear her voice crying: "Hear me out, *Tateh*-Father!" I tried to stop my

317

ears so as not to hear her, I shut my eyes not to see her; I chanted the *Shmin-esra* and could not hear my own voice, I beat my breast and called myself a sinner and did not know what my sin was; my life was in a muddle and I myself was bewildered. I told nobody of this encounter and spoke with nobody of Chava, asked nobody about her, although I knew very well where she was and where he was and what they were doing, but nobody would find out anything from me. My enemies won't live to see the day I complain to anyone. That's the kind of person Tevye is!

I should like to know whether all men are like this, or whether I alone am so crazy?

You know, for example, it sometimes happens... You won't laugh at me? I am afraid you will...

For instance, it sometimes happens that I put on my Sabbath coat and set off for the railway station; I am ready to get on the train and go out there, to them, I know where they live. I go to the ticket-window and ask the man to give me a ticket. He asks, "Where to?" "To Yehupetz..." So he says, "I know of no such city." So I say, "Then it is not my fault..." And I turn and go back home, take off my Sabbath coat and get down to work, to my dairy wares and the horse and wagon. As it is written: *"Each man to his labor"*—the tailor to his shears, the cobbler to his last.

Yes, you are laughing at me! What did I tell you? I even know what you are thinking. You are thinking: This Tevye, he is something of an imbecile!

Therefore, *"Up to here and no further"*—it's enough for today, I mean... Be well and strong, and write me letters. And, for God's sake, don't forget what I asked you: keep silent concerning this, don't make a book out of it. But if you do happen to write, write about someone else, not me. Forget about me. As the passage goes: *"And he was forgotten"*—no more Tevye the Dairyman!

1906

318

"I knew very well where she was and what they were doing."

Shprintze

I owe you a most hearty greeting, Mr. Sholom Aleichem, peace be with you and your children! Oh my, my—a good many years have gone by since we last met, how much water has flown under the bridge since then! The anguish both we and our people have had to put up with during these years! Kishinev, a "cosnetution," pogroms, troubles, evils*—oh, dear God, Almighty Lord of the World! But I am surprised—don't take it amiss—you haven't changed a hair, knock on wood, knock on wood! Now take a look at me: *"Behold, I look like a man of seventy,"* while I am not yet sixty. Do you see how white my hair has grown? Ah, it's *"the pain of bringing up children"*—what you have to endure from children! Is there anyone who has suffered so much pain from his children as I have? A new misfortune befell me—what happened to my daughter Shprintze is more terrible than all my other troubles. However, as you see, life goes on, for it is written: *"Perforce you must live."* Go on living, even though your heart is breaking as you sing this little song:

> *Of what use is my life, what's the world to me,*
> *When I have no luck and no money do I see?*

In short, as it stands written in Perek: *"The Holy One, blessed be He, wanted to grant merit..."*—God wanted to do his Jews a favor, so we were blessed with a new trouble, a cosnetution"! Oh, what a "cosnetution"! All of a sudden a tumult, a commotion broke loose among our rich ones, a stampede began from Yehupetz to foreign health resorts, allegedly on account of their nerves, to take warm baths and salt-water cures—all of it last year's snow and other non-

---

*Kishinev, "cosnetution", pogroms, troubles, evils. In 1903 a Jewish pogrom was instigated by the tsarist government in Kishinev, followed by numerous other pogroms; in 1905 the government was forced to cede a Constitution under pressure of the growing revolutionary movement in the land, but it did little to improve the life of the toiling masses.—*Tr.*

sense! When Yehupetz was deserted, Boiberik with its air and its woods and its *dachas* went to pot! As we say in the morning prayer: *"Blessed be He who bestows mercy..."* So what happened? We have a great God who rules the world and watches out for his poor wretches and makes sure that they suffer a little more on earth.

What a summer we had, oh my! Boiberik began to fill up with people running away from Odessa, from Rostov, from Yekaterinoslav, from Mogilev and from Kishinev—thousands of rich people, money-bags, millionaires! In their towns the "cosnetution" was, apparently, fiercer than with us in Yehupetz, because they kept coming and coming. One might have asked: Why do they come running to us? The answer is: Why do our people run to them? It has already become, thank God, a custom among us that no sooner do rumors of pogroms begin to spread than Jews start running from one town to another; as the Holy Book says, *"They journeyed and they encamped, they encamped and they journeyed"*—which means: you come to me and I'll go to you...

Meanwhile, as you may well imagine, Boiberik became a big town overflowing with people, with women and children. Now, children like to peck at foods, so dairy produce was in high demand. From whom, if not from Tevye, were dairy foods to be bought? So Tevye became the fashion. From all sides you heard nothing but Tevye and Tevye. Reb Tevye, come here! Reb Tevye, come to me! When God wills—why question it?

"And it came to pass..." It all began one day before *Shabuoth*. I bought some dairy goods to one of my customers, a rich young widow who had come to us from Yekaterinoslav with her sonny-boy, Aronchik, for the summer. You understand, of course, that her first acquaintanceship in Boiberik was with me.

"I've been told," she said, the widow, I mean, "that yours are the best dairy products."

"How could it be otherwise?" said I. "It is not for nothing that King Solomon says that a good name lets itself be heard, like the sound of a *shofar*, throughout the world, and if you like I can tell you what the *Midrash* has to say about that."

So she interrupted me, the widow, I mean, and told me that she was a widow and was unversed in such things. She didn't even know what it was eaten with. The main thing was that the butter should be fresh and the cheese tasty... Well, go talk to a female!..

In short, I began to come along to the Yekaterinoslav widow twice a week; every Monday and Thursday, punctually as a timetable, I would bring my dairy foods, without asking whether they needed them or not. I became an intimate in the household, as I usually do, and began to take a closer interest in the domestic affairs: stuck my nose into the kitchen, and told them a few times what I found necessary to tell them about running the house. The first time, naturally, I got a scolding from the servant-girl—she told me not to butt in, not to peep into stranger's pots. Next time my words were heeded, and by the third time they already asked my advice, because she, the widow, I mean, had by then realized who Tevye was.

It went on in this way until the widow disclosed her trouble, her affliction, her misfortune—Aronchik! He, a young man of twenty-and-something years, said his mother, cared for nothing but horses, bicycles and fishing, and beyond that—nothing! He wouldn't even hear of business, of making money. His father had left him, she said, a handsome fortune, almost a million rubles, but he took no notice of it at all. He only knew how to spend, he was foolishly open-handed!

"Where is he," I asked, "this boy of yours? You just turn him over to me, I'll have a little talk with him, edify him, quote a few proverbs, tell him a *midrash*."

So she laughed: "A *midrash?* You'd better bring him a horse, not a *midrash!*"

Suddenly, as we were talking, *the lad arrived*—in came the young man, Aronchik, a lad stately as a pine tree, strong and good-looking, the picture of health. He wore a wide belt right over his trousers, begging your pardon, a watch was stuffed into a pocket in the belt, and his sleeves were rolled up above his elbows.

"Where have you been?" asked his mother.

"Out in a boat, fishing," he answered.

"A fine occupation," I said, "for such a lad as you. Back at home everything may be going to wrack and ruin while you catch fish here!"

I took a look at my widow—she was red as a beet. She must surely have thought that her son would grab me by the collar, deal me a couple of slaps and then throw me out like a piece of broken crockery. Nonsense! Tevye is not afraid of such things! I, when I have something on my mind, I go ahead and say it!

"And so it was." The young man, upon hearing such words, stepped back a little, crossed his hands behind his back, looked me over from head to toe, emitted a queer whistle, and suddenly burst

out into such laughter that both his mother and I feared he had lost his mind for a minute!

What shall I say? From that time on we became friends, real good friends! I must tell you that the longer I knew the lad, the more I liked him, even though he was a scamp and a spendthrift, far too free with his money, and something of a dolt, too. For instance, he could meet a poor man, thrust his hand into his pocket, pull out some money and hand it over to this man without counting it. Who ever heard of such a thing? Or he could take a good new coat off his own back and give it away. Talk about folly! I was really sorry for the mother! She used to complain to me, asked me what she should do, beg me to try and hammer some sense into his head. I, of course, did not begrudge her this favor—why should I? Did it cost me any money? So I began to sit down with him and tell him stories, give him examples, quote passages from the Torah and roll off *midrashim,* as Tevye knows how to do. He really became interested and seemed to enjoy listening to me. He kept asking me all sorts of questions: how did I live, what kind of a home did I have?

"I should like," he once said, "to pay you a visit some day, Tevye!"

"If anybody wants to visit Tevye," I answered, "he just picks himself up and drives over to Tevye's farmstead—you have enough horses and bicycles. And in a pinch it's no big deal to come over on foot   it's not far, you only have to cut through the woods."

"When," he asked, "are you at home?"

"I can be found at home," I answered, "only on the Sabbath, or on a holiday. Wait! You know what? Next Friday, God willing, is *Shabuoth.* If you want to stroll over to our farm, my wife will treat you to *blintzes* such as—and I added in Hebrew—*'our blessed ancestors never ate in Egypt!'*"

"And what does that mean?" he asked. "You know that I'm not at all strong in Hebrew quotations."

"I know," said I, "that you are weak. If you had gone to *heder,* as I did, you would know even *what the rebbitzen said*—what the rabbi's wife said."

So he laughed and said: "Done. You shall have me as a guest. I'll come to you, Reb Tevye, on the first day of *Shabuoth* with a couple of friends to eat *blintzes,* but you see to it that they are hot!"

"At *white heat, inside and out*—from the frying pan right into your mouth!" said I.

When I got home I called out to my old woman: "Golda, we'll have guests for *Shabuoth!*"

She immediately came up with: "*Mazl-tov*, congratulations, who are they?"

"That you'll find out later," said I; "you get a batch of eggs ready—we have plenty of cheese and butter, thank God. I want you to make enough *blintzes* for three guests, people that approve of eating and don't even begin to know anything of Rashi's commentaries."

"Oh, you must have picked up some *shlimazls* from the hungry lands?" said she.

"You're a fool, Golda," said I. "First of all, it wouldn't be such a calamity if we should, God forbid, feed a poor man with *Shabuoth blintzes*. Secondly, be informed, my dear spouse, my modest and pious wife Madam Golda, that one of our *Shabuoth* guests will be the widow's boy, the one who is called Aronchik—I told you about him."

"Oh," she said, "that's a different story."

The power of millions! Even my Golda, when she gets a whiff of money, becomes an altogether different person. That's the way of the world, what do you think? How does it go in *hallel?* "*Gold and silver, the work of man's hands*"—money is the undoing of man...

Well, the bright, green Holy Day of *Shabuoth* came. How beautiful, how green, how bright and warm it is out in the country when *Shabuoth* arrives I don't have to tell you. Your richest man could only wish to have such a blue sky, with such a green forest, with such fragrant pines, such lush green, pasture land for the cows that stand chewing their cud and looking at you as if to say: "Give us such grass all the time and we won't begrudge you any milk!"

No, you may say whatever you like, tempt me with the best livelihood to move from the country to the city—I won't exchange places with you. Where have you such a sky in the city? As we say in a *hallel: "The Heavens are the Heavens of the Lord"*—it's God's own sky! when you look skyward in town what do you see? A brick wall, a roof, a chimney—but where will you find such trees? And if some wretched tree does manage to survive, you cover it over with a cloak!..

However that may be, my guests were full of admiration when they came to my farm on *Shabuoth*. They came, four young men, on horseback, their horses—one better than the other! As for the prancer Aronchik was seated on, it was a real gelding, the likes of which you wouldn't be able to buy even for three hundred rubles!

"Welcome, guests," I greeted them. "Is it in honor of *Shabuoth* that you've come on horseback?* No matter, Tevye is not too pious, and if, with God's help, you should be whipped in the next world the pain won't be mine... Hey, Golda," I called, "see to the *blintzes,* and let the table be carried out here into the fresh air. There is nothing inside the house I could boast of to our guests... Hey, there, Shprintze! Taibl! Beilke! Where are you? Get a move on you!"

My orders were obeyed: the table was carried outside, chairs were placed around it, a tablecloth laid, plates, spoons, forks, salt brought out, and very soon Golda appeared with the *blintzes,* piping hot, right from the frying pan, plump and tasty! My visitors couldn't praise them enough...

"What are you standing there for," I said to Golda, "go and repeat the same verse over again. Today is *Shabuoth*," I said, "so the same prayer has to be said twice!"

Golda immediately filled up another platter and Shprintze served the *blintzes* at the table. Suddenly I saw, as I glanced at Aronchik, that he couldn't take his eyes off my Shprintze! What had drawn his attention to her? "Eat," I said to him, "why aren't you eating?"

"What else am I doing if not eating?" said he.

"You are looking at Shprintze," said I.

At this everybody began to laugh, my Shprintze too. Everybody felt so happy, so good—a good, joyous *Shabuoth*... Go and foresee that from this merrymaking would spring a misfortune, a lament, an evil, God's punishment on my head, the blackest misery and suffering on my soul!

But man is a fool. A sensible man mustn't let anything get to his heart, he must understand that things are as they should be, for if they should have been otherwise, they wouldn't have been as they are! Don't we say in the Psalms: *"Put thy trust in God."* Put your faith in God and He will already see to it that you are doubled up

---

*Jewish religious laws forbid riding on anything or in any conveyance on the Sabbath and on holidays.—*Tr.*

under your load of misery and still keep on saying: *"This too, is for the best."* Listen to what can come about in this world, but listen carefully, because this is where the real story actually begins.

"It was evening and it was day." Late one afternoon I came home, dead-tired after my day's work, exhausted by the running from *dacha* to *dacha* in Boiberik. Hitched to my front door I saw a familiar horse. I was ready to swear that it was Aronchik's prancer, the one I had then judged to be worth three hundred rubles. I went up to the horse, slapped his rump, tickled his neck and ruffled his mane. "Well, well, my beauty," I said to the horse, "What are you doing here?" The animal turned his winsome face to me and looked at me with his clever eyes, as if to say: "Why ask me? Ask my master."

I went inside and began to question my wife. "Tell me, Golda my love, what is Aronchik doing here?"

"How should I know," she answered, "he is one of your buddies, isn't he?"

"So where is he?"

"He went with the children for a stroll in the woods," she answered.

"Why suddenly a stroll?" said I and asked her to give me supper. When I had eaten I began to think: what is it, Tevye, that upsets you so? When a person comes to visit you, do you have to get so rattled? Quite the opposite...

As I was thinking this I looked outside and saw my girls walking with the young man, holding bouquets of freshly-picked flowers, the two younger ones, Taibl and Beilke in the lead, followed by Shprintze and Aronchik.

"Good evening!"

"The same to you."

Aronchik stood there with a strange look on his face, patting his horse and chewing a blade of grass. Then he turned to me:

"Reb Tevye! I want to do business with you—let's exchange our horses."

"You haven't found anyone else to play jokes on?" I asked.

"No," said he, "I'm in earnest."

"So you're in earnest," said I. "How much, for instance, does your horse cost?"

"How much would you value it at?" he asked.

"I value it," said I, "at three hundred rubles, and perhaps even a bit over that."

326

He laughed and said that the horse cost more than three times that sum, and then asked: "Well? Is it a deal?"

This talk was not at all to my liking: What did he mean by offering to exchange his expensive horse for my outspent *shlimazl* of a hack? So I told him to put off business for another time and jokingly asked him whether that was really the reason for his visit. If that was so, I said, it was a waste of his travel expenses...

To this he answered me quite seriously: "Actually, I came for another reason. If you like, let us take a little walk."

Why this urge for walking? I thought to myself as I accompanied him to the nearby grove.

The sun had gone down some time ago, it was already darkish in the green grove, the frogs were croaking at the dike, and the fragrance of the grass was balm to the soul!

Aronchik walked and I walked along with him. He was silent and so was I. Then he stopped, cleared his throat, and said:

"Reb Tevye! What would you say, for instance, if I told you that I love your daughter Shprintze and want to marry her?"

"What I would say? I would say that one madman's name should be erased and yours put in its stead," I answered.

So he looked at me and exclaimed: "What do you mean?"

"Just what I said!"

"I don't understand you."

"That's a sign," said I, "that you are not so very bright. As it is written: *'A wise man hath his eyes in his head,'* which means that a smart man understands a wink, while a fool needs a stick."

This rather offended him. "I speak to you plainly and you answer me with witticisms and quotations!" he said.

To this I said: "Every cantor sings as he can, and every preacher preaches for himself. If you want to learn what kind of preacher you are, talk this thing over with your mother first, she will make everything quite clear to you."

"Apparently," said he, "you take me for a child that has to ask his mother what to do?'

"Of course you have to ask your mother," said I, "and she will certainly tell you that you are an imbecile, and she will be right."

"She will be right?" he asked.

"Of course she will be right," said I. "What kind of a husband are you for my Shprintze? Is she your equal? And, what is most important, what kind of a relative-by-marriage am I for your mother?"

"If that's the case, Reb Tevye," said he, "you are greatly mistaken! I am no eighteen-year-old youngster, I seek no in-laws to please my mother. I know who you are and who your daughter is. She suits me, and that's the way I want it to be and that's how it will be!"

"I beg your pardon for interrupting you," said I. "I see that you've already finished with one side. Have you already made sure of the other side?"

"I don't know what you mean."

"I mean my daughter, Shprintze. Have you already spoken to her about this, and what does she say?" I asked him.

This seemed to offend him, but he laughed and answered: "What a question! Of course I have spoken to her, and not just once but several times—I come here every day."

You hear that? He'd been coming here every day and I knew nothing! You're a cow, Tevye, in human likeness! You should be given straw to chew! If you permit yourself to be led by the nose you'll be bought and sold before you know it, you donkey!

Thinking thus, I walked back to the house with Aronchik; he said goodbye to my gang, mounted his horse and *"departed like Moses"*—trotted away to Boiberik.

And now let us, as you say in your books, leave the prince and turn to the princess, to Shprintze....

"Listen, daughter," said I, "there is something I want to know: you tell me how come that Aronchik talked to you about such a matter without my knowing anything about it?" Do you get any answer from a tree? I got the same answer from her! She lowered her eyes and blushed like a bride, but didn't as much as utter a word!

Bah, I thought to myself, you don't want to talk now, but you'll talk a little later...Tevye is not a woman, he can wait!

I waited for some time, for, as it is said, *"his day will come"*; then at a moment when the two of us were alone, I said: "Shprintze, answer my question: do you at least know him, this here Aronchik?"

"Of course I know him," was her answer.

"Do you know that he is a whistler?"

"What do you mean—a whistler?"

"An empty nutshell that whistles when you blow into it."

To this she said: "You are mistaken, Arnold is a fine person."

"I want you to tell me, but quite openly, how much this will cost us, all told."

"He is already Arnold to you," said I, "not Aronchik the charlatan?"

"Arnold," said she, "is no charlatan, Arnold has a kind heart. Arnold lives in a house of mean-minded people who know nothing but money and money."

"Oho," said I, "so you, too, Shprintze, have become an enlightened philosopher. You also despise money?"

In short, from this talk I understood that things had gone pretty far with them, and that it was a little too late to undo them, for I know my children. Tevye's daughters, as I already told you once, when they fall in love, it's with heart and soul and body! And I thought: Fool! Why should you want, Tevye, to be wiser than the whole world? Maybe it is God's will that through this shy little Shprintze you should be succored, be rewarded for all the blows and pains you have endured; maybe it was ordained that you should live well in your old age and learn how good life can be in the world? Perhaps it was fated that you should have a millionairess for a daughter? And why not? It doesn't suit you? Where is it written that Tevye must be a poor man forever, that he must always drag himself around with his nag, delivering cheese and butter to the rich Yehupetz gluttons!? Who knows, perhaps it was destined from above that in my old age I should redress the wrongs of the world, become a benefactor, a hospitable host, and maybe even sit down with Jewish scholars and study the Torah?

These and other shining, golden thoughts entered my mind. As it is said in the morning prayer, *"Many thoughts are in man's heart,"* or, as the peasants, begging your pardon, say: *Duren dumkoyo bogateyet*—a fool gets rich only in his thoughts.

I came into the house, took my old woman aside and started a conversation with her: "What, for instance," I asked, "would happen if our Shprintze became a millionairess?"

So she asked: "What is a millionairess?"

"A millionairess means the wife of a millionaire."

"And what is a millionaire?"

So I explained: "A millionaire is a man who has a million."

"How much is it, a million?" she asked.

To this I said: "If you're such a simpleton and don't know how much a million is, then what is there to talk to you about?

"Who asks you to talk?" was her retort. And that was also true.

Well, a day went by and I came home in the evening. "Has Aronchik been here?" I asked. "No, he hasn't...."

Another day went by: "Was the lad here?" "No, he wasn't."

To go to the widow on some pretext was unbecoming; I didn't want her to think that Tevye was eager for the match. Actually I felt that for her all this was like *"a rose among thorns,"* like a fifth wheel to a wagon. Although I couldn't understand why. Just because I didn't have a million? But now I had a relative-by-marriage who was a millionairess! But whom was she getting for a relative? A poor Jew, a pauper, a Tevye the Dairyman. So who had more reason to be proud, she or I? I'll tell you the plain truth: I began to want this match, and not so much because of the match itself as for the satisfaction of getting the better of them.

Damn them all, the rich Yehupetzers, let them know who Tevye is! Up to now one heard nothing but Brodsky and Brodsky, as if all the rest weren't human beings at all!

Thus I reflected, driving home from Boiberik. When I came into the house my wife welcomed me with good news: "A messenger was here just now from Boiberik, from the widow. She wants you to come there at once, without fail; even if it is the middle of the night, you must hitch up the horse and go to her; they want to see you very badly!"

"What's got into them?" I asked. "What's the great hurry, why haven't they got any time?" I looked at Shprintze—she was silent, only her eyes spoke, and how they spoke! Nobody could understand what was in her heart as I could....

I had been afraid all the time—anything was possible—that the whole affair might come to nothing, so I said everything I could think of against him, that he was this and he was that; however, I saw that it was like being up against a blank wall, and my Shprintze was wasting away like a candle.

I hitched up the horse again and set off towards evening for Boiberik. As I went along I thought to myself: Why should they summon me in such haste? To say something? About the betrothal? He could have come to me for that, I think. I am, after all, the girl's father. But this notion made me laugh: Who in the world has heard of a rich man coming to a poor man?! It could only happen when the end of the world came, in the time of the Messiah. The time that will soon come, as those young whelps wanted to convince me, when the rich and the poor will be equal, share and share alike, mine is yours, yours is mine and other such nonsense! It seems to me that ours is a clever world, and yet such fools live in it! Well, well, well!

With these thoughts I reached Boiberik and drove directly to the widow's *dacha*. I stopped the horse—where was the widow? No widow! Where was the young man? No young man! Then who sent for me?

"I sent for you!" said a roly-poly little man with a plucked beard and a thick golden chain across his pot-belly.

"And who are you?" I asked.

"I am the widow's brother," said he, Aronchik's uncle... I was summoned by a telegram from Yekaterinoslav and have just arrived"

"If that is so, then *sholom aleichem* to you," said I and sat down. When I had seated myself he said: "Sit down."

"Thanks," said I, "I am already sitting. So how do you do, and how does the 'cosnetution' do in your part of the world?"

To this he gave me no answer, plumped himself down in a rocking-chair, his hands in his pockets, his pot-belly with the golden chain bulging out, and addressed me with the following words:

"You are called, I think, Tevye, aren't you?"

"Yes," said I, "when I am called up to read the Torah they say: 'Arise, Reb Tevye, son of Shneyer-Zalman.' "

"Listen to me, Reb Tevye," said he, "of what use are long discussions? Let us go right to the issue, to the business at hand."

"With pleasure," said I. "King Solomon said a long time ago: *'For everything there is a time'*—when business has to be spoken of, let it be business. I am," said I, "a businessman."

"It's evident that you are a man of business. That is why I want to talk to you as one merchant to another. I want you to tell me, but quite openly, how much this will cost us, all told?.. But speak quite frankly!"

"If," said I, "we are to speak openly, frankly, then I must own up that I don't know what you are talking about."

"Reb Tevye!" said he, without taking his hands out of his pockets. "I am asking you how much, all told, this business will cost us?"

"That depends," said I, "on the kind of wedding you have in mind. If you decide upon a swell wedding, as is fitting for you, I'm not in a position to foot it."

He stared at me in surprise and said: "Either you are playing the fool, or you really are a fool... Although you don't look like a fool, because if you were one you wouldn't have managed to lure my nephew into this morass. You invited him to your home allegedly for *Shabuoth blintzes*, showed him a pretty girl who may or may not be your daughter—I don't care to go into such details—and he fell in love with her, that is, he liked her. Well, and that she, too, liked him, that of course goes without saying, we are not questioning that. I don't know, perhaps she is an honest child and is in earnest, I won't go so far into the matter... But you mustn't forget," he went on, "who *you* are and who *we* are. After all, you are a sensible person, how could you even presume that Tevye the Dairyman who brings us cheese and butter might become related to us by marriage?.. So what if they gave each other their word? They can take their word back! There is no great misfortune in that, and if his breach of promise has to cost us something we have nothing against paying. A girl is not a boy, whether she is your daughter or not, I don't care to go into such details."

God Almighty! What does the man want? thought I.

Meanwhile, he doesn't stop talking over my head for a moment; I needn't think, says he, that I could contrive a scandal, spread it about that his nephew, says he, had proposed to Tevye the Dairyman's daughter... And I should knock out of my head the notion that his sister was the kind of person from whom money might be pumped... If there was no trouble she wouldn't mind paying a few rubles: she would put it down to charity... We are human beings, after all, sometimes you have to help a person...

You want to know how I answered him? I said nothing, woe is me. *"My tongue clave to the roof of my mouth"* I lost the power of speech! I got up, turned my face to the door—and fled, as if escaping from a fire, from prison!

There was a buzzing in my head, a shimmering before my eyes, and the man's words seemed to repeat themselves in my ears: "Speak openly..." "A daughter or not a daughter..." "A widow to be pumped..." "Put it down to charity... "

I went to my horse, covered up my face and—you won't laugh at me?—I burst into tears. I wept and wept! When I had had a good cry I got into the wagon and laid into my horse, and only then did I ask God a question, as Job once asked: "What hast Thou seen in old Job, dear Lord, that Thou never leavest him be for a moment? Are there already no other people in the world?"

When I got home I found my gang, knock on wood, in a merry mood. They were eating supper, only Shprintze was missing. "Where is Shprintze?" I asked.

"What happened," they asked, "why were you sent for?"

333

"I sprang from my wagon...but when I got there it was already all over..."

So I repeated my question: "Where is Shprintze?"

And they again asked: "What happened?"

"Nothing, why should anything happen? Thank God, all is quiet, nothing is heard about any pogroms."

At these words Shprintze came in. She took one look into my eyes and sat down at the table, just as if the whole thing had nothing to do with her... Her face showed nothing, only this quietness of hers was a bit too much, unnatural.

I didn't like this sitting of hers, lost in thought, and her blind obedience. Told to sit—she sits, told to eat—she eats, told to go— she goes, and when her name is called she jumps. When I looked at her, my heart ached and an anger burned in me—I didn't know against whom. Oh, dear God in Heaven, Almighty Lord, why do you punish me so, for whose sins?!!

Well, shall I tell you the end of the story? Such an end I wouldn't wish on my worst enemy, and it would be wrong to wish it on anyone, for the misfortune of children is the worst curse in the chapter of *Admonitions!* How do I know, maybe someone did put that curse on me? You don't believe in such things? So what else can it be? All right, let me hear what you think. But what is the good of such a discussion. Listen to the end of my story.

One evening I was returning from Boiberik with a heavy heart. Just imagine the sorrow and the shame, and how I pitied my child! And what about the widow, you may ask? And her son? What widow? What son? They left without even saying goodbye! It's a shame to admit it—but they didn't even settle their debt to me for cheese and butter... But that is not what I'm talking about; they probably forgot. I'm speaking of the way they left without even saying goodbye!.. What the poor child went through, no other human being except me knew, for I am a father, and a father's heart understands...

Do you think she said even a single word to me? That she complained? Or wept even once? Eh! Then you don't know Tevye's daughters. Quiet, withdrawn, she kept her grief to herself, but she flickered and melted away like a candle! Once in a while she would sigh, but that sigh was enough to tear my heart asunder!

So I was driving along homeward, deep in sad thoughts, asking our Heavenly Father questions and answering them myself. It wasn't God who was bothering me so much—with Him I had already made it up, one way or another. People, that's who worried me; why should people make life bitter both for others and for themselves, when they could live well and happily? Could it be that God created Man so that he should suffer on earth? Of what use was that to Him?...

With such thoughts I drove into my farmstead. From afar I saw a crowd of people by the dike—men, women, lads, girls and small children without count. What could it be? It was not a fire. Maybe somebody had drowned—went bathing by the dike and found his death? Nobody knows where the angel of Death awaits him, as we say in the hymn describing the Day of Judgment.

Suddenly I saw my Golda running, her shawl flying, her hands stretched out before her, and in front of her my daughters Beilke and Taibl, all three of them screaming, wailing: "Daughter! Sister! Shprintze!!!"

I sprang from the wagon—I don't know how I didn't break my neck—and ran to the river, but when I got there it was already all over....

What did I want to ask you? Oh, yes! Have you ever seen a drowned person? Never ?..

When a person dies he usually dies with his eyes closed...The eyes of one who has drowned are open—do you know the reason for this?...

Please excuse me, I've taken up too much of your time, and I myself am also not a free man; I have to go to my horse and deliver my wares. The world is a world. One must think about earning a living, too—and forget what has been. Because it is said that one must forget what the earth has covered, and while a man lives he cannot part from his soul. Witticisms are of no help, and we must return to the old adage saying that as long *"as my soul abides within me"*—plod on, Tevye!

Goodbye, be well, and if you think of me sometimes, don't think ill of me.

1907

Tevye Goes to Palestine

As told by Tevye the Dairyman while traveling in a train

Look who's here! How are you, Reb Sholom Aleichem? What fine company! I never even dreamed of it! My best greetings, and peace be with you! I wondered all the time and thought and thought: What's happened, why is it that he is seen neither in Boiberik nor in Yehupetz such a long time? Anything could've happened: maybe he has settled all his accounts and left us altogether—moved to the place where black radishes and chicken fat are not eaten? On the other hand, I thought, can it be possible that *he* should do such foolishness? He is, after all, a sensible person, as I live! Well, thank the Lord for seeing you in good health, as it is written: *"A mountain with a mountain…"*—a man with a man….

You are looking at me, Panie*, as if you can't recognize me. I am your good old friend, Tevye. *"Look not at the vessel but at its contents"*—don't let my new coat deceive you. This is the same *shlimazl* Tevye as before, to a hair, but when you get dressed up in your Sabbath clothes you begin to look as if you were somebody, maybe even a rich man. When you go out among people you can't do otherwise, especially if you are going on such a long journey, to Palestine, no small matter.

You look at me and think: How come such a simple little person as Tevye, who dealt all his life in dairy foods, should suddenly get such an idea into his head, a thing only someone like Brodsky could allow himself in his old age? Believe me, Mr. Sholom Aleichem, *"it is altogether puzzling"*—this expression is all around true. Please move your valise a little and I'll sit down here opposite you and tell you my story—just listen to what the Almighty can do….

---

*Panie—Sir, Mr. (Polish) —*Tr.*

"I am your good old friend Tevye…don't let my new coat deceive you."

But before I begin I must tell you that I have for some time now been a widower, may this never happen to you. My Golda, God rest her soul, is dead. A simple woman, without learning, with no pretensions, but she was very devout and pious. Let her intercede in the other world for her children; they made her suffer enough in this one and perhaps were even the cause of her leaving before her time. She couldn't bear their having scattered in different directions—one this way, the other that way. "Alas," she would say, "what is left of my life, neither child nor chick! Even a cow," she said, "longs for its calf when it is weaned away from her..."

That's how she spoke to me, my Golda, shedding bitter tears. I watched the woman waning from day to day like a candle; my heart went out in pity for her, and I said to her: "Eh, Golda darling, in our *Rosh Hashono* prayer it says: *'Im k'vonim im k'vodim'*—whether we're like children or like slaves. With children or without children—it's all the same! We have a great God, a kind and strong God, but still," said I, "I should have as many blessings as the times the Almighty plays one of His tricks, my enemies should have such luck."

But she, may she forgive me, was, after all, only a woman, and so she said to me: "You are sinning, Tevye, you mustn't sin."

"Oh, come on," said I, "did I say something bad? Did I say anything, God forbid, against the ways of the Almighty? For since He has created His world so wonderfully, so that children are not children and parents are no better than dirt," said I, "then He, of course, knows what He is doing."

But she didn't understand me, her mind was wandering: "I am dying, Tevye," she said; "who will cook supper for you?"

Her voice was barely audible and she looked at me with such eyes that even a stone would be touched. Tevye, however, is not a woman, so I answered her with a saying, with a quotation from the Bible, with a *midrash* and another *midrash:*

"Golda," I said, "you've been a faithful wife to me for so many years, so you won't make a fool of me in my old age."

As I said this I took a look at my Golda—it was the end!

"What's the matter, Golda?"

"Nothing," she barely whispered.

I saw that the game was in favor of the devil, so I hitched up my horse and drove to town and brought back a doctor, the best doctor. When I got home—oh my, oh me! My Golda was already stretched out on the floor with a candle burning at her head; she

339

looked like a little mound of earth raked together and covered with a black cloth.

I stood and thought: *"That is all that man is!"*—so this is the end of a human being!? Oh, Almighty God, the things you've done to your Tevye! What will I do now in my old age, a wretched and miserable man? And with that I fell to the ground.

But go weep and wail! What's the use? Listen to what I want to tell you. When you witness death closely you become a heretic and begin to think: *"What are we and what is our life?"* And what is this entire world, with the wheels that turn, the trains that rush along crazily, with its entire tumult and bustle all around, and even Brodsky with his millions—vanity of vanities, altogether nonsense and trash.

Well, I hired a man to read *kaddish* for her, for my wife Golda, may she rest in peace, and paid him for a whole year ahead. What else could I do, if God had punished me, given me no males, only females, only daughters and daughters, no good man should ken them! I don't know if everybody has such trouble with their daughters, or if, perhaps, only I am such a miserable *shlimazl* who has no luck at all with them? That is, I have nothing against my daughters themselves, and luck is as God wills. I should have at least half of what my girls wish me. Quite the opposite, they are too devoted to me, and everything that is "too" is in excess. Take, for instance, my youngest, her name is Beilke. What idea can you have of the kind of child she is? You have known me, thank God, for a year and a day, and you are aware that I am not the kind of father who sits down and begins to praise his children just for the sake of talking. But since I've mentioned my Beilke, I must say just this: Since God began to deal in Beilkes he never created *such* a Beilke! Her beauty we won't even discuss. Tevye's daughters, you know that yourself, are famous far and wide as great beauties. But she, Beilke, puts all the others into the shade! A beauty of beauties! But that is not all. In regard to my Beilke, one may truly quote the words from *A Woman of Valor:* *"Charms are deceitful"*—I am speaking not of looks but of character. Gold, pure gold, I tell you! From the first I was always the cream of the crop with her, but since my Golda, may she rest in peace, passed away, I became the apple of Beilke's eye! She wouldn't let a speck of dust fall on me. I already said to myself: the Almighty, as we say in our prayer, *"precedes anger with mercy"*—God sends remedies for a scourge. However, it's hard to tell which is worse, the remedy or the scourge!

Go be a prophet and guess that Beilke would, on my account, sell herself for money and send her father in his old age to Palestine! That's only in a manner of speaking, of course. She is just as much to blame for this as you are. The whole fault is his, her chosen one's. I don't want to curse him, may a barracks collapse over him! Then, perhaps, if we should want to think the matter over carefully, to dig a little deeper, it might turn out that I am more guilty than anyone else, for there is a passage in the *Gemara* that says: *"Man is obligated..."* but it's a fine thing, as I live, that I should have to tell you what the *Gemara* says!

Well, to make it short—I don't want to keep you too long. One year went by, then another, my Beilke grew up, became, knock on wood, of a marriageable age, while Tevye went on with his trade, driving, as always, his horse and wagon, and delivering cheese and butter to Boiberik in the summer, to Yehupetz in the winter—may a deluge flood it, as it once did Sodom. I can't stand that city, and not so much the city itself as the people, and not all the people, but one man—Ephraim the Matchmaker, may the devil take him and his father's father! Now listen to what a matchmaker can do to you.

"And there came the day..." I come to Yehupetz once in the middle of September with my wares. I give a look— *"Haman approacheth"*—Ephraim the Matchmaker is coming towards me! I once told you about him. Although Ephraim is a pesky person, but no sooner do you see him than you must stop—that's the kind of power this man has.

"Ho, there, my sage," I say to my horse, "stand still a while, I'll let you have something to chew." I stop Ephraim the Matchmaker, greet him, and begin to talk to him in a roundabout way:

"How is business?"

He answers, with a deep sigh: "Bad."

"How come?"

"Nothing to do," says he.

"Nothing at all?"

"Nothing at all!"

"What's the matter?" I ask.

So he says: "The trouble is, that matches are no longer concluded at home."

"Where then are matches concluded now?" I ask.

"Somewhere out there, abroad," says he.

"So what, for instance, should a man like me do, whose grandfather's granny never set foot there?"

"For you, Reb Tevye," says he, offering me his snuff-box, "I have a piece of goods right here on the spot!"

"Namely?" I ask.

"A widow without children, has a dowry of a hundred and fifty rubles, used to be a cook in the very best houses," says he.

I give him a nasty look. "Reb Ephraim, for whom do you propose this match?"

"For whom should I propose it if not for you!" says he.

"Of all the wild and crazy notions—may they fall on my enemies' heads!" I shout and give my horse a taste of the whip, meaning to drive away, but Ephraim stops me:

"Please excuse me, Reb Tevye, perhaps I have offended you. But tell me, who did *you* have in mind?" he asks.

"Who should I have in mind," says I, "if not my youngest daughter?"

At this he suddenly springs back and slaps his forehead: "Wait! It's a good thing you reminded me, a long life to you, Reb Tevye!"

"Amen, the same to you, may you also live until the coming of the Messiah. But what's the matter with you," I ask. "Why the great rejoicing?"

"It's good, it's unusually wonderful, Reb Tevye, it couldn't be better in the entire world!" he cries.

"What, namely, is this goodness, tell me?"

He answers: "I have a match worthy of your youngest daughter, a piece of luck, a grand prize, a rich man, very rich, a millionaire, a Brodsky. He is a contractor and his name is Padhatzur."

"Padhatzur? A familiar name from the Bible," said I.

"What Bible," says he, "where Bible? He's a contractor, this Padhatzur, he builds houses, brick buildings, bridges. He was in Japan during the war and brought back heaps of gold. He drives around in carriages drawn by fiery steeds, he has footmen at his door, there is a bathroom right in his own house and furniture from Paris, and he wears a diamond ring on his finger. He is not at all old, not married, a real bachelor, top quality! What he is looking for is a pretty girl; it doesn't matter who she is, she may be naked and barefoot, as long as she is a beauty!.."

"Whoa, there!" say I to him. "If you fly so fast, without stopping to graze your horse, we'll find ourselves, Reb Ephraim, at the other end of nowhere. Besides, if I am not mistaken, you once tried to fix up this very same match for my older daughter, for Hodel."

342

Upon hearing these words of mine, he, Ephraim, began to laugh so hard that he had to hold his sides. I thought the fellow would have a stroke!

"Oh," he exclaimed, "you're thinking of the time my grandmother was brought to bed with her first child! That fellow went bankrupt before the war and ran away to America!"

"May the memory of a righteous person be blessed," said I. "Maybe this one will run there, too?"

This outraged the matchmaker terribly:

"What are you talking about, Reb Tevye? That one was," said he, "a good-for-nothing, a charlatan, a spendthrift, while this one is a contractor since the war, with a business, with an office, with clerks, with... with... with..."

What can I say—the matchmaker got so excited that he pulled me off my wagon, grabbed me by the lapels and began to shake me, and he wouldn't let go until a policeman came up and wanted to take both of us to the police station. A lucky thing it was that I remembered the Biblical passage which says: *"You may take interest from a stranger"*—you've got to know how to handle the police...

In short, why take up so much of your time? This Padhatzur became my youngest one's, my Beilke's, betrothed. And *"the days were not long"*—I mean, it did take quite some time before we raised the wedding canopy. Why do I say that it took some time? Because she, Beilke, was as eager for this match as one is eager for death. The more this Padhatzur showered her with gifts, with gold watches and diamond rings, the more loathsome did he become to her. Things don't have to be spelled out to me, you know. I understood this very well from the look in her eyes and on her face, and from the tears she shed in secret. I thought it over and once remarked, as if in passing:

"Listen, Beilke," I said, "I'm afraid that your Padhatzur is just as much to your liking as to mine, as sweet to you as he is to me, isn't he?"

She turned fire-red and asked:

"Who told you that?"

"Why then do you cry all night?' I asked.

"Do I cry?"

"No," said I, "you don't cry, you sob. You think that if you bury your head in a pillow you'll hide your tears from me? You think that I, your father, am a little boy, or that my brain has dried up and I don't understand that you are doing this for your old

343

father? That you want him to be provided for in his old age, so that he should have a place to lay his head, and wouldn't have to, God forbid, go begging from house to house? If that is what you think," said I, "then you are a big fool. We have a great God and Tevye is not one of those ten loafers who sits down to the bread of charity. Money is worthless, as it says in the Bible. Take, for instance, your sister Hodel, a pauper, one might say, and yet," said I, "look what she writes, from the devil knows where, from the ends of the earth, and how happy she says she is with her *shlimazl* Feferl!"

Now, you try and guess what she, Beilke, replied!

"Don't compare me with Hodel," she said. "Hodel's time was a time when the whole world rocked on its foundations, it was on the verge of turning upside-down; people were concerned about the world and they forgot about themselves. Nowadays, the world is a world again, so that each one is concerned with himself and the world is forgotten..."

That is how Beilke answered me—try and understand what she meant!

Well, you are something of an expert on Tevye's daughters aren't you? But you should have seen her during the marriage ceremony! A princess! Gazing at her in delight, I thought to myself: Is this Beilke, Tevye's daughter? Where did she learn to stand so, to walk so, to hold her head so, and to dress so that her clothes looked as if they had been poured out over her body?

However, I wasn't allowed to admire her for long; on the very day of the wedding, about half-past five in the afternoon, the newlyweds got up and left; they departed by an express train for the devil knows where, for "Nataliye"*, as is fashionable among rich people. They returned when winter had already come, around *Hanukkah,* sent me a message saying that I was to come to them in Yehupetz *immediately* and *without fail.* This made me think: If they had just wanted to see me, they would simply have asked me to come, that's all. But why the *immediately* and *without fail?* Probably something important was up—but what? All sorts of thoughts, both good and bad, flitted through my mind: Maybe the couple had already quarreled out there, and were on the verge of divorce? But at once I reproached myself: You're a fool, Tevye, why do you always expect bad things? How do you know why they

---

*Italy (distorted).—*Tr.*

have sent for you? Maybe they miss you and want to see you? Or perhaps Beilke wants her father to be near her? Or it may even be that Padhatzur wants to give you a job, take you into his business and make you a supervisor over his contracts?... Anyhow, I had to go. So I got into my wagon and *"went forth to Heron."* To Yehupetz.

Along the way, I let my imagination run free. I saw myself abandoning the village, selling the cows, the horse and wagon, all my goods and chattels, and moving into town. There I would become first a supervisor in Padhutzur's business, then his cashier, and then the manager of all his building contracts, and after that a partner in all his business affairs, fifty-fifty, and I would drive around just as he did, behind a pair of fiery steeds, one a bay, the other a chestnut. And I began to think in amazement about myself: *"What is this and what is it all for?"* How come such a modest little man, Tevye, to deal with such important affairs? What do I need all this hullabaloo for, this never-ending day-and-night fair with its bustle and tumult? How does it go— *"to seat them with the mighty"*—to hobnob with millionaires? Let me be, I want a quiet and peaceful old age, I want to be able to look into a volume of the *Mishnah* from time to time, to read a chapter from the Book of Psalms—one has to have the next world in mind sometimes, too, isn't that so? As King Solomon said: Man is verily like the cattle, he forgets that no matter how long he lives he will have to die some day...

With these thoughts and visions I arrived in Yehupetz and drove directly to Padhatzur's house. To boast to you of his *"grandeur and wealth"*—that is, of his home and its furnishings— of that I am not capable. I've never had the honor of visiting Brodsky in his home, but I am certain that there can be nothing finer than my son-in-law's house! You will understand what sort of mansion it was if I tell you that the man who guarded the door, a lanky fellow with silver buttons, would by no means let me in, do what you will. So how was I to get in? Through the glass door I could see him, may his memory be forgotten, brushing clothes. I winked at him, spoke to him in sign language, showing him by gestures that he should let me in, for the master's wife was my own daughter... But he understood nothing, the lout, and motioned to me, also in sign language, to go to blazes, to go my way, that is. Such a pig-headed idol! Just think, to visit your own daughter you've got to have pull?

345

Woe unto your gray head, Tevye, look what you've lived to! Such was my thought as I looked through the glass door. Then I noticed a girl moving about inside. Must be one of their housemaids, I decided, marking her shifty eyes. All housemaids have shifty eyes. I am a frequent visitor in many wealthy houses and I know all the maids in them. So I winked at her: "Open up, kitty!" She obeyed, and opened the door and asked me, in Yiddish, "Who do you want?"

"Does Padhatzur live here?" I asked.

"Who do you want?" said she in a louder voice.

But I said, still louder: "When you are asked a question you should answer. *First things first*—does Padhatzur live here?"

"He does," she answered.

"If that is the case we speak the same language. Go and tell your Madam Padhatzur that she has a guest, her father Tevye has arrived, and he's been standing outside for quite a while like a beggar at the door, because he didn't have the honor," I said, "to find favor in the eyes of that Esau with the silver buttons who isn't worth your littlest fingernail!"

Having heard me out, the maid giggled impudently, slammed the door in my face, ran upstairs, then downstairs again, opened the door for me and led me into a real palace, such as my grandfathers' grandfathers never saw even in their dreams. Silk and velvet, gold and crystal, and when you walked you didn't even hear your own footsteps, for your sinful feet were treading on the most costly rugs, soft as snow. And clocks! Clocks on the walls, clocks on the tables, clocks without end! Good Lord! Have you many more of this kind in the world? What does a person need so many clocks for? Such were my thoughts as I walked, my hands clasped behind my back, a little further on. Suddenly I saw several Tevyes at once on all sides, one Tevye going here, another going there, one coming towards me, another walking away from me. Confound it! Mirrors on all four sides! Only such a bird as this contractor could afford so many clocks and so many mirrors!

Here Padhatzur came to my mind, a fat, roly-poly little man with a bald head who speaks in a high voice and doesn't laugh but snickers. I recalled how he came to me in the village for the first time with his fiery steeds; he made himself at home at once—as if he were in his father's vineyard! Got acquainted with my Beilke, then called me aside and whispered a secret into my ear—but so loudly you could have heard it on the other side of Yehupetz.

What was this secret? The secret was that my daughter had found favor in his eyes and he wanted "one-two-three and a wedding canopy." That my daughter had found favor in his eyes was not difficult to understand, but this "one-two-three" was *"like a double-edged sword"* to me—as if a blunt knife had pierced my heart. What did he mean by "one-two-three and a wedding canopy"? And what about me? And what about Beilke? Oh, didn't I just long to give him a couple of quotations from the Bible and a *midrash* to remember me by! But on the other hand, I thought, why should you, Tevye, interfere? Did it help you a lot with your elder daughters, when you tried to advise them against their choices? You rattled like a drum, poured out your whole Torah, and who was the fool at the end? Tevye!

Oh, well, as the story-books say, let us leave the prince and turn to the princess.

Well, so I obliged them and came to Yehupetz. They greeted me affectionately: *"Sholom aleichem!" "Aleichem sholom!"* "How are you?" "How are things with you?" "Be seated!" "Thank you, I'm quite comfortable." And all the other ceremonies, as is the custom.

It didn't seem proper to ask them first why, *"Today of all days,"* they had sent for me. But Tevye is not a woman, he can wait.

Meanwhile, a tall man-servant in enormous white gloves came in and said that lunch was already on the table, so all three of us got up and went into a room entirely made up of oak: an oaken table, oaken chairs, oaken wainscotting, an oaken ceiling, everything elaborately carved and painted and designed. On the table was a royal spread: tea and coffee and chocolate, shortbread and pastries, fine cognac, the best appetizers, salted and pickled dainties, and all manner of other delicious foods, fruits, and vegetables. I'm ashamed to say this, but I'm afraid that at her father's table my Beilke never saw such delicacies.

Well, they poured me a drink, then another. Drinking to their health and looking at her, at Beilke, I thought: At last you have lived to see the day, Tevye's daughter, as we say in *Hallel: "Who raiseth up the poor out of the dust"*—when God helps a poor man—*"and lifteth up the needy out of the dunghill,"* the man becomes altogether unrecognizable. She seems to be Beilke, and yet not Beilke.

I remembered the other Beilke, from the past, and I compared the two Beilkes—and my heart ached. It was just as if I had struck a bad bargain, had done something that couldn't be undone. Let us say, for instance, I felt as if I had exchanged my hard-working

"Suddenly I saw several Tevyes at once, on all sides."

little dobbin for a colt without being able to tell what would become of it in the future—a horse or a block of wood.

Eh, Beilke, Beilke, thought I, what has become of you? Remember how you used to sit at night by a smoky lamp, sewing and humming to yourself, or how you would go out and milk two cows in a flash, or roll up your sleeves and cook me a simple borsht, or a dish of dough pellets with beans, or cheese-filled dumplings, or bake me some poppy-seed cookies, and you would say: "*Tateh,* go wash your hands!" This was, for me, the best of all melodies!

Now she sat there with her Padhatzur like a queen; two footmen were waiting at the table, clattering the plates—and she, Beilke? She didn't say a single word! He, Padhatzur, talked for both of them, his mouth didn't shut for a moment! Never in my life have I seen anyone who was so fond of jabbering, of chattering the devil knows what, without stopping his snickery laughter. Of such types it is said: he makes his own jokes and laughs at them himself.

Besides the three of us there was a fourth person at the table, a red-cheeked character. What and who he was I don't know, but that he was no mean eater was self-evident. All the time Padhatzur talked this guest went on gorging himself; as it says in Perek: "*Three who have eaten*"—he certainly ate enough for three.

This one ate and that one talked, and all of it such empty things, I couldn't care a hoot about: podryad*, gubernskoye pravleniye**, udelnaya vedomost***, kaznacheistvo†, Japan...

Of all this the only thing that held some interest for me was Japan, because I had had something to do with that country. During the war, as you know, horses were in great demand and were sought for high and low. Of course, the authorities got to me, too, and they took my horse to task, measured him with a yardstick, drove him back and forth and then gave him a white card††. Well, I told them that I'd known beforehand that their trouble was in vain, for, as the Bible says: "*The righteous man knoweth the soul of his animal.*" Tevye's horse is not a horse that goes to war.

But please excuse me, Mr. Sholom Aleichem, I get one thing confused with another and am apt, God forbid, to stray from the

---

*Contract (Russian).—*Tr.*
**Provincial Board of Directors (Russian).—*Tr.*
***Royal Family Real Estate Register (Russian).—*Tr.*
†The Exchequer (Russian).—*Tr.*
††A certificate giving exemption from military service.—*Tr.*

highway. As you say, let us get back to business—to my story.

Well, so we ate and drank our fill, as God bade us. When we got up from the table, he Padhatzur, took my arm and led me into a separate chamber—his "study"—a royally decorated room with rifles and spears on the walls, and tiny cannons on the table. He seated me on a sort of sofa, soft as butter, took out, from a golden box, two thick, aromatic cigars and lighted them, one for himself, one for me. Then he sat down opposite me and said:

"Do you know why I have sent for you?"

Aha, thought I, he probably means to have a talk with me about business. But I played dumb and said "*Am I my brother's keeper?'*—how should I know?'

"I wanted to have a talk with you—about you yourself," said he.

Must be about a job, I thought to myself, and said: "If only it is something good—my pleasure, let's hear it."

He took the cigar out of his mouth and began a whole speech:

"You are," said he, "no fool and so you won't take offense if I speak to you frankly. You must know that I do business on a large scale, and when one engages in such big business deals..."

Yes, thought I, he has me in mind. And I interrupted him and said: "As the *Gemara* says in the Sabbath chapter: *'The more business, the more worries.'* Do you know," I asked him, "how this passage from the *Gemara* should be explained?"

He answered me quite frankly: "I'll tell you the honest truth: I never studied any *Gemara* and I don't even know what it looks like."

That's how Padhatzur answered me and burst into his snickery laughter.

How do you like that? I would think that if God has punished you by making you an ignoramus, then let it at least be covered up, why go boast about it? Thinking so, I said to him:

"I did figure that you hadn't much to do with such things, but let's hear what you have to say further."

So he went on: "Further, I wanted to tell you that with my business and my name, with my *polozheniye**, it doesn't suit me that you are known as Tevye the Dairyman. I want you to know that I am *lichno*** acquainted with the Governor, and it is quite

---

*Standing, social status (Russian).— *Tr.*
**Personally (Russian).— *Tr.*

350

possible that Brodsky might come to visit me, or Polyakov, or maybe even Rothschild, *chem chort nye shutit?**"

That's what he said to me, this Padhatzur, and I just sat there looking at his shiny bald head and thinking: It may very well be that you are personally acquainted with the Governor, and that Rothschild might come to your house some day, but you talk like a despicable cur... And I said, with a bit of resentment:

"So what can be done if Rothschild does indeed come to see you?"

You think he understood the dig? *There was neither bear nor woods*—he understood nothing!

"I wanted you," said he, "to give up this dairy business and occupy yourself with something else."

"Namely with what?"

"With whatever you like," he said, "there are lots of businesses in the world! I'll help you out with money, if only you stop being Tevye the Dairyman. Or, hold on," said he, "why not pick yourself up one-two-three and go to America? Eh?"

After saying this he pushed his cigar back into his mouth and looked me straight in the eye, his bald head glistening...

Well? How does one answer such a crude fellow? My first thought was: Why are you sitting, Tevye, like a clay *golem?* Get up, kiss the *mezuzah,* slam the door and get out without as much as a goodbye! It really made my gall rise! The impudence of this contractor! What does he mean, telling me to give up my own respectable business and go away to America? Just because Rothschild might visit him some day, Tevye the Dairyman must fly to the ends of the world?!

My heart was boiling with anger like a kettle, and I was already upset from before this talk. My wrath was directed against her, against my Beilke: Why are you sitting there like a queen amidst the hundred clocks and the thousand mirrors, while here your father, Tevye, is running the gauntlet over live coals? As I live, I thought, your sister Hodel made a better marriage than you! It is true, of course, that she doesn't have such a house with so many expensive gew-gaws as you have, but she has Feferl for a husband, and he is a fine human being, a man who doesn't think of himself—his concern is for the whole world... And, in addition, he has

---

*"What doesn't the devil joke about?" A Russian saying, which means, "you never can tell."—*Tr.*

a head on his shoulders, not a pot with a shiny lid on it! And what a tongue he has, this Feferl—gold and gold! He, when you give him a passage from the Bible, comes back at you with three! Just you wait, my dear contractor, I'll quote you a passage that'll make your head spin!

That is what I thought, and then addressed him with the following words:

"Well, it's no great matter that the *Gemara* is a closed book to you—this I forgive you. When a Jew sits in Yehupetz and his name is Padhatzur and he is a contractor," said I, "the *Gemara* may well be forgotten in the attic. But a simple passage even a peasant in bast shoes will understand. You know, of course, what the *Targum* says about Laban the Aramaean: *'Hafromtah lapigstailah hakanmaknoh lafurhatah.'*"

He stared at me and asked: "What, then, does it mean?"

"It means," said I, "that from a pig's tail no fur hat can be made."

"In regard to what do you say that?"

"In regard to your bidding me to go to America."

Emitting his snickery laughter, he said:

"If not to America, then perhaps to Palestine? All old Jews go to Palestine..."

No sooner had he uttered these words than they sank into my brain as an iron nail sinks into wood: Stop! Maybe this isn't at all so bad, Tevye, as you might think? Maybe it is a good plan? Because rather than have such pleasure from children as you have, Palestine is perhaps better? What do you risk and whom do you have here? Your Golda, may she rest in peace, is already in the grave, while you yourself, God forgive me, haven't you suffered enough? How much longer can you tread the earth?

Actually, Mr. Sholom Aleichem, I must confess that I have for a long time cherished a dream to visit Palestine: I would like to stand by the Wailing Wall, by the tombs of the Patriarchs and Mother Rachel's Tomb, and see with my own eyes the river Jordan, Mount Sinai and the Red Sea, the cities Pithom and Raamses, and other such things. My imagination carried me away to the blessed Land of Canaan, *"the land flowing with milk and honey,"* but he interrupted my reflections, this Padhatzur, right in the middle, saying:

"Well? What is there to think about so long? One-two-three..."

"With you, praise the Lord," said I, "everything is one-two-three... For me it's a difficult piece of the *Mishnah,* because to pick oneself up and travel to Palestine one has to have the wherewith-al..." At this he emitted his snickery laughter, got up, went to his desk, took a purse from a drawer and counted me out a goodly sum of money. I immediately understood what he meant, took the wad—the power of money!—and put it deep down into a pocket. I wanted to quote a few passages and a *midrash* for his edification, to round everything up, but he paid no attention at all to my words and said:

"This will be more than enough to get you there, and when you arrive at your destination and need more money, write us a letter and it will be forwarded to you one-two-three... I hope you won't have to be reminded again about leaving, for, after all, you are a man of honor, a man with a *sovest.**"

That is how my son-in-law Padhatzur spoke to me with his snickery laughter that crept right into one's entrails.

I suddenly caught myself thinking: Why not fling the money right back into his face and quote a passage to the effect that Tevye is not to be bought for money, and with Tevye you don't speak of honor and of conscience?

However, before I could open my mouth to say something he rang a bell, called in Beilke and said to her:

"*Dushenka***, you know what? Your father is forsaking us, he is selling everything he has and is going away one-two-three to Palestine."

"*I dreamed a dream but I do not understand it*"—I dreamed it the other night and last night! So I thought to myself and looked at my Beilke—not a trace of any emotion on her face. Stood there as if rooted to the floor, not a drop of blood in her face, looking from him to me, from me to him—and not a single word! I watched her and also said nothing, so the two of us were mute, as it is written in the Psalms: "*...my tongue clave*"—we had both lost the power of speech. I felt dizzy, a pulse was beating in my temples as if I had breathed charcoal fumes. What could be the reason? Perhaps, thought I, it's from that fine cigar that he gave me to smoke? Yes, but he is also smoking, this Padhatzur! Smoking and talking, his mouth doesn't shut at all, although his eyelids are drooping as if he's ready to fall asleep.

---

*Conscience (Russian)—*Tr.*
**Dearest, darling, sweetheart (Russian)—*Tr.*

"First you've got to go," said he, "from here to Odessa on the express train, and from Odessa by sea to Jaffa. Right now is the best time for traveling by sea, because later the winds and snows and storms begin and—and—and..." He mumbled, his words were getting jumbled as if he were falling asleep, but he didn't stop his chatter: "and when you are ready for the journey you'll let us know and we'll both come to the railway station to see you off, because who knows when we'll see each other again?"

These words were followed by a gaping yawn, begging your pardon; he got to his feet and said to her, to Beilke: "*Dushenka,* you sit here a while and I'll go and catch forty winks."

You've never said a better thing, as I live! At least now there is someone on whom I can pour out the bitterness of my heart! This is what I said to myself, intending to take my Beilke to task, to give her a good scolding for everything that had piled up in my heart that morning, but now she, Beilke, fell on my neck and began to weep. How do you think she wept? My daughters, may no evil befall them, are brave, they keep up their courage, but then, when it comes to something, they suddenly break down and the tears begin to flow from them as the sap flows from a tapped birch. Take, for instance, my older daughter Hodel. How she carried on, how she wept when she had to leave to share her Feferl's exile in the cold lands! But there is no comparison: that one can't even hold a candle to this one!

I'll tell you the honest truth: I myself, as you already know me, am not a man who is ready with his tears. I wept long and bitterly only once, when my Golda, may she rest in peace, was lying on the ground, and once more I wept when Hodel went off to join her Feferl and I was left standing by the station like a big fool, all alone with my little horse; then, maybe another couple of times it happened that I, as you say, blubbered a little, but I don't remember that I ever made a habit of weeping. Now Beilke and her tears wrung my soul so that I couldn't restrain myself and I didn't have the heart to say even one cross word to her. To me you don't have to explain things. My name is Tevye. I soon understood the reason for her tears. They weren't just tears; they were, please understand me, tears for *"the sin I have sinned before thee,"* for not having listened to her father... So instead of giving her a piece of my mind and pouring out all my wrath against her Padhatzur, I began to console her with such an example and such an example, as Tevye can. She listened to me, my Beilke, and then said:

354

"No, *Tateh,* that is not why I'm crying. I have no complaints against anyone, I am crying because you are going away on account of me and I can do nothing about it. This is what torments me so."

"There, there," said I. "You talk like a child, you've forgotten that we still have a great God and that your father still possesses all his senses. For your father," I continued, "it's no big deal to travel to Palestine and come back, as it is written: *'They journeyed and they encamped'—tuda i nazad—*there and back again."

I tried in this way to comfort her, but to myself I thought: Tevye, you're lying! When you leave for Palestine it'll be *"may he rest in peace"*—no more Tevye!..

Just as if she could read my thoughts, Beilke said to me:

"No, *Tateh,* that is how you comfort a little child. You give it a doll, some plaything to hold and tell it a pretty story about a little white kid... If it comes to storytelling," said she, "let *me* tell *you* one. But the story I want to tell you, *Tateh,* is more sad than beautiful."

That is how she spoke to me, my Beilke. Tevye's daughters don't speak in vain. She gave me a whole song and dance, told me a saga, a story from the *Arabian Nights,* how this Padhatzur of hers had lifted himself from the lowest depths to the highest levels, all by his own wits, and now he sought the glory of having Brodsky visit his house; to achieve this he was handing out donations, simply pouring out rubles by the thousand in all directions. However, money alone was not enough, you had to have "lineage," too, so he, Padhatzur, that is, was moving heaven and earth in order to show that he was not just anybody. He boasted that he was descended from the great Padhatzurs, that his father was also a famous contractor. "Although," said Beilke, "he is fully aware that I know that his father was a poor musician. Now he tells everybody that his wife's father was a millionaire..."

Whom does he mean?" I asked. "Me? Maybe I *was* once destined to have millions some day, but that will have to suffice me!"

"Oh, *Tateh,*" said Beilke, "if you only knew how I blush when he introduces me to his acquaintances and starts telling them what important people my father, my uncles and my whole family are— pure fantasy! But I have to endure all this, listen and keep mum, because he is very capricious in these matters."

"You call it 'caprice,' " said I, " but to me it sounds like abomination and downright chicanery."

"No, *Tateh*," said Beilke, "you don't know him, he is not at all as bad as you think. Only he is a man whose moods change frequently—one minute he is like this, the next like that. He is really kindhearted and generous. A mournful mien on a person's face will prompt him, if the moment is propitious, to do anything for this person. As for me—why, nothing is too good for me! You think I have no influence at all with him? Not long ago I persuaded him to rescue Hodel and her husband from their distant exile. He swore to me," she said, "that he would spend thousands on it, but on one condition—that they go from there directly to Japan."

"Why to Japan," said I, "why not to India, or, for instance, to *Padan-Aram**　to visit the Queen of Sheba?"

"Because he has business in Japan," she answered. "He has business dealings all over the world; what he spends in a day on telegrams alone, our whole family could have lived on for six months. Yes, but what good is all this to me when I am no longer myself!"

"It comes out," said I, "as we read in the *Perek: 'If I am not for myself who will be for me?'*—I am not I, you are not you."

So I spoke to her, here a saying, there a quotation from the Holy Book, although my heart bled to see how my child suffered *"in riches and in honor,"* as we say.

"Your sister Hodel," I said, "would have done differently." But she, Beilke, interrupted me:

"I've already told you, *Tateh*, that you shouldn't compare me to Hodel. Hodel lived in Hodel's time, and Beilke lives in Beilke's time... From Hodel's time to Beilke's time the distance is as great as from here to Japan."

Do you understand the meaning of such strange talk?

Oh, I see that you are in a hurry, Mr. Sholom Aleichem. Another two minutes and all my stories will end. Satiated with the worries and anguish of my lucky youngest daughter, I left the house *"in mourning and with bowed head"*—completely crushed and beaten. I flung away the cigar, the fumes of which had made my head spin, and shouted after it—after the cigar, that is:

"Go to limbo, damn you!"

"Whom do you mean, Reb Tevye?" asked a voice behind my back. I turned my head and took a look—it was he, Ephraim the Matchmaker, may the Evil One catch him!

---

*A place mentioned in the Bible. Here meant in an ironical sense—"to some other place". —*Tr.*

"Welcome, whom do I see!" I exclaimed. "What are you doing here?"

"What," said he, "are *you* doing here?"

"I am visiting my children."

"And how are they?" he asked.

"How," said I, "should they be? We should be as lucky!"

"As I see," said he, "you are quite pleased with my merchandise?"

"And how pleased!" said I. "May God repay you many times over."

Thanks for your kind words; perhaps you might add a gift to your blessings?" he said.

"Why, didn't you receive your matchmaker's fee?" I asked.

"He shouldn't have more himself, this Padhatzur of yours."

"What was wrong," I asked, "too small a sum?"

"Not so small a sum as the 'goodwill' that went with it!"

"What do you mean?"

"I mean," said he, "that it's all gone already—not a single *grosz* left!"

"Where did it go to?" I asked.

"I married off a daughter," he answered.

"Congratulations," said I, "may God grant them good luck and you should live to have joy from them."

"Great joy," he retorted, "I have already lived to have from them. I landed me a scoundrel of a son-in-law. He beat and tortured my daughter, picked up the few rubles, and went off to America."

"Why did you let him go so far?"

"What should I have done with him?"

"You should have sprinkled salt on his tail," said I.

"You are evidently in a cheerful mood, Reb Tevye?"

"God grant you at least half of it, oh, Lord Almighty!" said I.

"So that's how it is? And I thought you were a rich man! But since you aren't—here's a pinch of snuff for you!" said he.

Having gotten rid of the matchmaker with his pinch of snuff, I drove home and began to sell off my household goods, objects that had accumulated over the years. Mind you, such things aren't done as quickly as you speak of them. Every pot, every trifle cost me a piece of my health. This reminded me of Golda, may she rest in peace, that reminded me of the children, God Bless them. But nothing hurt me so much as parting from my horse. Looking at him I felt guilty. So many years we had toiled together, suffered together, gone hungry together, and suddenly I take and sell him! I sold the horse to a water-carrier, because from teamsters you get nothing but insults. I went to them to sell my horse, so they said:

"God be with you, Reb Tevye, do you call this a horse?"

"What then is it—a candlestick?"

"No," they said, "it's not a candlestick you have here, it's a *Lamed-Vovnik*—one of the Thirty-Six Saintly Ones."

"What is that supposed to mean?"

"It means," they said, "an ancient creature of thirty-six years without a vestige of teeth, with a gray lip and trembling sides— like an old woman on a frosty Sabbath eve!"

How do you like such teamster-talk? The poor horse, I could swear, understood every single word, as it is said in the Holy Book: *"The ox recognizes a buyer"*—an animal knows when it is being put up for sale. You want proof? When I closed the deal with the water-carrier and said "good luck to you," my little horse suddenly turned his winsome face to me, and the look in his patient eyes seemed to say: *"So this is my lot for all my labors?"*—this is how you thank me for my service?.." I looked for the last time at my horse as the water-carrier led him away to teach him a harsh lesson, and I remained standing there all alone, thinking: Almighty God! How wisely You manage Your little world! You have created a Tevye and created his horse, and the same good luck befalls both of them! A human being, however, has a mouth and can at least complain, unburden his heart, but what can a horse do? Alas, it is but a dumb beast and, as it is said, herein lies *"the advantage of man over beast."*

You are looking, Mr. Sholom Aleichem, at the tears in my eyes, and you probably think: This Tevye apparently grieves for his horse? Why, dear man, for my horse? I grieve for everything, and I will miss everybody. I will miss the horse, I will miss the village, I will miss the village elder and the village policeman, I will miss the Boiberik summer people, the rich Yehupetzers, and even Ephraim the Matchmaker, a plague on him, because when all is said and done, what is he but a poor wretch trying to make a living?

When, God willing, I get safely to the place I am going to, I don't know what I will do there; but it's as clear as day that first of all I will go to Mother Rachel's Tomb. I will pray there for my children, whom I will probably never see again, and I will also keep Ephraim the Matchmaker in mind, him and you and all the Jews. Now let us shake hands, be well, a happy journey to you, and give my regards to each and every one.

1909

The "Fiddler on the Roof"—an American imagination.

Get Thee Out

My heartiest greetings to you, Mr. Sholom Aleichem! *Peace be with you and your children!* I've long been looking out for you, I have a whole pile of "merchandise" collected especially for you. I've asked: *"Where are you?"*—why don't I see you anymore? I was told that you have been traveling all over the world, in faraway lands, as it is said in the *Megilah,* the Book of Esther: *"The one hundred and twenty-seven provinces of Ahasheurus..."*

But it seems to me that you are looking somewhat strangely at me? Apparently, you are thinking: Is it he or not he? It is he, Mr. Sholom Aleichem, it is he! Your old friend Tevye, Tevye the Dairyman in person, the same Tevye, but no longer a dairyman, just an ordinary Jew, an old man, as you see, although in years I am not so old. As it is said in the *Haggadah: "Here I am, a man of seventy..."* but it's still quite a way off to seventy! Oh, why is my hair so white? Not from joy, believe me, dear friend. Partly my own troubles are to blame, not to complain, and partly the troubles of our people—a bad time! A bitter time for Jews...

However, I know what's pinching you—it's something else. You've probably recalled that we once said goodbye to each other when I was about to leave for Palestine. You must therefore be thinking that you see Tevye after his return from Palestine, and you probably already want to hear about my visit to Mother Rachel's Tomb and the Cave of Machpelah and other such things? Rest assured, if you have the time and want to hear a remarkable story, then listen attentively, as it is written: *"Hear ye!"* You will see for yourself that man is a mute beast and that we have a mighty God who rules over the world.

What portion of the Torah is being read in the synagogue this week? *Vayikro*—"Leviticus"? But I've been introduced to an altogether different chapter—*Lech-lecho*—"Get thee out!" "Get thee out, Tevye," I was told, *"begone out of thy country"*—out of your village where you were born and lived all your life, *"to the land which I will show thee"*—wherever your eyes lead you... And when was Tevye given this lesson to learn? When he had already become old and weak and forlorn; as we say in our prayers on *Rosh Hashono:* *"Do not cast us off in our old age!"*

But I'm running ahead of my story, I clear forgot that we were speaking of how things were in Palestine. How should things be going on there, my friend? It is a fine country—both of us should be as lucky— *"a land flowing with milk and honey,"* as it is said in the Torah. But the trouble is that Palestine is in Palestine, while I, as you see, am still here, *"outside of the Promised Land."* In the *Megilah,* Esther says: "If I perish I perish." These words, I tell you, must have been written about Tevye. A *shlimazl* I was and a *shlimazl* I'll die. There I stood, one foot almost on the other side, in the Holy Land, it only remained to buy a ticket and board a ship— and away! So what does God do? He thinks up something else for me. Just you listen.

My elder son-in-law, Motl Kamzoil, the Anatovka tailor, Heaven preserve us, lies down hale and hearty and goes and dies! That is, he never actually was what one might call robust. How could it be otherwise? He was, alas, only a poor workman, day and night he sat either *"absorbed in study or in worship of God"*—plying his thread and needle, patching, I beg your pardon, pants. So he sat and worked until he got the chest disease, and once it began, he hawked and coughed until he coughed up the last bit of his lungs. Nothing helped him, neither doctor nor medicine, goat's milk nor chocolate with honey. He was a fine person; it's true he was no scholar, but he was an honest man with no pretensions, and how he loved my daughter—simply adored her! He sacrificed himself for the children, and would have given his life for me!

So, *"Moses passed away."* Motl died and left me holding a bomb: how could I ever think of Palestine then? I already had a fine Holy Land right in my home! How, I ask you, could I leave a widowed daughter and her little orphaned children without a piece of bread? On the other hand, one might think, how could I help her when I myself was a sack full of holes? I couldn't bring her husband back to life, return their father from the other world to her children, and, besides, I myself am also nothing more than a sinful man: in my old age I wanted to rest my bones, to feel myself a human being, not a beast of burden. Enough fuss and bother! Enough of seeking the pleasures of this world! Some thought must be given to the next world, too, it's already high time! All the more so, since I had already played havoc with my bit of chattels: the horse, as you know, I had let go some time before, sold off my cows, and had only a pair of bull calves left that might perhaps become something worthwhile in the future if properly tended and foddered... And now suddenly go and become, in my old age, a provider for orphans, a father to small children!

But do you think this is all? Wait a while! The most important part is still to come, for if one trouble strikes at Tevye you may be sure that another one is following fast on its heels. For instance, once a misfortune befell me— one of my cows fell, so right after that—such a thing shouldn't happen to you—a second one lay down and died....

That is how God created His world, and so it will remain— nothing can be done about it!

Well, you remember the story of my youngest daughter Beilke, the grand prize she won, the big fish she caught—that Padhatzur, the bigshot, the contractor who made a fortune in the war and brought sackfuls of money to Yehupetz and fell in love with my daughter—he wanted a beautiful wife; he sent Ephraim the Matchmaker to me, may his name be forgotten... implored on his knees that she marry him, almost had a stroke, took her as she stood, without any dowry, and bedecked her from head to toe with gifts, diamonds, jewels... Great luck, wasn't it? Yes, well, all this luck flowed away like a river, and what a river! A river and a bog, God save us! When God orders the wheel of fortune to turn back, everything starts falling buttered side down; first, as we say in a *hallel,* it is *"who raiseth up the poor out of the dust,"* but before you know it—bang—and it becomes *"That looketh down low upon Heaven and upon the Earth"*—into the pit together with the traces!...

God loves to play with a human being. Oh, how He loves it! How many times did He play in this manner with Tevye: up and down! The same thing happened to my contractor, to Padhatzur. You probably remember how proud he was of his house in Yehupetz, with his thirteen servants, with his mirrors, clocks, and gew-gaws? Faugh, fah, fie! I think I told you, if you remember, how I tried to get my Beilke to make him buy this house in her name? They paid as much attention to my words as Haman does to a rattle—what does a father understand? He understands noth- ing! So what do you think the outcome was? My enemies should

362

have such an outcome: in addition to going bankrupt, losing everything, having to sell all the mirrors and clocks and his wife's jewelry, he also got mixed up in some messy business, and had to flee the country and go to where the holy Sabbath goes—to America, that is. All heavy hearts go there, so they went, too. At first they had a very hard time in America. The little cash they had was soon used up, and when there was nothing to chew, the poor things had to go to work; they worked at all kinds of backbreaking jobs, toiled as the Jews toiled in Egypt, both he and she! She writes that now things are easier, thank God: they operate a stocking machine and are "making a living"... That's what they call it out there, in America, but here we would say "living from hand to mouth." It's a lucky thing, she writes, that there are only two of them, with neither chick nor child. *"That too is for the best."*

So now I ask you, doesn't he deserve to be cursed with the foulest curses—I mean Ephraim the Matchmaker? For the wonderful match he arranged for me, for the dirty mess he got me into! Would she have been worse off if she had married, say, a workman, as Tzeitl did, or a teacher, as Hodel did? Oh, they didn't have it too good, either? One is a young widow, the other is in exile with her husband at the back of nowhere? But that's as God wills it—what can man foresee?..

You know, she was really a wise woman, my Golda, may she rest in peace: she took a look around in good time, said goodbye to this foolish world and departed to the next one. Don't you think that rather than endure *"the pain of bringing up children"* I have suffered on account of my daughters, it is a thousand times better to lie peacefully in the grave?.. However, our *Perek* says: *"Perforce you must live"*—a man cannot take his fate into his own hands, and if he does he gets rapped over the knuckles...

Meanwhile we've strayed from the road and therefore *let us return to our original subject*—let us leave, as you say in your story-books, the prince and return to the princess. Where were we? At lesson *Lech-lecho*—"Get thee out!" But before we begin *Lech-lecho* I want to ask you to be so kind as to stop with me for a while at *Balak*—the lesson of Vengeance. It has been the custom, since the world began, to first study *Lech-lecho* and later *Balak,* but with me it was the other way round: I was taught *Balak* first and then *Lech-lecho.* You might as well hear how *Balak* was taught to me; it might come in handy some day.

It happened some time ago, soon after the war, at the height of

"We've come, Tevel, to beat you up."

the "cosnetution," when *"salvations and consolations"* for the Jews—the pogroms—began, at first in the big cities, later in the small towns. But they never reached me, nor could they have done so. Why? Very simple! When you live for such a long time among Gentiles, down-to-earth Esaus, you are on friendly terms with all the householders of the village. *"Friend of the soul and Father of mercy"*—*"Batiushka** Tevel" was held in high esteem! Advice is needed—"whatever Tevel says," a medicine against a fever—"go to Tevel," a loan without interest—again Tevel. Then why should I think about such things, about pogroms? Nonsense! The peasants themselves had told me many times over that I had nothing to fear, they wouldn't let anything happen to me! But *sure enough*— I'll tell you a fine story, just listen!

One day I came home from Boiberik—I was still hale and hearty then, in full feather, as they say—I still dealt in cheese and butter and various greens, too; I unharnessed my horse, threw it some hay and oats, and all of a sudden—I hadn't even had time to wash my hands before eating—my yard was full of peasants. The whole community had turned out, from the *starosta*—the village elder—Ivan Poperilo, down to the cowherd Trokhim, and they all, to my mind, had a strangely festive look...At first my heart even missed a beat—what sort of a holiday was this all of a sudden? Could they have come to teach me a harsh lesson? But on the other hand, I immediately had a second thought: Feh, Tevye, you should be ashamed of yourself! All your life you've lived here, one Jew among so many Gentiles, in peace and in friendship, and nobody ever did you the slightest harm!...

So I went out into the yard and greeted the crowd warmly: "Welcome, my dear friends, what brings you here? What's the good word? What news have you for me?..!"

The *starosta,* Ivan Poperilo, stepped forward and said, quite openly and without any preliminaries at all:

"We've come, Tevel, to beat you up."

How do you like that? "Beating about the bush" is what we call it, language of implications, that is....

You can imagine how I felt. But to show them my feelings— oh, no, quite the opposite! Tevye is not a little boy...

"*Mazl-tov!* Congratulations, children!" I exclaimed quite cheer-

---

**"Father," also "my dear fellow"—an obsolete respectful form of address; also "Father" in addressing a priest (Russian).—*Tr.*

fully. "But why so late? In other places they've already almost forgotten about such things!..."

Ivan Poperilo, the *starosta,* that is, now said, very earnestly:

"You've got to understand us, Tevel. We're been hesitating, trying to decide whether we should give you a beating or not. All around, in other places, your people are being scourged, so why should we leave you out? So we, the whole village, have decided that we must punish you... But we don't know exactly what to do to you, Tevel: either only knock out all the window-panes and rip up the feather-beds and pillows, or burn down your house and barn, and all your goods and chattels?"

These words really brought a chill to my heart. I looked at these neighbors of mine as they stood there leaning on their long staffs, whispering to each other. It looked as if they really meant business. If so, I thought to myself, as it says in the Book of Psalms: *"The waters are come in even into the soul"*—you are in real trouble, Tevye! Something must be done, but what? *"Do not give Satan an opening."* Eh, Tevye, I said to myself, with the Angel of Death one plays no games, I must think of something to tell them!

Well, my dear friend, I won't go into all the details, but a miracle was apparently ordained and the Almighty kept up my courage; I said to them, to the peasants, good-naturedly:

"Please listen to me, gentlemen! Hear me out, my dear neighbors: since the whole community has decided so, it means that you probably know best that Tevye deserves to have his entire property and chattels ruined by you... Only you must know," said I, "that there is a Higher Power than your village community! Are you aware that there is a God in the world? I do not mean *my* God or *your* God, I am speaking of the God who is everybody's God, who sits up there in Heaven and sees all the meanness and vileness that goes on down here... It may be," I went on, "that He Himself has marked me down to be punished for nothing, innocently, through you, my best friends, but it may also be that, on the contrary, He by no means wants any evil to befall Tevye... Who can know what God wants? Perhaps one of you will undertake to find out?.."

In short, they apparently understood that they wouldn't get far with Tevye; the *starosta,* Ivan Poperilo, addressed me as follows: "It's like this, Tevel. Actually, we have nothing against you. You are a Jew, of course, but not a bad man. However, that is neither here nor there—we must do something to you. The community passed such a decision—we can't go back on it! At least," he said, "we'll smash your windows. This we must do, for it somebody drives through our village, let them see that we've punished you, otherwise we'll be fined..."

Such were his exact words, just as I told them to you, so help me God in all my undertakings! Now I ask you, Mr. Sholom Aleichem, you are, after all, a man who has traveled all over the world—isn't Tevye right when he said that we have a mighty God?..

So that is the end of section *Balak.* Now we'll go back to section *Lech-lecho*—"Get thee out!" This lesson was taught to me not long ago, and in real truth. No fine speeches or moralizations could help me this time. But this story I must tell you in detail, with all the particulars, as you like stories to be told.

It was in the days of Mendel Beiliss—at the time when Mendel Beiliss, our scapegoat, suffered the torments of the damned for someone else's sin, and the whole world was in a turmoil over the affair. One day I was sitting on the *prizba,* lost deep in thought. It was a hot summer day, the sun was baking my head as I meditated: But how, how could this be possible? In our times! Such a wise world! Such great people! And where is God! The ancient Jewish God? Why is He silent? How does He permit such a thing? How, and why, and wherefore!!! Such thoughts about God lead one to ponder over Heavenly things, to speculate: What is *this* world? What is the *next* one? And why doesn't the Messiah come? Eh, I said to myself, wouldn't he do a smart thing, the Messiah, if he came riding along on his white horse right now! Wouldn't that be a wonderful sight! It seems to me that our Jewish folk never needed him so badly as they do today! I don't know about the rich people, the Brodskys, for instance, in Yehupetz, or the Rothschilds in Paris. It may well be that they don't give a hoot for him; but we, the poor Jewish people of Dasrilovka and Mazepovka and Zlodeyevka, and even of Yehupetz, and even of Odessa, are looking forward to his coming. Oh, how we wait for him! Our eyes are practically popping out of our heads from the strain of watching out for his arrival! Our only hope now is that God will perform a miracle and the Messiah will come!..

Meanwhile, as I sat lost in such thoughts, I looked up and—a white horse was approaching, with a rider on its back. The man pulled up his horse right at my gate. Whoa! He got off, hitched the horse to a gatepost and came right up to me.

"Zdravstvui, Tevel!"*

"Zdravstvuite, zdravstvuite, vashe blagorodiye,"** I answered,
quite warmly, while my heart said, *"Haman approacheth"*—you are
looking forward to the Messiah so the *uryadnik*, the village policeman, arrives...

I stood up to greet him, the *uryadnik*, that is:

"Welcome, welcome, be my guest, what's new in the wide
world and what good word will you say to me, Your Honor?" But
my heart was almost springing out of my chest, so anxious was I to
know what his business with me was. However he, the *uryadnik*,
was in no hurry. He lit up a cigarette, blew out the smoke, spat,
and then asked me:

"How much time, for instance, do you need, Tevel, in order to
sell your house and all your belongings?"

I looked at him in amazement: "Why should I sell my house?
In whose, for instance, way is it?" I asked.

"It's in nobody's way," said he, "but I've come to send you
away from the village."

"Is that all, nothing else? For what good deeds? How did
I come to earn such an honor?" I asked.

"It isn't I who am sending you away," he answered. "It's the
guberniya—the provincial authorities."

"The *guberniya?*" I asked. "What has it noticed on me that it
doesn't like?"

"It's not you alone," he said, "and not from here alone—from
all the villages around, from Zlodeyevka, from Grabilovka, from
Kostolomovka***, and even from Anatovka that was up till now a
shtetl but has also become a village. All, all your people will be driven out."

"Even Leizer-Wolf the Butcher?" I asked. "And Naftole-
Gershon the Lame, too? And the Anatovka *shokhet?* And the
Rabbi?"

"All, all of them, everybody!" said he and even made a cutting
gesture with his hand, as if he were holding a knife...

This made me feel a little better. As we say, *"The troubles of the
many are a half-consolation."* However, I was greatly vexed by the

---

*"Hello, Tevye!" (Russian.)—*Tr.*
**"How do you do, Your Honor!" (Russian.)—*Tr.*
***The names of the villages are derived from the Russian words *zlodei*—villain,
grabitel—burglar, and *kostolom*—bone-breaker.—*Ed.*

368

injustice of the thing, and an anger burned in me, so I said to him, to the *uryadnik:*

Tell me, do you at least know, *vashe blagorodiye,* Your Honor, that is, that I have lived in this village much longer than you? Do you know that my father, may he rest in peace, lived right here, in this corner, as did my grandfather, may he rest in peace, and my grandmother, may she rest in peace?" I counted out my whole family by their names, told him where they had lived and where they had died...

He heard me out all right, but when I finished talking he said:

"You're a funny Jew, Tevel, and you've got nine measures of speech in you. Of what good are your stories about your grandmother and grandfather? Let them enjoy their rest in Paradise. And you, Tevel," he went on, "you go pack your bag and baggage and clear out—march-march to Berdichev!"

This made me still angrier: wasn't it enough that he'd brought me such good tidings, this Esau, so he has to pile insult on injury, jeer at me—"march-march to Berdichev!" Let me at least give him a piece of my mind... So I said: "Your honor! In all the years since you became the Chief here, how many times did you hear any neighbor of mine complain that Tevye stole something, robbed him, cheated him, or just took something? You just ask among the householders whether we haven't always been on the friendliest terms? Haven't I come to you, Your Honor, many times to intercede for the peasants, begging you not to be so harsh with them?"

This, apparently, he didn't like! He got to his feet, crumpled his cigarette, threw it away, and said:

"I have no time to engage in idle chatter with you. I received a paper and the rest is none of my business! Here, sign this paper, you're given three days to sell off your belongings and get ready to leave."

I saw that things were bad and nothing could be done, but I said:

"You're giving me three days, that's what you're giving me? For that may you live three years in honor and in riches. May God repay you manifold for the good tidings you've brought me!"

I let him have it, as Tevye knows how! What's the difference, I thought, since I have to leave anyhow. What is there to lose? But had I been at least twenty years younger, and had my Golda, may she rest in peace, been alive, and if I were the same Tevye the Dairyman as in olden times I would have fought until blood flowed! But now? *"What are we and what is our life?"* What am I today and who am I? Only half the man I used to be, a splinter, a broken vessel!

Oh, Lord of the Universe, God Almighty! I thought to myself. Why do You always pick on Tevye? Why don't You sometimes play a game—just for fun—with, say, a Brodsky or a Rothschild? Why aren't they taught the lesson *Lech-lecho*—"Get thee out!"? It would be more to the point with them than with me. First of all, they would get the real taste of what it means to be a Jew. Secondly, let them, too, feel that we have a mighty God....

Oh, well, this is all empty talk. With God you don't argue, and you don't give Him advice on how to run the world. When He said: *"Mine is the Heaven and mine is the Earth,"* it means that He is the Master and we must obey Him. Whatever He says is said!

I went into the house and told my widowed daughter the good news:

"Tzeitl, we are moving out of this village, someplace to a town. We've lived in a village long enough," I said. " *'He who changes his place changes his luck....'* Go and start packing the bedding and bedclothes, the samovar and all the rest of our junk, while I go out to sell the house. A paper has arrived which orders us to clear out of here in three days. Three days from now, not even a whiff of us must remain here!"

These tidings made my daughter burst into tears, and looking at her, her little children, for no reason at all, also began to cry. Our house was full of wailing and laments as if it were *Tishab b'Ab,* the day on which we mourn the destruction of the Temple! This made me good and angry, and I poured the bitterness of my heart out on my poor daughter:

"What do you want from my life?! What's all this blubbering for all of a sudden? Like an old cantor at the first prayer on a fast-day?.. What am I—God's favorite son? Am I the only one to be so honored? Aren't plenty of Jews being driven out of the villages now? You should have heard what the *uryadnik* said! Even your Anatovka that was a *shtetl* up to now has, with God's help, also become a village—probably on account of the Anatovka Jews, so that all of them could be driven out. If that's how it is, then how am I worse than all the other Jews?"

In this manner I tried to comfort her, my daughter, that is. But being a woman, she said:

"Where will we go to, so suddenly? Where will we go to look for towns?"

"Fool!" said I. "When God came to our great-great-grandfather, our Ancestor Abraham, and said to him *'Lech-lecho'*—'Get thee out of thy country!'—did Abraham question Him then, did he ask: 'Where shall I go?' God told him: *'Go unto the land which I will show thee'*—which simply means 'to all the four corners of the world...' We'll go," I said, "wherever our eyes lead us, wherever all the Jews go! Whatever happens to the Children of Israel will happen to Reb Israel. Are you a greater aristocrat than your sister Beilke who was a millionairess? If it suits her now to be with her Padhatzur in America and 'make a living' there, then what we'll have here is good enough for you... Thank the Lord that we at least have the means to move. A little is still left over from before, the cattle and chattels we sold also brought us something, and something will come in from the sale of the house. From a speck and a speck you get a full peck—and *'that too is for the best'!* But even if, God forbid, we had nothing," I said, "we'd still be better off than Mendel Beiliss!"

In a word, I managed to persuade her not to be so obstinate. I made it clear that when an *uryadnik* comes and brings a paper saying you must go you can't be a swine and you have to go. After that I went out into the village to fix up the matter of the house. I went directly to Ivan Poperilo, the *starosta,* the elder, that is, of the village. He was a well-to-do man and had long had his eye on my house. I went into no explanations—I'm no fool—I simply said:

"I want you to know, my dear Ivan, that I'm forsaking you."

"Why so?" he asked.

"I'm moving into a *shtetl.* I want to live among Jews. I'm no longer young. What if, God forbid, I should go and die?.."

"Why can't you die right here? Who is preventing you?"

I thanked him kindly and said: "You'd better do the dying here yourself, you'll find it more handy, while I'd rather go and die among my own people... But my house, Ivan, my house and kitchen garden. To another person I wouldn't sell, only to you."

"How much do you want for your house?"

"How much will you give me?"

"How much," he repeated, "do you want for it?"

Again I asked how much he was willing to pay. So we haggled and bargained and slapped each other's hands until at last we came to terms. I took a good down payment so that he shouldn't, God forbid, change his mind—I was too smart for him. And that was how I sold off in one day—dirt-cheap, of course—my whole property, turned everything into money, and then went to hire a wagon to cart off the remaining odds and ends of poverty.

But what happened after that—only to Tevye do such things happen! Listen attentively, I won't keep you long, I'll tell it to you in two, as they say, words.

Just before it was time to leave, I entered the house. It was no longer a home, it was a ruin. Bare walls that literally shed tears! The floor was strewn with bundles, bundles, and bundles! On the stove sat the cat, a poor, orphaned creature—it looked so mournful, it cut me to the heart and brought tears to my eyes...If I weren't ashamed of showing such weakness before my daughter I would have had me a good cry. After all, as one says, my father's house!.. Here I grew up, this is where I struggled and suffered all my days, and now, suddenly—*Lech-lecho!* Say what you will, it is a sorrowful thing!

But Tevye is not a woman, so I restrained myself and pretended to be in a cheerful mood. I called out to my daughter the widow: "Come here, Tzeitl," I said, "where are you?"

She came out from the other room, her eyes red and her nose swollen. Aha, I said to myself, my daughter has started her lamentations again, like an old woman on the Day of Atonement! These women, I tell you, the least excuse and they cry! Tears come cheap with them.

"Fool!" I said to her. "What are you crying for again? Aren't you silly? Just think of the difference between you and Mendel Beiliss."

But she paid no attention to my words and said:

"*Tateh,* you don't know why I am crying."

"I know the reason very well, why shouldn't I know it? You are crying," said I, "because it grieves you to leave your home. Here you were born, here you grew up, so it hurts you to part from it!.. Believe me, if I weren't Tevye, if I were someone else, I would kiss these bare walls and these empty shelves... I would drop down to this ground!.. I am just as sorry as you are for every last bit! Foolish child! Even this cat—do you see how it sits there on the stove like a poor orphan? A mute tongue, an animal, and yet—what a pity, it is being left behind all alone without a master, *tsar-balekhaim*—a pity for living things..."

"There is someone else who is still more to be pitied," said Tzeitl.

"Namely?"

"Namely," she said, "we are going away and leaving one person here, lonely as a stone."

I couldn't understand what she meant. "What are you babbling about? Where's the fire? What person? What stone?" I asked.

"*Tateh,*" she answered, "I am speaking about our Chava."

When she said these words I felt, I swear, as if I'd been scalded with boiling water or clubbed over the head! My anger aroused, I began to shout:

"Why all of a sudden Chava?! How many times have I told you that Chava was never to be mentioned or remembered!"

Do you think this scared her? Tevye's daughters have a power in them!

"*Tateh,*" she said, "don't get so angry, better remember what you yourself have said many times. You said that it stands written that a human being must have compassion for another human being, as a father has compassion for his child."

How do you like that? Her words exasperated me still more, and I cried:

"You're speaking of compassion? Where was *her* compassion when I cringed like a dog before the priest, his name should be blotted out, when I kissed his feet while she was probably in the next room and heard every word?.. Or where was her compassion when her mother, may she rest in peace, was lying—this shouldn't happen to you—right here on the floor covered with a black cloth? Where was she then? And what about the nights when I couldn't sleep? And the heartache I suffered all the time and still suffer when I remember what she did to me, for whom she exchanged us—where was her pity for me?" I couldn't talk any more, my heart was pounding so...

Perhaps you think that Tevye's daughter found no words to answer me with?

"You yourself, *Tateh,* say that even God Himself forgives those who repent."

"Repentance?" I cried. "Too late! The twig that has once torn itself away from the tree must wither! The leaf that falls must rot, and don't you dare speak to me of this any more—'*Up to here and no further!*'"

In short, when Tzeitl saw that words availed her nothing— Tevye is not a person who can be won over with words—she fell on my neck, began to kiss my hands and cry:

"*Tateh,* may evil befall me, may I die right here on the spot if

373

"Our exile is her exile...Look, Tateh, here is her bundle!"

you repulse her as you did that time in the woods when she stretched out her hands to you and you turned your horse in the other direction and fled!"

"Why are you heckling me so?! What a nuisance, what a misfortune on my head!"

But she wouldn't let go of me, she held me by the hands and went on protesting: "May evil befall me, may I drop dead if you don't forgive her, she is your daughter just the same as I am!"

"What do you want from my life!" I cried. "She is no longer my daughter! She died a long time ago!"

"No," said Tzeitl, "she never died and she is again your daughter as before, because from the very first minute she learned that we were being sent out she told herself that we were *all* being sent out—she, too. Wherever we went—Chava herself told me this— she would also go. Our exile is her exile... Look, *Tateh,* here is her bundle!"

All this my daughter Tzeitl said in one breath, as we recite the names of Haman's ten sons in the *Megilah,* she didn't let me put in a word. She pointed to a bundle tied up in a red shawl, and immediately opened the door to the other room and called: "Chava!"

That is how it was, as I live...

So what shall I tell you, dear friend? She, Chava, just as they write in the story-books, appeared in the doorway, healthy, strong, and as beautiful as before. Hadn't changed the slightest bit, only there was a worried look on her face and her eyes were a little clouded. She held her head up proudly and looked at me—and I at her. Then she stretched out both hands to me, and could utter only one single word, almost in a whisper:

"*Ta-teh...*"

Please forgive me, but when I remember that day tears come to my eyes. But you shouldn't think that Tevye, God forbid, dropped a tear, or showed that he had a soft heart—nonsense! That is, what I then felt deep in my heart—that's something else. You yourself are also a father of children and you know as well as I do the meaning of the words, *"A father hath mercy on his children."* When a child, however it may have sinned, looks right into your heart and soul, and says *"Tateh!"*—come on, just try and drive it away!.. But on the other hand, I recalled the fine trick she had played on me... Fedka Galagan, damn him... and the priest, may his name be

375

forgotten... and my tears... and Golda, may she rest in peace, stretched out on the floor, dead... Oh, no! Tell me yourself, how can one forget, how can one forget such things?.. But on the other hand again... how is it possible! After all, she was my child. *"A father hath mercy on his children."* How can a man be so cruel when God says of Himself that he is a *"long-suffering God and slow to anger..."* Especially since she had repented and wanted to return to her father and to her God!..

What have you to say to this, Mr. Sholom Aleichem? You are, after all, a man who writes books and you give the world advice, so tell me, what should Tevye have done? Should he have embraced her and kissed her, and said to her, as we say on Yom Kippur at Kol Nidre: *"I have forgiven thee in accordance with thy prayers"*— come to me, you are my child? Or perhaps I should have turned the shafts, as I did that time in the woods, and said to her: *"Lech-lecho"*—begone, that is, go back in good health to wherever you've come from?.. No, suppose you were in Tevye's place, tell me frankly, as between good friends, what would you have done? If you cannot answer me at once I'll give you time to think it over... Meanwhile, I must go— my grandchildren are already waiting for me, looking out for their grandfather. You must know that grandchildren are a thousand times more precious than children. *"Children and children's children"*—no small matter!

Please forgive me if I have given you a headache with my talk; at least, you'll have something to write about... And now—good-bye. If God wills it we shall probably meet again some day.

1914

[*Yekhalaklakoys*—"Slippery Places"—is a very short story previously never translated from the Yiddish,* written in 1916, just before that author's death, as an addition to "Get Thee Out!" In it Tevye, meeting the author by chance in a train, elaborates on how he managed to avert the lesson *Balak*—Vengeance—when the peasants came to beat him up or burn down his house. He told them that if they were in the right they would be able to repeat God's own words, hence the story might be called "Tongue-twisters." The following is the last paragraph of the story.]

---

*Our translator, Miriam Katz, apparently overlooked Curt Leviani's translation of this story as "Tevye Reads the Psalms" in Old Country Tales (1966)—The editors.

I have become a wanderer, one day here, another there. Ever since the lesson *Lekh-lekho* was read to me I have been on the move and know no place of rest where I could say, "Here, Tevye, is where you shall remain." Tevye asks no questions—he is told to go, he goes... Today, Mr. Sholom Aleichem, we meet in a train, tomorrow we may find ourselves in Yehupetz, next year—in Odessa, Warsaw, or even America—unless the Almighty looks around and says: "You know what, children? I'll send you down the Messiah!" Oh, how I wish He would play such a trick on us, He, the Ancient Lord of the Universe! And now—farewell. I wish you a happy journey, give my regards to all our people, and tell them not to worry: *Our ancient God still lives!*

1914—1916

The Three Great Novels/Characters

THE ADVENTURES OF MENAKHEM-MENDL

Menakhem-Mendl

Drawing by B.I. Inger

INTRODUCTION TO
MENAKHEM-MENDL

One of Sholem-Aleykhem's epistolary works, *Menakhem-Mendl* consists of a series of letters to and from Menakhem-Mendl in the big cities (Odessa and Kiev) and his wife, Sheyne-Sheyndl, in their *shtetl,* their little town, poor Kasrilevke.*

Menakhem-Mendl is one of a trio of Sholem-Aleykhem's greatest characters, the other two being, of course, Tevye and Motl, the son of Peysi the Cantor.

If Tevye represents the traditional *shtetl* Jew struggling to come to terms with modernity (and also struggling, simply, to survive and provide for his family), Menakhem-Mendl represents a *shtetl* Jew with both feet in the modern world, but one who doesn't really quite understand it, exists on the fringes or margins of it, and is always trying to explain it in his letters back home to the shtetl, to his wife, Sheyne-Sheyndl, who certainly cannot make heads or tails of it (and therein lies much of the humor).

Menakhem-Mendl also represents the struggling East-European Jewish "luft-mentsh," the Jew who "lives on air," who has "no visible means of support," but must twist and turn, run hither and yon, back and forth, up and down, trying to make hay out of nothing.

But he also represents the undying optimism, the refusal to be downcast for long or to give up in the face of defeat of these *"luft-mentshn."* For Menakhem-Mendl goes from one absurd business venture to another, each one more profitless and illusory than the one before. But he's always optimistic at the start. When one of his bubbles bursts, he may be deeply dejected for a time, but he's just as enthusiastic and sure of success at the start of the next venture.

There is a great deal of Sholem-Aleykhem in Menakhem-Mendl, for Sholem-Aleykhem, before he turned to writing as his only source of income, wheeled and dealed on the Kiev stock exchange, where he lost a fortune—his wife's inheritance. He continued to speculate at the exchange even after that—after his mother-in-law had paid off all his debts while he escaped to Paris, Vienna, and Chernovits. His writings and letters often reflect his desire to somehow win back those losses, and there is no doubt he saw his writing as one way to do that. Sholem-Aleykhem himself, judging from his letters and the accounts of others, was always somewhat

---

*Originally Sholem-Aleykhem gave the name Mazepevke to Menakhem-Mendl's *shtetl;* later, probably because his popular Kasrilevke stories made that fictional name so familiar, he changed it to Kasrilevke.

Menakhem-Mendl-ish, always looking forward to his next huge success, one that would surely pay off this time.

Sholem-Aleykhem published the Menakhem-Mendl letters over many years in many scattered places, starting with the first one in 1892, and ending with the last one in 1909. *The Adventures of Menakhem-Mendl* in Tamara Kahana's (his granddaughter's) translation consists of six "books," each of which contains a number of letters ranging from 1 to 24, for a total of 60 letters, the book itself containing, in her translation, 222 pages.

The nine letters included below are from "Book I - London."*

---

*The following passage from Tamara Kahana's translation of *Menakhem-Mendl* may make it easier for the reader to follow Menakhem-Mendl's twists and turns around the stock exchange:

> …a few words about Menahem-Mendl's transactions on the stock exchanges of Odessa and Yehupetz. "London" must be understood as used in the sense of "sterling." The petty money speculators in Odessa were buying and selling Russian rubles (gold) against British pounds (sterling), making their profits out of rises ("hausses") or drops (baisses) later in the day or, by the end of the day, in the value of the currency which they had sold. A "stallage" is an operation by which the speculator sells and buys the money of one country against the money of another country in the hope that by the time the sale or purchase is completed (whether at the end of the day or on any future specified date), the prices will rise or fall, so that he has a profit. A stallage, then, is actually a double operation, consisting of a buy *a la hausse* together with a sale *a la baisse* (from which Menahem-Mendl derives the corrupted terms "hausses" and baisses"). For instance, if the speculator purchases rubles with pounds sterling in the hope that the price of the ruble will go up by the time of delivery, then he is buying *a la hausse;* at the same time (or a little later), fearing that he might have made a bad guess on the rise in the price of the ruble and that it might go down, he protects himself—that is, he hedges, by telling his broker to sell some rubles for him *a la baisse,* so that if indeed the rubles do go down in price by the time of the end of the deal, then he has cut his losses or even managed to make a small profit, depending on whether the two differences came out in his favor or against him. But the main thing to remember is that if the terms and operations seem confusing, *they were certainly confusing to Menahem-Mendl himself!*

Book I: London

THE STOCK EXCHANGE IN ODESSA

3.

Menahem-Mendl from Odessa to his wife,
Sheineh-Sheindl, in Kasrilevka

To my dear, wise, and modest helpmeet, Sheineh-Sheindl, long may she live!

Firstly, I am come to inform you that I am, by the grace of God, well and in good cheer. May the Lord, blessed be His name, grant that we always hear from one another none but the best, the most comforting, and the happiest of tidings—amen.

And Secondly, I want you to know that it does not surprise me in the least that you cannot make head or tail of London. Because if experienced merchants, Jews with long beards, get snarled up in it, what can one expect of a woman? I shall therefore try to make it clear to you so that you'll understand exactly what it's all about. You see, London is a very delicate kind of merchandise. It is sold neither by the yard nor by weight, but on a word of honor. What's more, you cannot see it with your eyes. It changes every minute: Today it's expensive, tomorrow it's cheap; today it's a hausse, tomorrow it's a baisse; today it's high, tomorrow it's low. That is to say, over there in Berlin our ruble either rises to the sky or else plunges to the ground. It all depends on Berlin—whatever Berlin says goes. The exchange keeps swinging up and down like mad; telegrams fly back and forth, Jews scramble about like at a fair, buying and selling, rushing, pushing, shouting, making business and getting rich—and me in the middle. There is such a noise and tumult, it can shatter your eardrums. For example, only yesterday I made a little stallage which cost me a fifty, and today, exactly at noon, it evaporated like last winter's snow. But I don't suppose you even know what it means to make a stallage, so it must be explained to you. For example, you put up fifty for a day; the other fellow "sets the exchange," and you have the right to choose the kind of stallage you want—two hausses or two baisses. Or you can simply mark time, in which case the other fellow buys blind until the "close" (that's what we call twilight here in Odessa, which is just about the time that evening prayers are said in Kasrilevka). And if the exchange drops, you can kiss your fifty good-bye—and that's what is called making a stallage. But you are not to worry, my dearest wife! It's no great shakes to lose a fifty. The good Lord willing, everything will turn out for the best, and then, please God, the right moment will come, and I'll make money, and maybe even a lot of it!

And as for what you say about Uncle Menasheh's promissory notes, you are making a big mistake. Uncle Menasheh's sun has not gone down yet, and he is still a good risk. If I wanted to make a small reduction, I could find plenty of customers. But I don't want to. If I need any cash, I can get plenty. All I have to do is sell a couple of hausses or a couple of baisses. But I don't feel like doing that either. I'll do better by buying another stallage. The more stallages, the better. When you go to bed with a stallage, you sleep all the sweeter. And since I am pressed for time, I must cut this short. Please God, in my next letter I'll write you everything in detail. For the time being, may the Lord grant health and success,

From me, your husband,
Menahem-Mendl

Just remembered! You asked where I'm staying and what I'm eating. To tell you the truth, my dearest wife, I myself don't know where I am. The city of Odessa is terribly big, everything is expensive, and here the houses are as tall as the sky—you have to climb an iron staircase for half an hour before you reach your lodging, which is right under the clouds, and the window is a tiny one, like in jail. I'm happy to see daybreak when I can escape from this jail into Greek Street, and that's where I always eat, standing up. That is to say, you grab whatever comes your way, because who's got the time to sit down properly to eat when you have constantly to watch the Berlin exchange? However, fruit is very cheap here. You don't eat grapes here like in Kasrilevka, where you eat them only on New Year's when you say grace: here everybody eats grapes every single day, right in the middle of the street, and nobody is ashamed of it.

As above

4.

Sheineh-Sheindl from Kasrilevka to her husband, Menahem-Mendl, in Odessa

To my dear, esteemed, renowned, and honored husband, the wise and learned Menaham-Mendl, may his light shine forever.

In the first place, I wanted to let you know that we are all, praise the Lord, perfectly well, and may we hear the same from you, please God, and never anything worse.

In the second place, I am writing to say that I believe you must have gone out of your mind. May I be spared ever seeing head or tail of your wonderful Odessa, if I can make head or tail of all your chatter about stallages and baggages, hausses and baisses and all other messes, the devil knows what they are! And fifties are flying out of your hands like hot doughnuts. Money seems to mean nothing to you; it's just dirt! I'm sure anybody can bathe in gold if they engage in such business deals! Even if you were to chop my head off, I still wouldn't understand what kind of merchandise it can be if it's invisible. A cat in a sack?... Listen to me, Mendl, I don't like it. In my father's home, I wasn't accustomed to such airy affairs, and may the Almighty continue to preserve me from them. As Mother says, God bless her, "From the air, all one can catch is a cold...." You write: "When you go to bed with a baggage, you sleep all the sweeter...." Whoever goes to bed with a baggage? What strange expressions you use—they sound Turkish to me! And as for what you say about cashing in Uncle Menasheh's notes, if I refuse to believe you, nobody will consider me an infidel. As Mother says, God bless her, "Until you count your pennies twice, you can never be sure...." You know something, Mendl? Listen to me, to your wife—finish off with this Odessa of yours, and come home to Kasrilevka! Have you got fifteen hundred in your pocket? Does Father, God bless him, give us a place to live in? Are there shops for rent? So what else do you want! Why must I be on the tip of everyone's tongue and have my enemies whisper that you've run away from me to Odessa and abandoned me, may you never live to see that day! In the meantime, your Odessa can answer for the sins of our Kasrilevka, with all your tall houses and iron stairs that have to be climbed like mad! Is it worth it, to spoil your stomach for Odessa's sake? What's all the excitement about! Because grapes are terribly cheap? Do you have to gorge on grapes—are plums poison? This year we have plenty of plums, a penny a bucket! But you don't seem to care very much about what goes on at home. You don't even ask what the children are doing. It looks as if you've quite forgotten that you are father to three little ones, God bless them. As Mother says, "Out of sight, out of mind...." You can burst if you will, but she is always right. Meanwhile, be well, and the best of luck to you, which is the heartfelt wish of your really devoted wife,

Sheineh-Sheindl

5.

Menahem-Mendl from Odessa to his wife,
Sheineh-Sheindl, in Kasrilevka

To my dear, wise, and modest helpmeet, Sheineh-Sheindl, long may she live!

Firstly, I am come to inform you that I am, by the grace of God, well and in good cheer. May the Lord, blessed be His name, grant that we always hear from one another none but the best, the most comforting, and the happiest of tidings—amen.

And Secondly, I want you to know that just now there is a terrific upswing of baisses, I have therefore stuffed myself up with London, and I've made a stock of seventeen baisses and eight stallages. Besides, since I'm to get several hundred rubles in differences, I'll be able to make some more baisses, please God. If, my dearest wife, you could only see how business is conducted here on a word of honor, you'd immediately understand what is Odessa; a nod of the head is as good as a signature to a contract. I go for a stroll along Greek Street, walk into a "cafe," sit down at a small table and order a glass of tea or coffee or something. Up comes one broker, then another, and then a third. There's no need of a contract or a receipt, not even pen and ink! Every broker carries a little

384

notebook and a pencil. He takes out his notebook and writes that I'm down for two baisses with him, and all I have to do is pay him several shekels. It's a pleasure! And a few hours later when, God willing, the news arrives from Berlin about the rate of exchange, that very same broker comes running and gives you a twenty-five. A little later, when you already know the opening price, he forces a fifty on you, and still later, at the close, it grows to a hundred, please God. And sometimes it can be two hundred, and even three hundred—why not? That's the stock exchange for you! The stock exchange is a game of chance, a matter of luck.

And as for what you write about not believing in Uncle Menasheh's promissory notes, I have news for you: I've already found customers for them. If you want proof, here it is: Where else did I get the money for so many baisses and stallages? By the way, it is stallage and not baggage as you call it. And since you ask how one can go to bed with a stallage, I can see that you still don't understand what it's all about. A stallage is a piece of paper on which the other fellow writes that when the "ultimo" (that is, the end of the month) comes, he is obliged to give to you—or perhaps the other way around, to take from you—a certain number of pounds according to a certain exchange. That is to say the choice is up to you: If you feel like it, you pay; if you don't feel like it, you receive. Now do you understand the science of stallages? If, please God, there are strong "variations" in London, and for example, the newspapers start talking about war, then the russian ruble takes a flying dive into the depths of the earth, and London gives a leap till you can't see it above the clouds. Only last week they were saying about the English Queen that she wasn't in the best of health. Immediately the Russian ruble dropped and stallages jumped to the roof. Now the newspapers are saying she is feeling better, so the Russian ruble is up again, and today you can get as many stallages as you want. In short, you are not to worry, my dearest wife, for, God willing, as we say in Odessa, "Everything is going to be Class A"! And since I am pressed for time, I must cut this short. Please God, in my next letter I'll write you everything in detail. For the time being, may the Lord grant health and success. Please greet the children, God bless them, and give my kindest regards to everyone, to old and young, to big and small.

From me, your husband,
Menahem-Mendl

385

Just remembered! It is so hot in our Odessa, that during the day you sizzle, and at night you melt like wax. Therefore, as soon as it gets dark, the city empties completely. Everybody goes away to the springs—either the Big Spring or the Little Spring. There you can have everything your heart desires: You can bathe in the sea, and you can listen to music free of charge, without paying a penny!

As above

6.

*Sheineh-Sheindl from Kasrilevka to her
husband, Menahem-Mendl, in Odessa*

To my dear, esteemed, renowned, and honored husband, the wise and learned Menahem-Mendl, may his light shine forever.

In the first place, I want to let you know that we are all, praise the Lord, perfectly well, and may we hear the same from you, please God, and never anything worse.

In the second place, I am writing to say that I am again having trouble with my teeth, may all your wonderful Odessa music makers, big and little, enjoy such a pain! I have to suffer here from toothache and worry myself sick over his children, and he—nothing at all! He is living happily ever after in Odessa; he is riding around on springs, bathing in big and little fountains, while musicians play for him! What else does he want! As Mother says, God bless her, "I'd have him ride on a broom, not on springs...." Make up your mind! If you are a merchant and if you are dealing in that wonderful merchandise called London, then attend to your business, and not to the English Queen! Better think of your wife—you've got a wife till a hundred and twenty years, and three little children, God bless them. As Mother says, "Think of your own and yourself—leave the rest on the shelf...." And as for all those successes you write me about, I must confess they make my head spin. Somehow, kill me, but I still can't believe that hundreds of rubles are popping straight into your pockets. Is it some magic over there or sorcery, or a spell, or something? Better take care that with all your triumphs you do not touch a penny of the dowry money, because if you should, you won't hear the last of it from Mother, God bless her! You'd think he could give a thought to what's needed at home, at least. You know well enough that I can't possibly do without a silk coat and some serge for a dress and two pieces of linen cloth. I have to remind him of every little thing—the poor wretch has lost his memory; you'd think his brains have dried out! As Mother says, God bless her, "If a dig in the ribs doesn't work, try a brick...." Which is the heartfelt wish of your really devoted wife,

Sheineh-Sheindl

7.

Menahem-Mendl from Odessa to his wife,
Sheineh-Sheindl, in Kasrilevka

To my dear, wise, and modest helpmeet, Sheineh-Sheindl, long may she live!

Firstly, I am come to inform you that I am, by the grace of God, well and in good cheer. May the Lord, blessed be His name, grant that we always hear from one another none but the best, the most comforting and the happiest of tidings—amen.

And Secondly, I want you to know that I've made very good headway. That is to say, I'm up to my neck in baisses, and I am now very busy with London. This means that in one shot I hand out, or receive, as much as ten thousand pounds, twenty thousand pounds—on an "option," of course. Already I have access to all the business offices and am even privileged to sit in Café Fanconi, side by side with all the big speculators at the white marble tables, and order a portion of ice cream, because in our Odessa it is the custom that as soon as you sit down, up comes a man dressed in a coat with a tail and orders you to order ice cream. And since you cannot be an exception, you have to order it. And when you finish your portion of ice cream, he orders you to order another portion—if you don't, you're not allowed to remain. Then you have to loiter in the streets, which isn't quite nice for a speculator, and besides, there's a policeman in the street who looks for loiterers ... however, since Jews do have to loiter, we try to evade him. We play hide-and-seek with him and generally manage to fool him. But if he succeeds in catching anyone, he pounces on his precious prey and takes the treasure straight to the police station, as one might say, "Look, I've brought you a Jew...."

And as for your saying that you don't believe in my "variations" and "differences," it only goes to show that you're weak in politics. For instance, in our Cafe Fanconi, there is a man we call Gambetta. Day in, day out, he talks politics and nothing but politics! In a thousand ways he can prove to you that there's a smell of war in the air. He says that every single night he can hear cannon shots—not here, but over there, in France. The French, he says will never forget that man Bismarck as long as they live. He says, war simply must break out soon—it can't be otherwise. If you listen to Gambetta preach, you feel you have to sell everything you own, down to your coat, in order to buy up stallages and baisses, baisses without end!

And as for what you write about me buying you a coat, well, my dearest wife, I've got an eye on something much better for you—namely, a golden watch with a medallion, a golden chain, and a brooch, and I also saw some bracelets in one shopwindow, as a matter of fact, not far from Fanconi's, and I tell you, they're Class A! And since I am pressed for time, I must cut this short. Please God, in my next letter I'll write you everything in detail. For the time being, may the Lord grant health and success.

From me, your husband,
Menahem-Mendl

Just remembered! There is such prosperity here, knock on wood, and people are so busy doing business that one loses sight of Sabbaths and holidays. For me, of course, Sabbath always is Sabbath. It can rain stones from the sky, but on Sabbath I've got to drop into the synagogue. The Odessa synagogue is something to see. First of all, it is called the Choir Synagogue because on top of it there's a round cap instead of a roof, and it hasn't got an East Wall. That is to say, everybody sits facing the cantor. And as for the cantor (Pinney is his name, and what a voice!), it's true he doesn't wear a beard, but he cannot be compared to that old drone of yours, Cantor Moishe Dovid! You ought to hear him pray—it can drive you out of your wits! As for his Sabbath day psalm, it is worthwhile buying a ticket to hear it. All the little choirboys stand around him in their little prayer shawls—what a pleasure! If Sabbath were to fall twice a week, I'd go twice a week to listen to Pinney. I cannot understand the Jews of Odessa—why don't they go to the synagogue to pray? And even those who do go to pray don't pray; they sit like puppets with their fat and shiny faces; they wear top hats on their heads; their prayer shawls are small and skimpy, and—shsh!—nobody even opens his mouth. And if some Jew should venture to pray a little louder, up comes the beadle with shiny buttons and says, "Quiet, please!" Funny Jews in Odessa!

As above.

8.

*Sheineh-Sheindl from Kasrilevka to
her husband, Menahem-Mendl, in Odessa*

To my dear, esteemed, renowned, and honored husband, the wise and learned Menahem-Mendl, may his light shine forever.

In the first place, I want to let you know that we are all, praise the Lord, perfectly well, and may we hear the same from you, please God, and never anything worse.

In the second place, I am writing to say, my dearest husband, that I cannot understand what's so wonderful about having to sit at marble tables in Franconi's, may she burn to an ash, and gorge on what-do-you-call-it from morning till night. Just to throw money away? And who is that madman who wanders around your Odessa dreaming about cannon shots—may he get shot full of holes himself! Wars—is that what he hankers after? As Mother says, God bless her, "What's blood to you is water to him...." Oh, so you've seen golden watches and bracelets in Odessa shopwindows! You can save them for your grandmother! What earthly use to me are presents which you see through windowpanes, Mendl? As Mother says, God bless her, "Pancakes seen in a dream aren't

389

pancakes, only a dream...." Better walk straight into a shop and buy me some linen for bedsheets and pillowcases, and a couple of woolen blankets, and some table silver for the house, and whatnot. Just imagine, Blumch-Zlateh finds it necessary to stick her nose up at me. He head is swollen twice its size with pride, may she swell till she bursts! And for why? Because she is wearing a string of pearls around her neck, may it choke her! Well, she has it sweet with her husband! Some people have all the luck; it's only me who was born in such a dark and miserable hour that I've got to remind him of every little thing! Try to imagine that you are spending your money on another baisse, another mess, and all those other things which only the devil knows what they are and which I cannot even pronounce. I keep telling him: Sell whatever you have and count your change—so he goes and buys more! What are you afraid of? That you won't get any of this merchandise later on? I can see it all very plain now—what kind of business you're doing and what kind of town Odessa is, where a Sabbath is not a Sabbath, and a holiday is not a holiday, and where the cantor struts around with a shaved chin, may all my sins fall on his head! To my mind, from such people and from such a town one ought to run away like from a putrid swamp. But there he is, wallowing in it without any intention of budging. As Mother says, God bless her, "The worm inside the radish thinks there's no sweeter place...." And so, my dearest husband, I am writing you to think over carefully what you are doing and to stop frisking around your sweet Odessa, may it burn to an ash, which is the heartfelt wish of your really devoted wife,

Sheineh-Sheindl

Oh, yes! Please tell me, Mendl, who is Franconi, with whom you seem to be spending all your days and nights? Is it a he or a she?...

9

Menahem-Mendl from Odessa to his wife,
Sheineh-Sheindl, in Kasrilevka

To my dear, wise, and modest helpmeet, Sheineh-Sheindl, long
may she live!

Firstly, I am come to inform you that I am, by the grace of
God, well and in good cheer. May the Lord, blessed be His name,
grant that we always hear from one another none but the best, the
most comforting, and the happiest of tidings—amen.

And Secondly, I want you to know that already there is a smell
of heavy money in the air! If the ultimo passes without a hitch, I'll
be on the top rung, God willing. Then I'll cash in all my "differences," start out for home and, please God, take you to Odessa
with me. We'll rent an apartment in Richelieu Street, buy some
nice furniture, and start the kind of life one can have only in our
Odessa. In the meantime, I'm having a little trouble with my
stomach, may you be spared the same. It looks as if all that ice
cream has upset it.... Now, when I come to Franconi's I don't eat
ice cream anymore. So what do I do? I order a drink which you sip
through a straw; it's sweet and a little bitter all in one, it tastes like
salty licorice, and you can't possibly manage more than two or, at
the most, three glasses of it at a sitting. So the rest of the time you
have to go loiter outside and have dealings with the policeman,
which isn't at all pleasant. He's had an eye on me for some days,
but the Lord has been good, and I've managed to evade him every
time and to hide from him. What doesn't a Jew do for a living? If,
with the help of heaven, the "settlement" goes without a hitch, I'll
buy you double of everything you want, please God, more than
you ever dreamed of.

And when you say that Gambetta is a madman, you are making a mistake; he is simply rather quick-tempered. Heaven preserve
anyone from saying something about politics that he doesn't fancy!
Then he is capable of tearing you limb from limb. He claims that
something is liable to explode any day now, and, he says, the mere
fact that at the moment everything is suddenly quiet certainly
points to war. "There is always," he says, "a lull before a storm...."
Yesterday I had a chance to sell several baisses, as well as two or
three stallages, and to make a good profit, but Gambetta wouldn't

let me do it. He said,"I'll break your head if at a time like this you let the tiniest bit of merchandise slip out of your fingers!" The hour is close, he says, when a fifty-ruble stallage will be worth two hundred, three hundred, five hundred, a thousand—and why not even two thousand?... If it is as Gambetta says—or even half of what he says—I'm bound to get rich! Right after the settlement, I hope, please God, to switch back to hausses, start buying up rubles, and give London a fine runaround. I'll show them the difference between London and a ruble! And since I am pressed for time, I must cut this short. Please God, in my next letter I'll write you everything in detail. For the time being, may the Lord grant health and success.

From me, your husband,
Menahem-Mendl.

Just remembered! As for what you ask about Fanconi (not "Franconi" as you say), it's neither a he nor a she. It is simply a coffeehouse where you drink coffee, eat ice cream, and deal in London. I wish I had at least half the money that changes hands there in a single day!

As above.

11.

Menahem-Mendl from Odessa to his wife,
Sheineh-Sheindl, in Kasrilevka

To my dear, wise, and modest helpmeet, Sheineh-Sheindl, long may she live!

Firstly, I am come to inform you that I am, by the grace of God, well and in good cheer. May the Lord, blessed be His name, grant that we always hear from one another none but the best, the most comforting, and the happiest of tidings—amen.

And Secondly, I want you to know that the ultimo arrived and turned everything upside down, may heaven preserve us. The great variations, which I awaited like the Messiah's coming, went up in smoke. Bismarck, they say, caught a cold, so a terrible panic started up in politics, and nobody knows what's what. London is now actually worth its weight in gold, and our ruble has actually dropped down into the deepest cellar, and a terrible baisse has set in! So you're sure to ask what happened to all my baisses and my stallages? The answer is that baisses aren't baisses, and stallages aren't stallages—nobody wants to take; nobody wants to give—and what are you going to do about it? As in spite, I got my affairs entangled with little people who were choked by the first squeeze. In a word, this is an earthquake, a disaster, a catastrophe—you wouldn't recognize the place! Oh, had I made an about-face in time! But who can be a prophet? All the people are scurrying around like poisoned rats. There's a panic everywhere. Everyone is yelling, London! Where is my London? Give me London, London! But where is London? What is London? Slaps are flying, blows, insults, curses—and me in the middle. The point is there is no London and there never was!

In short, my dearest wife, everything looks dark and bitter. I've lost everything I made—profits, my capital, and the jewelry I bought you; I even had to strip off my Sabbath coat and pawn it—everything has gone down the drain.... You can't imagine the state I'm in, and I'm so homesick I am wasting away! A hundred times a day I curse the day I was born. Better to have broken both my legs before I ever came to Odessa, where a man counts for nothing. You can drop dead walking in the middle of the street, and nobody will even stop to look. How many brokers made a living around me and enjoyed plenty of tidbits on my account! And today not one of them even recognizes me! Before, I had a name here—they called me the Rothschild of Kasrilevka—and today they are making fun of me—those very same brokers! To hear them talk, I don't understand a thing about this business. "London," they say, "is an art that has to be understood." Where were they before, those sages? Things have come to such a pass that nobody talks about me anymore—I might as well be dead! And I wish I were dead rather than face such disgrace. And for spite, that cursed Gambetta sits there and doesn't stop dinning politics in my ear. "Ah," he says, "didn't I keep saying baisses?" "What good," say I, "are your baisses when nobody gives me London!" He laughs and says, "Whose fault is it? One has to understand the stock exchange. And if one doesn't know how to deal in London," he says, "one should stick to rags and old bottles...." I tell you, my dearest wife, I am so sick of Odessa, its stock exchange, its

Fanconi, and all those petty people, I'd be glad to run away anywhere! And since I am pressed for time, I must cut this short. Please God, in my next letter I'll write you everything in detail. For the time being, may the Lord grant health and success. Greet all the children, God bless them, and give my kindest regards to your father and mother, to old and young, to big and small.

From me, your husband,
Menahem-Mendl

Just remembered! There is a peculiar custom in this Odessa City—whenever anybody needs help, he doesn't go to a neighbor, a relative, or a friend, as we do in Kasrilevka, for example. Not because it's shameful, but simply because you know beforehand that you won't get even a fig, and that's all there is to it. So what does one do in time of need? They fixed up a place called pawnshop which gives you as much money as you want, so long as you bring them good security—it may be gold; it may be silver; it may be copper, or a suit, or a samovar, or a chair—even if you bring a cow, you can raise money on it! The only snag is that they put a very low value on anything you bring—less than nothing. On the other hand, there is one advantage: The interest they take is so nice and fat that it eats up your capital. So every two weeks they hold an "auction." That means, they sell all the securities which have not been redeemed, and people can get wonderful bargains and make a pretty penny on them. If I could lay my hand on some money now, I'd take a stab at doing business with a pawnshop, maybe get back what I lost, and perhaps even make a bit extra.... But what's the use? Without money, one should not be born into this world, and if one does get born, it is better to die.... I cannot write anymore. Let me know how you are feeling and what the children are doing, God bless them, and give my kindest greetings to your father and mother.

As above.

12.

*Sheineh-Sheindl from Kasrilevka to her
husband, Menahem-Mendl, in Odessa*

To my dear, esteemed, renowned, and honored husband, the wise and learned Menahem-Mendl, may his light shine forever.

In the first place, I want to let you know that we are all, praise the Lord, perfectly well, and may we hear the same from you, please God, and never anything worse.

In the second place, I am writing to say, you foolish simpleton, just look and see what you've done! What ill wind has driven you to Odessa? What was it that smelled so good to you there? Roast pigeons—is that what you were longing for? London! Ice cream! Vinegar and licorice! The moment you saw yourself getting stuck with London, why didn't you settle on a percentage in time and save at least part of your goods, you donkey? The way merchants do! And why don't you appeal to arbitrators, to a rabbi? God in heaven—ultimo—what has that got to do with business? You bought merchandise, didn't you? Well, what happened to the merchandise—where did it go? What a calamity! But didn't I feel it in my bones that nothing good would come of Odessa, may it burn to an ash? I keep writing to him: Leave that town, Mendl, send it to blazes together with London, and may a plague sweep over it! I say to him: Run, Mendl, run! As Mother says, "The higher the fool, the greater the fall...." But no, he won't listen to me, because who am I? I am Sheineh-Sheindl, worse luck! I am not Blumeh-Zlateh. Oh, my mother is really wise! How many times did she say that a clever woman mustn't give her husband too much rope, that a wife must keep such a firm hold on her husband that never for a moment does he forget he's got a wife! But what am I to do if it isn't my nature? I wasn't born coarse like Blumeh-Zlatch. I can't nag or scold or shout or curse like she! If you had Blumeh-Zlateh for a wife, may she never live to see the day, you'd find out quick enough what the Almighty can do!

And as for what you say about dying, you sage, it only shows what a dolt you are. Man doesn't live by his own will, nor does he die by his own will. What if one does lose a whole dowry—is that sufficient reason for a hasty act? You simpleton, where is it written that Menahem-Mendl has to get rich? Isn't Menahem-Mendl with money the same as Menahem-Mendl without money? Fool, can one defy God? Don't you see, He was against it? So stop squirming! Let the money be your scapegoat forever! Just imagine that robbers attacked you in the middle of a forest, or what if you fell sick, God forbid, and the dowry went to the devil on medicines? The main thing—don't behave like a woman, Mendl! Put your trust in the Eternal One. He is your staff and your sustenance. Come home and, please God, you'll be a welcome guest among your children....

I am sending you some money for traveling expenses, but see to it, Mendl, that you don't get involved in any deals, and don't buy rags and old bottles—that would be the last straw! As soon as you receive this letter with the money, for heaven's sake, hurry up and say good-bye forever to your Odessa, and the moment you leave that town, may it catch fire at all four ends, and may the fire burn and smoulder and splutter and crackle and rage till not a single stick or stone is left, not even an ash, which is the heartfelt wish of your really devoted wife,

Sheineh-Sheindl

The Three Great Novels/Characters

INTRODUCTION TO

ADVENTURES OF MOTL THE CANTOR'S SON

One of Sholem-Aleykhem's most endearing works is *Motl Peysi dem Khazn's (Motl, Peysi the Cantor's Son,* or, as Tamara Kahana, his granddaughter, translated the title for her English edition, *Adventures of Mottel the Cantor's Son).*

Motl, alongside Tevye and Menakhem-Mendl, stands as one of Sholem-Aleykhem's three greatest characters.

Sholem-Aleykhem himself, as is evident from his letters (see "Letter to Byalik," for example) and from his autobiography *(From the Fair),* had a playful, childlike quality in his character. He often saw the world in a bemused, whimsical way—the way a child might.

In *Motl,* he is expert at showing us the world from a boy's-eye-view. To a child, what is to an adult a tragic event, can often be a source of fun and adventure. If the breadwinner of the family must go out on strike, to Motl that's fun. Even becoming an orphan has its up side: "Mir iz gut, ikh bin a yosem!" says Motl ("Things are great for me—I'm an orphan!").

The structure of the Motl stories is, again, episodic. Sholem-Aleykhem published them over many years, a piece at a time in newspapers and in journals, starting with the first series of stories in 1907 and the second and last series in 1916, with Motl and his family in America. It was first published in book form in its entirety in two volumes in 1920 in New York.

The last thing Sholem-Aleykhem was working on a few days before he died in May of 1916 was a chapter of *Motl;* he never finished it.

We have chosen for this anthology Chapters 2 and 6. (*Adventures of Mottel the Cantor's Son* in Tamara Kahana's translation contains 39 such chapters and comprises 224 pages.) The chapters chosen contain the well-known "It's Grand to Be an Orphan" segment and a typical Motl kind of escapade which turns out badly but is lots of fun as it runs its course: a business venture for Motl and his brother Eli—the making and the selling of *kvas,* translated below as "apple cider" (although the dictionary tells us *kvas* is "a Russian fermented drink resembling sour beer, made from rye, barley, or other grains").

II. IT'S GRAND TO BE AN ORPHAN!

1

Never do I remember having been such a grand and important person as now. What is it all about? Well, as you know, my father, Peissi the Cantor, died on the first day of *Shevuoth,* and I was left an orphan.

From the first day after *Shevuoth,* we began to recite *Kaddish,* that is, my brother Eli and I. It was Eli who taught me to say it.

My brother Eli is a devoted brother but a poor teacher. He is an irritable fellow. He smacks me. He opens the prayer book, sits down with me and starts the lesson.

"Yisgadal, v'yiskadash shmei rabo..." he wants me to know it all by heart from the very start. He goes over it with me once, and once again, from beginning to end, and then he makes me say it all by myself. I say it all by myself, but somehow it doesn't turn out right. I manage about half of it pretty well, but in the middle I get stuck. Eli treats me to a dig of his elbow and says that it's obvious my head is somewhere out of doors (how did he guess?) or somewhere with the calf (he might have read my thoughts!). Still, he doesn't lose hope and repeats it with me again. I manage another bit, and not a step farther. He takes hold of my ear and says that father ought to rise up and see what a son he has!

"Then I wouldn't have to say *Kaddish!*" I answer and catch a sound slap on my right cheek from Eli's left hand. Mother gets wind of this and reads him a sermon: he mustn't hit me because I'm an orphan.

"God preserve you, what are you doing! Whom are you hitting! Have you forgotten that the child is an orphan?"

I sleep with Mother on father's bed—the only piece of furniture left in the house. She gives me practically all of the quilt.

"Cover yourself," she says, "and fall asleep, my poor orphan. There's nothing to eat."

I cover myself, but I don't sleep. I repeat the *Kaddish* by heart. I don't have to go to school; I don't have to study; I don't have to pray; I don't have to sing. I'm free of everything.

It's grand to be an orphan!

398

Congratulate me! I know all of the *Kaddish* by heart. Even the *Special Kaddish*. In the synagogue, I stand on a bench and rattle off the *Kaddish*. I have a good singing voice, too—inherited from father, as you know—a real soprano. All the boys gather around me and envy me. Women weep. Men give me pennies.

When the time comes for the *Special Kaddish*, rich Yossi's son, Henich-with-the-Eye (a terribly envious boy), sticks his tongue out at me. He's trying to make me laugh—simply dying to do so. But, just in spite, I won't laugh! When Aaron the beadle catches Henich at it, he takes him by the ear and conducts him to the door. Good for him! since I have to say *Kaddish* in the morning and at night, I don't have to go to Hersh Ber the Cantor any longer and I don't have to fuss with his Dobtzie. I am free.

I spend the whole day at the river fishing and swimming. I learned how to fish all by myself. If you wish, I can teach you. You take your shirt off and tie the sleeves in a knot; then you slow-ly walk into the water until you're up to your neck in it. You have to walk a pretty long way for that. When you feel your shirt get-ting heavy, that's a sign it's full. Then you climb out as fast as you can, shake out all the grass and mire and examine your catch. Little frogs often become entangled in the grass—these you throw back into the water. You've got to be merciful to animals!

In the thick mire, you may occasionally find a leech. Leeches are money; for ten leeches you can get three coppers—a penny and a half—which is not to be sneered at. You needn't look for any fish. Once upon a time, there used to be fish here, but no longer. I'm not interested in fish. I'm happy if I find leeches. Leeches aren't to be found everywhere, either. This summer, there hasn't been a single leech!... How my brother Eli discovered that I go fishing—I can't imagine. He almost tore one of my ears off thanks to my fishing. Luckily, Fat Pessie, our neighbor, caught him at it. A mother couldn't have defended her own child as she did me.

"So that's how you beat up orphans!"

My brother Eli is shamed and lets go my ear. Everyone takes my part. It's grand to be an orphan!

Our neighbor, Fat Pessie, has fallen in love with me. She presses mother to let me live with her.

"What do you care?" she argues. "Twelve go to my table—so he'll be the thirteenth!" She wouldn't have persuaded mother, if my brother Eli had not stepped in.

"Who'll see to it that he says *Kaddish?*"

"I'll see to it myself. Have you anything else against me?"

Pessie is far from wealthy. Her husband is a bookbinder and is called Moishe. He has a reputation for being a first-class workman. But that isn't enough. One's got to have luck. So says Pessie to mother. Mother agrees with her. She says that even to be unlucky, one must have luck! She takes me for an example: here I am—an orphan—and everybody wants me. There are some who even want to take me for good, but her enemies won't live to see the day when she'll give me away! So says my mother and weeps. She has a conference with my brother Eli.

"What do you think? Should he stay with Pessie for a while?"

My brother Eli is a grown-up already, else he wouldn't be consulted. He fondles his clean, hairless face with one of his hands, just as if he had a beard, and talks like a grown-up.

"Why not? As long as he doesn't do any mischief."

So it's decided that for a time I'm to live with our neighbor Pessie on condition that I do no mischief. According to them, everything is mischief! To tie a piece of paper on a cat's tail in order to make her spin is mischief. To bang a stick on a priest's fence and make all the dogs run out is mischief. To pull the stopper out of Leibkeh the water-carrier's barrel and make most of the water flow out is mischief!...

"*Your* luck that you are an orphan!" says Leibkeh to me, "else I'd break you, hand and foot. You may believe that I'm not lying!"

I believe him. I know that no one will touch me because I am an orphan.

It's grand to be an orphan!

Our neighbor, Pessie, may she forgive me, has told a big lie. She said that twelve go to her table. According to my reckoning, I am the fourteenth. She evidently forgot to count blind uncle Boruch.

Maybe she didn't include him with the eaters because he's very old and has no teeth to chew with. I won't argue the point. It's true that he can't chew, but, on the other hand, he gulps like a goose. Besides, he grabs. Everybody grabs. Their grabbing is simply extraordinary—unnatural. I grab, too, but they hit me for it. They kick me under the table with their feet. More than from anyone do I catch it from Vashti. Vashti is a bandit. His real name is Hershel, but because he has a boil on his forehead, he's been nicknamed *Vashti.* Everyone here has both a name and a nickname: "Barrel," "Tomcat," "Stork," "Wild Ox," "Mumble-Jumble," "Give-Me-More," "Smear-With-Butter"...

Don't be surprised—there is a reason for every nickname. Pinney is called *Barrel* because he's as fat and round as a barrel. Velvel is as black as a tomcat. Chaim is wild; that's why he's called Wild Ox. Mendel has a pointed nose—so he's a stork. *Mumble-Jumble* is the name given to Faitel because he can't speak properly. Berel is greedy; when you give him a piece of bread smeared with goose-fat, he says, "Give me more!" Zorach has a nasty nickname: *Smear-With-Butter,* and for a nasty reason. Because he has such greasy hair.

In brief, it is a house of nicknames. What is more, that cat—a dumb creature, mind you, and surely an innocent animal—she is called *Gossip Feiga Leah.* Do you know why? Because she's fat and Feiga Leah, the trustee's wife, is also fat. You can imagine how many thrashings they get for calling a cat by a human name! But it slides from them like water from a duck's back. Once they invent a nickname—it's the finish.

5

They gave me a name, too. Guess what? *Mottel-With-The-Lips!* Evidently they don't like my lips. They say that when I eat, I smack my lips. I'd like to see anyone eat without smacking his lips! I'm not one of those high and mighty fellows who sticks up for his honor, and yet—I don't know why—the name doesn't appeal to me at all. And just because I don't like it, they tease me and keep calling me by it. You've never seen worse pests. At first they called me *Mottel-With-The-Lips.* Then they shortened it to *With-The-Lips.* Later they shortened it further to *The Lips,* and still later to simply *Lips.*

401

"Lips, where have you been?"

"Lips, wipe your nose!"

I'm vexed and I cry. Once their father, Pessie's husband—that is, Moishe the bookbinder—caught me in tears and asked me why I'm crying. I told him, "How can I help crying when my name is Mottel and they call me *Lips?* He asks, "Who?" I say, "Vashti." He wants to thrash Vashti, but Vashti says, "It isn't me—its Tomcat...

One points to the other, the other to the third...There's no end to it. Moishe hesitates for a moment and finally stretches all of them out, one by one, and thrashes them with the cover of a prayerbook, saying.

"Scoundrels! I'll teach you to make fun of an orphan! Devil take your forebears!"

That's right. Everyone takes my part. Everyone, everyone takes my part!

It's grand to be an orphan!

VI. MY BROTHER ELI'S DRINK

1

"For one Rouble—One Hundred Roubles!"

"One hundred roubles a month and over can be earned by anyone who acquaints himself with the contents of our book which costs only one rouble plus postage. Hurry! Buy! Take advantage of this opportunity or you will be too late!"

My Brother Eli read this advertisement in some newspaper shortly after he left his father-in-law. As you know, Eli did not leave him because his term expired; he was to be supported by his father-in-law for three years. Actually, he had lived with him not more than three-quarters of a year. But you know what happened to Jonah the biscuit man. I never tell a story twice, unless one begs me. But now even begging won't help because I'm terribly busy. I'm earning money. I'm selling a drink which my brother Eli makes all by himself. He learned how to make it out of a book which costs only one rouble and which can teach you to earn one hundred roubles a month and over. As soon as my brother discovered that such a book existed in the wide world, he sent the rouble—his very last rouble—and told mother she need not worry any longer.

"Mother, thank God, we are saved! Now we are assured an income—up till here..." and he pointed to his throat.

"What is it all about?" Mother asks, "did you get a job?"

"Something better than a job!" answers my brother Eli and his eyes shine with happiness. He asks her to be patient for a few days until the book arrives

"What book?" asks mother.

"Wait and see!" says my brother Eli and inquires whether she would be satisfied with the hundred roubles a month. Mother laughs and says she'd be satisfied with a hundred roubles a year, as long as it's sure money. My brother remarks that she is not very ambitious and goes to the post office. He goes to the post office every day to inquire about the book. A week has passed since he sent the rouble and the book has not come yet. In the meantime one's got to live.

"You can't spit your soul out," mother remarks. I can't quite understand how one could spit one's soul out...

2

At last, the book is here! No sooner did we unpack it than my brother Eli sat down to read it. Goodness, what didn't he read out of the book! So many methods for making money by all sorts of recipes! A recipe for making one hundred roubles a month by preparing first-class ink. A recipe for making one hundred roubles a month by making shoe blacking. A recipe for making one hundred roubles a month by exterminating mice, cockroaches and other nasty things. A recipe for making a hundred roubles a month by preparing liqueurs, sweet brandies, lemonade, soda water, cider, and other drinks...

My brother Eli decided upon the last recipe. First, because with this one, one can earn *more* than a hundred roubles a month. That's what it says in the book. Secondly, you don't have to mess around with inks and shoe blacking, and you needn't have anything to do with mice, cockroaches, and other nasty things. The question remains: which of the drinks to choose? To make liqueurs

403

and sweet brandies, you've got to have the fortune of a Rothschild. To make lemonade and soda-water, you've got to have a machine, a kind of stone which costs goodness knows how much. So there remains cider. Cider's a drink which costs little and sells well. Particularly during such a hot summer as this. I must inform you that Boruch, the cider man, has got rich on cider. He makes "bottled" cider. His cider is famous throughout the world. It shoots from the bottles with a bang. Nobody knows how the shooting is done. That's Boruch's secret. They say he puts something in it that makes it shoot. Some say raisins, others say hops. When summer comes along, both his hands aren't enough to handle his trade. He makes piles of money.

The cider which my brother Eli makes from the recipe isn't "bottled" cider and it doesn't shoot. Our cider is quite another kind of drink. Just how it's made, I cannot tell you. My brother Eli doesn't let anyone come near him when he's working. We only see him pour the water in. But when he's really making the cider he shuts himself up in mother's room. Neither mother, his wife, nor I is allowed in. But if you promise to keep it secret. I can tell you what is in the drink. I know what he prepares. There is lemon peel, thin honey, something that's called *cremotartar* which is sourer than vinegar, and the rest is—water. There's more water in it than anything else. The more water, the more cider. All this is mixed together with an ordinary stick—that's what it tells you to do in the book—and the drink is ready. Then you pour it into a large pitcher and you throw in a piece of ice. Without ice cider is good for nothing. I needn't tell you why. Once I tasted cider without ice and I thought I'd expire...

3

When the first barrel of cider was ready it was decided that the one to sell it on the streets would be I. Who else but I? It wouldn't be proper for my brother to do it—he's a married man. Mother, of course, is out of the question. We'd never allow mother to go around the market with a pitcher, crying, "Cider, cider, people, cider!" Everyone agreed that it would be my job. That's what I thought, too. I was delighted when I heard the news. My brother Eli started to teach me how to do it. With one hand I had to hold the pitcher by a rope, with the other a glass, and in order to attract attention, I had to sing out loud,

> *"Jews, here's a drink!*
> > *A sweet glass costs a penny!*
> *Sweet, nice and cold!*
> > *You can't drink too many!"*

As I mentioned before, my voice is a good one—a soprano, inherited from my father, may he rest in peace. I started singing and turned the song inside out:

> *"Drink, here's a glass!*
> > *A Jew costs a penny!*
> *Sweet, nice and cold!*
> > *And don't drink too many!"*

I don't know whether it was because they liked my singing, or because the drink was really so good, or because the day was so hot, but I sold the first pitcher in half an hour and came home with three-quarters of a rouble. My brother Eli gave the money to mother and another pitcherful to me. He said if I could do this five or six times a day we'd earn exactly one hundred roubles a month. Figure it out for yourselves: omitting the four Sabbaths in a month and counting the original cost of the drink, what would be the percentage we'd make on it? The drink costs us almost nothing. All the money goes on ice. Therefore, you've got to try to sell the cider so quickly that the ice lasts for the second pitcher, the third, and so on. To do it quickly enough you've got to run. And after me runs a whole crowd of kids. They mimic my singing. But they can't disconcert me. I get my pitcherful sold rapidly and run home to fetch more.

I don't know myself how much I made on the first day. All I know is that my brother, his wife, and my mother praised me to the skies. For supper they gave me a slice of cantaloupe, a slice of watermelon, and two prunes. As to cider, I hardly need mention it. We drink cider as if it were water... When it's time to go to sleep, mother arranges my bed on the floor and asks me whether my feet hurt. My brother Eli laughs at her. He says I'm the kind of boy whom nothing hurts.

"Certainly!" I say. "Give me a pitcher and I'll go sell cider in the middle of the night!"

Everybody laughs at my boast, but in mother's eyes I see tears. That's an old story: a mother's got to cry. What I'd like to know is whether all mothers cry all the time, like mine?

4

Our business has been going on swimmingly. Each day is hotter than the last. It sizzles. People wilt with the heat, children drop like flies. If not for a glass of cider, they'd all burn to a cinder. Ten times a day I return with the pitcher and with money. My brother squints into the barrel and sees that there is little left. He hits upon a bright idea and pours in more water. But I had discovered this bright idea before he did. I must confess I've done the trick several times. You see, practically every day I go to our neighbor Pessie to give her a taste of our homemade drink. I gave her husband two glasses—he's a good man. The children get a glass apiece so they should know what sort of drink we can make. The blind uncle gets a glassful, too—one must have compassion for the unfortunate... I give cider to all of my friends, and to all of them free of charge. And in order to make up the loss I add water to the pitcher. To every glass of cider, I pour in two glasses of water. Everybody does the same at home. For instance, when my brother Eli drinks a glass, he adds water immediately. His wife drinks a couple of glasses—she adores my brother's cider—and adds some water. Mother takes a sip of cider after a lot of coaxing, and fills up the barrel with water.... So we really do not lose a drop of cider, and we're making lots of money. Mother paid off many of our debts. She got a few necessary things out of pawn. A table has reappeared in our house, a bench, and some bedding. On Sabbath we have fish, meat, and white bread for dinner. And they promised me new boots for the holidays...Who's better off than me?

5

Who would ever guess that such a thing could happen to us, and that our drink would become as worthless as a straw? Might as well pour it into the slop pail... At least, thank God, I wasn't arrested....

Listen to this: one day I took the cider to our neighbor Pessie. Everyone took a glassful. Me, too. Figuring that I was short twelve or thirteen glasses, I went into the room where they keep water. But instead of the water barrel, I evidently hit upon the barrel where they wash clothes and filled my pitcher with twelve or thirteen glasses of soap-suds. I went out into the street with a new song which I made up all by myself:

"Jews, here's a drink:
  Cider from heaven!
If you order just one,
  You'll ask for eleven!"

A man stops me, pays me a penny and orders a glass. He gulps it down and makes a grimace.

"Boy, what sort of drink is that?"

I pay no attention to him. There are two others waiting for me to pour. One of them drinks half a glass, the other a third of a glass. They pay, spit and walk away. Another man takes the glass to his lips, sips it and remarks that it smells of soap and has a salty taste. A fourth looks at the glass and hands it back to me,

"What have you got there?"

"A drink."

"A drink? That's a stink, not a drink!"

A man comes up, tastes the cider and splashes it all into my face. In a minute around me appears a whole crowd of men, women, and children. All of them chatter, wave their hands around and fume. Spying a crowd, a policeman comes up and asks what's the matter. They tell him. He looks into the pitcher and orders a drink. I pour out a glassful for him. He takes a sip, spits it out and becomes purple in the face.

"Where did you get these soap-suds?" he demands.

"Out of a book," I say. "My brother makes it all by himself."

"Who is your brother?" he asks me.

"My brother Eli," I answer.

"Which Eli?" he asks me.

"Dullard!" several Jews call out to me in Hebrew, "Utter not the name of thy brother!" There starts a row, noise, excitement. More people join the crowd. The policeman holds me by the hand and wants to take us—that is, me and the cider—to the police station. The noise increases. "He's an orphan! Spare the orphan!" I hear from all sides...My heart tells me that I'm in a mess. I look around, "Jews, help me out!" Somebody wants to give the policeman a bribe. The policeman refuses it. An old man with sly eyes, suddenly calls out to me in Hebrew,

"Youth! Remove thy hand from the watchman's, lift they limbs and show him the soles of thy feet!"

I tear my hand from the policeman's, lift my limbs and show

407

him the soles of my feet…. More dead than alive I burst into our house.

"Where is the pitcher?" asks my brother Eli.

"In the police station!" I reply and fall weeping into mother's arms.

Two shtetl types on the town.

VI
Other Novels

INTRODUCTION TO
IN THE STORM

As were so many of Sholem-Aleykhem's works, *In the Storm* was first published in serial form in periodicals, starting in 1907, when it was entitled *Der Mabl (The Deluge)*. When it appeared, reworked, in book form, Sholem-Aleykhem changed the title to *In Shturem (In the Storm)*.

In 1905, it was clear a storm was approaching, a storm which presaged the deluge to come. In that fateful year, Russia suffered a humiliating defeat at the hands of the Japanese. Bowed under the tyrannical yoke of the czarist regime, cold and hungry, the Russian masses yearned for bread and freedom. Students, intellectuals, Marxists, revolutionary leaders spurred the people on to act in their own behalf: for a constitutional form of government, for socialism, for more humane working conditions, for education and enlightenment. The czarist government responded with secret police, repression, imprisonment, interrogations, and executions.

In the Russian Jewish world, Jews suffered under a double burden: not only did they have to bear the common lot of hunger and oppression, but they were also persecuted, pogromized, for what they were, for being Jews. Assimilation, nationalism, socialism, or some combination of these, vied with each other among Jews as a solution to the "Jewish problem."

It is at this historical moment in Russian and Jewish history that Sholem-Aleykhem sets his story. And although Sholem-Aleykhem shows his broad human understanding and sympathy for all the Jewish solutions to the Jewish problem, there is no doubt that his strongest sympathies are with the Jewish nationalists, the Zionists. In some ways the whole novel is an attempt to make a case for Zionism as the best solution, as against socialism, Marxism, or assimilationism.

409

It is also a *roman* (novel) with a romance—with a love story.

The story is developed in two parts. In Part I we are introduced to three Jewish families living at the same address, an apartment building in Kiev at No 13 Vasilchikover Street. Each of the three families represents a different social class, as well as a different way of dealing with the problems of the day. Each family also reveals the philosophical gap between the two generations, between the parents and their children.

The first family, Itsikl Shostepol and his wife Shivka, represent the Jewish bourgoisie: Itsikl is an entrepreneur, provisions-supplier, tradesman, relatively well-off, traditional in his Jewishness; his wife is called Shivka-the-rich-woman.

The second family consists of the widower Solomon Safronovitch and his son Sasha. Safronovitch is a pharmacist, assimilationist in his bearing, with little regard for Jewish traditionalism. He is afraid to display any signs of his Jewishness openly. He considers Itsikl Shostepol, who is open about his Jewishness, a pious hypocrite.

The third family represents the bottom of this social microcosm. Appropriately, they live in the cellar of the apartment building.

There is a fourth Jewish family that is also very important to the playing out of Sholem Aleykhem's story, although they do not live on Vasilchikover Street. This family consists of the very poor and humble wood-hauler, Lipa Bashevits, whose humility is offset by his boundless pride in his beautiful daughter, Miriam-Gitl, or Masha.

She is now off in St. Petersburg studying medicine. She is also a fiery revolutionary leader, renowned for her bravery and resourcefulness, beloved both by the common people and the revolutionary intelligentsia.

The selection from *In the Storm* below consists of Chapters 3 through 7 (the book consists of twelve chapters in all, and 220 pages in Aliza Shevrin's translation). In these five short chapters you will meet Lipa Bashevits, the humble wood-hauler; Masha, his gifted and heroic daughter; Yashka Vorona, the turncoat, lowlife, and czarist secret agent; Tamara, the idealistic and socialist daughter of Itsikl, the Jewish petit-bourgois; Masha's revolutionary commune, consisting of a variety of students and intellectuals; and Abram Markovitch, artist, poet, Tolstoyan, dreamer, along with his loving wife, Rosa, and their adorable four-year-old, Zusya, destined to be one of the first victims of the impending storm.

FROM *IN THE STORM*

3. *MASHA BASHEVITCH*

Lippa Bashevitch the wood-hauler was a hardworking Jew who supplied homes with wood, from which he made a living, raised children and educated them.

"Raised children and educated them"—that's easy to say. But considering his circumstances, if you will permit me to say so, how could a wretched pauper like Lippa Bashevitch raise and educate children when his mind was always taken up with the struggle to earn a crust of bread for himself, for his wife and children, a struggle that was hardly successful? The impoverished Bashevitch tried everything, going from house to house offering to sell a full load of wood, a whole klafter, measuring three and a quarter by three and a quarter, for a mere fifty-two vershuk. And it could even be paid off in installments, only a ruble a week. Do you hear? Have you ever heard of such a thing? In installments!

In spite of all these inducements, once he had succeeded in finding a customer and they had agreed on a price and the wood had been ordered from him, had been measured out three times in the width, and his son-in-law had checked the measurements (the son-in-law was a young man who was good at figures, a mathematician who knew algebra), and a neighbor was also asked to double-check, and then, with God's help, the wood had been cut up, stacked, and was already being used to heat the house for a week—then, when they came to collect the first ruble, they were greeted by complaints from the woman of the house, complaints that darkened his life.

"A fine load of wood you gave me! May my enemies be so lucky! You call that wood? Till you live to see even a spark, your eyes can fall out of your head!"

"What are you talking about, Madamenyu, may you remain strong and healthy," the poor wood hauler pleaded. "It's gold, not wood! It's real aged hardwood, not just scrap or softwood!"

"You're a strange man," her husband broke in. "We're telling you that the wood is damp—and damp wood won't burn—and you insist that the wood is dry!"

"The wood must have come from a green tree," volunteered

the son-in-law, the one who was good at figures, the mathematician who knew algebra.

The miraculous strokes of good fortune that Jews experienced in that crowded, dark, dismal, filthy ghetto where the Diaspora had flung them together helter-skelter were so great and wondrous that each individual could have told a story to rival the exodus from Egypt. Each could have described how God had dealt with him, how he had survived a year and then another year, raised and married off one child, and another child, and yet another child— miracle upon miracle!

Lippa Bashevitch would have more to tell than anyone. Eight children God had granted him, and all eight were gifted. They knew everything and were informed about everything. You might ask when and where they had had the chance to study. Did they ever receive any education at all? Only to the extent that the father himself used to teach them a little at night. Did they ever have a teacher? Only to the extent that one assisted the other. And in spite of that, as fate would have it, they had all entered Gymnasium, studied well, and so excelled that the anti-Semitic teacher, the elder Romanenko, managed not only to exempt them from tuition but furnished them with clothing and shoes, because Lippa's children went half naked and barefoot till the age of fifteen.

If Lippa Bashevitch had had to depend on others to say a good word about his children he would have had to wait a long time. He had a daughter Masha about whom he said, "Since God had created this Masha, He has never created another such. The way she accomplishes her chores at home—golden hands! Not to mention her studies—the highest grades! Have you ever seen her diploma? You haven't? I haven't shown it to you? Here, I'll show it to you, then you'll first *see* a diploma! And by herself, all by herself. I'm telling you, this is a Masha sent from heaven, blessed by God! A one-in-a-million Masha!"

That's how Lippa Bashevitch crowed to all his neighbors and acquaintances, boring them to tears with his Masha. And needless to say, when Masha finished Gymnasium and brought home a gold medal, her proud father, poor as ever, almost went out of his mind and almost drove all his neighbors and acquaintances and even strangers out of *their* minds. He would stop everyone, show off the medal, and tell of Masha's outstanding scholarship, how she had impressed the director and the teachers, and how proficient she was at home, teaching the younger children, and what an excellent essay she had sent to the minister that she, Marsha herself, had written. And without a moment's pause he would pull out the essay and recite it in a lofty voice, rising and falling in tone: *"Yevo visakaprevoshoditelstvo Gospodinu Ministru naradnaha prosveshtshenya..."*—His Most Esteemed Sir Minister of Public Education...

The neighbors were relieved to be rid of Lippa Bashevitch when his daughter Masha went away to Petersburg. Now, they reckoned, he would stop pestering them about his Masha. But they were sadly mistaken. They now had to hear every word of Masha's correspondence to her parents from Petersburg. Remarkable letters! She was working very hard, mending laundry to earn the bare necessities, and was studying medicine. She wrote of a new life that would soon prevail in all the land, a life of freedom, of equality based on a constitution. In every letter she spoke of some sort of constitution; it got to the point where the neighbors gave Lippa the nickname "Constitutzia." Instead of Lippa Bashevitch they began to call him Lippa Constitutzia. People made jokes about Lippa's daughter and her constitution. But Masha, for whom it was no joke, worked incessantly for the constitution and believed that someday—if not today, then tomorrow—they would have that wonderful long-awaited, hoped-for constitution! "They will have to give it to us," Masha argued. "A deluge of blood will flow! The deluge will drown the sinful earth and rinse away all the evil, and the skies will clear and the sun will shine and it will become light in all the land!"

So preached Masha Bashevitch at every opportunity among the youth and among the workers, becoming well known in certain circles and beloved by the common people. "Our Masha"— that's what she was called in those circles, and many were prepared to follow her through fire and flood to the very ends of the earth.

No letter carrier in the great city of Petersburg walked as many miles a day as our Masha Bashevitch. After awakening early in the morning and dispatching at least ten letters to various friends about various matters, she would walk miles from the edge of the city to the Institute, from the Institute again a fair distance to the Dyeshavke market, where one could always find the cheapest lunch, and from there again several miles to work at the factory, and from there to friends, from the friends back home to the edge of town, all on foot. To use the public transportation would

413

require "Rothchild's fortune and Korach's riches," Marsha said, and she tore through Petersburg like a racehorse, not allowing herself to cease her work for a moment.

What Masha Bashevitch's work consisted of no one except the Party and her closest friends knew or needed to know; it was political conspiracy. But the police knew about all of her activities and exactly what she had been doing, and they were searching for her intensively; thus far they had been unable to find her.

But there was one man who had sworn to trap her. He was the notorious spy named Yashka Vorona.

4. *YASHKA VORONA*

On his papers it said "Yaakov Vladimorivitch Voronin, thirty-two years old." His real name was Yankel Voroner, and he came from a small town in Grodno Province. His life story is interesting, and we relate it here as briefly as possible.

His father a teacher... His mother a baker... Starved till the age of five... From the age of five helped deliver food to cheder children, earned a groschen, bought a bagel from his mother for supper... Delivered Purim *shalach-mones*... Went barefoot summers till age thirteen... After his Bar Mitzvah refused to say prayers... Beaten by his father, who broke his arm... Ran away to Grodno... Slept in the streets... Learned Russian and mathematics from a madman... Stole a Gemorah from a shul, was imprisoned for stealing half a loaf of bread... Ran away to the Mir Yeshiva... Masqueraded as an Orthodox Jew, prayed from morning to night... Was fed by charitable Jews... Stole rolls from the table of his hosts... Was caught smoking in the bathroom on Shabbos... Was flogged... Ran away to Bialystok... Became a teacher... Charged a gulden a week to teach two hours a day... Starved... Married a girl who was stone-deaf... Received fifty-five rubles dowry... Bought himself a pair of boots (his first pair of boots!)... Ran away to Vilna... Passed the sixth-level examination... Fell in with thieves... Wrote Yiddish dramas... Tried to sell them to a publisher... Publisher proposed they be bought by weight: two gulden a pound... Tore up the dramas, wrote a satire on the publisher... Showed it to friends... All were delighted... Sent it off to a Yiddish periodical... Never saw it again... Fell in love with a girl... An ugly business... Wanted to drown himself in the Velikaya... Was informed his father dead, his mother starving... Vowed to study law... Worked for a pharmacist... Spent two years there... Sent his mother money—a ruble a week, two rubles on holidays... Pharmacist accused him of handing out free perfume to poor girls... Had an affair with the pharmacist's wife... Ran off to Petersburg... Wanted to study medicine... Starved... Tried to get an interview with Baron Guinzburg... Stood for hours in the cold... Attracted the attention of police... Was arrested... Was to be shipped with convoy of convicts to Grodno... Converted... Gave up hope of introduction to Baron Buinzburg... Could not send money anymore to his mother... Went hungry himself... Got a job in an arsenal... Attended lectures at the university... Participated in all meetings... Became acquainted with all the students and workers... Concealed the fact he had converted... Was involved in a dynamite plot... Almost got to visit Siberia... Compromised himself... Informed on a few comrades, quickly released... Wanted to hang himself... Was offered work as a spy... Overjoyed to receive his first hundred... Fell in love with gentile washerwoman...Had two children... Served loyally... Authorities highly pleased with him... Bought his own house... Kept advancing... Suspected by some of the workers... Feared for his life... Tried to save his skin... Had the honor several times to report personally to highest authorities... Won assignment in Warsaw... Accomplished mission in best form... Won an award and permanent post in Petersburg... Would be completely happy if workers didn't threaten his life...

That is the up-to-date biography of Yashka Vorona.

Yashka Vorona had to admit that the job of finding the hidden Masha was his most difficult, and he would never forget her as long as he lived! He suspected a girl with short hair who once left a meeting with a crowd late at night, stopping every so often to have a discussion (it was during those happy times when three people could talk together freely in the streets without fear). After leaving the group this girl took a droshky and asked to be taken to one of the dark streets of the great city of Petersburg. Naturally Yashka quickly took another droshky and followed her to her destination, where she stopped, paid the driver, got out, rang the doorbell, and entered the courtyard. Our agent waited a while, rang for the watchman, entered the courtyard, showed the man his credentials, and asked to be shown the tenant register. Yashka leafed through the register several times and stopped at the name Miriam Gitl Bashevitch, living with a former resident of Orsha, Moishe Malkin.

"Ah??? Malkin?... A familiar name. I should learn something from him."

5. *THE LITTLE COMMUNE*

Malkin had for a long time been known to the police because of his finagling to obtain residences for Jews in neighborhoods where they were not allowed and through his constant applying for permits. Nothing could stop him—neither being arrested nor being sent off to prison. Malkin stubbornly decided once and for all that the town of Orsha was too small for him and he wanted to be a Petersburger. And he succeeded. He brought with him from Orsha a "document" stating he was a businessman, a shoe-polish maker, and settled in Petersburg as a shoe-polish maker.

There were two forces working in favor of Malkin's becoming a Petersburg resident: one force drove him from Orsha, because there was nothing to do there; the other force drew him to Petersburg, because he had heard that in Petersburg Jews were becoming rich, enormously rich, from the war (this was the time of the Russo-Japanese War). But Malkin was too late. Because of his shady dealings with illegal residences and because he had been away in prison, he had missed the most prosperous times, the golden times, and had arrived in Petersburg when they were already talking of peace, and our shoe-polish maker had gone through a great deal of trouble for nothing.

Malkin would have starved to death if his wife hadn't come to his aid with her great talent for cooking fish and baking challah. He opened a low-cost pension, hung out a shingle, and prospered. In a short time, by word of mouth, people found out that at Malkin's you could get delicious fish and fresh challah every day and cheaply. And Malkin's rooms, which were located right under the roof, on the very top floor, were soon occupied by regular boarders, young people of different professions, or rather, without any professions at all, who were called "proletarian intelligentsia." Such people would prefer to be doing whatever was useful—working, toiling, anything to earn a piece of bread—not for money, mind you, but enough to keep body and soul together in order to be able to further their great work in behalf of the sacred ideas that had brought them all together, right under the roof of Malkin the shoe-polish maker.

These are the boarders who lived at Malkin's, under the roof.

Meyer Gridell: Twenty-two year old, a Bundist. Studied in three Gymnasia; didn't finish any of them because of mathematics, which for him was a bourgeois joke. Quarreled with his parents. Ran away to Petersburg, registered as a typesetter, entered the university. Of short stature, swarthy, pockmarked face, nearsighted.

Chaim Broida: Thirty-four years old. Had been a teacher. Taught himself languages. Read a great deal. A fierce anti-Zionist and antinationalist. Secretly read banned periodical *Hashalach.* Registered as a tailor. Only God and he alone knew on what he lived. Tall, slender, with a hoarse voice, appeared to be a candidate for tuberculosis, but perhaps not.

Mischa Berezniak (Real name Moishe Fiedler): Around forty years old. Escaped from Siberia. Had two degrees. Exceptionally strong. Talked with a droning voice. Very much wanted by the police. Made his living by singing in a church choir every Sunday. Hard to tell he was Jew. Large, hairy, looked like a Russian priest. Had a wild temper.

Nissel Avrutis: Nineteen-year-old youngster. Never studied anywhere. Possessed rare gifts. Published poems in the best Russian newspapers, signed himself "Kolivri." A fiery anarchist. Registered as a dyer. Pale as a girl, with soft cheeks.

Etka Vayrach: Twenty-four years old. A Litvak from Bobruisk. Registered as a wigmaker. Completed Gymnasium. Studying dentistry. Made her living gluing cardboard cartons. Dark complexion, quite attractive. Fiery-eyed.

Chava Vahl: Twenty-one years old. Came from an aristocratic family. Her father boasted his ancestor was the Jewish-Polish king Shaul Vahl. Threw over a rich suitor. Taught herself massage. Registered as a hatmaker. A dangerous revolutionary. Not attractive.

Masha Bashevitch: We already know.

417

Now we must introduce you to Malkin's three older boys. One should say "men" rather than "boys" because they were three tall, healthy brutes, with stout legs and strong arms, who worked hard and ate heartily. They had the kind of appetite that a millionaire could not support. One developed an appetite by merely watching them eat. Seventeen holiday feasts, eighteen wedding suppers, a hundred banquets, dinners, and buffets given by multimillionaires couldn't compare with one weekday's meals of that proletarian-intelligentsia bunch upstairs under the roof. No one stood on ceremony. No one sat at the head of the table. They sat and talked and ate, all on the same footing, like partners, like a commune.

With time it actually did become something of a commune, thanks to the new boarder, Masha Bashevitch. When Masha Bashevitch came to her first meal to arrange her room and board she immediately felt at home. After meeting the group and learning each one's name, Masha tossed off her hat and coat, and, dinner over, she rolled up her sleeves and started helping Frau Malkin wash the dishes. Malkin himself tried to protest, but Masha cut him off.

"It's none of your business! If I have the time, I'll help you. If I don't have the time, you'll help *me.* Here, for example, my shoe is torn, do you see? Be so kind, Herr Malkin, take my shoe to the shoemaker. I saw a shoemaker in your courtyard. Ask him what he wants to repair it, and while you're at it, I would appreciate it if you would pay him, as I'm short of cash today."

Several minutes later Masha heard a child crying from behind the stove and she turned to Frau Malkin and said, "Is that one of yours? So show me that crybaby and we'll see what the matter is." And Masha took the child on her lap, gave him the nickname of "Pempek," for his fat tummy, bounced him and jounced him and danced with him till the crying baby stuck his pink little tongue out, showed six newly cut teeth, and laughed gleefully.

"Why are you sitting like clods, with your hands folded?" Masha shouted at the two girls who were studying dentistry and massage.

"What should we be doing?" the girls answered with a questioning laugh.

"What should you be doing! Take an automobile drive through the Nevski! There's a broom—take it and sweep out the rooms."

418

As one could imagine, that first night at supper all of them wanted to impress Masha Bashevitch with their own liberal ideas and their fine oratory. A discussion ensued about principal economic issues, and the words poured forth: Karl Marx, LaSalle, proletariat, Koitski, class struggle...

"Be quiet, all of you!" shouted Masha, covering her ears. "If you want to carry on a debate like people, not like geese, you have to do it according to parliamentary rules—elect a president and ask to be recognized. This time I am your president. Herr Berezniak, you have the floor!"

And that's how a small commune evolved at Malkin's, and its leader was Masha Bashevitch.

6. THE BIRD SHOT AT AND MISSED

It was not yet dark, and not all the streetlights had been turned on, when the small commune located right under the roof of Malkin's apartment began gathering one by one to exchange with one another the day's happenings. Each one had a bundle of news to untie—one about a secret meeting, one about a fight over the workers, another about a new strike that was being planned—and each one wanted to be heard first. But Malkin, the landlord himself, cut in, shouting to be heard over the others.

"Do you know what I have to tell you, friends? Just listen to me and I'll tell you something really funny. First of all, I'm older than all of you. I'm not even mentioning the fact that I'm the landlord here, because I know the word 'landlord' means very little to you. And second of all, I promise you, you will have a good laugh!"

"If we'll have a good laugh, Herr Malkin, then you can go first, you can have the floor."

Obviously these words were spoken by Masha Bashevitch, who all this time was sitting preoccupied and troubled, drumming her fingers on the table—a sure sign she wasn't in a good mood. And the landlord Malkin started to tell his story.

"This morning, when all of you had vanished as salt dissolves in water and I remained all alone with little Pempek here"—he gestured toward his small son, who was sitting on the masseuse's lap, pulling her nose—"the door opened and in came a delivery man carrying books and sat himself down to chat with me. As usually happens, little Pempek here didn't let anyone get a word in. To make a long story short, it turns out he is a sympathizer, and a committed one too, selling banned books. And while he was at it he confided to me that the girl who had broken into the typesetter's and printed those proclamations—Masha is her name—was his daughter. So? Didn't I say you would have a good laugh?"

"So? What did you tell him?" asked Masha.

"What *could* I tell him?" said Malkin. "I told him he was really a big liar. He tried to contradict me and to convince me that it was indeed his daughter's work, and this really annoyed me. So I disabused him and revealed to him the secret that this Masha was a different Masha and that I knew her and that she was living here in my house."

As if an angry bee had stung her, Masha Bashevitch sprang up! She slapped her hands together and cried out to Malkin, "What have you done? You're really a child, an overgrown child, and a foolish child at that! Who asked you to prattle on with that loose tongue of yours? Ach, Malkin! Malkin!"

And Masha began pacing back and forth, storming through the apartment, muttering angrily and wringing her hands. The entire commune and Malkin himself were terrified by her; as long as they had known Masha Bashevitch they had never seen her so distraught and upset. All attempts to calm or soothe her were of no avail. Masha Bashevitch didn't allow herself to be mollified. And it was Malkin who was the object of her rage.

"What right did you have to discuss things that are none of your business with a total stranger you don't know at all? I am convinced he is one of them, the police. Our doorman mentioned to me this morning that after I came home last night, some character was looking for someone—he wasn't sure whether it was for me or another woman. Children, do you know what I will tell you? I'm going to have to move to other lodgings, and immediately. Don't try to talk me out of it, stop making long faces and sad speeches. Better help me pack my bags, and if one of you would be so kind, please tell the doorman to cross my name off the register and tell him I've gone to Vilna. If they want to find me, at least let them go out of their way. Take care, little Pempek, give me your dirty little face. I hope you grow up to be at least a bit smarter than your father. Adieu!"

One's own sister would not be so warmly sent off as Masha was by the little commune. They were all moved and downcast at this unexpected turn of events. Frau Malkin couldn't control herself and burst into tears. And the two female boarders, the dentist and the masseuse, were ready to accompany her, but Masha wouldn't have it.

When she was already out the door, she turned around to face the commune and said to them: "What else have I forgotten to tell you, children? Oh, yes. If you should hear that I've been arrested—who can tell?—don't any of you dare to visit me. Things are getting hotter. Get rid of any evidence as you would get rid of chometz before Pesach—any scrap of a letter, any piece of paper, a proclamation, a pamphlet. Burn them. Whoever feels he needn't remain here had better get out as soon as possible. Take care of yourselves, all of you! Be well, little Pempek, you I will miss."

As could have been predicted, a heated debate erupted among the members of the commune immediately after Masha's departure. Some were highly critical of Masha's leaving and going into hiding; others defended her and got to work burning letters and pamphlets. Malkin's sons helped with the task, and Frau Malkin was happy to be saving wood. Even little Pempek enjoyed the fire, never taking his eyes off it, as if it were burning for his sake alone.

The fire in the stove had long been dead and the ashes from the burned papers had long ago been swept out by Frau Malkin. The remaining members of the commune had each gone to his corner to rest from the work and worry of that day. Only Malkin and his wife sat together next to little Pempek's crib, worrying about where the following day's grocery money would come from. The husband asked the wife and the wife asked the husband, "Where can we get some money?" "It's not good!" Malkin said. "Not good," Frau Malkin repeated, and at that very moment there was a knock on the door, and another knock, and still another, each one louder and more insistent than the previous one.

"Who's there?" asked Malkin.

"Friends," a voice answered from the other side of the door.

"What do you think it can be, a raid?" Malkin asked his wife, but there was no time for an answer, because before Frau Malkin could open her mouth to reply the door burst open and in came the visitors—the chief of police, several security police, and an officer between them. Terrified, Malkin sat frozen at the table, while Frau Malkin remained by the crib.

"*Zarastvoy, golubchik*—How are you, my dear friend?" the chief of police said to Malkin, whom he had seen more than once in his local precinct office. "How's business?"

Malkin was so stunned he couldn't open his mouth. The local policemen, the security police officers, went about doing their work—they woke up the entire commune and dragged them out of their beds half naked. A soldier stood alongside each one and an interrogation began.

"Masha Bashevitch!" called out an officer, still a young man not yet out of his teens, with two fine curly muttonchops growing on his cheeks à la Pushkin. "Which one of you here is Masha Bashevitch?"

"Masha Bashevitch is not here," Malkin forced himself to say at last.

"What do you mean, she's not here?"

"She's gone."

If someone had thrown a bomb he could not have created a greater effect or have surprised them more than with the news that the one they had been sure of finding was gone.

"Your bird has flown the coop!" the officer with the Pushkin muttonchops said with a bitter little smile to a man who was standing unnoticed near the door dressed in an overcoat of a nondescript color—it was hard to say whether it was gray or brown or yellowish. It would be easier to say it was all three colors at once. All this time the unnoticed person in the three-colored overcoat had been standing on the side like someone who had been called in as a witness. But upon hearing that Masha Bashevitch was not there this man suddenly came to life, went over to the table, looked around angrily through his ash-tinted spectacles, his face frozen, his hands trembling. He went right up to Malkin, looked right into his eyes, and with a quiet but intense voice said to him in Yiddish, "Malkin! Where is Masha Bashevitch? I know that you know. It will be healthier for all of you if you tell the truth."

Malkin recognized his guest of the previous morning, the delivery man.

It was Yashka Vorona.

7. *MASHA SEEKS A REFUGE*

When Masha Bashevitch left Malkin's small commune right under
the roof, she took her bag, a small felt valise held together with a
rope, hailed a droshky, and asked to be taken to one of the outly-
ing streets of greater Petersburg. Since it was a long drive, Masha,
as was her habit, engaged in conversation with the coachman, a
strong, healthy Orlovsker peasant with the face of a bear. She discovered that he owned a bit of property in Orlovsk Province which
didn't provide him with so much as a crust of bread, and so he was
forced to be a coachman, his wife had to take in laundry, and his
children—ach, the children! He had three sons and a daughter,
and one of the sons, the eldest, a reservist, had been killed in
Manchuria and another had just joined the army that year.

"Why so many soldiers?" Masha asked him. "Are you provid-
ing the Russian Army with soldiers?"

"What can one do?" the coachman answered her. "They ask
and we have to give."

The coachman turned his face to her, trying to see to whom he
was speaking, whether she might be an informer. But Masha's face
told him she was no informer, and on the coachman's face there
appeared a grimace that could be interpreted as a smile. He felt
free to speak to her, telling her he was not a dim ignoramus as she
might suppose but that he was also aware of what was going on in
the world. He himself was illiterate, but others read pamphlets to
him. Sylvester read to him and explained what they meant. Who
was Sylvester? Sylvester was a worker from an iron foundry who
shared his living quarters with him. Sylvester told him what was
going on at the foundries. They were planning a strike. Even he
and his horse would have to go on strike if Father Gapon told
them to.

"Who is this Gapon?" Masha asked him in order to find out
how well informed the coachman was about what was going on at
the foundries.

"Father Gapon," the coachman explained in his own language,

"is the priest who was sent to wage war against that black evil spirit, the Antichrist, who has stolen into our country and refuses to leave. No matter how much he is smoked out with incense, no matter how many prayers and curses and pleas and oaths have been heaped on him, yet he refuses to budge, that black spirit, that Antichrist, may he perish from the plague!"

With these words he inflicted on his horse what he wished to inflict on the Antichrist. Masha wanted to find out from this poor soul exactly who he thought this Antichrist was.

"The devil knows!" he answered her. "I think he must come from the Jews."

"Why the Jews?" Masha asked him, astounded.

"Where else if not from the Jews?" the peasant replied with authority. "Everything is because of the Jews. Isn't the war because of the Jews?"

"How do you know that?"

"I *don't* know, but I believe it."

Masha was faced with the task of enlightening him about Gapon, the Antichrist, the Jews, and who had really caused the war. And a difficult bit of work it was; woodchopping was much easier! Nevertheless she was satisfied with her work, because when they arrived at her destination and she paid the coachman for the hour and a half ride, a broad, simple smile appeared on his bear-like face which seemed to express "Now it's all as plain as day!"

They had driven up to a high, gray-painted outside wall, and Masha rang the bell on the door at the entrance. A watchman appeared wearing a white apron and a white badge on his hat. Masha learned from him that the person she was looking for had been arrested and she could not stay there because the landlord had told him not to rent any rooms to students or young women. "Better to let the rooms remain empty," he had said, "or burn them to the ground before the police accuse me of harboring a nest of students, thieves, crooks, and socialists in my place!"

Poor Masha had to pick up her felt valise and look for another place to stay three streets away. The doorbell was answered by a woman wearing a red kerchief with green flowers—the watchman's wife apparently—who told her in a singsong voice to leave as soon as possible, because the whole neighborhood was crawling with police. They were looking for someone.

Obviously our heroine had to make a sharp about-face and quit the area at once, because she was not about to let the police stand in the way of her mission; she had much, much more to do! Suddenly (all good ideas came suddenly) a good idea came to her. Tamara! Tamara Shostepol!

Masha Bashevitch and Tamara Shostepol, though they had been friends from the same city and had graduated from the same Gymnasium, hardly saw each other—not because there were any bad feelings between them but for reasons neither could explain. In her heart Masha admitted she disliked Tamara's bourgeois parents and their bourgeois home. Masha remembered the strong impression Tamara's home had made on her whenever she visited. Tamara's mother would serve her a glass of tea as if it were costing her her last cent. What's to be done? Sometimes you *do* have to serve a guest a glass of tea! And every time the maid forgot to add sugar Tamara's mother would curse her for forgetting.

As for her father, Itzikl Shostepol, she truly despised him. She remembered how once, having come to see Tamara and not finding her at home, she had met the father at the door.

"Who is this girl?" Itzikl had asked his wife, scratching himself under his collar.

"A friend of Tamara's," the wife had answered, not wishing to refer to her by name. Masha was in the sixth-level Gymnasium at the time and could already win an argument with smarter people than Itzikl Shostepol. She said to him proudly, "I am Lippa's daughter."

"What Lippa?"

"Lippa Bashevitch," Masha answered him.

"What Bashevitch?" Itzikl asked again, not removing his hand from his collar.

"The wood hauler," Tamara's mother volunteered. Itzikl turned his back on Masha, and Masha left there in a rage, vowing never to visit Tamara again. But not long after, she ran into Tamara, who insisted she visit, and she talked to her so long that she persuaded her to change her mind.

Once they met in Petersburg at a meeting, and Tamara reprimanded Masha for not coming to visit her. To this Masha replied, "Why don't you come to visit *me?*" But then she realized what she had said and quickly stopped herself. "Besides, you can't come to my place."

"Why?"

"Because Malkin's residence, where I live, is too small for you."

That hurt Tamara's feelings, so she made a *point* of paying her a visit, met Malkin and the whole proletariat bunch, even carried on a discussion with the members of the commune, who all fell in love with her, from the youngest, Avrutis, to the eldest, the former Siberian exile, Berezniak. Tamara liked them all, even the women of the commune, Etka and Chava.

"Now I hope you will visit me too," said Tamara to Masha.

"At the first opportunity," replied Masha, but no sooner had Tamara left than she forgot about her. She remembered Tamara's invitation only at that moment when she was walking the streets of the great city of Petersburg, bag in hand, seeking a refuge.

After walking several more miles our heroine paused at a brown outside wall and rang the doorbell. Responding to the bell was a small barefooted shikseh with large beads around her neck and a ready smile on her face. Masha handed her the bag and asked her what her name was.

"They call me Masha," the little shikseh with the large beads said, laughing.

"If that's so, we have two Mashas here," Masha Bashevitch said to the little Masha and asked to be taken to Miss Shostepol's room.

"Who's there?" a man's voice called from the next room.

"It's me!" Masha Bashevitch answered him as she unpacked her bag and made herself at home in Tamara's room.

"Who is 'me'?" the same man's voice asked again, and not receiving an answer, the man himself appeared, a forty-year-old, sleepy-eyed and disheveled, without an undershirt and wearing a buttoned-up kind of vest, without suspenders, so that his trousers kept slipping down and he had to hold them up with both hands at his belly, yanking them up frequently. At the same time he had to keep adjusting his pince-nez, which refused to stay put on his nose in spite of the fact that it was a hooked Jewish nose. Apparently it was the fault of the spectacles—not of the nose—or perhaps of the owner of the nose, who looked as if he were an absentminded character, one of those poor souls who are always exhausted and disorganized, who start twenty thousand projects and never finish them.

Seeing an unfamiliar visitor in Tamara's bedroom, the sleepy-eyed man with the drooping trousers sprang back, and bending down as far as his spectacles would allow him to, he asked the banal question, "With whom do I have the honor?" He had a mild speech impediment (instead of "r" it came out "kh").

"The honor is not so great." Masha answered him bluntly, as

426

was her manner, and went about her work—putting away her handkerchiefs, combs and brushes, pillowcases, and little collars as if she were at home. "I'm a hometown friend of Tamara's. My name is Masha Bashevitch."

The name "Masha Bashevitch" went through the sleepy-eyed man like an electric current. A friendly smile spread over his entire face. He became another person! He clasped her hand and held onto it all the while he spoke, and he spoke at great length without pausing, connecting one subject with the next so cleverly that it was impossible to interrupt him unless one were to leave in the middle of a sentence or shout louder than he. Those who knew him did exactly that—they had no other choice.

"Are you *the* Masha Bashevitch? Ay-ay-ay! When Tamara comes she will jump for joy! We hear about you every day, ten times a day! You are a heroine! Not everyone can do what you are doing. We all have to learn from you. We are children, school-children compared to you! My name is Abram Markovitch. Everyone knows Abram Markovitch! My profession is painting, but I am also a bit of a poet, a vegetarian, and a Tolstoyan. What do I think of Tolstoy? I think very highly of him. You probably think he is a greater poet than a philosopher? I don't agree with you!"

Whether Masha Bashevitch agreed with Abram Markovitch's opinion of Tolstoy or not was another matter, but that she had to remove her hand from his was obvious, and this she did in time, trying to get a word in but finding it impossible, because Abram Markovitch was going strong and it would have been as much a pity to interrupt him as it would be a pity to waken a soundly sleeping person. Luckily for Masha, Tamara Shostepol arrived. And when Tamara arrived she politely sent Abram Markovitch from the room, asking him to tell Rosa she had a guest for tea.

"Not for tea," Masha corrected her, "but for a week or for two weeks, until I find a safe refuge. I hope you don't mind bringing in another bed?"

Tamara reddened, Itzikl Shostepol's daughter was not sufficiently democratic to deal easily with a situation that came so naturally to the genuinely democratic Masha Bashevitch. Tamara told her she would be happy to have her stay not only two or three weeks but two or three months, the entire winter. And she soon changed the subject to the commune. How was it going there? How was Malkin? And she talked about Abram Markovitch, what

427

a babbler he was but nevertheless a good person, a jewel, but a babbler, and about his wife, Rosa, who was a relative of hers.

"I'm not saying this just because she is a relative," said Tamara, "but when you get to know her better, you yourself will say that she is not just a woman but an angel! They have a child—that is to say, they have many children, but they have this one child, Zusya is his name, a four-year-old boy, and I can't imagine what he will grow up to be! Smart as a whip, good as an angel, and is he beautiful! Have you ever seen Raphael's self-portrait? Ah! I forgot that you are a...a...that you don't approve of art."

"You are greatly mistaken, Tamara. I love true art and little children too," said Masha, and Tamara responded with a sigh. She reminded herself that she, Tamara Shostepol, had been in Petersburg for quite a while and had still accomplished nothing, and she was envious of her friend Masha, deeply envious, but she didn't have the courage to say this. She opened the door, looked out and called, "Zusya! Nana! No one's here." And then she said to Masha, "Do you have any letters from home? Do they write?"

"Very often!" Masha answered her with a laugh. "Too often. Almost every day I get letters from my family, from my brothers, from my parents—especially from my father! He writes to me every other day and I have to write *him* every other day. And not just short letters but long megillahs full of details—what's happening and especially about the 'revolution.' He's become a revolutionary, a fanatic revolutionary!"

Masha burst out laughing, displaying her fine white healthy teeth that no dentist had ever had the opportunity to touch with his shiny instruments, and again Tamara was envious of her, because she was in such frequent touch with her family and because of her perfect white teeth.

"Here's the samovar!" announced the little barefooted shikseh Masha, the one with the large beads.

Other Novels

INTRODUCTION TO
MARIENBAD

Sholem-Aleykhem wrote *Marienbad* in 1911. It is the second novel in which he used the epistolary form. The first, *Menakhem-Mendl* (begun in 1892), is a dialogue-in-letters between Menakhem-Mendl and his wife, Sheyne-Sheyndl (an excerpt is included in this anthology [see p. 378]). *Marienbad* consists of a series of letters, notes, and telegrams to and from a group of close friends and relatives who are quite different from Menakhem-Mendl and Sheyne-Sheyndl.

Unlike the poor shtetl Jews that populate most of Sholem-Aleykhem's tales, the Jews in *Marienbad* are well-off city dwellers, successful business-men and their wives and families. Marienbad was a fashionable spa in Bohemia frequented by some of these Jews from Warsaw and other cities in Russia and Poland. They bathed in the mineral waters, played cards, spent time in the cafes, tried to arrange marriages for their eligible daughters, and became involved in flirtations and intrigues. The 36 letters, 14 love notes, and 46 telegrams comprising *Marienbad* give us a humorous and satirical glimpse of that life.

In the introduction to her English translation of *Marienbad*, Aliza Shevrin makes the following point:

> ...The value of this work lies in its unique representation of a people who always existed in an isolated and dissident relationship to the surrounding dominant culture. In this important respect Eastern European Jewry reflected in its daily experience what has since come to be appreciated as the plight of minority and Third World cultures in our own day. What is noteworthy is the tenacity with which they struggled to maintain their eth-nic identity in the face of powerful examples of an entirely different way of life. It took the madmen of the Third Reich to destroy them.

In translation, *Marienbad* consists of 96 communications and is 222 pages long. Presented below are the first five letters.

FROM *MARIENBAD*

1.

BELTZI KURLANDER FROM BERLIN
TO HER HUSBAND, SHLOMO KURLANDER,
ON THE NALEVKIS IN WARSAW.

To my dear husband the learned Shlomo may his light shine forever.

I want to let you know that I am still in Berlin. I am hoping to be able to leave for Marienbad after Shabbes. I really don't owe you any explanation. You must believe me that it's not my fault I've had to stay on an extra whole week. When you hear what I've been through, you will have to agree that it's never possible to figure things out beforehand. As they say, "Man proposes and God disposes."

I had counted on spending one day or two days at most in Berlin. How long should it take to see a specialist? It might have worked out if he had come to see me. But I thought to myself, Why should I make you spend an extra thirty marks which can come in handy for something else? You are always reminding me that we spend too much money. The times, you insist, are not the best—you go on and on. Maybe that's why I didn't want to stay at that hotel on Friedrichstrasse where my cousin Chava'le made reservations for me. How can I compare myself to Chava'le Tchopnik? Chava'le can spend as much as she likes and no one will complain because Chava'le isn't her husband's second wife, as I am, and her husband doesn't have any children from his first wife, as my husband has, and Berel Tchopnik doesn't tremble over every groschen, as you do, and he isn't afraid to remain a pauper in his old age, as you are. I don't mean, God forbid, to say anything against you, but I tell you frankly that I hate to run up extra expenses. So that is why I decided to stay at a place where many of our Nalevkis friends stay, at Madam Perelzweig's. The woman is a widow, a very capable person and an honest one. She is a good cook, charges reasonable prices, and her place is not far from everything. For just ten pfennigs you are on Leipzigerstrasse, at Wertheimer's. And how is it possible to be in Berlin and not step

430

into Wertheimer's for a minute? If you would see Wertheimer's just once, you would say that it is not to be believed. I had already heard of Wertheimer's back in Warsaw, but never did I imagine that on this earth there could be such a store. What can I tell you, my dear husband? It can't be put into words! You can't see enough, you can't say enough! And people! The mobs—so packed together you couldn't squeeze in a fingernail. And everything dirt-cheap, exactly half of what we have to pay on the Nalevkis. Just picture it—two marks for a dozen handkerchiefs! Or for ninety-eight pfennigs you can get a pair of silk stockings that you can't buy for a ruble and twenty in Warsaw. Or, for instance, a wall clock for sixty-eight pfennigs—tell me, is it possible? I figure that with God's help, when I am all better, on my way home I will return through Berlin, not Vienna—Vienna is, they say, a provincial town, a nothing compared to Berlin—and then I will really be able to spend some time at Wertheimer's and, with a clear head, do some serious shopping for the house—some glassware, some faience and other household articles, some silk goods, furniture and perfumes. Don't worry at all about customs; I'll manage somehow. Chava'le Tchopnik brings over whole cratefuls every year. In the meantime, I've hardly bought anything except some underwear, a pair of summer shoes, a little hat, a nightgown made entirely of ribbon, a halfdozen petticoats, a green umbrella, handkerchiefs and a few odds and ends which I must have for Marienbad. And while I was already at Wertheimer's, I couldn't resist the excellent buys and asked them to pack in a half-dozen tablecloths, two dozen napkins and a special machine for making butter. I could kick myself for not listening to you and taking along an extra few hundred rubles. It was so stupid of me to want to show off to you that I am not as big a spendthrift as you think. Better to spend it at Wertheimer's than on that doctor, may he suffer for it! Just what I needed in Berlin—a doctor! As if we don't have enough of them in Warsaw. You can bet the Berlin doctors would have to wait a long time before I would send for them. But fate had to arrange a misfortune. Just listen.

I had barely arrived at the lodgings—at Perelzweig's, as I told you. Even before I had had a chance to change or wash up properly, I was immediately asked the question—what kind of doctor do I want called in? So I said, "First of all, who told you that I need a doctor? Am I so sick that you can see it on my face? And second of all," I said, "I have brought with me from back home the address of a specialist." Then this old bachelor, a man with red pimples on his nose, spoke up. "Don't be offended, Madam," said he, "at what I will tell you. It's because," said he, "you have the address of a specialist that you must first see," said he, "a regular doctor. Because there's a big difference," said he, "between what you would tell the specialist and," said he, "what the doctor would tell him in his doctor's language." It turns out that this old bachelor with the red nose actually lives at the widow Perelzweig's, whom I told you about, and he arranges appointments with doctors. That means his job is to get a doctor if you need one and then the doctor gets the specialist or he even takes you to the specialist's office himself. So I politely let him know that nobody was taking me anywhere. "I am still," said I, "thank God, strong enough to walk a mile." So this doctor-arranger with the red pimples retorted, "Madam! As far as I'm concerned," said he, "you can walk three miles. But I must tell you ahead of time that you're wasting your time. If you visit a Berlin specialist on your own," said he, "without first seeing a regular doctor, then the specialist won't spend so much as half a minute with," said he, *"fee-foo-fah,* a poke with the finger one-two-three and out you go! Finished! But if you come," said he, "with your own doctor, then it's another story. A doctor he can't refuse; a doctor he has to listen to. Have you gotten the point yet," said he, "or not?"

To make a long story short, he called in a doctor for me. Right off, he didn't appeal to me. He didn't look me in the eye, he didn't have enough time for me, and he spoke in a squeaky voice. Would you like a doctor who doesn't look you in the eye and talks with a squeak?

First he questioned me thoroughly—who and what and when—and examined me all over. Then he insisted, this smart doctor, that I stay in bed till the following day when he would, said he, examine me again and then he would tell me, you see, which kind of a specialist he would refer me to. When I heard that he wanted to confine me to my bed, I let him know in no uncertain terms that he should forget about anything like that. "I didn't come," said I, "to Berlin to lie in bed. I have to go," said I, "to shop at Wertheimer's and at Teitz's and furthermore, I want," said I, "to go everywhere. If you wish," said I, "to come tomorrow, you are welcome, but for me to stay in bed—that," said I, "won't do!" He thought he had found himself some dummy from the Nalevkis from whom he could make a fortune. I could tell right away this was no doctor but a leech. As proof, just listen to what this blood-sucker did. It makes my hair stand on end!

In the morning, the two of us went to see the specialist and it turned out that it wasn't at all the specialist that Chava'le Tchopnik had told me about but another specialist for completely different ailments. This I discovered only after I had been put through torture and we were on our way home. That is, I *thought* we were going back home. It turns out we were going to yet another specialist and still not to the one I had in mind. This time he brought me to a woman's specialist! So I became quite properly indignant and started to make a fuss. The doctor then scolded me in his squeaky voice, I should remember that I wasn't in Warsaw on the Nalevkis but in Berlin and that I shouldn't make such a fuss and that he had no time and that he knew better than I what kind of specialist I needed. How can you argue with that? And so, as I'm telling you, we visited, if you can believe it, three specialists, and all three specialists, as if they had agreed ahead of time, said the same thing, "Marienbad!" So tell me, did I need three specialists to tell me that? Marienbad I had already heard about in Warsaw. In short, a waste of time, a waste of money. But what's done is done.

I went back to my lodgings so exhausted that I could barely stand on my feet. I simply had to lie down. Do you think I was allowed to rest for long? The doctor should only live as long as I rested! You can't imagine the bill I was presented with by this highway robber. I jumped out of bed as if struck by a thunderbolt. I should pay him, said he, eighty marks! Why eighty marks? "A simple addition," said he. "Two visits at ten marks each—is twenty. Three consultations with three specialists at twenty apiece—is sixty. Sixty and twenty are," said he, "always and everywhere, eighty." I must have made such an uproar that the whole house came running, the widowed landlady, the old bachelor—that *shlimazel*—and all the other guests. "Where are we?" I screamed at them, "In Berlin or Sodom? It's a thousand times worse here," said I, "than it is in Russia! You don't have doctors here, but hooligans! *Pogromchiks!*" I tell you, whatever came into my head, that's what I said to them. Try to picture the scene—people came crowding around us, and finally, finally they worked it out between us so that I would only have to pay him fifty-five marks. Fifty-five boils should fester on his face, that fine doctor! Do you think I'm finished? Hold on. Remember there's still that old bachelor with the red nose and the pimples. He wants fifteen marks too. What for? "That," said he, "is my commission for recommending the doctor." What do you say to such a lout? This made my blood boil so that it brought on my old symptoms and I had to take to bed with a migraine till the following day. It's no small matter—to throw out so much money and, I ask you, for what? For whom? Wouldn't it have been ten thousand times better to have spent it at Wertheimer's? I'm eating myself up alive for not coming here a week earlier. I would have been with my cousin Chava'le—a relative, after all, and I wouldn't have fallen into the hands of these leeches. It's just lucky that Berlin is a city in which there is a great deal to see or else I would die of boredom. You can see more in Berlin in one day that you can see in thirty years in Warsaw. In addition to Wertheimer's and Teitz's and other big stores, there is a Wintergarden and an Apollo Theater and a Schumann Circus and a Busch Circus. They even say there is a Luna Park that's not to be described! I'm planning to go there, God willing, in the morning, so I'll write you about it in my letter tomorrow.

Meanwhile, be well and tell Sheva-Rochel to take care of things—not only the kitchen but the rest of the house as well. Before leaving I forgot to write down on the laundry list a little collar and two pillowcases. Also I opened a jar of jam the day I left. She should use that one for cooking and not dare to touch the jams on the balcony under the chest. And remember to write me, for God's sake, in Marienbad, Poste Restante, as we agreed.

From me, your wife,
Beltzi Kurlander

2.

SHLOMO KURLANDER
FROM THE NALEVKIS IN WARSAW
TO HIS FRIEND CHAIM SOROKER IN MARIENBAD.

My dear friend Chaim,

I must ask you, my dear friend, for a small favor. It's really not a small favor. In fact, it is a big one. A very big one. Something awful has happened to me—my dear friend, my Beltzi must go to Marienbad. Why suddenly to Marienbad? Ask me something easier. She says she's not well and has to go to Marienbad. And the doctor also says she's not well and must go to Marienbad. Well, if two say a third is drunk, then the third starts to feel dizzy....But confidentially, I'll tell you—between the two of us, and I beg you to let it remain that way—I understand what's behind Marienbad. If Madam Tchopnik goes to Marienbad, why shouldn't Madam Kurlander also go to Marienbad? She compares me to Berel Tchopnik! She doesn't know, apparently, that what Tchopnik can afford *I* can't afford, *you* can't afford, *no one* can afford. Tchopnik can sit around an entire year in the finest apartment like a king and forget altogether that for an apartment you have to pay rent. I remember the time when Tchopnik rented one of my apartments. I thought I would have apoplexy. Every day he would demand new repairs and he would order me around like a janitor. Anyone else I would have thrown out on his ear but because of Beltzi I had to take a bellyful from him and be silent. How come? Because his Chava'le and my Beltzi are third cousins, you know, a grandmother's sister's granddaughter. Really close relations! What I had to put up with that year from Berel Tchopnik would take a week to tell. When a butcher would come to collect, Berel Tchopnik wouldn't open the door more than a crack, shouting, "The nerve of a butcher to come asking for money!" And Madam Tchopnik, when you would try to present *her* with a bill, you'd wear out two pairs of shoes trying to collect, and after a while you'd quit trying. When it comes to tailors and shoemakers—forget about it. They already know you don't go to them to collect because you won't get anything. Need I say more? Just recently they gave a dinner party on the occasion of Madam Tchopnik's birthday, just before they left for Marienbad. Well, you should have seen what went on! I wasn't there, but my Beltzi told me that it was such a big spread it was enough to marry off two daughters. The food was catered by Hekselman's Restaurant and the meal was fit for a king: fish and meat and roasts and wine and beer and whatever your heart desired. Wineglasses were clinking, the servants were running about, it was lively. They played a game in which Tchopnik was banker, of course. Somehow, he always manages to come out on top; he knows how to work it. According to my Beltzi there were hundreds in the kitty. Nevertheless, when Hekselman came the following morning to collect, they heaped such ridicule on his head that he's still ashamed to talk about it. But I got carried away talking about Tchopnik and almost forgot my request.

My request is simply this: Since my Beltzi is traveling to another country for the first time in her life—she can't even open a door for herself and doesn't know the language—I was wondering if you would be so kind and help her out, recommend a good lodging, a good doctor, a kosher restaurant—in a word, be her guide. By the way, I'd also like to ask you to keep an eye on her, see whom she meets there and with whom she socializes. I want, you understand, that she should keep some distance from Madam Tchopnik. You might wonder what I have against Madam Tchopnik. She's never hurt me. I just don't want my Beltzi to be too cozy with Madam Tchopnik, even though they *are* third cousins. I don't want her to be a model for Beltzi, so that whatever Madam Tchopnik says is good and whatever Madam Tchopnik wears is pretty and whatever Madam Tchopnik does my Beltzi will also want to do. Believe me, dear friend, it's not the money that matters to me. You know that I'm not, God forbid, a miser. My Beltzi gets her way with me, whatever she wants. She is, after all, a second wife, and a second wife, they say, like an only daughter, gets her way in everything. So you must wonder what the problem is? I don't want my wife to follow the crowd. Is that so terrible? I have, as it is, enough enemies on the Nalevkis who would be happy to drown me in a teaspoon of water. And especially since I married Beltzi, they'd like to avenge themselves on me, don't ask me why. It's as if I was ruining someone's reputation or business. They say she's young enough to be my daughter-in-law. Why should that bother them? Troublemakers have already tried to stir up fights between us. I ask, what have I done to them? All this fuss because she's pretty. To hell with all of them. Would they have been happier if I had remarried an ugly woman?

And so, dear friend, I don't have to say anything more, you understand what I mean. I want you to keep an eye on her and to write me a letter occasionally telling me how you are and what you are doing and how Beltzi is and what she is doing. If she should come to you for money—I gave her your address—give her on my account whatever she asks—naturally, not all at once, but a little at a time—because money to her, just between us, has no value. I knew beforehand that if I gave her too much money to take along, as soon as she got to Berlin it would probably disappear into thin air. And it was just as I predicted. I've already received a letter from Berlin (on the way to Marienbad she stopped in Berlin), sending me regards from someone by the name of Wertheimer who owns some kind of store, this Wertheimer, where you can find, she says, even "bird's milk." She's already been there, she writes, and she gives me to understand that this Wertheimer wasn't disappointed in her. She compares herself to Madam Tchopnik. Berel Tchopnik boasts that when his Chava'le went abroad, he gave her five hundred for the trip and when she arrived in Berlin she already wrote for more money and he had to send her another five hundred the following week. He throws five hundreds around, this Tchopnik! Do you have any idea what he does for a living? This man has been living in Warsaw for twenty years and I dare you to find anyone who can tell me what Berel Tchopnik's business is. He is a natty dresser with a prosperous paunch and a fancy accent who won't say one word more than is necessary. While he's looking at you, he is thinking how to trick you into lending him money he'll never repay.

In a word, this Tchopnik isn't worth the time spent talking about him. Again, I beg you, Chaim, you know how much my Beltzi means to me. I'm very disturbed that she's traveling alone. I would accompany her but how can I abandon my business? It's the height of the season. I'm putting up a few buildings and, God willing, in about a year I imagine I will be doing all right. As I see it, apartment houses should be making more money this year than last. But my Beltzi doesn't need to know this. Rather, if you have the opportunity, you can tell her the opposite—I don't need to teach you what to say; you already know. There's no other news.

You get our newspapers there so you probably know that things are not going too well here. I can give you news of your Esther. I saw her from a distance and she looks as if she's about to give birth any day now. If it's a boy, how can there be a *bris* without you? So see to it, my friend, that you do what I ask and answer me soon.

From me, your best friend,
Shlomo Kurlander

3.

BELTZI KURLANDER FROM BERLIN
TO HER HUSBAND, SHLOMO KURLANDER,
ON THE NALEVKIS IN WARSAW.

To my dear husband the learned Shlomo may his light shine forever.

I promised you yesterday that I would describe the Berlin Luna Park as soon as I got back from there, so I am doing it for you even though it's an impossible task. If I sat here and wrote all night I would not be able to convey one tenth of what you can see in that Luna Park. Now, that's really some place! Picture in your mind a huge park ablaze with light wherever you look. Every building is lit up from top to bottom. As soon as you arrive, you step right into a Funny House. Once you enter this special hall you are completely overcome by laughter. You laugh so long and hard that you come close to bursting. Wherever you turn, you see your own face in the weirdest shapes. Then after buying a ticket you sit down in this silly train which flies crazily uphill and downhill. One minute it lifts you up above the houses, the next minute it hurls you down, down into hell itself till you feel you are about to explode. People start shrieking and screaming. Up it goes again taking you high up a hill and then *zoom!* down you go again toward the ground, till you return to where you started from and come to a stop, feeling like an idiot. The German ticket-taker tells you to step out and you do, totally bewildered. Then you come to a lake and you see people sliding downhill in these little boats. They dive straight into the water and don't drown! You get the urge to try it and climb up the steps to the top. You buy another ticket and sit down in a little boat and down you go like a lunatic right into the water. You get out of there soaking wet wondering why a German would ask you to pay for this. From there a little further on you see these wild dark gypsies from Egypt who dance and sing, leap and tumble, lick red-hot irons with their tongues, stab themselves with swords and wiggle their bellies. And for this they make you pay! They will take you, if you want, right into Gehenem itself where they show you corpses, devils and ghosts, snakes, scorpions and other hideous things. You thank God to get out of there alive! Cafes, restaurants, cabarets, music boxes, movies, sideshows, photographs and more—they are as plentiful as the stars in the sky. If you let yourself go and take whatever these Germans offer you, you can come out of there more dead than alive. The whole thing, all in all, didn't cost me a single pfennig. How is that possible, you'll ask? You'll really like this.

Remember that bachelor, that lout with the pimples who gouged fifteen marks out of me for recommending that "fine" doctor? It was he who took me to Luna Park at his expense. He also treated me to Seltzer water, chocolate and whatever I wanted. I suppose he realized this made me feel ill at ease and he said to me, "For pretty young women who need a doctor, I am," said he, "an arranger. But to see Berlin, I am," said he, "no longer an arranger but a cavalier and a gentleman." What do you say to such a *shlimazel?* On the way back he said to me, this smart aleck, his face lighting up like the sun in July, "Madam! If you promise you won't be offended, I would like to tell you something." Said I, "Only if it's something clever." Said he, "I don't know if it's clever," said he, "but it will certainly be interesting to you." Said I, "If it's interesting, why not?" Said he, "Only on the condition, Madam, that you give me your reaction afterward." Said I, "Why shouldn't I?" Said he, "No, I mean I want you to be frank and not put me off." Said I, "Why should I put you off?" Said he, "No, I mean, if you don't like what I have to say," said he, "I want you to say so." Said I, "So talk. Stop pestering me like this." He stopped walking and this is what he said: "Listen, Madam, this is the way it is. Will you believe me or not? Maybe you'll believe me and maybe not,

439

although I don't know why you shouldn't believe me. I am," said he, "a sincere person and what I have to say," said he, "I say. I hate," said he, "being wishy-washy. I come right out with it, one-two-three and it's over. I have to tell you, Madam," said he, "that I am the kind of person who, if I have something to say, I say it right out. I can't hold it in too long. I have wanted to tell you for a long time," said he, "that I have found you very attractive," said he, "from the moment," said he, " that I first saw you. What do you say," said he, "to that?" "What," said I, "can I say? You're lucky," said I, "that we're in Berlin on the Friedrichstrasse. Otherwise, I would show you," said I, "what I think of fresh men like you!" With that, our conversation ended right on the spot. From then on I remained without an escort and have had to go everywhere alone. But it's no problem. Berlin is not a wilderness and the Germans are the kind of people who are willing to stop and listen to you, show you the way and answer your questions. On the contrary, if you ask them something they don't know, you can see that it really irks them. A German remains a German.

So I've written you all that I promised. God willing, when I arrive safely in Marienbad, I will write you more news from there. Meanwhile, be well and be sure to keep me up on all the Warsaw news when I'm in Marienbad. How is Esther Soroker? Has she given birth yet? And if so, what did she have, a boy or a girl? Some devoted husband she has, I mean, Chaim Soroker—to leave a wife when her baby is due and go off to Marienbad. Whoever heard of such a thing? He's the one who wants to "give birth," by losing that fat belly of his. If it were me, I'd never let him come back to the Nalevkis. I would make him stay in Marienbad forever. I would make him "give birth," all right, but it wouldn't be just his belly he would lose. Say what you like— I know he's a good friend of yours—but that's not the way to behave. It broke my heart when I went over to say goodbye to her. She's not the type to complain, but you could tell. They have the worst luck, those two sisters, both Esther and Chan'tzi. Chan'tzi, they say, is treated even worse by her Meyer. They told me here in Berlin that Meyer Mariomchik is also in Marienbad. And Broni Loiferrman and Leah'tzi Broichshtul and Madam Yamayichke with her daughters are already in Marienbad. All of Nalevkis is in Marienbad. Not bad. I hope to find letters from you in Marienbad. Just don't forget to write what's doing at home. Don't leave everything to Sheva-Rochel. You should check every day on what she brings from the market and be sure to reweigh the meat she gets from the butcher and, for God's sake, pay cash for everything because even the most honest shopkeeper will add on a bit if you charge it. And if Leah, the dressmaker, comes to you complaining that I didn't pay her enough for her work and appeals to your good nature, don't you dare fall for it. She's threatened to take me to court. Let her try! And don't forget, I beg you, to send me money in Marienbad. I'll send you my address as soon as I get there. I'm praying to God to arrive safely.

From me, your wife,
Beltzi Kurlander

4.

SHLOMO KURLANDER
FROM THE NALEVKIS IN WARSAW
TO HIS WIFE, BELTZI KURLANDER, IN MARIENBAD

To my dear wife, Beltzi, long may she live.

I received both your letters from Berlin and can tell you, dear Beltzi, that I am, thank God, well and that everything is all right at home. I just wish the tenants would pay their rent on time so that I wouldn't have to sue them. Besides losing the rent money, there are expenses, lawyers, papers and other complications. And to make matters worse, there is the indignity I would suffer because some of these ingrates threaten to "expose" me in the newspapers if I evict them and I don't want to have my name in the papers. I hate it. These days the construction business eats up so much money that I don't know how I will ever break even. On top of that I have to deal with craftsmen and laborers, who talk back to me and have no respect for a boss.In short, what can I tell you, Beltzi dear? One trouble leads to two others. And then your letters arrive from Berlin. You can't possibly imagine how sorry I am that you didn't go to Vienna instead of to Berlin. Oh, well, I suppose you wanted a specialist's diagnosis. All right. I would never stop

441

you and you know I would never scrimp on any amount of money when it comes to your health or welfare. It's bad enough to get entangled with those bloodsuckers and to need three specialists who will confuse you so that in the long run *they* will make you sick, but, I ask you, Beltzi dear, how can you risk your health by running around to Wertheimer's and Teitz's looking for bargains? I believe you when you say everything is half price, but your health is far more important, and besides you can get those same bargains in Warsaw. As they say, "For money you can get everything." Is it really a good idea to be pushed around in crowds? So you'll buy a few pairs of stockings and a wall clock—do you have to jeopardize your life for it? I ask you, Beltzi, you're not one of those Nalevkis *yentas,* so how come you did such a foolish thing? And to run around all over Berlin—I must say, Beltzi dear, I can't begin to understand what there is to see in Berlin. I picture a big city, three times, five times, ten times as big as Warsaw with nicer, taller buildings, a great deal nicer, a great deal taller. So what's so wonderful about that? Or, as you write, you went to the theater and the circus and other such places—that doesn't bother me. Quite the opposite—when you are in a foreign country you have to go everywhere and see everything. Why not? But one thing *does* bother me—that you jeopardize your own reputation and status by allowing yourself to be led around by any loafer whom you neither know nor should want to know. It's a good thing the idiot respected you. What would you have done if you had met a hooligan or a scoundrel? In strange places, Beltzi, you have to be even more cautious than at home. The worst embarrassment or misfortune might happen, God forbid. For this reason, I've written a letter to my good friend Chaim Soroker, in Marienbad, asking him to be available to you occasionally for advice or a little encouragement. He's been abroad several times and is familiar with foreign ways and customs and, as we've had business dealings in the past, I've indicated to him that he should let you have as much money as you need. To send money by mail is expensive and runs the risk of getting lost en route; there's no sense in mailing money. Be sure to get in touch with Chaim Soroker, give him my regards and tell him I'm awaiting an answer to the letter I recently wrote him. Tell him that there's still no news from home. His Esther hasn't given birth yet. One more thing I'd like to ask of you, Beltzi dear—keep some distance from your cousin, Chava'le Tchopnik. Not because she doesn't have a good reputation on the Nalevkis—I laugh at those things—but just because I don't want tongues to wag about you and fingers to point at you. As you yourself said, Marienbad has become a miniature Warsaw. All of the Nalevkis, you said, are there this summer. You see that Broni Loiferman and Leah'tzi Broichshtul and even Madam Yamayichke and her daughters are already in Marienbad. What other proof do you need? You have to avoid them like the plague because they are terrible gossips. Better to break a leg than to fall into Madam Yamayichke's mouth. I will never know why it is so important for Broni Loiferman and Leah'tzi Broichshtul to drag themselves off to Marienbad. Alright, Loiferman, they say, hit it rich this year in the lottery, and the rubles are burning a hole in his pocket. But Broichshtul? Just last week he came to see me about getting an interest-free loan and I told him where to get off. Asking for an interest-free loan and sending your wife to Marienbad—for that you really have to have nerve!

As for your writing that I should look after everything in the house—don't you worry about a thing. You just see to it that you get better and come home safely and then everything will be all right. Your worries about Sheva-Rochel are a waste of time. First of all, she's proven many times over that she's honest, even if there were gold lying around, and second of all, I really am keeping a close eye on everything; not only the sugar canister but the bread is under lock and key. I too am reluctant to buy on credit at the market. True, we deal with honest folks, with virtuous folks, but let's face it, some of them can be real thieves at times. Again I urge you, Beltzi dear, not to begrudge yourself anything. You should enjoy yourself there and get the best of everything for yourself. Just one thing I ask—don't go bargain-hunting in the shops. When you come home, I will, God willing, I promise you, buy you anything your heart desires. Why do you need such junk—tablecloths and handkerchiefs—don't you have enough of those already? Why do you need a special machine to make butter? And where will you put a wall clock? I'm just afraid, Beltzi, that when you arrive at the border you'll have such aggravation that all the good that Marienbad did will be thrown out the window and all my money would be wasted. Remember the humiliation Madam Karalnik from the Nalevkis suffered three years ago when she showed up at the border looking a little to plump and was made to go into a separate room where she was stripped down to her undershirt. They unwound from around her body over four hundred yards of silk ribbon. From that time on she was dubbed by all of us on the Nalevkis "the Karalnich'ke with the ribbons."

See to it that you get well soon and return home safely.

Wishing you only the best, I remain,

Your husband,
Shlomo Kurlander

5.

CHAIM SOROKER FROM MARIENBAD
TO HIS FRIEND SHLOMO KURLANDER
ON THE NALEVKIS IN WARSAW.

Dear friend Shlomo:

I received your heartwarming letter and am so pleased that you write so openly and consider me as a true friend. It will please me even more if I can be of real service to you. That your Beltzi is coming to Marienbad, I knew even before your letter arrived. You might want to know in what way and from whom I found out? Actually from Madam Tchopnik. How, you say? Let me tell you exactly how it happened. Since there really is nothing to do here— one can go crazy from boredom—let me try my hand at being a writer. I ask only one thing from you, Shlomo, that everything I write about this place be strictly confidential. You trusted me to be discreet, so I too trust you in matters I would not trust anyone else, not even my own wife. I am positive these matters will remain between us.

First I must describe Marienbad to you so that you will know precisely what this place is like. The people who come here are those whom God has blessed with an abundance of money and punished with an abundance of flesh. Perhaps it is really the very opposite—punished with an abundance of money and blessed with an abundance of flesh. These people are the most miserable on earth. They crave food and aren't allowed to eat. They yearn to travel and can't. They desire nothing better than to lie down and aren't permitted. "You must walk, the more the better," say the doctors. "You must lose weight," they say, "the more the better." "Lose weight," translated, means "Lose your ugly, fat belly, slim down." And for fat bellies there is one remedy—Marienbad. Here you lose weight as if it were removed directly by hand. There's nothing surprising about that. For food they give you next to nothing. The doctor forbids you to eat. You survive only because you are permitted to drink a little spring water, or as they call it, *Kreutzbrunen,* in the morning. Drunk warm on an empty stomach, it has the flavor of tepid dishwater. After your drink, you must walk, *exercise,* as the doctor calls it. After such drinking and such exercise you long to bite into something solid. You return to your hotel to eat and they serve you what they call *frishtik,* which turns out not to be food at all. What does this *frishtik,* consist of, I ask you? Meat? No. Eggs? No. Rolls? No. A mug of cocoa and a dry zweiback—that's what they call frishtik. After *frishtik,* the doctor makes you do more *exercise,* and that's when you work up a real appetite. When dinnertime comes around you imagine you could swallow an ox, horns and all. But the doctor says, "No, no, dear man, if you eat like that," says he, "you won't lose so much as an ounce, not an inch of fat, and you won't ever get rid of that excess baggage!"

In a word, it's hell, believe me. Luckily, you can stick your tongue out at the doctor. He orders you to eat nothing—let *him* eat nothing; he insists that you walk—let *him* walk. We're better off sitting down and playing a game of Preference. The problem is that there aren't always the necessary three players, so you have to play Sixty-six with a partner. You know that I really enjoy card-playing, but there is no one else around with whom to play Sixty-six except for Madam Tchopnik. As unbelievable as you think Berel Tchopnik is, he's nothing compared to his wife. I tell you, there is only one Madam Tchopnik. And she doesn't play half badly either. She can outplay any three men. So why am I complaining, you ask? She hates to lose more than anything in the world. And if she loses, she doesn't pay up. "You know who I am," she says. "You can trust me and, if necessary," says she, "my husband will pay you." What do you say about depending on *him* to pay up? It wouldn't be so bad if playing Sixty-six were the only thing she wanted to do. The problem is she likes to have you stroll with her through Marienbad. Just strolling with her would be tolerable, but the problem is she wants to do more than stroll. To her strolling involves going shopping, bargain-hunting, outwitting a German or two—and before you know it, you are lending her money which you will never see again. What a nuisance, I tell you! You can't hide from her. And just my luck, I'm the only one she seeks out. There's not one other man here from the Nalevkis. Only women. Broni Loiferman, Leah Broichshtul, Madam Sherentzis and Madam Pekelis. There's Madam Yamayichke with her three overgrown mam'selles who are the laughingstock of Marienbad because of their falsified ages. They would be perfectly fine mam'selles if not for their noses. Marienbad this season is full of wives. Everywhere you turn, wives—young wives, old wives, countless wives. Most of them are the ordinary sort from Bialystok, Kishinev, Yekaterinoslav, Kiev, Rostov and Odessa. Wherever they are from, they are here for the so-called "cure." But their main purpose is to corral husbands for their daughters, their ripe mam'selles. These chaperons are dressed in rich silks and satins, they wear pearl necklaces. Their daughters are put on display. The mothers speak pidgin German and inspect every man as if to say, "If you're a bachelor, come here; if you're married, go back to where you came from." Buzzing around these mamas like a bee around honey, is this character with a top hat who is called Svirsky. This Svirsky is a marriage broker, but he calls himself an international matchmaker. He's Jewish but he refuses to speak Yiddish, only German. His word for a successful match is a *partie,* a potential bridegroom is a *bräutigam;* he will never say "your wife," but *eure Frau gemahlen.* I tell you it's quite a sight to see these over-stuffed mamas in their pearl necklaces chasing after Herr Svirsky, chattering to him in their bad German while he boasts about his successes, how many parties he's arranged, and all based on love. I've met our Madam Yamayichke from the Nalevkis with her three daughters several times strolling about with this Herr Svirsky, who never removes his top hat—not Shabbes, not weekdays. May God help her, I wish with all my heart that Svirsky might arrange a *partie* for her, three *parties,* three *bräutigams* for her three noses even if it's without love, and the sooner the better. You can bet the youngest will have to start lying about her age soon because she's already past thirty. And if we were to add to her age the years her older sisters have subtracted, it would altogether, I'm afraid, add up to a total of more than a hundred, poor things! As much as possible, I avoid Madam Yamayichke—you know what a gossip she is.

So now that I've described a little of Marienbad for you, I can tell you how I found out your Beltzi was coming.

Yesterday morning I went to the "watering trough" where I met Madam Tchopnik, Madam Loiferman, Madam Broichshtul, Madam Sherentzis, Madam Pekelis and Madam Yamayichke with all of her three noses, as well as some other women—the whole Marienbad Nalevkis crowd! "Good morning," "Good day," How is it going!" "What's new!" Meanwhile Chava'le Tchopnik said to me, "Do you know we're expecting a guest in Marienbad tomorrow!" Said I, "God love you and your guest. Who is it?" Said she to me, "Aha, see how clever you are and figure it out." Said I, "What makes you think I can figure is out?" Said she, "I'll give you a clue." Said I, "By all means, let's have a clue." Said she, "Not one clue but several. First of all, she is," said she, "pretty, the prettiest of all the Nalevkis women." That really irked the other women. They exchanged glances and hurled such fiery looks at Madam Tchopnik, you could have burned down a small town in Poland. Madam Tchopnik was oblivious to their reaction and started enumerating the virtues of this pretty newcomer to Marienbad. "Enough of these virtues," said I to her. "Give me another clue." "The other clue, she said, "is that she has a husband who is more than twice her age and she's not even twenty years old."

At this point all the other ladies burst out laughing, "Not counting Saturdays and holidays!" Seeing this could go on all day, I said to Madam Tchopnik, "Enough of this backbiting," said I, "let's hear," said I, "who is coming to Marienbad." Said Madam Tchopnik to me, "Hush! One more clue and that will be all. She is," said she, "a relative of mine." "Is that so!" said I, "so why are you beating around the bush? Just say," said I, "that Beltzi Kurlander is coming to Marienbad and make an end of it." There then ensued a discussion among the women about your Beltzi, and, as usual, talking more than all the others was Madam Yamayichke. What can I tell you, Shlomo? I can't begin to put it down in writing and really don't want to repeat it. You must know yourself what Madam Yamayichke can think up about your Beltzi. And not just about Beltzi, but also about you! If an outsider were to overhear her, he would surely conclude you had ruined her life or done something awful to her.

Fortunately, Herr Svirsky with his top hat joined us and called Madam Yamayichke away to whisper something in her ear, probably about a *partie* or a *bräutigam*.

447

That's how I found out that your Beltzi was coming to Marienbad. Then when I went home in the evening, I found your letter. You were correct in writing to me. Rest assured, dear friend, that I will do everything you ask of me on your behalf and on hers. You can rely on me. I won't spare any effort and will write you everything as it happens. But you too must not be lazy. Write more often what the news is from Warsaw. But try to write only good news—I hate sad letters. It's a matter of necessity. If I'm here for the cure, I have to forget all about my troubles and misfortunes. There are enough troubles at home the rest of the year. Believe me when I tell you that when I am abroad, I do not even read a newspaper. I do exactly as I please—I eat and drink and sleep and take my stroll and try to lose weight and play a game of Preference if I can find a third hand and if I can't—I play Sixty-six with a partner. So be well. God willing, tomorrow morning, when your Beltzi arrives, I will most likely let you know about everything in greater detail. Again, be well, and continued success in your business. Wishing it so,

Your best friend,
Chaim Soroker

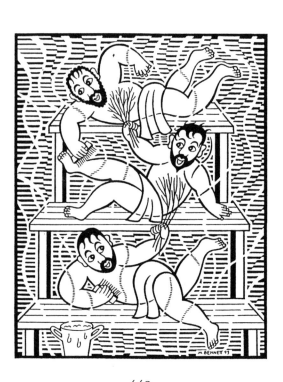

Other Novels

INTRODUCTION TO

THE BLOODY HOAX

The idea for *The Bloody Hoax* (subtitled, "An Extraordinary Novel") had been germinating in Sholem-Aleykhem's mind for many years when something happened in 1913 which almost certainly must have pushed him to start working on it in earnest. That something was the trial of Mendl Beylis (Mendel Beilis), a Russian Jew accused (in 1911) of murdering a Christian child so as to use its blood in the baking of the *matses* (matzohs) for the feast of Passover. This was the age-old ritual-murder charge, called by Jews in Yiddish the "blut bilbl" (the blood libel). It had been discredited many times in its long history, but it was being revived now in the twentieth century in Kiev as part of a widespread antisemitic move organized by the czarist regime and joined by other Jew hating segments of the Russian population, such as the Black Hundreds.

The case received world-wide coverage in the press. Jews everywhere followed the progress of the trial as it unfolded in the newspapers day-by-day, Sholem-Aleykhem among them. And although in his fictionalized account of it at the end of *The Bloody Hoax,* Sholem-Aleykhem followed the twists and turns of the Mendel Beylis trial closely, the novel (written in two parts, consisting of almost four hundred pages altogether) is, of course, about much more than just that trial. It is really about antisemitism in Russia in general and a plea for understanding between the Russian and Jewish peoples.

In the course of the novel various cultural and historical currents eddying through and around the Jewish people at the time are discussed—Zionism, assimilation, and the Yiddish language among them.

And, of course, *The Bloody Hoax* is also a love story, told in Sholem-Aleykhem's special, tender, endearing way.

At the very beginning of the novel (the selection reproduced here), two young students, graduates of the same Russian *gymnasium,* make a wager,

449

agreeing to exchange their identities for one year: the Russian student, Popov, using his friend's documents to pass himself off as the Jew, Rabinovits, and the Jewish student, Rabinovits, passing himself off as Popov. As a result, Popov, in the guise of Rabinovits, discovers that (1) in spite of his gold medal for superior grades, he is refused admittance to the university, and (2) he cannot remain in Kiev without a special residence permit, required of all Jews. He finally finds a room with a Jewish family. The head of this household, David Shapiro, gains him admittance to a dental school which qualifies him for a residence permit.

Popov discovers what living like a Jew in the Russian Pale is really like, as he finds himself, along with the Shapiro household, subjected to various humiliations, including middle-of-the-night searches reminiscent of the kinds of searches and expulsions performed by the Immigration and Naturalization Service here in American cities. He also falls in love with the beautiful Jewish daughter of David Shapiro. As you can imagine, similar complications occur with Rabinovits, who is now masquerading as Popov. At the end, the real Popov is accused, like Mendl Beylis, of slaughtering an innocent Christian child so as to use its blood for baking matses.

Finished in 1914, Sholem-Aleykhem turned *The Bloody Hoax* into a play in that same year called *Shver Tsu Zayn A Yid (Hard to Be a Jew)*. It was staged by Maurice Schwartz in New York in 1920. Paul Muni (then Muni Weisenfreund) played the Russian student.

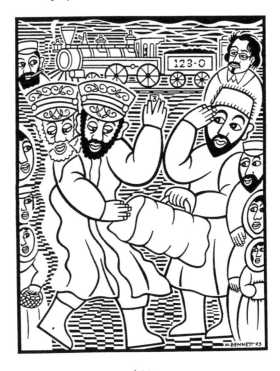

450

FROM *THE BLOODY HOAX*

1.

LET'S CHANGE PLACES

It was long past midnight.

In a private room of an elegant restaurant, The Elephant, under recently invented electric lights, amid loud music, chitchat and laughter, a dozen or so young men barely out of their teens were carousing—drinking, smoking, arguing, bantering, and joking while someone was banging away at a piano.

It was the celebration of a group of classmates who had just completed *gymnasium*—secondary school—and were enjoying one last evening together before bidding one another farewell for a long time, perhaps for good. In a few days each would be heading home, and only God knew if they would ever meet again.

The thought of never meeting again was so new to each of them, so alien that they had to imagine it could only be a dream. For eight years they had been as one! In those eight years, not a single day had gone by without their seeing one another. And now suddenly they would all be going their separate ways, and who knew where or when they would meet again!...

"And that's why, my friends, we have to down another glass of wine!"

Another glass of wine and another glass, and after each glass cheeks flushed deeper, eyes grew drowsier, foreheads glistened with sweat. It was time to begin parting in earnest.

"More wine!"

"Champagne!"

"Champagne! Champagne!"

For the tenth time they sang the traditional student song:

Gaudeamus igitur
Juvenes dum sumus...

This was sung in a fine baritone by a cheerful, dark-haired young man with rosy cheeks and lively eyes, and the rest of the delighted young men joined him:

451

Post jucundam juventutem,
Post molestam senectutem
Nos habebit sumus...

"Hey, Hershke! Why so downhearted? Why that hangdog look?" the cheerful dark-haired young man with the rosy cheeks called out to another young man who was sitting by himself off to the side staring down at his feet, making it impossible to see his face.

"Leave him alone, Grisha, he's a goner. He really polished off a couple of good ones!" one of the bunch exclaimed to the dark-haired young man.

"You're an ass!" the fellow called Grisha cut him off, "Hershke can't be drunk. He belongs to a people who stay sober on principle."

With those words, the dark-haired Grisha went over to the solitary young man called Hershke, who belonged to that sober people, and tapped him lightly on the head. The other one lifted his face. None of his features were at all Semitic. On the contrary, the cheerful, dark-haired young man who called the other one Hershke and was himself known as Grisha looked more like a Jew and more likely to be called Hershke because his hair was dark and his eyes too lively. He was also endowed with a small bend to his nose. But only on the real Hershke's pale forehead were to be found a few more wrinkles than one would expect for his twenty years, and his eyes revealed a suppressed, ever present sorrow, a sadness which carries over among our people from generation to generation on which only a Jew can be an expert because a Jew feels more with his heart than he perceives with his eyes...

"What's the matter, Hershke?" Grisha asked him, pulling up a chair and seating himself close to him while the rest carried on—drinking, smoking, laughing, making an uproar and reveling merrily.

The young man named Hershke made an effort to smile weakly and the two boys started to converse.

"Nothing's the matter, Grisha. It's just that my head hurts a little."

"You're lying, you're worried about something. I've been noticing it all night. You can't fool me, Hershke, I know you too well."

"I'm glad you know me. But I wish you knew me a little better. If you did..."

452

The rest was expressed with a gesture and Grisha asked him, "Then what?"

"Then you wouldn't have to ask me. Then you would know that I'm not like the rest of you. I can't celebrate as you do."

"Why?"

The young man named Hershke smiled, gesturing with his hands expressively. "For the reason that when you celebrate, you celebrate with your whole being, with every part of your body and all your senses."

"And you?"

"And I? I don't dare... I can't... Before my eyes there is always the *memento mori,* reminding me that I am a Jew..."

"That's ridiculous!"

Grisha pushed his chair back from Hershke, looked him directly in the face and said warmly, "Hershke! You certainly can't accuse any of us. We, your friends, who..."

"Don't be a fool! Who's talking about you and our friends? Do you really think this is the way the world is? Outside the *gymnasium* is the real world. There are other people out there besides you. You don't know what kind of hell is out there. If you were in my shoes for just one year, then you would know, then you would feel..."

The young man known as Grisha was thoughtful a while. Then he tossed his dark hair back and said, "Do you know what I'm going to tell you, Hershke!"

"What are you going to tell me?"

"Let's change places."

The two of them burst out laughing at the notion. Then Hershke said to Grisha, "It's easy for you to make jokes, but if your name were Hershke, not Grisha..."

"Let's trade places," Grisha said again, seriously now, but Hershke wasn't listening and continued, "You would, for example, have to be subject to the quota system."

"You're talking nonsense, Hershke. What quota! What system? You've won a gold medal. What do you care about quota systems?"

"Some reasoning! Do you know how many of last year's medalists are without jobs no matter what they try to do about it? They sell their last pair of pants to scrape up enough money to send off a wire to the minister, a whole song and dance, full of heartrending feelings, crying out to the heavens."

"Nu?"

"Nu-nu."

"What 'nu-nu'?"

"Fool that you are! They don't even get an answer. Yids sending wires! Those pushy people! Lucky they don't get themselves arrested! They get off easy if they're just driven out of the city and their residence permits revoked. And the same thing will most likely happen to me."

"You're wrong! It won't happen to you. You won a medal."

"Again with the medal? What an ass! You can't get that medal out of your head, can you!"

"That's why I'm telling you—let's change places."

"The whole problem is that you aren't really hearing what I'm saying. It's going in one ear and out the other."

"Go to the devil! I've worked myself into a sweat over this."

Grisha mopped the perspiration from his forehead and with a laugh moved closer to Hershke, taking his arm.

"Listen carefully to what I'm saying to you, Hershke. Let's trade places!"

Hershke finally heard what was being said to him and seemed to wake as from sleep.

"What do you mean 'trade places'? What can you possibly mean by that?"

"We can switch diplomas. You give me your diploma with those top grades of 'fives' and your medal and I'll give you my diploma with its 'threes.' You'll be Grisha and I'll be Hershke. Has that gotten through to you yet, or not?"

"Have you gone mad? Or are you pulling my leg?"

Grisha crossed himself and Hershke burst out laughing. Then they both began laughing together, and finally Grisha said to his comrade in all seriousness, "You said that I should try being in your shoes for a year. And I'm telling you that the devil himself isn't as bad as he's portrayed. We're not changing places forever, just for a year. Why not! You be Grisha Popov, and I'll be Hershke Rabinovitch. Do you understand yet or not? We'll exchange diplomas and names and passports. I'll be you and you'll be me. Why are you looking at me that way? I'm not joking with you. I'm being very serious." (And Grisha put on a serious face for his friend.) "I'm well acquainted with you and with other Jewish students and all I ever hear from you is: 'Jews... Jews are a tragic people,' and other such statements. I don't understand it. My brain registers it but I can't say I really know what it means. Do you understand that or not? I want to be in your skin for a little while. For one year I want to be a Jew and feel what it's like to be a Jew, understood? Let's shake hands on it and give our word before all our friends that whatever may happen during this year will be past and forgotten and not a soul must know that you are you and I am I, I mean, that I am I and you are you—Hell! I mean, that I am you and you are me. So is it agreed?"

Grisha offered his hand as Hershke rubbed his forehead and looked at his comrade like a person who isn't sure whether the other one is a bit crazy of whether he himself is in his right mind. Nevertheless, he put his hand out to his friend, and his friend Grisha helped him to his feet, led him over to the rest of the group, who were still caught up in their revels. With one hand he slapped the tabletop so hard that the bottles and glasses clinked together loudly and with his other hand pointed to Hershke, who was standing in a state of confusion, and cried out at the top of his lungs in his rich baritone voice, "Silence, comrades! Be quiet! I don't want to hear a pin drop!"

Suddenly it did become quiet. All eyes turned toward Grisha and at his apprehensive friend, Hershke. Grisha assumed the stance of an orator and began to give a speech.

2.

THEY CHANGE PLACES

"Friends!" Grisha began in a quiet voice, hooking his thumb in his vest like an experienced speaker, his eyes looking downward at first. Then as he raised his head slowly, his voice grew louder and louder. "Friends! At this very moment, the man you see before you is not your friend Grisha Popov, but your other friend, Rabinovitch. Don't think I am out of my senses or that it is the wine speaking. I assure you I have all my wits about me and I swear to you that I have never been as sober as I am at this moment.

"I shall clarify what I mean in a moment. Our comrade, who was known as Hershke Rabinovitch and who will now be known as Grisha Popov—you will soon see why—belongs to a people which the world does not love and which is persecuted almost everywhere on the face of the earth. We don't know the whys or wherefores of this powerful hatred and it is not our task at this time to decide which party is more to blame—the oppressors or the oppressed, the persecutors or the persecuted. Possibly both sides are in the right according to their points of view, or perhaps they are both in the wrong. We only know that the stronger of the two brings down every evil on the heads of the weaker, accusing them of every sin, while the weaker protests that these are all lies and that they are no worse than others and perhaps even better. For better or worse, this is not a matter easily settled and I don't know who has the right to settle it.

"I can believe one way, you another. I myself believe that both sides have exaggerated their positions. For instance, I am convinced that we, as Christians, don't hate the Jews nearly so much as the Jews imagine we do, and I am of the opinion that the Jews don't suffer nearly so much as they would have us believe. True, it isn't pleasant to be persecuted and hated by the whole world. But there remains a certain satisfaction, a special pride, one might say, a kind of sweetness, in the word 'martyr.' It is more convenient to believe I am being pursued for no reason than to believe I am pursuing someone else for no reason. In any case—the devil is never as bad as he is portrayed. I expressed this opinion to my friend Hershke here... pardon! our friend Grisha, and he answered that it was easy for me to say because I have never been a Jew. If I were to find myself, he says, in his skin for at least a year, then I would, he says, know what it's really like. That gave me an idea. Perhaps he isn't entirely wrong. One has to be in another's place in order to really experience what it's like and only afterward can you judge, either blaming or justifying... And so with this idea in mind I suggested to my friend Hershke that we exchange diplomas, names, and passports for no more than a year. In other words, at this very moment, this is no longer Grigori Ivanovitch Popov who is speaking to you, but Hersh Movshovitch Rabinovitch, and he, Hershke, is no longer Hersh Movshovitch Rabinovitch, but Grigori Ivanovitch Popov. He will leave here with my documents and will enter the university, and I will leave here with his documents. He insists that with his documents it will be difficult for me even to be admitted to the university because he is a Jew, and I say, nonsense, with a medal I can laugh at the whole world."

"Bravo!" the boys shouted as one, and began to applaud enthusiastically. But Grisha didn't let them applaud long. He raised his hand for silence and went on.

"Comrades! I have entrusted you with a secret, a deep secret, and I am asking two things of you: first, that you congratulate us both for our new exchanged roles. And second—quiet! Hold on, I haven't finished yet. And second—give me your word of honor and swear that no other human being alive besides us here will know of this, not now, or later, even when the year is up. The whole plan has to be, I insist, a secret, a holy secret that we must take with us to our graves!"

"We swear! We swear!" they cried out in many different voices, and Grisha ended his speech.

"I swear you to secrecy by all that is holy to all of us. He who bares this secret to an outsider will be considered a traitor and a criminal. Friends! I propose we fill our glasses and drink a toast to our new-born comrade who was once called Hershke Rabinovitch and today will be called Grigori Ivanovitch Popov. Let us all wish him good luck. Long live Grigori Ivanovitch Popov! Hoorah!!!"

*   *   *

The excitement and enthusiasm that this totally unexpected toast aroused among the young classmates cannot be described. That they all took it upon themselves to keep the holy vow without wavering—of that there was no question. And that they all agreed with the sentiment of the toast was evident from the way glasses were emptied to the last drop. The crowd was so taken with the idea that a Hershke had turned into a Grisha and a Grisha into a Hershke that they made the two of them exchange not only their documents but their clothes as well right in front of their eyes. And once they had changed clothes, there was such glee among the group that they proceeded to embrace both of them, their voices ringing to the rafters. Then one of them sat down at the piano and started to play a waltz, to which they all danced. And when they had had their fill of dancing, Hershke Rabinovitch, now known as Grigori Ivanovitch Popov, stood up and spoke to the crowd.

"Friends! Our comrade Grisha Popov, or, as he is now called, Hershke Rabinovitch, started out with a joke which has now

457

turned serious. We can't be so clever as to know in advance how this joke will turn out or what terrible consequences may come of it. Furthermore, it is obvious which one of the two of us will profit more (as the former Hershke, I can't restrain myself and must use the word 'profit'). That much I know, as you must also be well aware of if you have any brains at all. And if you don't realize this, then it's not my fault. But I must make one request of you, my dear friends. Since our friend Grisha, I mean Hershke, has taken a vow and has made me take a vow for a year that he will be me and I—him, and since we cannot know in advance what can befall us in our new lives into which we are now entering, I therefore wish to state a condition, that should one of us come out of this looking badly, that is..."

"No conditions!" called out the former Grisha Popov, now Hershke Rabinovitch, springing up from his seat, "No conditions! It's decided and no going back!"

"No going back!" echoed the rest of the crowd.

"*Byt posyemu*—So be it!" added the new Hershke Rabinovitch.

"So be it!" repeated the crowd.

When our new Grigori Ivanovitch Popov realized he was being out-voted, he stood up from the table, went over to the former Popov, now Hersh Rabinovitch, and with a smile on his lips put out his hand.

"Remember now, Hersh Movshovitch Rabinovitch, no regrets."

"Regrets?" the former Popov replied forcefully and with pride. "The Popovs, I mean the Rabinovitches, know no regrets. I come from a people, *chort vozmi,* which has gone through fire and water! My forefathers kneaded clay in Egypt, built the eternal pyramids, erected the famous cities of Sodom and Gomorrah...pardon I mean Pitum and Ramses, suffered until they settled in the land of Canaan. And when we settled in the land of Canaan, there came Balshazar... Tphoo! I mean Nebuchadnezzar, who burned down our holy temple and dragged us off in iron chains, brought us, together with our sisters and children, to the idolatrous Babylon, and from there—I am taking a giant leap, my friends, and leaving out Haman and Ahashueros and other such fine folks because it's already daylight outside—and from there they chased us to Spain, to that accursed Catholic Spain where the Inquisition was awaiting us. Just bear in mind, my friends, what my blessed ancestors suffered in the Inquisition! They were burned at the stake; on the scaffold they were slaughtered, stabbed, axed, drawn and quartered!..."

"Bravo, Hershke, bravo!" burst out the entire group of youths, the true Hershke Rabinovtich among them, applauding loudly and laughing even louder, so impressed were they with their comrade Grisha Popov, who had entered into the role of Hershke Rabinovitch so skillfully and so naturally that one wanted to embrace and kiss him. "An artist, a true artist! Look how his eyes light up! And how do you like that serious face? He doesn't allow so much as a smile. Would you be able to tell, even if you had the brains of a genius, that this is Grisha Popov, not Hershke Rabinovitch? No, look at his Jewish face, his Jewish eyes, even his nose seems to have bent into a Jewish nose, ha-ha. Bravo, Hershke, bravo! Bis!! Bisss!!!..."

*   *   *

It was already broad daylight when the classmates left the elegant restaurant, The Elephant, and seated themselves in droshkies which took them off in different directions. Grisha and Hershke boarded the same droshky, Grisha in Hershke's clothes, Hershke in Grisha's clothes. Even though Grisha Popov was now Hershke Rabinovitch and Hershke Rabinovitch was now Grisha Popov, they had much to talk about. They had to give one another personal information, background, and family history before each would go his own way, assuming his new role. In truth, it was the beginning of the great hoax.

3.

A ROOM TO LET

A pleasant excitement prevails in a large university town as the end of summer approaches and before the fall semester begins. Vacations are drawing to a close, and the *gymnasiums,* the polytechnicum, and the university itself prepare to open their doors for the new semester.

From nearby cities and towns, and places well beyond, parents with their offspring in tow arrive in the university town, some ready to begin a new grade and some to take entrance examinations in order to qualify for the temples of enlightenment and learning.

A special anxiety stirs the parents, even more than in the excited offspring. Young mothers, dressed in the latest fashion, beat down the doors of the directors' secretaries, administrators, and teachers. They are prepared to fall in a dead faint or throw three hysterical fits because their "Volodka" or their "Sashka" wound up with only a "two" on the entrance examination.

The booksellers and stationers display their latest and best selections, which they have prepared for the young people's delectation. They are ready to do business, to make a bit of money, to exchange old books for new ones—in a word, to serve the culture of the fatherland with integrity and loyalty like good, honest patriots.

The tailors and clothiers are also no mean patriots. They display in their show windows the finest and most up-to-date fashions they can muster, from elegant uniforms with shiny buttons to stylish trousers which seem to plead: "Come put us on and show us off!"

The hatmakers and milliners display entire collections of peaked caps and hats decorated with all varieties of white and yellow ornaments, eagles, bars, and decorative gold braid. In the luggage and variety shops, even the smallest satchels are given their place; they too are on display along with spats, galoshes, candy, and cigarettes. And the sausage makers—who are certainly not be found anywhere near the august Ministry of Public Education and who don't hold much by learning, but who also wish to partake, however distantly, in the culture of the fatherland—display in their shop widows thick, juicy slices of sausage and ham, meat pies and beef so fresh and redolent of garlic that the best student can quickly forget all about culture and the fatherland when hunger comes upon him and he takes a good whiff of that aromatic pork.

The hotels and inns, the restaurants and cafeterias are packed full with the newly arrived guests, fathers and mothers and children of all sizes. On the windows of almost all the houses are attached notices advertising "*Komnata Vnayom*—Room To Let."

Those who put up the notices know beforehand who will be occupying the rooms. It will be either a single male student who possesses but one pair of trousers, two shirts, and a mountain of books; or it will be a female enrolled in special courses, one who once wore her hair bobbed and now fancies short, tight frocks which in Paris are called "culottes." At any rate, each little room contains no more than one iron bed, hard as the notorious bed at the gates of Sodom, one iron washstand, which will not tolerate one's standing too close to it while washing, as it suffers, may such an affliction not be visited upon you, from a rusty rheumatism in its legs since the day it was brought from the factory.

The little room also contains a table and a chair, which have their good points and bad points. The little table can serve as a desk or as a place to eat or, for that matter, for whatever else you might wish. Those are its good points. The one bad point of the table is not to be blamed on the table itself, but on its drawer. Once you open the drawer, it doesn't want to shut; and once it is shut, under no circumstances can you open it—not from the front, not from the back, not from the sides. You can yank it as hard as you wish and the table will simply drag right along with you. Do you want to outsmart it and try to pull the drawer out from underneath with both hands? Go ahead and try. I can tell you ahead of time what will happen: the back legs will lift up and the whole table, with its books, inkwell, and carafe of water, will wind up together with you on the floor. So? What have you accomplished? You had better get along without a drawer. Where is it written that a table must have a drawer?

And what about the chair I was telling you about? A chair like any chair, this is one of those chairs called "*Wiener shtuhlen*—Viennese chairs." They are lightweight, strong, and comfortable to sit on because their seats are woven of straw—flat and smooth and soft. Those are the virtues of "Viennese chairs" in general. But the chair which is found in the room we have described has not one of the enumerated virtues. Suffice it to say we will share this secret with you—the chair lacks a seat. That is, it has a seat, but without straw, that is, it once had straw, when the chair was a chair. But let's not waste any more breath on this poor excuse for a chair. Let's talk about the landlady who was letting the little room, her husband, their daughter Betty, and about the person who came to rent this room—much more important matters.

Sara Shapiro—that was the name of our landlady—was still a young woman, pretty with attractive, dark features. She was standing at the stove, her sleeves rolled up, preparing lunch, while her

461

daughter, Betty, a true beauty with a fiery temperament, about eighteen to twenty years old, was sitting reading a Russian newspaper when the doorbell began to ring loudly.

"It must be another *shlimazel* for the room!" the mother announced to her daughter, indicating that she go open the door.

Unenthusiastically, the daughter laid aside the newspaper and ran down the three flights to open the door. In two minutes she returned with a clean-shaven young man carrying an almost empty satchel who wished to look at the room to let.

Carefully looking over the newcomer with the almost empty satchel, the mother quickly determined that he must be a poverty-stricken student from the hinterlands who couldn't rent the room in any case and consequently told her daughter in Yiddish to overstate the rent. The daughter obeyed and told the young man the rent. The young man didn't blink an eye and asked to see the room. At that point Madam Sara Shapiro laid aside her cooking, rolled down her sleeves, and went along to show the young man the room.

As they entered the previously described room, our guest carefully looked over the landlady and her daughter much more than he did the room and its furniture. After a short deliberation, he declared that, good, he was satisfied. Madam Sara Shapiro again found it necessary to remind him of the price. The visitor said the price was fine. If that were the case, Madam Shapiro felt she had to tell him that he had to pay for the first half-month in advance. The young man said he wouldn't mind paying a whole month in advance.

At this Madam Shapiro became a bit wary: what sort of customer was this? He comes along, takes one look, doesn't bargain; you tell him he has to pay half a month's rent in advance and he's willing to pay a whole month's rent! Who knows what kind of fly-by-night he is? She and her daughter exchanged glances. When she took a good look at the young man she noticed how fixedly he was staring at her Betty. This made her mistrust him all the more and she decided on what she had to do.

"Please don't be offended, but we have to be very strict... You understand, the police... if you wouldn't mind showing me your documents... Your passport..."

"Oh, my passport?..." Our young man withdrew his papers from a side pocket and with a gentle smile handed his passport to Madam Shapiro and then started to open his wallet.

But at that moment something occurred that stopped the young man from taking his money out. Madam Shapiro looked at the passport and read aloud: *Shklovskii Meshchanin Hersh Movshovitch Rabinovitch,* telling her he was a resident of Shklov and, from his name, a Jew. She gave her daughter a quizzical look, then said to the young man, "Please don't be offended... I'm not sure you can stay here. I didn't know that you were a..."

With a little smile the young man turned toward Madam Shapiro.

"That I am a what?"

"That you are one of ours... a Jew."

"And if I am a Jew, what of it?"

The young man put his wallet back in his pocket and the three of them looked at one another wordlessly.

4.

THE POWER OF A MEDAL

Up to that point the conversation had been carried on in Russian. But now that it became clear that he was a resident of Shklov whose name was Hersh Rabinovitch, well then, what would be the harm if they were to converse in "our" language? And Sara Shapiro directed herself to him in plain Yiddish.

"I'm surprised at you. You look to me like a worldly young man and yet you don't know that a Jew has to have a residence permit."

To this compliment the worldly young man had no response as he had understood not one word spoken to him. He answered Madam Shapiro in Russian, blushing a little.

"Excuse me, I'm afraid I don't understand Yiddish." Madam Shapiro could no longer contain her laughter.

"A Shklov resident with the name of Rabinovitch and you don't understand Yiddish?!..."

Betty, who till then had been standing off to the side seemingly uninvolved, interrupted the conversation to come to the aid of the young man who had rented the room. She addressed her mother in Russian.

"There aren't enough people nowadays, children of Jews, who don't understand any Yiddish?"

Then she explained to the young man, briefly and to the point, what they were speaking about: a Jew was forbidden to live in that city unless he had a special residence permit. If anyone were to allow a Jew to live there without that permit, they would be severely punished: their residence permit would be taken away and they would be sent from the city within twenty-four hours. "Now do you understand?"

All this was said with so sweet a smile and with so much charm that were her mother not by her side, the young man would have thrown his arms around her and kissed this enchanting young woman who was capable of such sweet and yet such mischievous smiles. And even though the regulation about residence permits was only vaguely known by our hero—he had heard that there were cities where Jews must have permits to live but he remembered it quite dimly—nevertheless, he acted as if he were well aware of it and said with a smile to the charming young girl, "I do know all about the permit regulation even thought I'm not from these parts. It's a regulation they should have gotten rid of a long time ago together with all the old trash. But I wish you could explain one thing to me—why did they require me to leave all my documents at the university?"

The word "university" burst upon both mother and daughter like a sudden bright ray of sunshine. Their faces lit up and the other slapped herself on the thighs.

"Is that so? Are you really a student at out university? Why didn't you say anything until now?"

"Didn't say anything? It seems to me that all three of us have been talking quite a bit," the student said smiling, all the while gazing at the daughter, not at the mother. The mother continued her interrogation.

"Does that mean you're already admitted?"

"Just about... I have a medal."

"Ah! You're a medalist? Is that so? Hear that?"

The last sentence was addressed in Yiddish to the daughter, with a sigh. But she quickly collected herself and said to the medalist in Russian, "I was saying to my daughter, she has a brother, that is, I have a son who is a gymnasium student, in the third class, and

464

I've been badgering him for almost three years, every morning and every night, 'A medal, a medal, a medal!' Does he listen to me? A Jew without a medal is like a... like a..."

Madam Shapiro looked around the room for something she could use as a comparison for a Jew without a medal, but there was nothing in the room that had any resemblance to a Jew with or without a medal. Her daughter felt this was entirely beside the point. Why did a stranger need to know whether her brother would earn a medal or not? She said to the student, indicating his half-filled satchel, "Is this all you have or do you have more?"

"What more do I need?" he answered, looking directly into her lovely, luminous eyes so intently one could interpret his look as saying, "What more do I need when you have such beautiful, kind, intelligent, lustrous eyes and such adorable dimples in your cheeks?..."

The mother, whose sole life's objective was to have her son win a medal, interceded for the new tenant and said to her daughter, again with a deep sigh, "He's absolutely right. What else does he need? If he has a medal, he needs nothing else. Nothing else!"

The words "nothing else" she clipped as with a knife. She suddenly became very attentive to the medalist tenant and asked him in a most friendly manner, "Do you have a father and mother?"

To our hero this question was so unexpected that for the moment he quite forgot whether Hershke Rabinovitch had a father and a mother or only one or the other. He was quite unable to answer the question. Luckily Betty again came to his rescue. She turned to her mother.

"That's enough cross-examining our roomer. It might be better if you asked him if he'd like a cup of tea."

And to the new tenant Betty said with a lovely little smile, "My mother likes to talk a little too much...You can order a samovar if you'd like some tea. Your rent includes two samovars a day."

"Why only *two* samovars a day?" her mother interrupted, "—three samovars. In the morning, in the afternoon, and at night."

"That's because you have a medal," Betty added with a laugh, and said to her mother in Yiddish, "Come!" And both daughter and mother left the room, leaving the medalist alone with his half-empty satchel and with his thoughts, which were revolving around the power of his medal, and even more, about the charm of the lovely girl with the pretty, clear, intelligent eyes, mischievous smile, and dimples in her cheeks.

—Translated by Aliza Shevrin

465

Sholem-Aleykhem with Khayim Nakhman Byalik in 1907

VII
A Letter

INTRODUCTION TO "A LETTER TO BYALIK"

In the summer of 1907, Sholem-Aleykhem spent some time vacationing in the countryside around Geneva, Switzerland. There he also met for a week with three other great names in modern Yiddish (as well as Hebrew) literature: Mendele Moykher-Sforim, Khayim Nakhman Byalik, and Ben Ami.

Sholem-Aleykhem describes their time together, hiking and conversing, in a short piece called "Fir zenen mir gezesn" ("The Four of Us, We Sat Together"). Out of this meeting came a memorable, if somewhat comic, photograph, posed in a photographer's studio against a landscape backdrop, with Sholem-Aleykhem holding up an oar.

Also out of this meeting came the following amusing letter to Byalik. From it we learn something of Sholem Aleykhem's humorous, playful character—even off the authorial page, so to speak—in his relations with friends, for he and Byalik became fast friends after their first meeting at the eighth Zionist Congress in 1907 at The Hague.

It seems when Byalik came to Geneva after the Congress to spend some time in the country (at Sholem-Aleykhem's invitation), he wound up staying with Sholem-Aleykhem's family. The following letter (our translation) concerns the fate of a pair of slippers Byalik left behind.

Summer 1907

Oy, Byalik, Byalik!

You left and—vanished, as if into a fog. How does a person not even write a little note?

I have, for your information, regards for you. Guess from whom? From your shoes; that is, your slippers.

The morning after you left Switzerland, I got up early, as always, and, as always, bent down for my shoes under the bed.

I take a look—a pair of shoes, quite unfamiliar shoes—boxy slippers with leather toes.

I examine the slippers—still in pretty good shape, new slippers!

Whose are these slippers? Finally, it appears, these are Byalik's slippers.

How do Byalik's slippers turn up here? Probably he forgot them. Or perhaps he left them for me as a present? In short, there arose a kind of commotion in the house: slippers-slippers, slippers-slippers!....

First, Tisse appeared with a claim that these shoes should belong to her. Her Berkowits is very close to Byalik, so the slippers should go to her.

So then my second one, Lyali, pipes up, the one who is studying to become

467

a doctor: the shoes should be, if there is justice, hers. What's her story? As fol-
lows. She has no slippers. She's had a desire for a long time already for slippers.

Says Emma—that's the third one—that the slippers should be hers because
she certainly doesn't have any shoes at all.

So then the younger one, Marroussia, contends that her soul is also not
made of clay, the slippers fit her too.

So then Numtshik hears talk of slippers, and doesn't want to hear anything
about what kind of slippers, and just shouts: Momma, I want slippers!

As a result of all this clamor, Misha wakes up and makes a pogrom: the
slippers, says he, are his because Byalik slept with no-one else but him, so the
slippers belong to him "according to what is just."

At that moment, Ben-Ami arrives with his daughter, Sarah, and finds out
about the slippers. Says he: the slippers belong to him because if the incident
with Rosh-Hashone hadn't happened,* Byalik would have stayed with him and
would certainly have left his slippers at his place.

Naturally, Sarah agrees with him and covets the slippers with her eyes.

So Micah and Tamara** come up with a compromise and say: You know
what—give me one slipper and Tamara the other.

To make a long story short, we went to the zeyde*** to ask for a judicial
decision: to whom should the slippers belong? After listening with his eyes closed
and a smile on his lips to the various claims to the slippers, the zeyde Reb
Mendele renders the following judgement: Since the slippers are forgotten slip-
pers, without owners, so to speak, and since all of you want them, let the slip-
pers be brought to him, to the zeyde himself, that is, and there let the slippers
remain till Elijah comes.

This judgement pleased only one, Ben-Ami: he remembered the verse, "Not
me, not you ..." But I am not happy, so in the meantime, the slippers remain
here with me.

I expect, God willing, to quickly dispatch the slippers to Odessa. Of course,
not both slippers at once. One slipper I will send you right after Sukkes, and
the other slipper I will send for Passover—so you'll have both slippers.

And since you might be missing your slippers I have had a photograph made
of both slippers; I enclose a picture of your slippers with friendly regards from us
all and from your slippers, which find themselves at the moment on my feet,
since I really do not have any, except for yours, and I thank you for the slippers,
and may you always come to us every summer with new slippers and may you
always leave us a pair of slippers, because I came to the conclusion that it is bet-
ter with slippers than without them, especially such beautiful slippers as yours
which are as slippers go (among slippers, compared to all other slippers) the best.

—Sholem-Aleykhem

---

*Byalik arrived in Geneva on Rosh-Hashone, which displeased the observant Ben-Ami.
**Ben Ami's younger children.
***"Grandfather": how Sholem-Aleykhem referred to Mendele Moykher-Sforim
(e.g., "the grandfather of modern Yiddish literature").

VIII
An Essay

INTRODUCTION TO
WHY DO THE JEWS NEED A LAND OF THEIR OWN?

Sholem-Aleykhem the ardent Zionist is not as well known to many of his readers as is Sholem-Aleykhem the writer of Yiddish short stories and novels.

Sholem-Aleykhem was a passionate Jewish nationalist, and his advocacy of Yiddish as a national Jewish language, and as a language which should be accorded the same status and respect as other modern European languages—and a language in which literature on a high level can and should be (and had already been) created—was part of his Jewish nationalism.

But his nationalism didn't stop there, didn't stop with what came to be called "Yiddishism." It also expressed itself in his passionate devotion to the cause of Zionism.

Early on in his life and career, Sholem-Aleykhem demonstrated his Zionist proclivities. Already in 1888, as a young man, Sholem-Aleykhem became a dues-paying member of Chovevei Zion, a forerunner of the modern Zionist movement, which began, formally, with the first Zionist Congress in Geneva in 1897.

After that Sholem-Aleykhem not only wrote many tracts, pamphlets, novels, stories, and essays presenting the Zionist case—he even served as an American delegate to the eighth Zionist Congress in 1907 held in The Hague, where he met for the first time another delegate by the name of Khayim Nakhmen Byalik (the two became fast friends through the few years left to Sholem-Aleykhem).

In 1981, Joseph Leftwich and Mordecai S. Chertoff translated into English from Yiddish an interesting anthology, published in Yiddish in 1978 and in Hebrew in 1981, in which they included as many of Sholem-Aleykhem's works as they could find having to do with the Zionist idea. The anthology appeared in English as *Why Do the Jews Need a Land of their Own?* (1981). It includes an unfinished short novel, records of a Zionist Congress, some political essays, pamphlets, short stories, one-acters, a stack of Menakhem-Mendl letters, biographies—as well as the one title essay which we present below, written by Sholem Aleykhem, in Yiddish, of course, in 1898.

469

Why Do the Jews Need a Land of Their Own?

(1898)

"For the Lord will have
compassion on Jacob,
and will yet choose Israel,
and set them in their own land."
—Isaiah 14:1

Why do Jews need a land of their own? Some question! There are people who would add another question. And they would be right. Why should Jews not want a country? If Jews are a nation, why should they be worse than all other nations? It's as though they were asking you what do you want a home for? Naturally everyone should have a home. What else? Stay outside? If you consider it at bottom, properly, it isn't just like that. The question is, what does one want a home for, a home of his own? Does a man need a home of his own?

Jews have a saying for it—better a rich tenant than a poor landlord. But when does that apply? When there are houses galore and houses are cheap, and landlords fight each other to get you as a tenant. Everybody after you, wants you! But what if the boot is on the other foot? What if you've been a tenant all over the place, and you've got a reputation—between ourselves—as a bad tenant, so that you can't get into a house anywhere, and you have nothing left but to stay outside, under God's Heaven! What do you do then?

More than eighteen hundred years we have been dragging around as tenants from one house to another. Have we ever tried

470

thinking seriously—how long? How much longer? What will be the end of it?

In these eighteen hundred years we have gone through all sorts of times. There was a time when houses were plentiful, and everyone was happy to have us as a tenant (Nobody, indeed, came to blows over us). It didn't last long. They soon got fed up with us, and we were told to pack up and clear out. Go and find another lodging!

In these eighteen hundred years we have had all sorts of times. Occasions when we pulled ourselves together and recovered from our wanderings, hoping that any minute now Messiah would come, we would get over all our troubles, and be on a level with everybody else. It didn't last long. Before we could look round to see where in the world we were, we were again miles under, in the depths of despair.

That's what happened with us in the last few years, when people became wise, and the world was full of knowledge. The word haskalah (education) brought us a lot of new words, noble, high-sounding words, like humanity, justice, emancipation, equality, brotherhood, and suchlike words that looked good and fine on paper and did your heart good to look at them.

What came of all these fine words you know by now. And if you don't know, try and read Dr. Max Nordau's speech at the Zionist Congress in Basel, and you will see that all these fine words remain no more than fine words. At bottom our position remained bitter and black. Worse than before. *

That our position is bitter and black we had known before. We heard the story from our grandfathers of old, terrible, wonderful tales, of a Pharaoh in Egypt who had plagued us, a Haman who had ended up in disaster, a Titus who had collapsed in ruin, an Inquisition, and the expulsion of the Jews from Spain and Portugal and other places. And more such tales with which our history is full. We witnessed many of them ourselves. Seen them with our own eyes, read about them in the newspapers. Only those who went to the congress opened our eyes, painted a picture of our position all over the world, and we discovered that even in those countries where we envied our brothers, thought they were living happily, it was nothing of the kind. We had been mistaken. It

---

*"The Jewish Congress in Basel," report by Doctor Mandelstamm, Yiddish by Sholom Aleichem (Warsaw 1897).

turned out that things are nowhere good for us; they are terribly bad. We are hated everywhere. They can't stand us anywhere. And as if to provide evidence for what we say, France came out with the notorious Dreyfus trial, and the hatred whipped up against the famous French writer Emile Zola, who wanted to put right the injustice committed against this innocent man Dreyfus. Who of you all hasn't read about that amazing trial? Who among you has been indifferent to the injustice committed before our eyes now at the end of the nineteenth century? And where? In France! "Spit on Zola!" "Death to the Jews!" That's what the anti-Semites shouted in Paris.

The Jewish Congress in Basel drew the right conclusions about the position of our brothers throughout the world, and considering these conclusions we learned three things:

1. They hate us everywhere, in the whole world.
2. The situation is so bitter and black that it can't go on any longer.
3. We must find a way, but one that will work.

A. Let's consider it well, why do they hate us? we ourselves know (we don't have to pretend among ourselves) that we are no better and no worse than the rest. We have all the good qualities and the bad that all people have. And if it happens sometimes that we go a little too far, we have, to compensate, other qualities that outweigh the faults. Only what? The hatred against us is so great and so deeply ingrained that no one will consider our good qualities, and our faults are flung at us at every step, all the time.

What is the cause of this hate?

We won't go into long discussions, turning the pages of history, to get to the bottom of it. Where does this hatred come from? It is an old, persistent disease, an epidemic, God forbid! that goes by heritage from generation to generation. It sometimes happens that our enemies can't themselves say why they hate us. It's a real tragedy. God's own curse that has come down on us these many, many years. And going back to this question, let us make a strict account. Why should they love us? Can we demand of people that they must love us? Who are we among the nations? What are we, and what big noise do we make amongst the other nations in Europe that they should love us?

Who are we? Sons of Abraham, Isaac, and Jacob, who once

had our own land. We sinned and were driven out and dispersed over the whole earth, and so we wander about among strange nations for nearly two thousand years, like a lost orphan child, who is kept only for pity's sake. He is thrown a crumb, tossed a bone, and little notice is taken of him. If there is anything someone wants to say to him, it is said straight out, without mincing words. And if he doesn't catch on, he gets it in the neck.

What does the orphan do then? He hides. He pockets the blow and wipes his lips as if nothing had happened. He's a stranger! Everywhere a stranger! So as long as the native, the one who belongs, finds things going well and easy, feels comfortable, earns enough for his needs, the stranger can get by, more or less. But when the native feels cramped, crowded out, with competition growing, and his earnings going down, then the stranger assumes enormous bulk, looks gigantic. All the troubles in the land seem to stem from him. And people begin to murmur. At first under their breath, then louder and louder. "What do we want these strangers here for!"

It only needs one to say it first, and the others follow. No arguments will help. No facts and figures, to show that the stranger too is a human being, that he has also to eat, and that he can help in the common task, can be of use. Nobody will listen. Nobody wants his usefulness. Take it somewhere else, they say. We don't want it. Get out!

So what are we? We are foreigners, aliens everywhere.

Now there is a second question—who are we? Meaning, are we a People, a nation, or not? What is called a nation, and what are the signs of a People? A People should first of all have a country. A people should have an ideal. That means an idea, a thought towards which the whole People will strive, devoted to it heart and soul.

We lost our land. Where is our ideal? To have a land we must want it. That means we must all have one wish, and will, one idea, and thought. That is unity. What unity we have now we all know well enough. Our enemies accuse us from the start, saying that we have too much unity. They say about us that all Israel are brothers. All Jews are one Jew. We, of course, know how much truth there is in that. Wish it on the anti-Semites to have our unity. If one of us says yes, the other will say no. If one says kosher, the other will say treif. And what one finds pleasing, the other dislikes. He wants it, so I want the opposite. Two Jews have three opinions. When one

473

says this, the other says yes, but not like that. The other man's opinion isn't worth a pinch of snuff. No need to listen when somebody else is talking. There is no elder, and surely no wiser. Because we are all wise. Kulone Chachomim. We are all wise men. We all know what is going on in the world. We knew it long ago, long before that other man is trying to tell us. So what's all this about an idea that will link us all together—our whole People? Take a ride, for instance, to Berditchev, a Jewish town. Stop a Jew there, in the street or in the synagogue and put the question to him— Excuse me, Mister Jew, what is your ideal? And what's going on here about Zion and Zionism?

He'll look at you as if you were mad, a man with time to think about ideals, a loafer, a drifter, a waster of time. Ideal, shmideal, Zion and Zionism. You tell me rather how's business! Have you anything in your mind to turn an honest rouble?

I said Berditchev not as an exception. But as an example. The same sort of place. The same sort of thing will hold good in Kovno, in Riga, in Shnipishok, anywhere you like. They say the whole world is one town. And I'm not saying that all Berditchev Jews or all Shnipishok Jews are all so taken up with the chase after the rouble. Or that nobody there is interested in Zion and Zionism. I'm only saying that most Jews are miles and miles away from such things, things that don't contribute to their takings. And if there are Jews in every town who devote themselves to things like Zionism, they are no more than a few single individuals.

The argument is that Jews are poor, badly off. They must all chase after the rouble to keep going. But that argument is false. To begin with, not all Jews are poor. Thank God, we have plenty of wealthy Jews (and I am not speaking of the magnates, the really, truly rich, for where does it say that aristocrats like these, millionaires, must read little booklets written in Yiddish?). I'm talking of the middle-class Jews who have both time and the mind to devote themselves to such things as Jewish affairs. And on the other hand, the worse things are with Jews, the more and more often they have to think of these things on which their own happiness and the happiness of the entire Jewish People depend. Bad times and bad conditions getting worse every day demand that all Jews must come together, be driven together, all with one wish and one will, one purpose, one ideal. Brothers, there is something missing. The spirit is missing, the folk-spirit that we lost all this time that we have been dragging around here and there.

So what are we? Well, we have our religion. We have our own language. And, of course, there are a few million of us, people who pray from the same prayer book, who keep the Sabbath, eat matzoth at Passover time, hamantaschen at Purim, a smear of honey at Tabernacles, and —

That's all? Nothing more? If so the world is almost right when it says we are not a nation, but just a lot of stiff-necked, stubborn people—what we are told we are, every day!

Again, what are we? How about our ideal? Where is our "Jerusalem thy city" that we repeat day by day? What of "Next year in Jerusalem" and "Ani ma'amin"?—Our "I believe"—our principles of Jewish faith? And our form of greeting to each other—"Live to see Messiah"!

True! Only we mustn't fool ourselves. We know well enough how a Jew speaks these words. Our question is, what has he in mind while he speaks those words—his shop, his mill, the forest where he has a lumber lease from the landowner, or his shares on the stock exchange, or far away in Yehupetz, at the Market Day Fair. As for living to see Messiah—good! Why not? If Messiah comes riding along to collect Jews and take them to Eretz Israel at his expense, on condition that each of us, all of us must go on that journey, and the moneyed ones go first!

Jews have such a delightful sacred ideal, and all they do is make fun of it!

No, brothers! We remember Jerusalem every day, but what we have in our minds is Yehupetz. Eretz Israel has till now been a place where old Jews go to die. Zion till now was a word, a fine, beautiful name that we find in our holy books, with other lovely old names, like Wailing Wall, and Mother Rachel's Tomb—all names that should move our hearts, should evoke memories, conjure up pictures of our glorious past.

"Zion, how fare your wandering children?" That's a line from a poem by one of our greatest Jewish singers and patriots, Rabbi Judah Halevi. That was his question to us!

But the words, alas, fly by swiftly, leave an impression with us for a moment, and vanish.

Judah Halevi was drawn to Zion all his life, till he went there and was killed there. "Where shall I find wings," he asked, "to fly there, to bring my broken heart to Zion, the Holy Land? That I should fall with my face to the ground, embrace the holy earth, kiss the dear stones, the sacred dust, the holy graves!"

475

And that is where he was killed.

Unhappily, our Jewish People know little of this great Jewish poet and his intense love of Zion. Our people no longer feel what they once felt about this majestic name Zion. It seems that the wound must be so old that the pain is no longer felt, insensible. That is not surprising, for after all, this long Golus, this wandering from one land to another, suffering such things as the Spanish Inquisition, and more, much more, and still retaining some fragments of humanity, is itself an achievement, a miracle. Such a miracle as only God can work, God and his Torah, this little Pentateuch, our spiritual Fatherland, this community of soul!

This fact alone, that we hold on to our Jewishness so long, that we have not been wiped off the face of the earth like many others, nations who have left no trace behind—that itself is proof that we can and with God's help will be a nation with all the signs and symbols of a nation.

That leaves us with the third question. What bonds have we with the other nations? No bonds at all!

There were times indeed when there was some talk of our being kindred, having bonds. Shem and Japhet wanted to marry into us. We were on the point of intermingling—assimilation. Both sides deluded themselves. It seemed that we were brothers, body and soul. We on our side were prepared for it, and to show how delighted we were with the match we started aping them in every way, with everything—dress, speech, behavior, manners in the house and outside. With our festivals. With our names—Abraham became Anton; Jeremiah, Jerzy; Getzl, Maxim. The women followed suit. Hannan became Gertrude; Esther, Isabel; and Dvoshe, Cleopatra! Everyone tried to outdo the other. All wanted to show that "I am not I."

What came of it? Nothing! Worse than that! It finished up with rows and scandals. What can we do if we are not really equal sides? we can't impose friendship by force. It won't work!

There are the three main reasons why they hate us, always and everywhere. They hate us because we are strangers and because we want to eat. They hate us because we are a nation without a land and without an ideal. They hate us because we do not have equal links with the nations. We only push the cart from behind, leaping and jumping and grimacing all the time to attract attention. In one word they hate us and hunt us more and more as time goes on, more and more brutally. I hope I'm wrong.

476

B. Because as we go on things keep getting worse, and things are becoming so dangerous that it cannot possibly continue as in the past. When they reminded us of our faults and revived all the old accusations against us, we responded by finding excuses, trying to justify ourselves, to show that we are not as bad as they made out. You will see that we are right if you give us a little more time, a little more freedom to speak. "Give us a chance to educate ourselves, give us education, and you will see that we are an entirely different people."

Now, when we see plainly that being on the defensive will not help, that self-vindication gets us nowhere, that since we are a nation like all other nations, that we will never mix and mingle with other nations, and that we are hated everywhere in the whole world, we must look for some other way to assure our existence; we must find our own remedy. Our help is in ourselves alone.

C. What is our help, what is our remedy? Our wise men have long pondered this question, have written a great deal about it, our scholars, our providers and protectors—and they have found only one way—Jews must have an ideal. And the ideal must be a land. In a word, Jews must have a land, their own land.

Only sixteen years ago a great man, Dr. Pinsker, published a little pamphlet with the name "Auto-Emancipation." It caused a stir in the Jewish world. "To end our troubles," Dr. Pinsker said, "we must have a land. But not to wait for someone to give us the land. We must find a land ourselves, a piece of earth, a corner, that is our own, no matter where it is, so long as it is ours."

Does a Jew realize what lies in these few simple words—"a piece of earth, a corner that is our own"? Does a Jew feel how necessary and how advantageous it is for each and every one of us, and for the whole community, for us all? Does a Jew ever think what we would have looked like among the nations of the world if we had a piece of land somewhere, our own small corner—that we would be no longer paupers, wandering gypsies, outcast and unwanted!

Dr. Pinsker had given a lot of thought to the subject, and he had concluded that only a land of our own can bring us salvation. He laid the first stone of that great structure which our people cre-

477

ated afterwards. For he was followed by other Jewish writers who discussed and considered the matter. It started a search over the world for a land where we could settle Jews who had got stuck like a bone in the throat in the countries where they lived. One said Palestine. Another Argentina. A third Brazil. Some thought Africa would be the place. Others plumped for Cyprus. Back of beyond! God knows where! There is an apt saying—a big world, but no room to sit down. None of the other nations came out to welcome us, to say Sholom Aleichem, were in no hurry to invite us in, but on the contrary fought over us like those seven towns when a synagogue cantor applied for a job, each wanting some other town to take him on. The conclusion was reached that if Jews wanted to live as a nation, there is no other way but to go there, to the ancient Holy Land of our forefathers, the land of the patriarchs. We were shown with all the necessary evidence that every other way was wrong, was false, that the Jewish People are too much divided already, split up, scattered, and dispersed. What we need is a merkaz, a center.

The question, "Wohin?" ("Where to?") ceased to be the question. Disappeared from the agenda. The organization "Chovevei Zion" was formed then, and it still exists. Though it is true that when the emigration started, more Jews went and still go to America, the heart of each immigrant lies over there, in the land of our Fathers, Palestine, Eretz Israel, Zion—those words are heard often among our people, everywhere, even in distant, free America. We already have in Palestine a good many fine colonies that Baron Edmond de Rothschild founded. We also have our own colonies there, where our brothers distinguish themselves with their work.

But time has shown that the colonizing of Palestine is proceeding too slowly. The number of Jewish people grows and their poverty grows more. Jews need, most of all, a land of their own, where they can go and settle openly, not having to sneak in as in the past. These are the words of Herzl, who convened the first Jewish Congress held in Basel.

Indeed, Dr. Herzl did nothing new by using these words. He said almost the same thing that Dr. Pinsker had said sixteen or seventeen years before. The difference was that Pinsker spoke in general terms, that Jews must have a country, and Herzl came out openly before the whole world with the demand that Jews must have a country, their own land, and pointed straight at Palestine. Dr. Pinsker poured out his bitter heart quietly, reasonably, without fuss or clamor. While Herzl demanded publicly, to the whole world, a ready-made Jewish state. I refer to Herzl's *Judenstadt,* which made a stir, not only among Jews, but also among other people.

"A Jewish state," Herzl said, "is necessary not only for us, but for the whole world. For it is the only way to get rid of the unhappy Jewish Question... Of course, as long as the idea of a Jewish state, a Jewish land remains the idea of one or a few people, it will be no more than a very fine idea, and that's that. But as soon as it becomes the idea of the whole People, it will not be difficult to carry it into effect."

"The Jewish People," Dr. Herzl proceeded, "cannot and must not be destroyed. We will not be destroyed because our enemies will not allow it. We will not be destroyed, and this is proved by our nearly two thousand years of suffering, and we are still here. We must not be destroyed, because that is not desirable. Some leaves may fall off, but the tree remains. And that we should not be destroyed, we must have a land. Our own land...Time now," says Herzl, "for us to reveal our mission to the world, for all we will do in our new land will be to the good not only of our people, but of everyone, all mankind."

"Palestine or Argentina?" Herzl asks, and this is how he answers his own question. "The Jewish people will say thanks for every piece of land that will be given them, to settle there freely, to develop their powers and their energies and abilities. The difference between Argentina and Palestine is that the Holy Land, Zion, is bound up with our ancient history. The very name Eretz Israel is enough to attract the love of the Jewish people."

Herzl went on to present his plan—how Jews should make their land purchases in Eretz Israel, and how in time a Jewish state would develop there, of course, with the consent of the sultan and of all the European powers.

It would take a whole book to reproduce the plan in its entirety. Yet everybody will understand that building a grand edifice like that is no easy matter. It is a work not for a year or even ten years. As the saying goes, "Things don't work as fast as we talk." Jews must first of all understand the idea properly, grow accustomed to it, get done with the question we posed before, "Why do Jews need a land of their own?"

"That means we must see to it that all Jews should feel and understand how necessary and useful it is. We must see to it that

479

this idea should be the ideal of the entire People. We must see to it that our wives and sisters should understand it, so that our children will be brought up under our national flag, so that our children should be Jewish children, who will not be ashamed of their People...Jews must return to the Jewish People before they return to the Jewish land."

Professor Schapira had this to say at the Basel Congress: "If our ancestors had contributed each year the shekel from the time we lost our state, we could by now have enough funds to buy the whole of Eretz Israel."

I think this is a mistake. With this amount of money we could have bought half of the whole world. Does it mean that because our parents didn't do it, we mustn't do it either? What a great legacy we would leave our children and our children's children. They will inherit this holy ideal from us, the ideal that will go with us, a heritage from generation to generation. A land, our own land— that will be the ideal among all Jews the world over. Our children, or our grandchildren may live to see it. We ourselves perhaps, too.

IX

Last Will and Epitaph

INTRODUCTION TO

SHOLEM-ALEYKHEM'S *LAST WILL AND TESTAMENT*
and

EPITAPH

In 1915, Sholem Aleykhem and most of his family were in New York, when he received a terrible blow. He was informed of the death (in Copenhagen, from tuberculosis) of his oldest son Misha.

It broke his heart and, as he says, Misha "carried off with him to his grave a piece of my life." It surely hastened his death in 1916.

Upon hearing the dreadful news, Sholem Aleykhem retired to his workroom to rewrite his will, first written in 1908, when he was himself fighting off tuberculosis in Nervi on the Italian Riviera.

It is a beautiful, sad, but heartwarming document, one of the world's great ethical wills. In 1916, the day after the funeral, it was reprinted in the *New York Times;* it was also reproduced in the *Congressional Record*.

Here it is, in our translation, reproduced below, followed by our literal (unrhymed, unmetrical) translation of the poem he wrote (1905) for his own epitaph. It is engraved on his tombstone in the Workmen's Circle cemetery in Brooklyn, New York.

THE LAST WILL AND TESTAMENT OF SHOLEM-ALEYKHEM

I request that this be opened and read on the day of my death.

-Sholem Aleykhem

11 Tishri, 5676; 19 September 1915, New York

Today, the day after *yinkiper,* a New Year has just begun, and a great misfortune has befallen my family—death took my oldest son Misha (Mikhail) Rabinovits, who carried off with him to his grave a piece of my

481

life. So it remains for me to rewrite my will, which I wrote in 1908, when I was ill, in Nervi (Italy),—

Being well and in full command of my senses, I write my will, which consists of ten points:

1. Wherever I die, I wish to be buried not among aristocrats, big shots, or wealthy people, but precisely among ordinary folk, workers, the real Jewish people, so that the gravestone which will be placed on my grave will beautify the simple graves around me, and the simple graves will beautify my grave, just as the simple, honest folk during my life beautified their folk-writer.

2. There should be absolutely no titles, or words of praise, or "our teacher" on my gravestone, except for the name "Sholem-Aleykhem" on one side and the Yiddish epitaph, enclosed, on the other.*

3. There should be absolutely no debates or discussions among my colleagues about immortalizing my name, about erecting a monument to me in New York, etc.: I will not be able to rest comfortably in my grave if my friends engage in such foolishness. The best monument for me will be that people will read my works and that patrons will be found among the wealthier segments of our people who will undertake to publish and distribute my works, both in Yiddish and in other languages, and in this way make it possible for the people to read them and for my family to live decently. If I was not decreed worthy or wasn't able to earn the honor of such patronage during my lifetime, perhaps I will be deemed worthy of it after my death. I leave this world with the full conviction that the people will not forsake my orphans —

4. At my gravesite, and every day for a year after that—and subsequently on the anniversary of my death—my remaining son, as well as my sons-in-laws, if they wish, should say *kadish* [the prayer for the dead] for me. And if they don't feel like doing that, or time will not permit, or it will be against their religious convictions, they can make up for it only by all of them gathering with my daughters and with the grandchildren and with just good friends and reading this last will of mine and also picking out a story from among my little stories, one of the very happiest, and reading it aloud in whatever language will be more understandable to them, and let my name be mentioned by them with a laugh better than never to be mentioned at all.

---

*This wish was not fully complied with. On one side of the gravestone is the Yiddish epitaph; on the other, instead of just his name, a Hebrew translation of the epitaph.

5. As to religious convictions, my children and my children's children may have whatever ones they want. But their Jewish heritage I beg them to safeguard. Those of my children who will cast off their background and go over to another faith will thereby themselves cast themselves off from their roots and their family and will have thus erased themselves from my last will—"and they shall have no portion and inheritance among their brethren."

6. Everything I own both in monies—if such will be found in my possession—and in books, printed or in manuscript, both in Yiddish and in other languages (except for those translated into Hebrew), belong to my wife Hodl Beys Elimelekh, or Olga Rabinovits, and after her death it goes to all my children equally: to my daughter Khaye Esther (Ernestina) Berkovits; to my daughter Sore (Lyalya) Kaufman, to my daughter Nemi (Emma) Rabinovits; to my daughter Miriam (Marroussia) Rabinovits; and to my son Nokhem (Numa) Rabinovits. And as to my works in Hebrew, they belong to their masterful translator, my son-in-law, I.D. Berkovits, and to his daughter, my grandchild, Tamar (Tamara) Berkovits—that should be her dowry. Of the royalties that might arrive for my plays both in Russia and America, half should go to my family and half should be put away in the name of my granddaughter Bella, the daughter of Mikhoel and Sarah Kaufman—let that be her dowry.

7. Of all the sources of income listed in the preceding paragraph, five percent of up to five thousand rubles a year should be deducted for a Fund for Jewish Writers (in Yiddish and in Hebrew). And if the annual income amounts to more than 5000 rubles a year, then ten percent should be deducted (e.g., from 6000 rubles, 600; from 7000, 700; from 8000 rubles 800 rubles, etc.). If at that time there will exist such a Fund here in America or there in Europe, the percentages should be paid into the Fund every year and the Fund will act according to its statutes. But if up to that time there will exist no official Fund, or such a Fund will exist which does not espouse my will as it is expressed at the beginning of this paragraph, the percentages should be distributed to needy writers by my family, directly, according to their mutual agreement.

8. If I do not succeed while I live to erect a tombstone on the grave of my just-deceased son Mikhoel (Misha) Rabinovits in Copenhagen, then let my heirs do it with a generous hand, and on the anniversary of his death every year, let the prayer for the dead be recited and eighteen crowns distributed to the poor as charity.

9. My wish is that my heirs should arrange their affairs in such a way that my works and my plays should never be sold, not here in America

and not in Europe, but that they should succeed in living on the income from them all the years that are rightfully theirs according to the laws of the land. Unless some time comes, or some fool may be found, who will pay for the rights an amount enough to support a family, then all the heirs should come to a mutual understanding, and if the majority is willing, let them divide the monies among themselves, share and share alike, according to paragraph six, but first of all, let the 10% be deducted for the Jewish Literature Fund, according to paragraph seven.

10. My last wish to my successors and my plea to my children: Watch over your mother, beautify her old age, sweeten her bitter life, heal her broken heart; don't cry for me, on the contrary, speak of me with joy; and the main thing—live in peace with one another, bear no enmity one toward another, help one another in bad times, think at times of the family, take pity on any pauper, and in good times, pay my debts, if there will be any. Children! Bear with honor my hard-earned Jewish name, and may the God which is in Heaven be your help. Amen.

—Sholem ben Menakhem Nokhum Rabinovits
(Sholem-Aleykhem)

SHOLEM-ALEYKHEM'S EPITAPH

Here lies a Jew, a plain one,
Who wrote in Yiddish for women,*
     and for plain folk;
His whole life he scoffed at everything,
Derided the whole world.
The whole world enjoyed itself,
and he—*oy vey*—he was in trouble.

And precisely when the crowd laughed,
     clapped, and amused itself,
He grieved—this only God knows,
Secretly—so none should see.

Sholem-Aleykhem

---

*Sholem-Aleykhem is echoing an old tradition here: in the early stages of the development of Yiddish literature, when Jewish women were not schooled to read Hebrew, Yiddish versions of biblical and religious wisdom literature were written for them; Yiddish was then considered a language for untutored women—although the truth was, men ("plain folk") read in it too (but might not have wanted to admit it).

SELECTED BIBLIOGRAPHY

Aarons, Victoria. *Author as Character in the Works of Sholom Aleichem*. New York: The Edwin Mellen Press, 1985.

Abramowicz, Dina. *English Translations of Yiddish Literature: 1945-1967*. New York: YIVO, 1968.

Berkowitz, I. D. *Dos Sholem Aleykhem Bukh*. 2nd ed. New York: Farlag YKUF, 1958.

---. *Undzere Rishoynim*. Tel-Aviv: Hamenora, 1966.

Butwin, Joseph and Frances Butwin. *Sholom Aleichem*. Boston: Twayne Publishers, 1977.

Fridhandler, Louis. "Guide to English Translations of Sholom Aleichem" in *Jewish Book Annual*, Volume 45, 1987-88 (New York: JWB Jewish Book Council 1987), 121-42.

Gittleman, Sol. Sholom Aleichem: *A Non-Critical Introduction*. The Hague: Mouton, 1974.

Halberstam-Rubin, Anna. *Sholom Aleichem: The Writer as Social Historian*. New York: Peter Lang, 1989.

Kellman, Ellen. "Sholem Aleichem's Funeral (New York, 1916): The Making of a National Pageant." *YIVO Annual*, Volume 20; ed. by Deborah Dash Moore. New York: Northwestern University Press and YIVO Institute for Jewish Research, 1991.

Madison, Charles. *Yiddish Literature: Its Scope and Major Writers*. New York: Schocken Books, 1971

Miller, David Neal. "Sholom Aleichem in English: The Most Accessible Translations." *Yiddish*, 2: 61-70. New York: 1977

Miron, Dan. "Bouncing Back: Destruction and Recovery in Sholem Aleykhem's Motl Peyse dem Khazns." *YIVO Annual of Jewish Social Science*, Volume XVII. Ed. by David G. Roskies. New York: YIVO Institute for Jewish Research, 1978.

---. "Shalom (Sholem) Aleichem (Shalom Rabinovitz). *Encyclopedia Judaica*. First printing. Jerusalem: Keter Publishing House Ltd., 1971.

---. *Sholem Aleykhem: Person, Persona, Presence*. New York: YIVO Institute for Jewish Research, 1972

---. *A Traveler Disguised: A Study in the Rise of Modern Yiddish Fiction in the Nineteenth Century*. New York: Shocken Books, 1973.

Mlotek, Eleanor Gordon. *Mir Trogn a Gezang!: Favorite Yiddish Songs of Our Generation*. 2nd ed. New York: Workmen's Circle Education Department, 1977.

Niger, Shmuel. "The Humor of Sholom Aleichem," translated by Ruth Wisse. *Voices from the Yiddish: Essays, Memoirs, Diaries,* ed. by Irving Howe and Eliezer Greenberg. Ann Arbor: the University of Michigan Press, 1972.

---. *Sholem Aleykhem: Zayne vikhtikste verk, zayn humor un zayn ort in der yidisher literatur.* New York: Yidisher Kultur Farlag, 1928.

Norich, Anita. "Portraits of the Artist in Three Novels by Sholem Aleichem." *Prooftexts 4.* Baltimore: The Johns Hopkins University Press, 1984.

Reyzin, Zalmen. *Leksikon fun der yidisher literatur un prese.* Warsaw: Tsentral, 1914.

Rosenfeld, Lulla. *Bright Star of Exile: Jacob Adler and the Yiddish Theater.* New York: Thomas Y. Crowell, 1977.

Samuel, Maurice. *The World of Sholom Aleichem.* New York: Alfred A. Knopf, 1943.

Sandrow, Nahma. *Vagabond Stars: A World History of Yiddish Theater.* New York: Harper and Row, 1977.

Shandler, Jeffrey. "Reading Sholem Aleichem from Left to Right." *YIVO Annual,* Volume 20; ed. by Deborah Dash Moore. New York: Northwestern University Press and YIVO Institute for Jewish Research, 1991.

Shmeruk, Khone. "Sholem-Aleichem and America." *YIVO Annual,* Volume 20; ed. by Deborah Dash More. New York: Northwestern University Press and the YIVO Institute for Jewish Research, 1991.

---. "Sholem-Aleykhem." *Leksikon fun der nayer yidisher literatur.* New York: Congress for Jewish Culture, 1981

Sholem-Aleykhem. *Ale Verk fun Sholem-Aleykhem.* New York: Sholem Aleykhem Folksfond Oysgabe, 1927

Trunk, I.I. *Sholem-Aleykhem: Zayn vezn un zayn verk.* Warsaw: Farlag "Kultur-Lige," 1937.

Warnke, Nina. "Of Plays and Politics: Sholem Aleichem's First Visit to America." *YIVO Annual, Volume 20;* ed. by Debora Dash Moore. New York: Northwestern University Press and the YIVO Institute for Jewish Research, 1991.

Waife-Goldberg, Marie. *My Father, Sholom Aleichem.* New York: Simon and Schuster, 1968

Weinreich, Uriel. "Guide to English translations of Sholom Aleichem." *The Field of Yiddish;* ed. by Uriel Weinreich. New York: Linguistic Circle of New York, 1954.

Wiener, Leo. *The History of Yiddish Literature in the Nineteenth Century.* London: John C. Nimmo, 1899.

Wisse, Ruth R. *The Schlemiel as Modern Hero.* Chicago: The University of Chicago press, 1971.

---. *Sholem Aleichem and the Art of Communication.* Syracuse, N.Y.: Syracuse University, 1979.

GLOSSARY

Ahaseurus—king of Persia in the Book of Esther.

alef—first letter of the Hebrew/Yiddish alphabet.

aleichem sholom—see *aleykhem-sholem*.

aleykhem-sholem—traditional reply to the greeting *"sholem-aleykhem,"* which see.

Asmodeus—evil spirit; the king of the demons. Sometimes depicted as a merry trickster rather than as an evil demon.

balak—see *bolek*.

blintzes—crepes filled with cheese or fruit.

blondzhen—stray, ramble (having lost one's way).

bolek—the leason of vengeance; teach/learn a harsh/impressive lesson.

borsht—beet soup.

britshke—half-covered, four-wheel, horse-drawn carriage.

britzka—see *britshke*.

chalah—see *khale*.

cheder—see *kheyder*.

dacha—a Russian country home; a cottage.

eynikl—grandchild.

frishtik—breakfast.

gabe—trustee or warden of a public institution, especially a synagogue; manager of the affairs of a Hasidic rabbi.

gabeh—see *gabe*.

gemara—see *gemore*.

gemore—the commentaries on the *mishne;* the *gemore* and the *mishne* together comprise the *Talmud*.

golem—see *goylem*.

goy—gentile, non-Jew; Jew ignorant of Jewish traditions.

goylem—a statue or artificial man into which life is breathed by supernatural means; dummy; clumsy fellow.

groshn—grosz; penny, small coin.

grosz—small coin of Poland (see *groshn*).

gvir—a wealthy man.

gvirte—a wealthy woman.

gymnasium—european school equivalent to high school and junior college.

haggadah—see *hagode.*

hagode—a booklet containing the home services for the *seyder* of Passover night.

halel—a hymn of praise; a group of psalms recited at synagogue services during various holidays.

hallah—see *khale.*

hallel—see *halel.*

Haman—in the Book of Esther, chief minister to Ahasuerus, king of Persia; he is the villain.

hanukkah—see *khanike.*

hashono rabo—literally, "the Great Hosanna," it is the seventh day of *sukes (sukkoth);* thought of as the day the final fate of the Jews in the year to come is sealed in the heavenly court of records, it comes at the end of the three weeks of penitence beginning on *rosheshone.*

hasid—see *khosed*

haskale—see *haskole.*

haskole—nineteenth century Jewish enlightenment.

hassidism—see *khsidizm.*

heder—see *kheyder.*

kaballa—see *kabole.*

kabole—cabala; Jewish mysticism; an attempt to fathom the mysteries of God and creation; medieval cabalists developed a complete philosophic system; influenced *khsidizm.*

kaddish—see *kadish.*

kadish—one of the most ancient prayers in the Jewish prayer book, generally recited in the synagogue during religious services, it became the mourner's prayer for the dead, especially that of a son for his dead parent; also the person who says the prayer.

khale—a braided white bread eaten on the Sabbath and holidays.

khanike—the midwinter eight-day festival commemorating the liberation of the temple in Jerusalem from the Syrians and Greeks in the second century B.C.E.

kheyder—the religious elementary school conducted by a *melamed,* usually in his own house.

kishke—section of intestine stuffed with flour and chicken fat.

klezmer—musician (player).

klezmorim—traditional Jewish musicians (plural of *klezmer).*

khosed—a follower of the Hasidic movement.

khsidizm—founded in eighteenth-century among east-European Jews; religious-mystical-revival movement; organized into groupings devoted to particular rabbis and generally stressing pious devotion and ecstasy more than learning.

knishes—a bun filled with meat, buckwheat, or potatoes, and served hot.

kosher—proper according to Jewish dietary laws.

kreplakh—boiled dumplings stuffed with meat or cheese.

l'chaim—see *lekhaim.*

legboymer—a joyous, although minor, spring holiday, commemorating the end of a dreadful plague among the students of Rabbi Akiva in the second century C.E.; celebrated by outings; usually transliterated as *Lag B'Omer.*

lekhaim—to life! often used as a toast.

luft-mentsh—man of air. Poor economic conditions, aggravated by anti-Jewish restrictions in commerce and in the trades, resulted in unemployed, unskilled Jews in the Pale, who were continually scrambling somehow for their existence, seemingly living on air; a ubiquitous Jewish type in czarist Russia.

ma-nishtane—the four questions, recited by the youngest child at the Passover seder, start out with the words *"ma-nishtane,"* meaning, literally, "How does it differ?"

manna—in the Bible, food eaten by the Israelites in the desert. It was found on the ground every morning except the Sabbath (a double portion was collected on Fridays), and as much as could be eaten was collected by the people.

maskil—literally, in Hebrew, "intelligent," "knowing"; in the nineteenth century , a follower of the *haskole* ("enlightenment") movement among the Jews of Eastern Europe to acquire modern European culture and secular knowledge.

mayven—see *meyven.*

mazl-tov—congratulations.

medresh—a particular manner of interpreting the verses of the Bible using parables, imaginative stories, and poetical interpretations; a body of post-Talmudic literature of Biblical exegesis; usually transliterated as *midrash.*

megilahs—see *megiles.*

megiles—literally, scrolls; applied more specifically to the five short books of the Bible: Song of Songs, Ruth, Lamentations, Ecclesiastes, and Esther.

megillahs—see *megiles.*

melamed—a teacher of religion and Hebrew to young children in *kheyder.*

meyven—expert, connoisseur, judge.

mezumem—currency, cash.

mezuzah—see *mezuze.*

mezuze—a piece of parchment containing twenty-two lines from Deuteronomy. It is rolled up in a wooden, metal, or glass cylinder and attached to the doorpost of Jewish homes. It is kissed upon entering and leaving the house.

midrash—see *medresh.*

mishnah—see *mishne.*

minhah—see *minkhe.*

minkhe—afternoon daily prayer; may be recited after noon and before sunset; usually combined with the *mayrev* or evening service.

mishne—part of the *Talmud.* A legal codification of basic Jewish law transmitted orally from early post-Biblical times to 200 BC.

perek—*pirkei avoth* ("The Ethics of the Fathers"), a collection of maxims and moral teachings taken from the Talmud.

purim—the feast of Lots. This joyful holiday commemorates the victory of the Jews over their persecutors. It celebrates the events described in the Bible's "Book of Esther."

rabiner—crown rabbi. In the employ of the Russian government; not required to be an ordained orthodox rabbi; one of his chief functions was to record births, deaths, marriages, etc.

rashi—Rabbi Solomon, the son of Isaac, one of the foremost commentators on the Bible; lived in Troyes, France (1040-1105). (Acronym for *Ra*bbi *Sh*loyme ben *I*tskhok.)

reb—mister; traditional title prefixed to a man's first name.

rebbe—hasidic rabbi; teacher; master (used in addressing a rabbi).

rosh-hashono—see *rosheshone.*

rosheshone—the Jewish New Year; it takes place on the first and second days of the Hebrew month Tishri, ushering in a period of ten days of awe, culminating in *yinkiper*.

schlimazl—see *shlimazl.*

seyder—the service and the festive meal eaten on the first two nights of Passover.

shabbes—see *shabes.*

shabes—sabbath, weekly rest-day observed from Friday sunset through Saturday sunset.

Shabuoth/Shavuoth—see *shevues.*

shalach-mones—see *shalakhmones.*

shalakhmones—traditional gifts (usually food) exchanged on Purim.

sheytl—wig worn by orthodox Jewish women after marriage.

shevuos—see *shvues.*

shvues—the Feast of Weeks, or Pentecost, celebrated seven weeks after Passover. An early summer holiday, it celebrates the Giving of the Law on Mt. Sinai, and simultaneously the gathering of the first fruits. Dairy food is eaten instead of meat during this holiday.

Shevuoth—see *shvues.*

shimenesre—the eighteen blessings which are said by Jews in the three daily prayers.

shiva—week-long period of mourning following the funeral of a close relative.

shlimazl—an unlucky person whose life is a series of misfortunes; the word often has an amusing connotation.

shmooze—an Americanized version of *shmuesn,* which see.

shmuesn—talk, converse, chat.

shmattes—see *shmates.*

shmates—rags.

shmin-esra—see *shimenesre.*

shofar—see *shoyfer.*

shokhet—see *shoykhet.*

shophar—see *shoyfer.*

sholem-aleykhem—a traditional Jewish greeting, meaning, "peace be with you," but through repeated usage simply signifying, "Hello."

sholom-aleichem—see *sholem-aleykhem.*

shoyfer—the ram's horn blown in synagogues on Rosh Hashonah and Yom Kippur.

shoykhet—ritual slaughterer.

shtetl—town.

simkhes-toyre—holiday on the day after Shemini Atzeret, the holiday marking the end of the *sukes* festival; it celebrates the completion of the year's reading of the toyre; usual transliteration, *Simchat Torah.*

suke—tabernacle erected in celebration of the *sukes* holiday; the family eats its meals there during this holiday.

sukes—the feast of booths. Four days after *yinkiper,* Jews observe *sukes.* During this holiday, lasting for seven days, the family gathers for meals in booths, or tabernacles, erected for the occasion. The booths recall the times when Israel wandered in the wilderness after the exodus from Egypt. It is also a harvest festival.

sukkah—see *suke.*

sukkoth—see *sukes.*

talmud—includes the work of numerous Jewish scholars. The writing of this work extended over almost a thousand years. Based on the teachings of the Bible, the Talmud interprets Biblical laws and commandments; contains laws, legends, ethics, comments on philosophy, medicine, agriculture, astronomy and hygiene.

talmide-khakhomim—a scholar whose study of the *toyre* and the *talmud* never ends; a truly learned person; scholar.

talmud-torah—see *talmud-toyre.*

talmud-toyre—traditionally, a tuition-free elementary school maintained by the community for the poorest children.

targum—the Aramaic translation of the Bible.

tate—father.

tateh—see *tate.*

tisha b'Av—see *tishe-bov.*

tishe-bov—a fast day which occurs on the ninth day of the month of *Ov,* a day on which both the first and second temples were destroyed.

torah—see *toyre.*

toyre—in rabbinic literature *toyre* is used in a variety of senses, all based on the general understanding of *toyre* as the guidance and teaching imparted to Israel by Divine Revelation. In its narrow, literal sense, *toyre* designates the Pentateuch, the Prophets and Hagiographa (i.e., the Bible)—but in a wider sense, it is also applied to Scripture as a whole, including the oral law, and finally to religious learning in general.

treif—see *treyf.*

treyf—not *kosher.*

tsene-rene—yiddish homiletical commentary and explanation of the *toyre,* written especially for women, and in wide use from the 17th century onward. Jewish women often spent Sabbath afternoons reading from the work.

Vashti—the wife of king Ahaseures in the Book of Esther, the Purim story.

vertutti—cheese fritters.

vey iz mir—my goodness! Woe is me!

vibores—election.

yinkiper—the day of atonement.

yisgadal, v'yiskadash shmey rabo—the first words of the prayer for the dead, the mourner's *kadish:* "Magnified and sanctified be His great name..."

Yom-Kippur—see *yinkiper.*

zloty—the standard monetary unit of Poland.

zeyde—grandfather.